Meet the

Meet the Bronies

The Psychology of the Adult My Little Pony *Fandom*

Patrick Edwards, Daniel P. Chadborn,
Courtney N. Plante, Stephen Reysen,
Marsha Howze Redden

McFarland & Company, Inc., Publishers
Jefferson, North Carolina

ISBN (print) 978-1-4766-6371-5
ISBN (ebook) 978-1-4766-3795-2

Library of Congress Cataloguing-in-Publication Data

British Library cataloguing data are available

Printed in the United States of America

McFarland & Company, Inc., Publishers
Box 611, Jefferson, North Carolina 28640
www.mcfarlandpub.com

This book is dedicated to the brony community. Without your participation, feedback, stories, and interactions, these studies would have never been possible. We also dedicate this book to Lauren Faust and to all of those who work on *My Little Pony: Friendship Is Magic* (voice actresses/actors, directors, writers, animators, etc.). Without your work, the brony fandom itself would not exist.

Table of Contents

Acknowledgments

There are too many people who have helped us over the last eight years to be able to name each one. Nevertheless, we will try.

Will Edwards, whose membership in the brony community and interest in *MLP:FIM* spurred the beginnings of Brony Study.

Dr. Jan Griffin, whose work with statistics and large data analysis was crucial in our investigations into the community and whose experience and knowledge propelled Brony Study into what it is today.

To all of the psychology conferences, editors, journals, and colleagues who were willing to hear us out, review our research, and offer us a platform to present our work and who did so with only a few odd looks when we explained bronies to them.

To both BronyCon for inviting us back to discuss our research year after year and to Equestria Daily for helping us pitch our research and ultimately reach fans across the world.

And, of course, our families, friends, and fellow fans of all types who have supported us in our work and development since the beginning of the project. Specifically, fellow fans in the University of Waterloo Bronies Club for being awesome, Susan Bressler Thomas for her technological assistance, and Michael and Jared for introducing one of the authors to ponies and ultimately sealing his fate.

Preface

Welcome to the culmination of eight years of psychological research on the brony fandom! You may be asking yourself, who are the bronies, what is Brony Study, and how do a bunch of psychologists wind up doing *this* with their careers? Worry not! You will find answers to *all* of these questions! And if, by chance, you find yourself wondering whether you *really* care about the psychology of the *My Little Pony: Friendship Is Magic* fandom, we'll tell you this: If you're a fan of *anything*, be it *My Little Pony*, an NFL team, video games, or pretty much anything else, this book will be relevant to you. Why? Because, as you'll soon see, many of the same psychological processes we've found in the brony fandom can be found in other fan groups.

Of course, we don't cover *everything* there is to know about fan groups in this one book.[1] Broader, more nuanced discussions about the psychological processes underlying various fandoms have been the focus of other books, studies, and lines of research. For now, we've chosen to focus on one fandom in particular, the brony fandom, and to follow them from their very beginning to the current day. We've also chosen to narrow our focus to the *psychology* of the brony fandom. For those interested in the *history* of *My Little* Pony as a show, the 2017 book *Ponyville Confidential: The History and Culture of My Little Pony, 1981–2016* by Sherilyn Connelly is a great start. If you're interested in various fan cultures (e.g., *Star Trek*) from a non-psychological perspective we might suggest authors such as Henry Jenkins (who is beyond prolific in the field).

But, if what you're looking for is a glimpse into the minds of those who like colorful friendship equines, you're holding the correct book, one chock-full of research studies, data, more graphs and tables than you can shake a stick at, and *way* too many pony-themed puns.[2]

So if you're still with us, we hope that you're rewarded for your inquisitive nature and your open mind. If you're a brony, some of these findings may reinforce your day-to-day experience, while others will no doubt surprise you. If you're here because you're not a brony, but you just *need* to understand them, we suspect that you'll come to the same conclusion that we have, that bronies are a diverse group of people who, despite seeming strange at first, are just like everyone else, except for their love of a show about colorful ponies.

If nothing else, we hope that by the end of the book you see, as we have, that the show and the fandom are a wonderful influence on the lives of those in the brony fandom. And you don't have to take our word for it: These same ideas have been articulated by Lauren Faust, Jayson Thiessen, Tara Strong, Ashleigh Ball, Andrea Libman, and the rest of the cast. Early on in our book-writing process we reached out to John de Lancie, who voices the character Discord on the show and had originally reached out to Drs. Edwards and Redden for their input in the documentary *Bronies: The Extremely Unexpected Adult Fans of My Little Pony*. In 2016 he shared with us some of his thoughts on coming into a fandom he knew nothing about and becoming one of the fandom's most vocal supporters.

> A few years ago, I got a call from my voiceover agent with an offer to voice an animated show. I read the script, thought it was good, and accepted the job. As with most voice-overs' jobs, I spent a couple of hours the night before preparing the material and then an hour recording in the studio the following day. Job completed, never to be thought of again. Three months later, I turned on my computer one morning and was astounded to discover 300 emails, all mentioning *My Little Pony*. Not remembering, I asked my wife what she knew about *My Little Pony*. "You voiced it a few months ago," she said, "and it's a cartoon for little girls." I pondered that statement for a moment and then, with raised eyebrow, responded in my most serious voice, "Well … let me tell you something … these are not little girls who are writing me!" Thus, my introduction to Bronies.
>
> Admittedly, I went through the usual stages of disbelief when it came to bronies. Why are twenty-year-old guys watching a cartoon intended for ten-year-old girls? But as I scratched the surface my initial negative opinion changed to acceptance and then to admiration. I even went so far as to produce a documentary on bronies. My hope was that this documentary would provide a visual record of a phenomenon that, frankly, I couldn't quite explain but was willing to embrace. Fandoms are created for many different reasons. *Star Trek*, a fandom with which I'm familiar, appealed to those who were interested in science, and a hope for a better future. Under the *Star Trek* umbrella, a generation of young adults emerged as the nascent "nerd" culture of today. *My Little Pony* has attracted its adult fans for a myriad of reasons that this book will fully explore, but the one that speaks most to me is a need for sanctuary. A place of refuge and safety, in an otherwise chaotic world, where one can be oneself for just a little while. I met a military drone operator who told me, "Given what I do everyday, I look forward to watching a show that is bright, colorful, positive, encouraging and fun." Amen.
>
> Many of the Bronies I've met are smart, progressive, secular, and creative. And, yes, they embraced a show that was not initially intended for adults and made it their own. But let's be frank; a show that espouses Honesty, Kindness, Laughter, Generosity and

> Loyalty should be watched by every person on our planet whatever their age or gender. As far as I'm concerned, the Bronies are on to something. Like the *Star Trek* generation before them, bronies long for a better, more tolerant future and, as far as I'm concerned, they are well on their way to making that future a possibility. Read on … this book is fascinating.

As you will soon see, Mr. de Lancie's response to the brony community is very similar to the experience of many who let their curiosity get the best of them and take the plunge to learn a bit more about this weird and wonderful fandom. We hope you come away from this book with more than just answers to your questions about the brony fandom. We hope you come away with a better appreciation of fan communities in general and the important role that they, along with the media we consume, play in our day-to-day lives, even though we're so quick to write them off as "mere recreation."

But enough of this preamble—let's get this carriage moving!

Chapter 1

Meet the Bronies!

"Isn't this exciting? Are you excited? 'Cause I'm excited, I've never been so excited!"
—Pinkie Pie (Season 1, Episode 1, Friendship Is Magic, Part 1)

Welcome to the weird and wonderful world of brony culture!

Chances are pretty good that you're picking up this book already having at least a *little bit* of knowledge about the brony fandom—whether it's being a brony yourself, knowing a brony personally, or simply having heard the term thrown around by the media. Regardless of *how* you know about bronies, the important thing is that your curiosity has gotten the better of you—you're looking to learn a thing or two about what the deal is with this often-discussed (and just-as-often-misunderstood) subculture. Well, you've come to the right place!

To start, let's briefly clarify what we mean by the term "brony." Different people will almost certainly provide you with different definitions. Some of these will be grounded in first-hand experience while others will be grounded in speculation, misconceptions, or outright ignorance. Our own definition is by no means an objective one, nor is it even the "best" one out there. Instead, our definition of the term "brony" reflects our own unique perspective of bronies. Or, to put it another way, our definition of "brony" is grounded in our experience as social scientists studying fan groups. It's tempered by both our own first-hand interactions with the brony community and by the experiences of two members of the team who self-identify as bronies.[1]

So just what *is* our definition of a brony? A brony is a fan of the animated television show *My Little Pony: Friendship Is Magic* (*MLP:FIM*). In addition to liking the show, a brony typically identifies with the *MLP:FIM* fanbase. Of course, as you'll see throughout this book, this definition is fairly broad, including, but not limited to, avid viewers of the show, online reviewers, fanfiction writers, artists, animators, musicians, performers, plushie makers, costume builders, forum posters, and convention attendees. The term "brony" is also used throughout this book to refer to *anyone* who self-identifies with this community, not just to *male* fans.[2]

In this first chapter we'll lay the groundwork for your understanding of what a brony is. We'll review some basic information to make sure everyone's on the same page, starting with a look at what it means to be a "fan" of something—both to laypersons to researchers. We'll then explain how bronies are just like any other group of fans—albeit fans of a somewhat unusual interest. After a brief review of the history of both the *MLP* franchise and the brony fandom, we'll end the chapter with a look forward to the rest of this book, outlining how we plan to take you through years of psychological research on the brony community in a not-too-chaotic fashion.[3]

First, let's start by looking at what it means to say someone is a fan of something.

What Makes a Fan a Fan?

When laypersons hear the term "fan," they often imagine a person who's obsessed with something, usually donning the (often ridiculous-looking) garb and accessories associated with that interest.[4] For example, what comes to mind when we think of a *sports fan*? Depending on where you're from, you might have pictured an (American) football fan with their face painted in their team's colors cheering loudly at a game they spent $100 to watch in person.[5] Alternatively, you might be imagining a crowd of teenage girls shrieking when their favorite boy band takes to the stage. Or you might have thought about a group of *Star Wars* fans donning head-to-toe stormtrooper armor and waving plastic lightsabers around.

It's no coincidence that whatever image came to your mind, it likely involved people acting in unusual or excessive ways. The term "fan" itself originates from the Latin word "fanaticus," referring to a person insane with divinely-inspired passion (e.g., a religious fanatic). The word's usage has evolved over the centuries and refers today to someone who is devoted to enthusiastically pursuing a specific interest or hobby. Nevertheless, the word retains some of its historical connotation of excess: When we think of fans, extreme behavior often jumps to the front of their minds.

To social scientists, however, the term "fan" simply means anyone who self-identifies by their interest in a particular hobby.[6] This has two important implications. First, it implies that fans are *self*-identified—no one can tell someone that they're a fan. In the same way that no one can decide for you whether or not you like licorice, no one can tell you whether or not you are a fan of something.[7] Of course, this doesn't mean we can't reasonably guess that you *might* be a fan of something based on your behavior (e.g., plastering your walls with science-fiction posters might suggest that you're a science fiction fan). But there are plenty of cases of people who like listening to a particular band, watching a particular show, or spending time on a particular hobby who wouldn't call themselves "fans" of these activities.

The second implication of the social scientific definition of the term "fan" is that it's an *identity*—a part of who you are. Calling yourself a fan of something is a way of communicating to others that your passion for this thing is a big enough part of your life that it's useful to help them understand who you are and why you behave the way you do.

To see what we mean by fan as an identity, let's use the example of one of the authors, Dr. Plante. He's a fan of video games and he also happens to like eating licorice. Over the years, he's spent thousands of hours (and thousands of dollars!) on video games. A lot of his social interaction takes place though multiplayer games. He wears t-shirts that often feature video game characters. He even *studies* the effects of video games on players! In other words, Dr. Plante's love of video games can tell us a *lot* about him: how he spends his time and money, who he interacts with, how he chooses to express himself, and what he does for work.

Let's contrast this with Dr. Plante's enthusiasm for eating licorice. He likes it a lot. It's been one of his favorite treats since he was a child, and it was always something he looked forward to at Christmas. His favorite flavor of tea is licorice and he would probably reach for the licorice-flavored candy first if he was buying a treat at the store. That said, Dr. Plante's love of licorice says very little about him in general. His love for licorice has minimal impact on his social life, the way he behaves, his work, or the way he expresses himself. Knowing that Dr. Plante likes licorice doesn't really help you predict what he does in his spare time, what sorts of clothing he wears, or what he's saving up to buy.[8]

This is why it makes sense to say Dr. Plante is a fan of video games, but not a fan of licorice. Sure, he likes both things, but only his love of video games tells you something important about him. This is why, when introducing himself to someone, Dr. Plante might say, "Hi, I'm Courtney—I'm a big fan of video games," but wouldn't say, "Hi, I'm Courtney—I'm a fan of licorice!" The second statement sounds absurd precisely *because* we recognize that we communicate our interests to someone as a way of helping them better understand us. And while most of us like a lot of different things, there are very few that we like *enough* that people can get an accurate picture of us by knowing about them.

Let's return to our earlier question about what comes to mind when we think of a fan. Were sports fans the first example to come to your mind? If so, you're certainly not alone in this regard: Studies suggest that when *most* people think of a typical fan, sports fans are the first thing to come to mind. They are the "prototypical" fan, so to speak (Reysen & Shaw, 2016). Because of this, the more a fan interest differs from a prototypical sports fan, the more *abnormal* it seems to us. This means that fans can be considered extreme not just because they have an extreme love of something (e.g., stalking behavior, bankrupting oneself pursuing one's interest), but also because they're a fan of something atypical or unusual. We'll return to this point and see how it applies to the brony community in Chapter 17.

Before we finish our discussion about what makes a fan a fan, it's worth briefly mentioning an important distinction made by researchers who study fans, the difference between *fanship* and *fandom* (Reysen & Branscombe, 2010). Fanship is the extent to which you identify as having a passionate interest in something. For example, a person might claim to be a *huge* fan of *Harry Potter* since they own every version of the books and films, write *Harry Potter* fanfiction, and know entirely too much trivia about it.

In contrast, fandom is the extent to which you identify with *other fans* of an interest—how much you consider yourself to be a member of the fan community. For example, our same *Harry Potter* fan might also consider themselves to be an active and participating member of both the local *Harry Potter* fan club and the online *Harry Potter* fan community. Fandom has less to do with how strong your own passion is and more to do with how strong your connection is to other fans.

Fanship and fandom often go hand in hand. Usually a person who considers themselves to be a passionate fan of *Star Trek* will also enjoy spending time hanging out with people who like talking about *Star Trek*. But the two are not one and the same. It's entirely possible, for example, that someone is high in fanship (e.g., watched every episode of *Star Trek*) but low in fandom (e.g., has no interest in meeting other *Star Trek* fans). The reverse is also possible (e.g., someone who's only casually watched some episodes of *Star Trek*, but who is strongly drawn to the fan culture surrounding *Star Trek*).

It's important to keep this distinction between fandom and fanship in mind as we discuss what makes bronies similar to, and different from, long-time fans or collectors of *MLP* in the next couple of sections.

A Crash Course in the History of *MLP*

To this point, we've discussed what makes a fan a fan and we've made it clear that there are fans of pretty much any interest you can imagine. But if you want to understand why sports fans wear jerseys of their favorite players, you need to know a thing or two about sports. Likewise, if you want to know why *Star Wars* fans wave around glowing plastic lightsabers, it helps to know a bit about the films. In the same vein, if you want to understand what it means to be a fan of *MLP*, you first need to know a bit about the show and its history.

To be clear, this is only a crash course in the history of *MLP*. This overview is largely based on the work of others who have painstakingly compiled the fandom's history based on hundreds of interviews, news articles, and memos from Hasbro, the company responsible for *MLP*. In particular, we highly recommend Sherilyn Connelly's excellent 2017 book *Ponyville Confidential: The History and Culture of My Little Pony, 1981–2016*, which we consider to be the *definitive* reference on the history of *MLP*.

To start, the *MLP* franchise has existed for more than 35 years. Since then it has changed dramatically in its presentation, appearance, focus, and target audience. As such, the *MLP* that many bronies consider themselves to be a fan of today is *very* different from the *MLP* of the early 1980s.

Something that's pervaded the *MLP* franchise from its inception, however, is its overarching goal of selling children's toys.[9] The franchise was created, and is still owned by, Hasbro, which sells a myriad of children's toys including Nerf guns, Play-Doh, board games, Mr. (and Mrs.) Potato Head, Easy-Bake Ovens and, perhaps most famous of all, media-influenced action figures (*Transformers*, *G.I. Joe*, Marvel). Throughout the 1980s, Hasbro created a series of television shows designed specifically to function as advertisements for their action figure lines. Nearly all of these toy lines, especially those promoted in television shows, were targeted toward boys.

In 1981, however, market researchers at Hasbro had begun to take an interest in a line of toys called the My Pretty Pony dolls. They were designed by Bonnie Zacherle, a contractor working for Hasbro's research and development department. The dolls were ten inches tall and made of hard plastic, designed to be realistic-looking. They were targeted at little girls who often spoke about wanting their own pet pony and were found to spend a great deal of time daydreaming about horses.

Aiming to improve the popularity of the My Pretty Pony dolls, in 1982 Hasbro created a set of six smaller, more colorful versions of the figures. They were made with softer plastic and sold under the brand "My Little Pony." The success of this newly-minted toy line led to the development of its own animated cartoon, which sought to grow their sales. The result was a 22-minute animated special simply called *My Little Pony*, aired in 1984. Two years later, a 65-episode animated series entitled *My Little Pony 'n' Friends* was developed alongside a full-length film entitled *My Little Pony: The Movie*. These, coupled with the 1992 series *My Little Pony Tales*, are considered by fans to be "Generation 1" or "G1" of the *MLP* franchise.

G1 was a highly-effective commercial for the popular *MLP* toy line. As a show, however, it was roundly panned by critics. Many saw the show as nothing more than a shameless cash grab, devoid of any artistry or substance. Adding to the criticism, G1 took place at a time when the Federal Communications Commission—the government agency responsible for regulating television in America—was being pressured to crack down on advertising directly targeted toward children.[10]

Beyond criticisms about the show's intent, the show itself was also panned by critics. It became an easy punching bag for critics. Many saw the show as gratingly saccharine-sweet, with characters designed around excessively feminine stereotypes (e.g., long flowing hair, long eyelashes, emotion-driven plots). Even *My Little Pony Tales*, which attempted to be more slice of life and to appeal to the types of real-world problems that viewers would be more familiar with, fell victim to these criticisms.

By 1992 the show stopped, effectively ending *MLP* G1. The end was due in no small part to the gradual decline in sales of *MLP* toys as popular competitors like Polly Pocket and Troll dolls came on the market. Despite its disappearance, however, the show would leave a lasting cultural legacy, one that would come back to "haunt" fans of later generations. The show would be forever remembered as a crass, cynical cash grab, a shallow, superficial series in an overly-feminine wrapper. This latter point was made especially poignant since the show was often contrasted against other popular, male-targeted shows such as *G.I. Joe*, *Transformers*, and *He-Man and the Masters of the Universe.* As Connelly put it in her book, the show became a cultural touchstone for anyone wanting to refer to a mindless, trashy children's show.[11]

Throughout the late 1990s and the 2000s, multiple attempts were made by Hasbro to revive the *MLP* franchise in one form or another. This included everything from McDonald's Happy Meal toys to the release of computer and video games (e.g., *My Little Pony: Friendship Gardens*, where players took care of their own pony as a pet). Much of this Generation 2 revival, which lasted from 1998 to 1999, focused on reminiscence of the past, trying to capitalize on mothers who had grown up with G1 characters. There was, however, little attempt to modernize or update the characters to cater to a new generation of kids.

Generation 3, released in 2003, was another attempted revival from Hasbro. This time, however, it focused this time on a newer, more innocent look to contrast itself against the heavily made-up Bratz and Barbie dolls of the time. G3 targeted a younger demographic (three- to six-year-old girls) than G1 did (a nine-and-under demographic). G3 also changed its focus from being a toy line to a "lifestyle" brand. This meant going beyond watching the show and buying the toys. Hasbro merchandised *MLP*-themed books, bedding, bath products, towels, backpacks, clothing, and music, wanting the show to permeate every facet of its viewers' lives.

In what was perhaps the most important change for what would later become the brony fandom, the franchise revamped the way fans interacted with the characters. In earlier generations, fans saw the pony characters almost like pets, as characters to be taken care of or admired.[12] In G3, however, backstories were written for the characters, who were given personalities and written to be more engaging. The writers wanted viewers to identify with the pony characters. This change would be amplified further in G4 of the show, marking one of the biggest draws of bronies to the show—the ability to identify with its characters (see Chapter 10).

In 2003, the first of a series of G3 films was released, called *A Charming Birthday*. It was followed by *A Very Minty Christmas* (2005), *The Princess Promenade* (2006), and even a touring live stage show called *My Little Pony: The World's Biggest Tea Party*. While there was no episodic content in G3, it *was* successful in rekindling interest in the series and, more importantly for Hasbro, toy sales. It was also around this time that collector conventions such as the My Little Pony Collectors' Convention in England and the My Little Pony Fair in Las Vegas popped up in 2004.[13]

It was at these same conventions that the media started noticing the occasional male attendee. This was also where the legacy of MLP as a trashy, hyper-feminized franchise reared its ugly head. These male attendees were often forced to justify their seemingly unusual interests, with media stories making them out to be deviants and questioning their sexual orientation or gender identity.

Despite such setbacks, however, there were a number of important positive changes in G3 that paved the way for the subsequent generation of *MLP*. For one thing, numerous characters were created in G3 who would go on to appear (in modified form) in Generation 4.[14] Perhaps even more important, however, in 2008 the franchise limited its focus from a myriad of different characters to a "core seven" characters. These seven characters would ultimately be fleshed out and given a greater sense of distinct identity.[15]

It was during this time, when *MLP* was fighting against its legacy of being a shallow, treacly, hyper-feminine, cynical cash grab while simultaneously trying to make changes for the better, that G4 took shape. Lauren Faust, a veteran in the animation industry (e.g., *The Powerpuff Girls*, *Foster's Home for Imaginary Friends*), was brought on as the creator of a new generation of *MLP*. This generation, G4, would go on to be called *My Little Pony: Friendship Is Magic*. Faust was a fan of *MLP* as a child. She sought to wrest the franchise from the negative aspects of its legacy while retaining the elements of fantasy and creativity it had inspired in her. Her changes to the show included greater focus on character-driven stories, developing fully fleshed-out, relatable characters, imbuing the show with complex moral ambiguity, and updating the show's aesthetics and quality of animation. Faust sought to tackle complex issues within the show and to inject a feminist message into it. She wanted girls to see well-rounded characters with a myriad of strengths and weaknesses and to move past the cutesy, goody two-shoesness that had plagued existing generations of the show.

The target audience was also far more nuanced and complex than it was for the original generations. Rather than appealing simply to young girls, Faust recognized that it would be important to foster co-viewing of the show—to get parents to watch the show with their children. She knew that many mothers—themselves fans of earlier generations—should be able to find something they found interesting and worth watching in the show. As such, the writers put considerable effort into targeting content not only to its youngest viewers, but also ensuring there was material that would appeal to tween and even adult audiences as well. This often included the clever use of cultural references, background details, and running jokes.

It was with these goals that *MLP:FIM*, Generation 4 of the *MLP* franchise, launched with a fresh new show and a brand-new philosophy aimed at toppling its legacy. The show itself launched in 2010, marking the first *MLP*-themed episodic series since *My Little Pony Tales* in 1992 on Hasbro's newly-created Hub Network. This is where, at last, bronies enter the scene. Shortly after the initial release of the show in 2010, regulars of the popular Internet forum 4chan's "Comics and Cartoons" board took notice of the show and began discussing it. At first, many were gearing up to give the show the same lambasting that critics had given earlier generations of the show. Forum members discussed the show with a hint of irony, watching it as a joke. Much to their surprise, however, many found themselves unexpectedly drawn to the quality of the show's writing and animation, identifying with its characters and compelled by the lore of the show's fictional universe.

In short time, the term "brony" was used to describe fans of the show. The term was a shortening of the term "Pony-bro" commonly used on the site (a portmanteau of the words "bro"—popular in the vernacular to refer sarcastically to males—and "pony"). Not long after, the popular Brony news site Equestria Daily was launched. In short order, it found itself getting in excess of 100,000 page views per day.

The fast and unexpected growth of this demographic—a proud and vocal community made up of predominantly young adult males from websites like 4chan—did not escape the notice of the show's creators. Faust herself personally thanked fans of the show, including bronies, on her DeviantArt journal shortly after the show's initial release. The show's creators and the brony fandom would continue to play off one another in the coming years. Bronies generated extensive amounts of fan-made writing, music, art, animation, costumes, and analysis and critiques of the show. The show's creators would, in turn, throw nods and references to the brony community into the show itself.[16] This is perhaps best exemplified in an episode entitled "Slice of Life," an episode consisting *entirely* of background characters popular with the brony community—complete with characteristics, backstories, and personalities reflecting, in whole or in part, those generated by the brony fandom. Here they were, the fandom's favorite background characters and recurring jokes, put front and center as the focus of an episode! A similar nod to bronies could be found in the character of Muffins (known as Derpy Hooves to bronies because of her first appearance in the show's background with a googly-eyed expression due to an animation error). Muffins could often be found in the background of scenes as an Easter egg for diligent fans to notice (or, as in the case of the *Equestria Girls* film *Rainbow Rocks*, appearing less subtly in ending credit artwork alongside the film's main characters).

The brony fandom would continue to grow and develop a significant real-world presence, including conventions worldwide such as BABSCon in San Francisco, California, BronyCon in Baltimore, Maryland (which exceeded 10,000 attendees in 2015), and Galacon in Ludwigsburg, Germany. Bronies would also be the subject of several documentaries about the fandom, including the 2012 *Bronies: The Extremely Unexpected Adult Fans of My Little Pony* and the 2014 *A Brony Tale*.

Unfortunately, media coverage of the brony fandom was largely unchanged from the judgmental and stigmatizing tone it had shown for male fans of G3. To this day, media stories about bronies tend to remain fairly negative, owing in no small part to the legacy of the show as trite, hyper-feminine, and a product of commercialism. As male G3 fans and attendees of *MLP* collector conventions were ridiculed by the media, bronies were roundly mocked by news media. They found themselves trivialized as immature or childish, had their sexual orientation and gender once again questioned, and were, especially online, treated as dysfunctional or suffering from mental illness (see Chapter 17 for more on this).

As a light-hearted example of the stigma bronies faced, Bill Clinton was "accused" of being a Brony after appearing on a 2011 NPR segment. On the segment, Clinton was asked a trio of multiple-choice trivia questions about the show. Despite having never watched the show, the questions were worded in a way that made the answers fairly obvious. The former president got all three questions correct and, for days afterward, was roundly mocked for being a "closeted brony."

As funny as it may seem to mock a non-brony former president for his knowledge of the show, the results of this stigma have far more dire consequences for bronies themselves. In 2014, two independent incidents occurred in rapid succession which illustrate the toll that stigmatization takes on the brony community. In one case, a nine-year-old boy attempted suicide due to repeatedly being bullied and harassed—including being repeatedly called gay—for liking the show. In the second case, an 11-year-old boy was bullied at school for wearing a Rainbow Dash backpack, something which he was told by school staff he could avoid by simply leaving the backpack at home. Both cases illustrate how the apparent acceptability of targeting bronies—especially male bronies—for liking a show "for girls" makes it socially acceptable for people to harass and bully bronies without consequence. On a more positive note, the brony fandom rallied together behind the victims in both cases, raising awareness, money, and support for the boys and their families. This is an excellent demonstration of several important norms within the brony fandom—kindness, compassion, charity, and acceptance (see Chapter 19 for more on prosocial norms in the brony fandom).

The brony fandom continues to exist, both online and at conventions. With *MLP:FIM* set to finish its ninth and final season in 2019, however, questions remain about the future of the fandom. With talks of a soon-to-be-launched Generation 5, many bronies find themselves wondering whether the fandom will continue, business as usual, following the new generation of the franchise, or whether the fandom itself will simply fade away.

Okay, So What *Is* a Brony?

Taking everything we've discussed in this chapter and putting it together, a clearer picture emerges for what, precisely, a brony is.

We can start by pointing out what a brony is *not*. Bronies, for the most part, are *not* simply "male fans of *MLP*." As we will see in Chapter 4, fans from all walks of life, irrespective of age, gender, race, and sexual orientation, self-identify as bronies. As such, it would be factually incorrect to define bronies simply as "adult male fans of *MLP*."

Moreover, it would be incorrect to define bronies as fans of anything from the *MLP* franchise. The brony fandom did not emerge (at least, the term "brony" did not) until G4 of the show. As such, there were no self-identified bronies in the 1980s, 1990s, or 2000s. This is not to say, of course, that there are no bronies who *are* fans of earlier generations of the show. It does seem accurate, however, to state that being a fan of *MLP:FIM* seems to be the closest there is to a *necessary* condition to being a brony.

Conversely, it's also not the case that *everyone* who is a fan of *MLP:FIM* is, by definition, a brony. As we pointed out in our distinction between fandom and fanship earlier in this chapter, a person can like something without self-identifying as a fan of it. Plenty of people watch *MLP:FIM* and would not consider themselves to be a brony. Whether it's because they are high in fanship but low in fandom, because they have no interest in the fandom (or actively avoid it due to the stigma associated with it), or simply because their interest in the show isn't a big enough part of their identity to use it as a label, they have their reasons for eschewing the label. Just as many people enjoy the *Star Wars* films without labeling themselves *Star Wars* fans, many people watch *MLP:FIM* without labeling themselves bronies.

Finally, a distinction needs to be made between *MLP collectors* and *bronies*. As we mentioned in our discussion of the history of the *MLP* franchise, there have long been collectors of *MLP* figures and toys—including those who have done so since *G1*. Many of these collectors, predominantly female, would reject the label of "brony" despite their interest in the *MLP* franchise as a whole. Again, it's informative to look to the distinction between fanship and fandom to understand why this may be the case. A person who goes out of their way to collect *MLP* figures would likely score high in fanship—a strong interest in the content itself (including the show, merchandise, etc.). One of the defining features of the brony fandom, however, is its powerful sense of *fandom*. In many ways, bronies are just as interested, if not more interested, in the Internet-based community which has sprung up around the show than the show itself (as we'll see discussed in chapters 13 and 14). Whereas a collector may see the show and collecting figures as central to their interests, a brony may consider their interaction with other bronies and fan-produced content as being central to their interests. This doesn't make either one "more" of a fan than the other, nor does it mean that there cannot be overlap between the two. But it does suggest that, at very least, they should not be treated as one and the same.

So what *is* a brony? A brony is, simply put, a fan. They're fans of the television show *MLP:FIM* who feel a particular connection to the fan community which has formed around the show. That's it—plain and simple. Anything else tacked onto this definition would only exclude people who call themselves bronies or include people who wouldn't call themselves bronies. For example, adding that bronies are people who "go to brony conventions" would unnecessarily exclude the many bronies who have never been to a brony convention. Ditto for definitions that include "people who draw *MLP*-themed art" or "people who watch fan-made content related to *MLP*." To be sure, a *lot* of bronies do these things—there's no end to the myriad of ways an interest in *MLP* can manifest. But they aren't what makes a brony a brony.

And, as we've said, we should be wary of adding features to the definition of brony that would make it *overly* inclusive. For example, defining bronies as "people who like the show *MLP:FIM*" would lead to calling *anyone* who likes the show a brony, regardless of whether or not they consider themselves to be a member of the brony community. Likewise, including things like "people who draw *MLP*-themed art" ends up including animators, commissioned artists, or people who work for the show in the brony fandom, despite the fact that their involvement is a job rather than a fan identity.

What's the Plan?

So where do we go from here? It might seem like, to this point, we've answered some pretty lofty questions about bronies. We've talked about how psychologists consider them to be fans (and what it means to be a fan) and we've talked about the origins of the term and the community itself!

But we've only just scratched the surface from a *psychological* perspective. It's one thing to be able to point to a definition of a brony or to know the history of the brony fandom as a whole. It's another thing entirely to get inside the head of a brony and to know what makes them tick. It's another thing *still* to look at the social psychology of the brony fandom to understand the norms of the brony community, how the group interacts (with itself and with others), and the ways being part of this group changes a person—for better and for worse. That's where the rest of this book comes in!

In Chapters 2 and 3 we introduce you to the nuts and bolts of everything you need to know about the research itself: who we (the researchers) are, where we're coming from, why we're studying this fandom, and how we do it. By laying out our backgrounds, our history of involvement with the fandom, and our techniques for conducting research with the fandom, we're "showing our work," so to speak. We're showing our biases and limitations, but also the strengths of our studies and our ability to draw some conclusions about the brony fandom based on a series of studies.

In Chapters 4–6 we'll paint as detailed a picture of the brony fandom as possible from a demographic perspective. Before we can get into the minds of the brony fandom, it's useful to know who we're dealing with as a group. We break down the group on a number of important demographic variables, showing the make up of the group as a whole, since it's largely a product of where the fandom originated (i.e., online forums such as 4chan). Getting a better picture of what the fandom looks like also allows us to form questions about what might drive the fandom—are these *really* people who are dysfunctional, people from broken homes, or people struggling to understand their gender or sexual orientation?

In Chapters 7–12 we look at a range of brony-related behaviors, trying to better understand what bronies *do*. This includes looking at what motivated bronies to watch *MLP:FIM* in the first place (Chapter 7), whether bronies engage in the sorts of consumerism that fueled *MLP* in the first place (Chapter 8), and the factors motivating bronies to keep viewing and engaging with the show (Chapter 9). In Chapter 10 we look at the nature of the relationships bronies form with the show's characters and whether those relationships tell us something about type of person they are. In Chapter 11 we dive into the more mature elements of the fandom, including pornography use and attitudes toward sex. Finally, in Chapter 12 we conclude this section on fan-related behavior by looking at the overlap between being a fan of *MLP* and being a fan of *other* interests.

In Chapters 13–15 we get to the heart of the brony fandom—the community itself. In Chapter 13 we look at how bronies interact with the brony fandom (e.g., conventions, online), while in Chapter 14 we look at the extent to which belonging to the fandom and making friends with other bronies drives their interaction with the fandom—and what they get out of it. In Chapter 15 we look at barriers to entry in the brony fandom, including gatekeeping, as well as factors that may explain the growth of the brony fandom—including evangelizing about the show and word-of-mouth recruitment.

In Chapters 16–19 we delve into the psychology of individual bronies, including their personality make up and what we can tell about bronies based on the type of person they are (Chapter 16). In Chapter 17 we examine the topic of stigma, looking deeper into what effect being a part of a bullied and picked-on fan group has on bronies. In Chapter 18 we delve further into the well-being of bronies, asking whether there's any truth to the popular idea that bronies are damaged, dysfunctional people. Finally, in Chapter 19 we talk about whether watching a show with powerful themes of friendship, compassion, and generosity can have a positive effect on bronies helping and charity behavior.

In the last chapters of this book we look to the future of the *MLP* fandom, speculating on where bronies think the fandom is headed next and what we might expect to see in the future. With the show set to enter its final season, it's informative to look back at where the fandom as come and to look at other fandoms for guidance regarding where we can expect the brony fandom to go next.

Okay, we've satisfied our inner Twilight Sparkle and made a list of things to do. Now let's get to it!

Chapter 2

Science Is Magic: The History of Brony Study

"Maybe the ponies in Ponyville have interesting things to talk about! C'mon, Twilight, just try!"

—*Spike* (*Season 1, Episode 1,* Friendship Is Magic, Part 1)

Before we dive into what years of studying the brony fandom has taught us, we think it's a good idea to give you an idea of who we are, where we're from, and how we got caught up in researching the brony fandom.[1] It's a way of laying our cards on the table, so to speak, and letting you know our own perspectives, biases, and motivations for doing this work. It's also a way for us to collect our thoughts and reflect on a project that started back in 2011 with the initial goal of studying bronies, but which grew to include writing a book for bronies and non-bronies alike![2]

We'll begin by telling you what the Brony Study is and how it came to be. Next, we'll give you a bit of background on who the individual researchers are—our backgrounds, credentials, and why we think we're qualified to write a book about the science if bronies. We'll finish up by talking a bit bout some of the methods we've used, how the study has evolved along the way, and what the future holds.

What Is Brony Study?

Brony Study was the brainchild of Dr. Patrick Edwards, a psychologist who wanted to understand the new and interesting fan community known as bronies from its very inception. While other fields (i.e., communications, sociology) had previously studied fandoms and fan experiences, they often did so using fandoms which had been around for years.[3] They also tended to study these fan groups in a *qualitative* fashion—conducting interviews on a handful of fans at a time. What was missing in the research literature was a study of a newly-formed fandom from a *quantitative* perspective—studying hundreds, even thousands of fans, using numbers to allow researchers to run statistical analyses.

With this in mind, the group had three main goals:

1. Understand who was taking part in the brony community.
2. Explore the differences and similarities between bronies and non-bronies and determine whether there was any truth to the stereotypes that existed about them.
3. Answer the question we get most often, "Why *My Little Pony*?"

Over time, we began to answer many of these questions. As we searched the existing research on fans and discussed our work with both colleagues and with bronies themselves, our focus began to shift. We went from getting an initial look at the brony fandom to testing specific hypotheses about the fandom, including questions about the function and meaning of the fan community, why bronies join, stay, and leave the fandom, and the negative and positive aspects of being part of the brony fandom. And, as of the completion of this book, we're still studying the brony fandom, publishing papers on those findings, and continuing a discussion that began back in 2010. But today we're far more confident in our ability to answer these questions—so much so that we're willing to put ink to paper and commit to our answers with a book!

The History

In the summer of 2011, Dr. Patrick Edwards was having a conversation with his son, Will, about what he'd been doing while off from school. Will explained to his father that he'd been drawing ponies. After a bit of clarification that he was not drawing real-life horses, but rather characters from the show *My Little Pony: Friendship Is Magic*, Will also announced that he was a brony. Dr. Edwards' initial response was similar to how most people react when they hear about bronies for the first time: "You have got to be kidding me." Yet, with an open mind and a bit of a push from Will, Dr. Edwards dove head-first into the online world of discussion, art, music, fiction, and the show itself.[4] Fascinated by what he found, and with the show preparing for its second season, Dr. Edwards rolled up his sleeves and got to work putting together what would ultimately become the Brony Study.

In the early stages of the first Brony Study survey, it became apparent that there would be some *neigh*-sayers and skeptics along the way. A typical response from his colleagues, upon hearing about his proposed study, was confusion and shock.[5] These responses likely stem from peoples' surprise at bronies' brazen rejection of two strong norms regarding age (cartoons like *My Little Pony* are "for children") and gender (shows like *My Little Pony* are "for girls"). In the wake these rejections, outsiders seek explanations, usually leading to assumptions about bronies' sexual orientation, sexual deviancy (e.g., pedophilia), or mental health problems (for more on stigma toward the brony fandom, see Chapter 17). While it wasn't at all surprising to hear these stereotypes bandied about by the hosts on Fox News, it *was* surprising to hear fellow psychologists and mental health professionals espousing many of the same beliefs. As scientists, we're truth-seekers; when confronted with an unexpected event or group, we want to know the *real* answer for it—not someone's hot-take or armchair speculation.

And so Dr. Edwards and his colleagues found themselves faced with the first task of trying to define what exactly a brony was and what made the brony fandom distinct. This included exploring what bronies did online and reading the testimonials of fans and their friends and family members. We also stumbled into anti-fans, who were quite open about their strong negative reaction to bronies as a group or to the discovery that their friends, family members, or neighbors happened to be one.[6]

This cursory look through the brony fandom revealed that bronies weren't a standalone phenomenon. Several of the authors had lived through the early *Star Trek* years, and we knew that in recent years fandoms had sprung up around TV shows like *Glee* and *Game of Thrones* and around video games like *World of Warcraft* and *League of Legends*. It also helped that Dr. Edwards himself had been an avid fan of Marvel comic book heroes as a child and was married to a dedicated fan of daytime soap operas. As we searched the social scientific literature, we discovered that no one else had studied the brony fandom. While the opportunity to break new ground is always an exciting one in science, there was another challenge: There also wasn't a tremendous amount of work in psychology on fandoms in general.[7] This meant that not only were we treading new ground, but there wasn't really a template for how to go about doing this research.

It was in this context that, armed with a handful of questions, Dr. Edwards and his colleague, retired clinician Dr. Marsha Redden, launched the first of the Brony Studies out of the Wofford College Department of Psychology in the fall of 2011. The study itself consisted of an online survey launched on the popular brony website EquestriaDaily.com.[8]

The survey launched on a Friday. The following Monday, the department head made a bit of a snarky comment to Dr. Edwards, asking him how that pony survey of his was going. When Dr. Edwards responded that over the weekend they had gotten nearly 1,500 participants, the department head's disbelief for this line of research vanished.[9] Weeks later, nearly 2,400 bronies had completed the survey, along with 500 more non-bronies who would form the study's comparison group. The plan was to analyze the data and present the findings at BronyCon in New York in January 2012.

Dr. Edwards was taken back and surprised at the level of suspicion the organizers of BronyCon voiced about his research efforts and their reluctance to allow the presentation of the initial research results, with one organizer stating, "When science gets involved they always mess things up!"[10] Dr. Edwards was able to get a spot at the convention to discuss the initial findings. Suffice it to say, it was one of the more unusual environments in which Dr. Edwards had given a talk about research—a far cry from the academic conferences he was used to. It was also at this first brony convention that the fandom further coalesced: fans mingled with artists, voice actresses, and even creators of an *MLP*-themed fighting game featuring characters from the show (which was eventually launched with the help of Lauren Faust herself[11]). It was amidst this backdrop that the first presentation of Brony Study data took place. It was a rousing success: a standing room only crowd, roaring applause, and a wave of questions and stories from the audience.[12] The success emboldened Dr. Edwards to continue the research, soon being joined by Dr. Marsha Redden with whom he would prepare and launch a second survey.

It was shortly after that the pair were contacted by Dr. Daniel Chadborn, who had been doing similar research on other fan groups.[13] He officially joined the team during the next BronyCon and worked to get the team's third study up and running. The team would continue to grow further with the addition of Dr. Jan Griffin to the team. By 2015, what represented the original team had more than doubled in size, spanned 14 surveys, and had collected over 50,000 participants worth of data. These efforts would form the basis of a multitude of conference and convention presentations at national and regional psychology conferences and form the basis for the yearly BronyCon panels offering both overviews of the data as well as the ever-popular chance to "Ask the Brony Psychologists." In addition, Drs. Edwards, Griffin and Chadborn involved a large number of undergraduate psychology majors in the projects research efforts, these students helped with data collection, analysis, and conference presentations. Several of them have used these experiences to spring board into graduate training programs in psychology.

By 2015 the work with the initial surveys was beginning to wind down, both under the weight of so much data to analyze and write about and with the researchers having developed additional interests. While this might have spelled the end for the Brony Study, in 2015 two additional researchers, social psychologists Dr. Stephen Reysen and Dr. Courtney Plante, expressed their interest in expanding their ongoing work with other fan communities—including half a decade of research on the furry community. With that, the project and data collection relaunched, this time with a focus on the social psychology of the brony fandom.

Since them, the team has continued to pursue a number of new projects, including five more major studies, eight publications in peer-reviewed scientific journals, and continuing plans for future research.[14] In 2018, everyone who had worked on the various brony studied officially came together to combine all of their work from the past seven years—old studies and new, published and unpublished, previously reported and newly-analyzed—into the book you're now holding, a book which, itself, has been several years in the making!

Who Are the Brony Researchers?

Anyone can put a survey up on the Internet and call it a study. But there are vast differences in the quality, content, and theoretical grounding of a study put up by a curious high school student and a carefully-produced, ethically-approved study put together by a team of researchers. It's with this in mind that we feel we should lay out our credentials. Not for bragging purposes, of course, but simply to underscore the fact that we're trained professionals (with the exception of the occasional student collaborator and insight, ideas, and information from Dr. Edwards's son Will).[15] As psychologists, we've spent years honing our craft, earning Ph.D.s in our respective fields. We have years, if not decades of experience carrying out and publishing academic research. This means we've learned through formalized education (and a healthy dose of trial and error!) the proper way to design and analyze studies to avoid the sorts of pitfalls that might otherwise invalidate a hastily-thrown-together study by a well-meaning but amateur fan.

Some of us are bronies who happen to be psychologists. Others are psychologists who knew fans or found connections to the brony community in other ways. Others still are simply researchers interested in understanding what makes fan groups tick. But all of us share the common goal of doing carefully-crafted research under the oversight of institutional ethics committees. In short, we're scientists trying to do good science by the book!

Below, we highlight the expertise each of us brings to the table and explain how each of us got into this project.

Dr. Patrick Edwards. As previously mentioned, Dr. Edwards is the founder of the Brony Study Project. He has a Ph.D. in clinical psychology from the University of Georgia and has been teaching graduate and undergraduate psychology for over 30 years. His general research interests include health psychology, patients' responses to therapy, and factors influencing the development and expression of brony fan identity. In addition to teaching, he has worked in both private practice and in psychiatric hospitals as a clinician. While he would not officially call himself a Brony (to stay unbiased), he is a self-proclaimed "Brony Booster" and an avid supporter of the community. Currently, he has also published a fantasy novel (soon to be series of books) about a group of individuals who come together due to their shared brony interests, in no small part influenced by his work with the brony community.

Dr. Marsha Redden. Dr. Redden earned her Ph.D. in Clinical Psychology at Louisiana State University in 1973 and soon after began an independent clinical private practice in a small community in South Louisiana. Before retirement she spent her time working general practice, helping clients of all ages with a variety of issues. She retired in 2008 after 31 years and had, from that point on, served as an adjunct professor at a small liberal arts college, where she taught classes on research methods. Today, she still maintains a small private practice and engages in volunteer work. Along with Dr. Edwards, she represents the clinical expertise on the team.

Dr. Daniel Chadborn. Dr. Chadborn joined the group in 2013 after completing his master's degree at Southeastern Louisiana University. He has since received his Ph.D. in psychology with a focus on social and experimental psychology from Texas A&M University–Commerce. His research interests include understanding how groups affect peoples' sense of identity and the way they think, the factors which motivate fans, and anything having to do with social psychology in general. His early interest in researching the tabletop roleplayer community and his introduction to *MLP* by a group of friends led him to contact Drs. Edwards and Redden and eventually join the team. Since then he has continued to work on the project along with Drs. Reysen and Plante, with a social psychological/fan studies approach to the project. Currently, he is an assistant professor of psychology at New Mexico Highlands University where he teaches both undergraduate and graduate classes.[16]

Dr. Jan Griffin. Dr. Griffin has a Ph.D. in psychology with specialties in personality psychology, social psychology, and statistics. She has been teaching and doing research since 1980 after receiving her Ph.D. from Northern Illinois University. Her research interests include stereotyping, social stigma, and social influence. She is currently a professor at the University of South Carolina–Upstate, where she teaches a variety of classes and works with students on a variety of research projects. Her statistical expertise and insight was crucial early on in helping to make sense of the study's larger data sets and performed the more advanced statistical analysis presented both at BronyCon for the fans and professionally at a number of conferences. Her additional work has involved recruiting and supervising a number of undergraduate research assistants over the course of studying the fandom.

Dr. Stephen Reysen. Dr. Reysen has had a longstanding interest in researching fan communities, doing work with many different groups, most notably the furry and anime communities. He received his Ph.D. from the University of Kansas and is currently an associate professor of psychology at Texas A&M–Commerce, where he joined the study alongside Dr. Chadborn. He teaches courses related to social psychology, intergroup relations, and multicultural diversity and his research interests include topics related to personal identity (e.g., fanship, threats to public identity) and social identity (e.g., fandom, global citizenship).

Dr. Courtney "Nuka" Plante. Dr. Plante received his Ph.D. form the University of Waterloo in 2013 and is currently an instructor at MacEwan University where he teaches courses on social psychology, introductory psychology, and media psychology. His research interests include the effects of screen media, the functions of fantasy, and fan cultures. He (along with Dr. Reysen and two other researchers) is the co-founder of the International Anthropomorphic Research Project (IARP),[17] which has studied the furry fandom for the better part of a decade. He joined the Brony Study research team because of his own work studying bronies within the furry fandom and because of his own interest as a brony himself.[18]

William Edwards. William Edwards. Will is the son of Dr. Edwards. As a teenager he was the impetus for the Brony Study. He recently received a BS degree in Microbiology from Clemson University with a minor in Japanese (JLPT certified). He currently works as a lab technician and hopes to attend graduate school in the future. Will is an avid gamer and the artist responsible for "ponifying" Drs. Edward, Redden, and Griffin.

So What Kinds of Studies Have We Done?

Since the launch of the first survey in 2012, the Brony Study project has launched 19 surveys. We briefly want to touch on what they entailed and what our goals were for each of them, since they serve as the backbone of the findings reported throughout this book. For the most part, we'll present these studies below in the order they took place, though some of the studies (e.g., the longitudinal study) took place over the course of several years. The first wave of studies were headed by Drs. Edwards, joined shortly after by Dr. Redden, with Dr. Chadborn and Dr. Griffin joining the team partway through. What this early focus represents is more of an exploratory study of fandom and the bronies. Our main goal in these early studies was to utilize questions we thought were important to ask and through factor analysis (a method to combine items into a single factor like extraversion or group identity) examined patterns to follow up on in future studies. These studies looked at the brony fandom as a stand-alone phenomenon to examine what we could about them.[19] This is also the study in which we launched our investigation into the fan typology, a categorization of bronies based on open disclosure as a fan and sense of meaning gained from the show/group.[20]

Since 2015 Dr. Chadborn has been working with both Drs. Reysen and Plante on the second wave of studies, which have taken a more social psychological approach to the study of the fandom. And while the earlier studies focused on understanding who the bronies are and exploring fandom from the bottom up, the second wave has looked into testing hypotheses and relating those findings to current psychological theory (a top down approach). An overview of the studies can be found in Tables 2.1, 2.2, and 2.3 at the end of this chapter.

Wave One: 2012–2016

Brony Study 1. This first survey was launched after season 2 of the show, shortly before the first BronyCon in New York. The main goal of the study was to gather basic information about the brony community, their reactions to the show, and the reactions of non-bronies to the brony community. This survey attained a sample of non-bronies by asking bronies to send the survey to non-fan friends and family. This allowed us to look at the differences and similarities between bronies and non-bronies.

Brony Study 2. This follow-up study was launched post NYC BronyCon to expand on the work started with the first survey. This survey was our largest to date, both because included the largest sample of bronies (nearly 15,000!) and also included the largest number of items of any study to date, with questions about demographic information, personality, fans' favorite characters, Internet use, bullying, humor, and much more.

Brony Study 3. Launched in 2013–2014, our third major study removed non-fans to focus more on what motivates bronies to engage with the community and the show. In this study we asked questions about daydreaming, consumption and production of fan content, morality, and the acceptance and consumption of *MLP*-themed pornographic content.[21] It was at this point that we felt we had a fairly good understanding of the demographics and basic opinions of the brony fandom. From this point on, our surveys focused on testing specific hypotheses and occasionally updating our findings as we came across updated methods and scales.

The Exposure Study. Seeking to expand on previous psychological research showing that exposing people to other groups improves their attitudes toward those groups, we had a number of undergraduate students watch an episode of *MLP:FIM*. We were interested in their reactions to the show and whether their beliefs about bronies would change after viewing. We also measured how bronies tended to react to the show, along with questions about why bronies thought people might want to leave the fandom. This marked our first attempt to examine how the fandom itself was changing over time.

How the Fandom Changed My Life. Collected at the end of 2014, this survey was based on numerous emails the team had received from fans and parents describing the influence of the show and the fandom on their lives. We measured how being a brony had affected bronies for better and for worse, examined their first reactions to the show, and asked several questions regarding the abundance of male fans compared to female fans in a fandom for a show that was supposedly "for little girls."

Longitudinal Study. Over the course of several years (following BronyCon 2013 and ending after season 6 of the show), we conducted a series of studies aimed at tracking changes in the brony fandom over time. While not a traditional longitudinal study, where the same questions are asked to the same groups over time, we did track a several of the same variables over time. In this book, we largely look at each of these studies in isolation, as they each asked unique questions that were rarely asked (or not asked at all) in the other studies.

Other Short Surveys. Numerous smaller surveys were collected over the course of the first wave of Brony Study surveys to test a number of smaller hypotheses:

1. The Brony Feedback Study helped us get information from the community about their thoughts regarding our previous surveys and suggestions for what questions or research paths they wanted us to take in the future.
2. The Big 5 Survey, examined personality traits using up-to-date methods. It also sought feedback about famous fans and creators in the community.
3. The Brony Meetup Survey was undertaken by Dr. Edwards through his interaction with numerous local and national meetup groups. It aimed to study how members of the community came together and interacted in person in their local communities.
4. The BronyCon 2016 Short Survey was the last official Wave 1 survey. It examined cosplaying in the fandom, demographic variables, and looked at the possible functions of brony identity.

Wave Two: 2015–2018

Fan Functions Survey. This survey represents the transition between the earlier Brony Study surveys and a more community/social psychological focus for the project. The survey was based on prior surveys of other fan communities, which allowed us to compare bronies to other fan communities (e.g., anime fans, furries). This study looked at the functions that *MLP* and the brony fandom fulfilled for bronies, as well as what motivates bronies. The survey also represents the first push to make the findings available outside of convention and conference presentations and into the realm of published work in peer-reviewed scientific journals.

Brony Study 2016. Like the previous study, this study was based on previous work done with the furries and anime fans. It featured an extensive look at what it meant to identify as a member of the brony community, reassessed many of the Wave 1 survey items to get an up-to-date look on factors such as the favorite characters and attitudes, and was the first study to involve an experimental manipulation—looking at how uncertainty of the community's future influenced attitudes toward negative fan behaviors.

Brony Study 2017. A pair of studies was launched in 2017. The first examined fan behavior, favorite character identification, morality, and views regarding sexism. The second survey looked at charity and helping behavior, comparing bronies to other groups (e.g., university students, fans of the popular YouTube creators Rooster Teeth). We also tested what, precisely, motivates helping behavior in bronies and in other communities.

Brony Study 2018. Our most recent study aimed to address rumors about the end of *MLP:FIM* and how fans were responding to the existential threat potentially facing the community. While still undergoing analysis and preparation at the time of writing this book, we will present some of those findings here.

While this is the most recent study we have conducted, it will certainly not be the last, as we are already in the process of preparing our 2019 Brony Study as we write this book.

What Does the Future Hold?

Many of the founding members of the Brony Study have moved on to other projects or are enjoying their retirement. Likewise, *MLP:FIM* is said to be approaching its final season in 2019, along with the announcement that the final BronyCon will take place in the summer of 2019. Despite many of

Table 2.1. Wave 1 Survey Timeline and Information

Survey	Year	Size*	General Focus	Chapter Inclusion
Brony Study 1	2012	4200	Demographics	4–6, 7, 12, 14, 15, 16
Feedback Survey	2012	88	General feedback about the first survey.	18, 19
Brony Study 2	2012	10615	Main comparison between fans and non-fans.	4–6, 7, 14, 16, 17, 18, 19
Brony Study 3	2013	4276	Motivations, Internet use, consumption, morality, community and many other factors.	4–6, 8, 9, 10, 11, 13, 14, 15, 18, 19
Exposure Study	2013	4042	Exposed students to an episode, also examined Bronies on factors such as why people leave the fandom.	4–6, 7, 9, 14, 16, 17, 20
FCML Study	2014	1898	How the fandom changed my life, looking at pre/post fandom changes.	4–6, 7, 9, 10, 13, 15, 17, 18, 19
Big 5/Famous Fans	2015	1363	Personality and open ended data on prominent fan creators.	9
Meetup Study	2015	405	Information on why fans meet and what differs between those that do and don't.	8, 10, 13, 20

*This represents the number of participants after we removed anyone under the age of 18 for ethical reasons (as we need parental consent for those 17 and under).

these endings, however, it is far from the end of the brony fandom and our research with it. In many ways, the end of the show marks the beginning of an exciting new era of research—studying a community and what holds it together long after the original material around which the community was brought together is gone. For many fan communities, including the *Star Trek*, *Dr. Who*, and *Sherlock Holmes* fandoms, we've seen how the end of a series does not mean the end of the fandom. Our current research interests will continue to evolve as the community itself evolves and changes, focusing on new questions like who stays and who leaves and what keeps the community together in the long run.

The story of the brony community we tell in this book is expansive, stretching from the earliest studies in 2012 through the work conducted in 2018, on the eve of the last season of the show. But it is still only a part of the story of the brony fandom. We will continue to study the fandom, presenting

Table 2.2. Wave 1 Longitudinal Survey Timeline and Information

Survey	Year	Size	General Focus
Post Season 3	2013	4275	Assessed of factors concerning change in the community.
Pre-Season 4	2013	1773	Short follow up to post season 3.
Post Season 4	2014	1531	
Pre-Season 5	2015	2681	Expansion examining more in depth ratings of the show.
Pre-Season 6	2016	2149	More ratings and thoughts on the Equestria Girls movie.
Post Season 6	2016	1229	A broader survey on multiple factors assessed previously

Longitudinal survey data are covered in the following chapters: 7, 8, and 19.

Table 2.3. Wave 2 Survey Timeline and Information

Survey	Year	Size	General Focus	Chapter Inclusion
Fan Functions	2015	2525	Broad survey understanding the functions and motivation in fandom.	9, 19
Brony Study 16	2016	1055	Social psychological focus also examined identity uncertainty theory in fans.	4–6, 8, 9, 10, 11, 12, 13, 17, 18, 20
Brony Study 17	2017	590	Re-examines favorite character and a number of additional social psych. factors.	5, 8, 17, 19
Prosocial Study	2017	1130	Examined fan motivations for prosocial giving in multiple fan communities.	5, 6, 8, 7, 13, 17, 19
Brony Study 18	2018	221	Used a mortality salience manipulation to assess feelings tied to the fandom ending.	8, 9, 13, 14, 15, 17, 18, 19, 20

and publishing our work and communicating with the fandom for as long as there is still a brony community.

It's been a heck of a ride so far, and we're looking forward to where the future takes us!

Chapter 3

Sampling, Statistics, Research Design and Other Nerd Stuff

"I'm doing scientific research. I'm observing Pinkie Pie, scientific name: Pinkius Piecus, in its natural habitat."
—Twilight Sparkle (Season 1, Episode 15, Feeling Pinkie Keen*)*

Before we dive head-first into what the research on bronies can tell us it be*hooves* us to talk a bit about research methodology itself. After all, what good is a book full of numbers if we don't know the first thing about how we got those numbers, what they mean, or whether they can even be trusted? Indeed, given the ease with which people make up statistics and post them online, it's worth taking a moment to educate ourselves on how science comes up with these numbers and whether they can be trusted in the first place.

You can treat this chapter as a brief summary of some of the things you would learn in an introductory undergraduate science course. We'll start off at the beginning with a brief review of what the goal of science is and why we do studies in the first place. We'll then discuss the messy business of turning day-to-day experiences into numbers that we can summarize, analyze, and draw inferences from—a process called operationalization.[1] After that, we'll discuss how scientists design and implement studies, in much the same way a craftsperson uses a set of tools to accomplish a particular job. Following that, we'll address specific concerns about sampling and how to make sense of statistics. Finally, we'll end the chapter with a brief discussion about the imperfectness of scientific studies and how, despite these imperfections, we can nevertheless learn something from them.

A Crash Course in the Scientific Method

The first mistake laypersons make when they talk about science is to treat science like a tool. For many people who don't work in a scientific field, science is a thing you swing around to add credibility to your point. For example, if you wanted to *prove* to someone that playing video games improved your intelligence, you might search the Internet for a scientist who claims that there's a link between playing video games and intelligence. Even better if they can give you an official-sounding number, something like "People who play video games are 53% smarter than those who don't!"[2] Others, seeing your statistic and the apparent blessing of science, would be forced to either concede that the science is on your side or, just as likely, would be forced to wade through science to find *their own* scientist with a *different* statistic!

As you can probably tell from our tone, this isn't how science is done by actual scientists. Science isn't a club you swing around to prove your point and win arguments. Instead, science is a process, a way of systematically studying the world around us. It's a way to objectively gather facts and interpret them in a manner that's as humble and self-critical as possible. Science is something you *do*, not something to be *used.*[3]

So how, exactly, does science work?

Well, it often starts with an observation about the world. An astute person will notice something about the world, like a tendency for objects to fall toward the ground or a tendency for people to pull their hands away from a burning stovetop. From these observations, they form a theory about how the world works.[4] If the theory is any good, it will be able to generate hypotheses-testable statements about what *ought* to happen if the theory is, in fact, true. As a simple example using the theory of gravity, one might say, "If the theory of gravity is an accurate model of how the universe works, then an apple released from my hand should fall towards the ground." In the realm of psychology, we might say, "If social identity theory is an accurate model of the way people form their self-esteem, then a person who strongly identifies with a group that they view in a positive light should experience higher self-esteem than a person who does not identify with such a group."

Ultimately, hypotheses exist to be tested. This leads to our next step in the scientific method, hypothesis-testing. Scientists craft studies aimed at systematically and objectively testing whether their hypothesis is false. At first, it seems a bit backwards to test whether a hypothesis is false, but that's because it's impossible to prove that a hypothesis is 100 percent correct. After all, if I dropped an apple and saw it fall to the ground, it would certainly *support* my hypothesis that gravity causes things to fall. But it could never prove that this was *always* the case. Remember, part of the process of being a skeptical scientist is acknowledging the possibility, however remote, that the *next* time I drop an apple, it might do something *entirely* different! Even if it were possible to drop apples for the rest of time, it would still not eliminate the possibility that at some point, in some place, something could be dropped that *wouldn't* fall to the ground. Because this possibility always exists, we don't try to prove our hypotheses correct—we try to prove them *incorrect*. If we can find an example of an apple that *doesn't* fall, our hypothesis is deemed to be false. Otherwise, we can treat it as functionally true ... *for now*.[5]

Let's assume that, after running our study, the evidence supports our hypothesis rather than disproving it. What now? It means that our original theory—our model for how the world works—is supported by our test. It means that we can use our theory to make useful predictions about what we can expect to happen in the world. It means we can be a bit more confident in our understanding of the natural world. And, if we're good scientists, we'll share our findings with other scientists, who'll then scrutinize our work, check it for mistakes or weaknesses, and possibly run studies of their own. If our theory conflicts with their theory, they may design a study pitting the two theories against one another, to see which of two hypotheses is more strongly supported by the evidence.

And if the data go *against* our hypothesis? It means that our original theory was flawed—it led to a hypothesis that doesn't match up with the real world. It means we have to go back to the drawing board, throwing away our theory entirely or, more likely, revising our theory to make it better match reality. Then, once we've tweaked it and worked the kinks out of it, we generate a new hypothesis and try it all again![6]

Rinse and repeat for a few centuries, and you have the scientific method as it's used to this day!

Operationalization: Putting Numbers to Experience

While the previous section nicely summarized the scientific method, it *did* gloss over quite a few details. One such detail is the question of how, precisely, we gather data about the world around us.

When we think about data, we're often talking about numbers. And when it comes to the physical world, there's no shortage of things we can measure: How fast is something moving? How tall is it? How much does it weigh? What temperature is it? How long does a chemical reaction last for? These are all physical properties about the world that we have, over the millennia, devised ways of putting numbers to (e.g., kilometers per hour, meters, kilograms, or degrees Celsius.)[7]

But not everything lends itself so easily to measurement. Let's say, for example, that we wanted to measure John's aggression. How, exactly, do we do that? It's not like we can crack open John's skull, grab a ruler, and measure the aggression inside with a ruler. John's aggression is not a physical, tangible thing, it's an abstract concept. And, as it turns out, psychology is full of such concepts: extraversion, motivation, group identity, happiness, and jealousy, to name just a few. None of these things are easily quantifiable—none of them have an obvious way of turning the abstract concept into a number.

One possible way out of this problem is to simply limit ourselves to only measuring things that we can see, touch, and measure. Doing so *would* skirt the problem of not having an easy, intuitive way to measure these abstract constructs.[8] However, this approach does have a downside—dramatically limits our ability to study most of human experience. This is unnecessary, we would argue. After all, while we may not be able to crack John's head open and measure his aggression with a ruler, we *can* measure the by-products or consequences of John's aggression: How many times has John punched someone? How angry, on a 1 to 10 scale, does John feel in this moment? How quickly do thoughts related to violence come to John's mind? How readily does John recognize and respond to violence-related words and images on a screen?

Of course, you might argue, all of these are proxy measures for the thing we *actually* want to measure—John's aggression. And we would entirely agree! But when you think about it, is it *really* all that different from how we measure other things in our world? How do we measure temperature, for example? Well, if you're using a mercury thermometer, you're measuring the amount of volume that a known mass of mercury takes up. This measure of volume is a proxy measure of what you're actually trying to measure—the average kinetic energy of the particles in an area.

And while you could certainly argue that measuring someone's aggression through the number of fights they've been in is an imperfect way to measure aggression, take a closer look at the other measurement devices science uses. Many of them have their own imperfections. Take a metal ruler, for example. You can use it to measure an object's height, sure, but the answer you get will vary depending on the temperature of the room: Metal expands when it's warm and contracts when it's cold. Likewise, all electronic scales involve a margin of error or a point in which they are no longer sensitive.[9] Put simply, there *are* no perfect measures in science!

Psychologists have the particularly difficult job of trying to figure out creative and valid ways to meaningfully measure abstract constructs. But over the years they have devised ways to do so. Sometimes they involve measuring behavior (e.g., How many dollars did someone donate to charity?) Other times they involve participants self-reporting their own feelings or beliefs (e.g., On a 1 to 7 scale from "Not at all" to "Strongly agree," how much do you agree or disagree with the statement "I strongly identify with the brony community?"). And while each measure may, itself, be imperfect, scientists have a long track record of learning a surprising amount about the world using flawed and imperfect measures. We'll talk more about this in the last section of this chapter on the fallacy of the imperfect study.

The Science (and Art) of Study Design

While science should be thought of as a process or a way of thinking rather than as a tool, it *does* make sense to treat individual studies as tools used by scientists. Studies are carefully crafted by scientists to fulfill a certain purpose, whether it's to test a particular hypothesis, to pit two or more competing hypotheses against one another, or simply to explore a particular topic and gather observations to help scientists form a theory.

When it comes to tools, it's important to use the right tool for the job. Studies are no different: Depending on its intended purpose, different studies will vary in their appropriateness. As an analogy, hammers work great if your job is to drive a nail into a wall to hang a picture. Hammers are terrible tools, however, if your job is to paint a wall or loosen a screw. In the same vein, certain types of studies are great if your goal is to measure the relationship between two variables (e.g., group identity and happiness) in a sample, but terrible if your goal is to determine a causal pathway (e.g., whether donating to charity *causes* people to feel happier).

Scientists have all sorts of study designs at their disposal. In fact, you can take entire courses and read textbooks on the subject.[10] For now, we'll spare you the nitty-gritty details and instead briefly go over three types of "tools" commonly used by psychologists—types of studies designed to fulfill one purpose or another.

By far one of the most common studies you'll read about (certainly in this book) is the *cross-sectional* study. It's a fairly simple, fairly intuitive study design aimed at testing whether there's a relationship between two or more things. The gist of the study design is this: If you want to know whether two things are related, get a large sample of people, measure both things, and then see whether people who scored high or low on one of the things differ in a predictable way on the other thing. So, for example, if we wanted to know whether watching *MLP* is related to donating to charity, we would get a sample of people, measure how much they watch *MLP* and how much they donate to charity, and then test whether those who watched *more MLP* also happened to give more to charity than those watched less *MLP*.

Cross-sectional studies have a number of benefits. First and foremost, they're fairly intuitive and simple to conduct. The study itself only involves contacting participants at a single point in time (e.g., a single survey). This means that researchers can give the survey out (via e-mail, in person) to *thousands* of people in a short amount of time. Another strength of the cross-sectional study is that it's fairly good at assessing "real-world" behavior (e.g., how often did you watch *MLP* last week?).[11]

But cross-sectional studies, like with any tool, have their own limitations. Arguably their *biggest* limitation is their inability to allow researchers to infer causal direction. To see what we mean, let's imagine that, in one of our surveys, we found that people who watch more *MLP* also reported that they were kinder people than people who watched less *MLP*. One possible interpretation of this finding is that watching *MLP causes* people to become more kind. But the reverse is also possible: Maybe being a kind person *causes* people to watch more *MLP*. But a third possibility also exists: Perhaps it's neither! Maybe some additional factor is causing *both* kindness and *MLP*-watching to *appear* to be related to one another. For example, perhaps having friends who are bronies *causes* people to watch more *MLP and* causes them to become kinder. In this case, watching *MLP* and kindness may have nothing to do with each other *directly*, but are only related because they're both related to having friends who are bronies.

This problem is commonly summarized by the statement "correlation does not equal causation," and it's a pretty considerable limitation of the cross-sectional study. The inability to definitively show the direction of the relationship between any two variables means that a cross-sectional study can only tell us, at best, whether a relationship exists. This is why you'll so often hear researchers talk about an *association* between X and Y rather than saying that X *causes* or *increases* Y. Scientists are very precise with their wording for this reason, to avoid making claims that are not supported by their data.

One way to partially overcome the problem of not being able to infer causal direction is with a second type of study, known as a *longitudinal* study. In a nutshell, these studies are identical to cross-sectional studies with an extra twist: Instead of doing the survey once, you do the survey *multiple* times in the same group of participants. For example, you might ask a group of 200 people how often they watch *MLP* and how kind they are in 2015. Then, two years later, you could track down the same 200 people and ask them the same questions again. As a result, you would be able to not only look at how much they watched *MLP* and how kind they were in 2015 and in 2017, but you would *also* be able to look at how those two variables *changed* over time.

This added element of time gives us a surprising amount of power to answer some interesting research questions. For example, we can test the hypothesis that as people *increase* in the amount of *MLP* they watch over time they also become *increasingly* kind in a proportionate fashion (i.e., bigger increases in watching the show yield bigger increases in kindness). It also allows us to pit both causal directions against one another: Does kindness at an earlier point in time predict watching *MLP* at a later point in time, or is the opposite true, that watching *MLP* at an earlier point in time predicts kindness at a later point in time?

Unfortunately, despite this strength of the longitudinal design, it has its own drawbacks. The first is that it's *much* harder to conduct a longitudinal design than a survey design. In a survey, it's only necessary to send out surveys to a group of people once. In a longitudinal design, it's necessary to track down the same participants at a later point in time—something that can be surprisingly difficult after just a few months, let alone a few years. For example, perhaps we studied 200 bronies in our first sample. It might be hard to track down and study the same bronies two years later. Some of them may not want to do our survey a second time. Some may have left the brony fandom altogether and thus not want to complete a brony-related survey. Some may have moved or changed their contact information, preventing us from finding them. In short, trying to get back even a fraction of the original sample can be surprisingly difficult!

A second weakness of the longitudinal study design is its inability to *completely* rule out the third-variable problem. Despite the fact that it is able to compare whether X causes Y or Y causes X, it cannot rule out the possibility that a third variable, Z, is causing both to occur. Without measuring Z in the study, it's impossible to know whether Z caused both X and Y to happen! And, as it turns out, there are an infinite number of potential Zs out there!

This leads us to our third type of study: the experimental design. Experiments are specifically designed to allow researchers to test causal direction—in fact, they are the gold standard for doing so! The logic of the experimental design goes like this: You take all of your participants and you assign them to two or more conditions completely at random. One condition might be to watch an episode of *MLP* while another might be to watch an episode of a different show. After viewing the show (or whatever the difference between the conditions happens to be), you then measure some outcome variable (e.g., kindness). If the two groups differ on the outcome variable (e.g., the *MLP* group scored higher on kindness after watching the show than the non–*MLP* group), the researcher can conclude that the difference between the groups was *caused* by whatever the researcher manipulated between the two conditions (in this case, the television show they watched).

But how can the researchers be so confident that it was the manipulation that caused the difference in kindness, and not the fact that the groups just happened to differ on kindness at the start of the study? That's where the random assignment comes in. Without getting into too many ugly statistics, assigning people to the two conditions completely at random means that there is no reason for one group to be higher on kindness (or any other variable). For example, because the groups were randomly assigned, there should be, statistically speaking, an equal number of men and women in both groups, as well as an equal number of older people, younger people, tall people, kind people, fans of the show, et cetera. To be sure, it *is* entirely possible that by sheer coincidence, we just so happened to have put all the "kind" people in the "*MLP*" condition and all the "unkind" people in the "not-*MLP*" condition out of sheer dumb luck.[12] While scientists acknowledge this possibility, however, they also acknowledge that this is highly unlikely—especially as the sample size gets bigger and bigger. It is thus far more reasonable to conclude, if participants were truly randomly assigned, that the difference between the two groups on kindness was *caused* by the manipulation of the television show.

While experiments are an excellent tool for testing causal direction, they are, like the other studies we have discussed, not without their own limitations. For one thing, experiments can be much more difficult to conduct than cross-sectional studies. For example, while it's easy to send a survey link out to 5,000 bronies, it's *much* more time-consuming to bring hundreds of people into a laboratory to have them watch an episode of a show. It *is* possible to make the manipulation part of a survey (e.g., to randomly assign people to read X or Y in a survey), and that's certainly something we, the researchers, have done before. But a second major problem with experiments is that they tend to involve less "mundane realism" than cross-sectional studies—that is, they *feel* less realistic than real-world conditions. For example—making a person watch an episode of *MLP* in the lab for research purposes may be *very* different from how the person watches the show on their own. In the lab, they may watch a single episode of the show in sterile white room on a TV screen, whereas at home they watch it on their computer with their friends, surrounded by their *MLP* merchandise, while munching on snacks. These sorts of differences can sometimes lead to results that tell us a lot about causal direction but say little about how the phenomenon itself occurs out in the "real world."

In the last section of this chapter we'll talk about how scientists deal with the limitations inherent in each of these research designs and how, despite these imperfections, we can still learn a lot about the world. But for now, let's switch our attention to a couple of other important facets of research: How we get our samples and how we analyze and make sense of our data?

Sampling: Who Are We Talking About

Once we've settled on what kind of study we're going to run, it's time to go out and find some willing participants![13] At first glance, this seems like this shouldn't be all that hard: Just find a group of people and ask them if they want to participate in your study. If you're interested in studying a particular group of people (e.g., bronies), then it's just a matter of going wherever bronies go (e.g., conventions) and asking them there, right?

Yes and no. True, if you want to study a group like bronies, it makes sense to recruit participants from places where you're bound to find lots of bronies. This would certainly raise your likelihood of finding brony participants (as compared asking random people on the street if hey happened to be a brony). On the other hand, researchers need to be concerned about something called *generalizability*. Generalizability refers to the extent to which we can take the results of a study and apply them to the group as a whole. Intuitively, you probably already have a fairly good understanding of this idea, even if you've never put it into words before.

To illustrate, let's imagine that we, as researchers working at a university, decided to conduct a survey of bronies to help us better understand the brony community. Conveniently, we learn that there is a weekly meeting of the university's brony club in the building next door! We attend one of these meetings and the club members agree to fill out our survey. After analyzing the data, we discover that 100 percent of our sample (unsurprisingly) has some university education! From this, we conclude that *all* bronies are university-educated.

Hopefully you see the problem here. Our sample of bronies did not reflect the entire brony population. While it *was* a convenient sample for us to use, using this sample sacrificed our ability to *generalize* from our study's findings to the entire brony population—at least when it comes to questions about education. At first glance this seems like a pretty obvious oversight, leading you to wonder how anyone can ever run into this problem. But keep in mind that this was a deliberately extreme example. The more you delve into the problem of sample generalizability, the more you realize just how subtle and difficult-to-avoid the issue can get!

For example, let's say you decided to get a far more generalizable sample of bronies by attending a large brony convention with more than 10,000 attendees. Great! Now we've got bronies from all walks of life, all types of education, and all sorts of backgrounds—surely the problem of generalizability is dealt with!

Well, not exactly. After all, there are geographical limitations when it comes to attending a brony convention. If the convention takes place in the Northeastern United States, it will tend to contain more people from the Northeastern United States than, say, people from the Southwestern United States. Moreover, it will be more likely to include North American bronies than, say, Australian bronies or European bronies. Each of those geographical biases will introduce new biases into your sample, including differences in language, culture, political beliefs, and socio-economic status. And speaking of socio-economic status, it's not exactly *cheap* to attend a convention. By drawing your sample from a convention, you're excluding bronies who may not have the money to attend (e.g., students, unemployed, in debt, medical bills, etc.).

Drawing your sample from an online source might help eliminate *some* of these problems, but it also introduces entirely new biases as well. Where do you advertise your survey? If, for instance, you advertise your survey on popular brony art websites, you may be missing bronies who aren't interested in fan-generated artwork. If you advertise on brony-related news websites, you exclude bronies who don't frequent those particular sites. Sampling from the Internet itself introduces the problem of missing bronies who don't own a computer or who lack reliable Internet access. It may also preferentially select bronies who are younger and more in touch with social media and Internet culture while excluding older bronies who may enjoy the show but be less adept when it comes to the Internet. And this isn't even *considering* the language your survey is being conducted in, because if it's only in English, you're going to miss out on a lot of bronies who only speak French, Spanish, German, Russian, or Japanese.

So does this mean that it's impossible to get a perfectly generalizable sample of bronies? In a word: yes. The very practice of sampling from a population means that researchers will inevitably have an imperfect picture of the group as a whole. Or, to put it another way, the only way to get an absolutely perfect picture of a group is to study every single member of the group. Anything less than studying everyone will *necessarily* involve some imperfections when trying to match your data to the entire population. The best that researchers can do is to be mindful of these limitations when designing their studies, balance convenience of a sample against its generalizability, and avoid, whenever possible, avoid drawing conclusions about topics from samples which are heavily biased on that topic (like "education" in our university brony club example).

We'll discuss more about the sorts of trade-offs and what researchers can learn from imperfect samples in the final section of this chapter.

Data Analysis: Making Sense of the Numbers

Don't worry, we *promise* this won't turn into a lecture about statistics! Instead, we're going to briefly look over the types of analyses that are commonly done in this area of research and what researchers are able to conclude from these analyses. Statistical analysis is something that's pretty unintuitive for a lot of people. Despite this, people are often persuaded by statistics without actually knowing where the numbers themselves come from! This is why it's so important for us to "show our work," so to speak, to let you know *how* we come up with the numbers we do and why we draw the conclusions we do in this book.

There are two general "flavors" of statistics: descriptive statistics and inferential statistics. Descriptive statistics are the sorts of statistics that the average person thinks about when they hear the word "statistics." Put simply, descriptive statistics *describe* some feature in a sample. For example, saying that 80 percent of a sample is over the age of 18 tells us something about our sample: It's mostly comprised of adults. Likewise, saying that the average person in our study is 5'11" or that the average participant rates chocolate a 9.1/10 on a "likeability" scale tells us something about the most common or general tendencies of our sample. Other things we can look at are now much variability is in our data (e.g., is everyone somewhere close to 5'11" in our sample, or are they all over the place with respect to their heights, and the average just happens to be 5'11"?) or the range of our data (e.g., how much of a difference is there between the shortest and the tallest person in our study?)

Descriptive statistics are fairly easy to understand and intuitive, and this book will include plenty of them. Any time we talk about what percent of our sample agreed with a statement, or what the average response of participants in our samples were, we're relying on descriptive statistics. They give us a handful of numbers to help us get a clearer picture of the group we're studying at a glance.

Inferential statistics are a bit more complex, but are also a lot more powerful and broad in their application. In a nutshell, inferential statistics allow us to answer important questions that typically involve comparing our descriptive statistics to other numbers in some meaningful way. For example, let's say we're comparing two groups: bronies and non-bronies. Let's say we find that bronies score an average of 6 on a measure of happiness while non-bronies score an average of 3 on that same measure. At first glance, we might conclude, "Well, clearly bronies are happier than non-bronies!"

But can we *actually* conclude that from just looking at the averages? Not exactly. Let's imagine, for example, that our samples only looked at one brony and one non-brony. Sure, the one brony that made up our sample scored higher than the one non-brony in our sample, but can we *really* conclude from this that the *entire* population of bronies score higher on average than the entire population of non-bronies? Probably not; after all, we could run the study again with a different brony and a different non-brony and wind up with dramatically different results!

We *could* increase our sample size to 100 bronies and 100 non-bronies, but it *still* wouldn't be enough to *only* look at the difference between the averages. What you need to do is look at how big the difference *between* the groups is and look at how much variability there is *within* each group. For example, let's say our sample of 100 bronies scored an average of 6 on the happiness scale, with every brony scoring somewhere between 5.5 and 6.5. And let's say our 100 non-bronies scored an average of 3, with each non-brony scoring between 2.5 and 3.5. In this case, the difference *between* the groups is 3 points, while the differences *within* each group is 1. This means there's a fairly large difference between the groups relative to how much variability there is *within* each group. Or, to put it another way, it means that if we were to grab *another* sample of 100 bronies and 100 non-bronies, their averages probably wouldn't differ all that much from 6 and 3—meaning you would probably find the same difference between the groups.

This is what inferential statistics allow researchers to do: to determine how likely it is that differences between a group and a point of comparison are due simply to random chance or due to a *real* difference. Different statistical tests allow us to compare two groups in this way (e.g., *t*-tests), three or more groups in this way (e.g., Analyses of Variance—ANOVAs), or to test whether a relationship between two variables is so much larger or smaller than zero that it's probably not due to chance (e.g., correlations, regression analyses, structural equation modeling).

So if we, as researchers trained in statistical methods, say something like "Bronies are significantly more kind than non-bronies," we're basing this conclusion on inferential statistics. It's not opinion, and it's more than just comparing which of the two averages is larger. It's shorthand for saying, "Bronies in our sample scored *so* much higher than the non-bronies in our sample on this measure of kindness that we wouldn't expect to see this big of a difference due to chance alone. If we were to run this study again and again, we'd only expect the non-bronies to beat the bronies maybe 1 out of 20 times!"

For the sake of brevity—and to spare you the gruesome details of the literally hundreds of pages of statistical output that went into this book—we've avoided putting statistical gobbledygook in the book. Where we think it might be interesting to readers, we provide basic descriptive statistics (e.g., percentages of bronies who agreed with a statement or average scores on a particular measure). But rest assured that behind every statement we make about bronies in this book, unless otherwise stated, there is a statistical test! It's what separates science from rumors, speculation, and opinion.

Limitations and the Fallacy of the Perfect Study

Up to this point we've learned a bit about how the scientific method works, how researchers pick their measures, design their studies, gather their samples, and analyze their data. If you're a skeptical or highly critical reader, however, you've probably noticed something—there are *all sorts* of places where flaws, limitations, and weaknesses can creep into our studies. And you're entirely correct in noticing this. In fact, let us spell it out so this frightening implication is crystal-clear to the reader.

There are no perfect studies.

It bears repeating: Nowhere in science is there a single example of a perfect study—one that is without flaws, alternative explanations, limited measurement devices, or potential biases. It's true, whether we're talking about psychology, chemistry, biology, or physics. The entirety of the human race's scientific understanding of the world is built upon this house of cards![14]

To help you understand how this can be true, we suggest thinking about research in the same way you'd think about designing a car: It isn't about designing something *perfect*. After all, there *is* no perfect car. The perfect car would be blazingly fast, completely safe, incredibly powerful, resistant to breakdowns, lightweight, comfortable, and affordable. It should become apparent to you that a car *cannot* be all of these things at once because some of these things completely contradict one another. As you put a smaller, lighter engine into the car, you're sacrificing its power and durability. As you put higher-quality parts into a car, you're also making it more expensive. As you make the car smaller and sleeker, you're also making it less comfortable and limit the passenger space inside. Car design, you could say, is about making a series of trade-offs to design the right car for the right job.

Research should be approached with the same mindset. There is no perfect experiment: It's impossible to design a study where researchers have complete control over every outside variable, while still creating a situation that feels perfectly natural to the participant. It's impossible to design a measure that perfectly captures every element of a person's personality without also being so long that participants get bored and stop paying attention. It's impossible to obtain a sample that perfectly generalizes to an entire population while also being affordable, reasonable, and able to be conducted in a timely fashion. Each time you design a study to have a particular strength, you necessarily sacrifice something the study can do well. It's not about creating the perfect study: It's about creating a study that tests the hypothesis you want to test in a *good enough* way.

But how can we *learn* anything from flawed studies? To understand this, you need to understand that a weakness in a study doesn't mean that the study itself needs to be thrown away entirely. In fact, if we took this approach, literally every single scientific study ever conducted would find itself in the trash bin of history. Instead, studies should be thought of as single pieces of evidence used to test and support theories. It all boils down to comparing the relative weight of the evidence for each theory. If Theory A has one study supporting its claims and Theory B has 10 studies supporting its claims, we can say that there is *more* evidence supporting Theory B than Theory A. The *wrong* approach would be to go through each of Theory B's studies and say, "Oh, this one has a weakness, throw it away … this one has a weakness too, throw it away."

This principle is known as *converging evidence*—the idea that while each individual study may have its unique flaws and limitations, different studies will have *different, overlapping* strengths and weaknesses. For example, a study of bronies conducted at a convention might conclude that bronies are a fairly agreeable and trusting group of people. But such a study is limited because it ignores bronies who cannot attend conventions. But if another *online* study of bronies comes to the *same* conclusion, we can be pretty confident that the conclusion is a valid one, because the studies, despite their different designs and limitations, nevertheless point to the same conclusion. This is why researchers often conduct a *series* of studies on a subject, rather than running one study and calling it a day. Very rarely do researchers ground an entire scientific theory on the results of a single study.

This is also why it's not enough for critics to simply poke holes in a study in order to "disprove" its conclusions. For example, let's say we ran a convention-based study of bronies and found that bronies are fairly outgoing, friendly people. A critic might say, "Yeah, but your sample is biased and ignores bronies who don't go to conventions!" This doesn't mean that our conclusion must therefore be *false*! It only means that we might need to do an additional study to see whether our results apply to *all* bronies or only apply to convention-going bronies. Likewise, if we find a link between watching *MLP* and kindness, a critic might say, "Yeah, but correlation doesn't prove causation!" This doesn't mean that it's *impossible* for watching *MLP* to cause kindness. It simply means that a follow-up study is needed to test how kindness and *MLP*-watching are related.

In sum, as we describe our findings from years of studying the brony fandom throughout this book, we very much encourage you read with a critical, skeptical eye. This is precisely what a good scientist *ought* to do! But being skeptical and critical is about more than finding flaws and burning it all to the ground. One of the most important skills a critic must have is to understand the implications of a particular criticism—what can a study tell us, and what can't it tell us? Only then can we avoid throwing the proverbial baby out with the bathwater![15]

Chapter 4

Just *How* Extremely Unexpected Are the Adult Fans of *My Little Pony*?

My character?! We are real ponies! This journal is a record of things that actually happened to us!

—*Twilight Sparkle (Season 7, Episode 14,* Fame and Misfortune)

For most non-bronies, their understanding of the brony fandom comes largely from the Internet rumor mill and news coverage of the community. In fact, the first major coverage of the brony fandom *combined* these two sources in the form of a Wired.com piece, "My Little Pony Corrals Unlikely Fanboys Known as 'Bronies,'" which sparked a series of shocked and generally negative responses (Watercutter, 2011). One year later, news outlets such as *The Guardian* (Angel, 2012) referred to bronies as rebels who bucked gender stereotypes.[1] Both of these pieces frame the brony fandom as being one defined by deviance. This framing of bronies as unusual or unlikely, along with all of the stigmatizing stereotypes associated with the fandom (for more on this, see Chapter 17) became one of the main driving forces of our study. We wanted to investigate whether there was any truth behind these characterizations of the community, and to do so using data instead of anecdote or baseless accusation.[2] We sought to do so in part because people tend to trust information, especially information collected by trusted individuals using trusted methods (Kaptein, Markopoulos, De Ruyter, & Aarts, 2015). It's also been shown that shedding light on a stigmatized group can help improve peoples' views and understanding about that group (Birtel & Crisp, 2012; Heijnders & Van Der Meij, 2006; Hughto, Reisner, & Pachankis, 2015).[3]

If the research presented throughout this book is our attempt to shed light on this often-misunderstood community, then the present series of chapters is our first step toward that goal. It represents some of the most basic data on the brony fandom, data which can help us get a mental image of what the average brony is like. This includes the more basic information concerning the bronies' age, country of origin, upbringing, day-to-day life, and everything in between.[4] Before we can understand the mind of a brony and how being a brony can affect someone's psyche, we first need to know who these people are and how they match up to against non-bronies. And, perhaps most importantly, a little understanding about the fan community can help us avoid jumping to conclusions about just how weird or "unexpected" bronies really are.

The Prototypical Brony: It Isn't the "Mane" Thing About Them

Once someone gets an idea into their head, it can be notoriously difficult to change their mind about it. Applied to the present discussion, once a person has an idea of what the "brony" label represents, the idea shapes everything else they think about the group. In principle, this isn't necessarily a problem. Normally we base our labels, stereotypes, and preconceptions about something on observations and first-hand experience. In other words, we might well assume that bronies are like X precisely *because* we've seen bronies who look like X.

The problem arises when these preconceptions don't accurately reflect reality. To see an example of this, let's imagine a large crowd of typical young adults. Chances are fairly good that at least *some* of them will be wearing a fedora. Some will live in their parents' basement or be unemployed/underemployed. Some might disassemble toasters and rebuild them into alarm clocks for fun. The point is, with a large enough group, you'll find examples of pretty much any behavior you can imagine, no matter how rare or unusual it is.

This same principle holds true if the large group in question happens to be a large group of bronies. As it turns out, with a large enough group of bronies, we can find pretty much any behavior we'd care to look for: sexual deviancy, criminal behavior, or social awkwardness. The problem is that the existence of *examples* of this behavior in a group doesn't mean that these behaviors are *common* in the group, nor do they mean that the behavior *defines* the group. Defining what a group is involves distilling a common essence from all of the group's members. Sometimes this can be done pretty well—especially for groups with a long history that rally behind a clear and oft-repeated goal. The Ku Klux Klan (KKK), for instance, has a decades-long history of espousing hyper-nationalist views and opposing immigration into the U.S. Because of the length of time these views have been espoused for and the consistency of these views among members of the group, it's a pretty safe bet to say that your average KKK member probably has some deep-seated racial biases and some pretty strong attitudes about what the U.S. ought to look like.

But can the same be said about bronies—or about fan groups in general? What "common essence" defines them? Well, about the only thing we can be pretty sure that they have in common is that they all happen to like the same thing: Mets fans like the New York Mets, Trekkies like *Star Trek*, and bronies like *My Little Pony: Friendship Is Magic*.[5] Unlike baseball and *Star Trek*, however, which have been around for long enough that people generally accept that a community of fans can (and do!) organize around these interests, the same cannot be said for bronies, who are still relatively new to the scene. Describing bronies as "people who like *MLP*" doesn't seem like "enough" of an explanation. It *can't* be the whole story: They seem so *unusual*, especially when framed by media stories as a bunch of deviants.

As such, people go out of their way to further "explain" bronies—something that, for any other fan interest or hobby, needs no explanation. This need to explain leads people to fixate on examples of particularly extreme bronies, particularly surprising pictures or images, or shocking anecdotes from non-bronies who've heard from a friend of a friend about something they saw a brony do once. In time, our definition of what a brony is becomes unnecessarily complex, since it becomes saddled with all sorts of extra characteristics and traits that may only describe a *fraction* of the group. It's how a group of people who just like a cartoon somehow become gay, fedora-wearing, basement-dwelling, socially awkward, gender-confused nerds.

All of this being said, there wouldn't be any need to explain who the bronies are if they were *exactly* like everyone else. Clearly, there are *some* things that make bronies different enough from the average person that people have taken notice. But we would caution that even if such differences occur, they're unlikely to be the differences that warrant the sorts of stereotypes that exist when it comes to the brony fandom. Nor are these differences part of the *definition* of what makes a brony a brony. And it would certainly be a stretch to assume that *every* brony has these characteristics—just as you wouldn't assume that every doctor, librarian, or psychologist matches the stereotypes of *those* professions. Everyone is different, and that's just as true for bronies as it is for any other group of people, up to and including those strange New York Mets fans.

Basic Demographics

Despite the fact that bronies are a fairly diverse group of folks, we *can* look at average tendencies within the group. These averages can help us piece together an image of what a typical brony looks like, where the majority of them are from, and a lot of information about their thoughts, feelings, and behaviors.[6] In the following section we'll be covering some of the basic characteristics of the brony community, including information on age and gender, how long they've been in the fandom, their membership in other fandoms, and much more. We'll follow this up with a discussion about differences between male and female bronies and some of the differences we've observed between fans and non-fans. We'll save some of the more in-depth questions about bronies, such as education, parental and peer information, and country of residence for the next chapter.[7]

Age and Sex[8]

In a single sentence, bronies are, as a group, predominantly young adult (18–25 years old) males (see Figures 4.1 and 4.2). It *is* worth noting that the fandom probably trends a bit younger than is observed in our samples. This is because we somewhat *overestimate* the age of the average brony due our need to exclude anyone under 18 for ethical reasons. It should also be noted that not all male fans of *MLP* would call themselves a brony and, as we will discuss a little later, female fans may well engage with the community *more* than male fans.

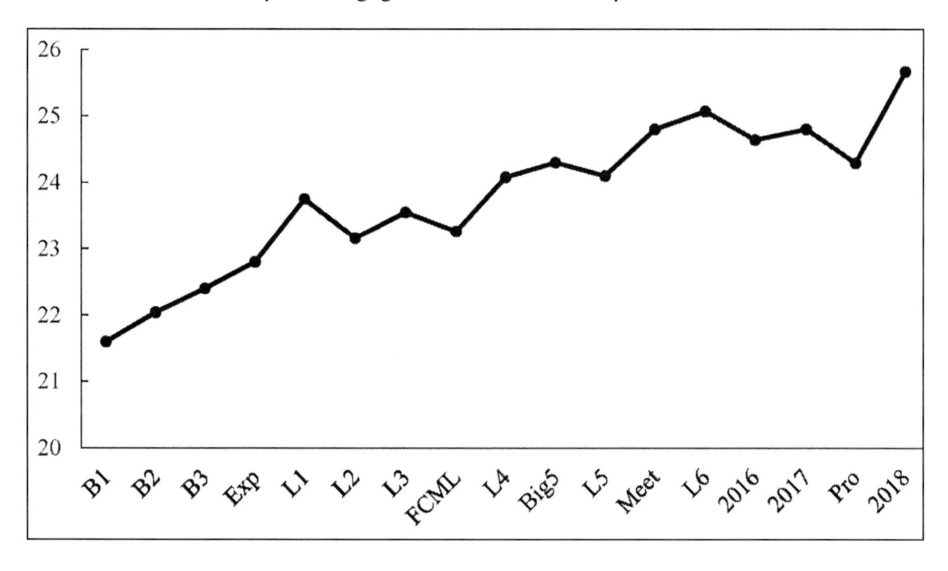

***Figure 4.1.* Average age of bronies for each study in chronological order.**

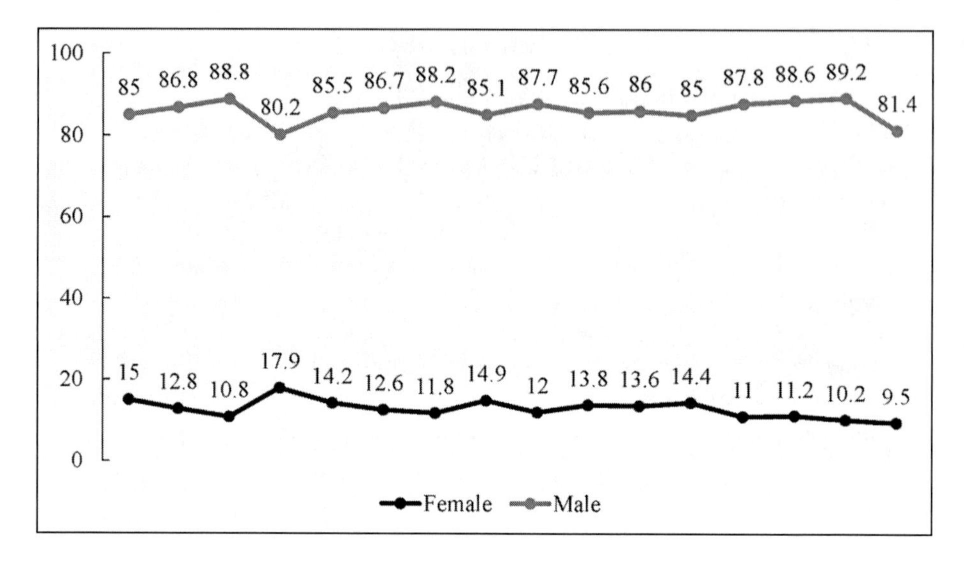

Figure 4.2. Sex composition of the brony fandom for each study in chronological order. (_Note:_ Numbers do not add up to 100 percent because of non-male/female categories [e.g., intersex]. Later surveys asked about these categories directly.)

Across all of our studies, the average age of bronies has ranged from about 21 to 26 years. More importantly, these results reveal an upward trend in bronies' age over time. What's likely happening is that fans of the show are aging with the show and sticking with the community as time goes on, rather than dropping out and being replaced with new fans—something we typically see in other fan communities (we'll discuss this more in a later sections). For contrast, work done on the furry fandom consistently finds that the average age of furries has remained fairly stable over the last decade, suggesting that older fans are leaving the fandom at about the same rate that younger fans are entering the fandom. In the case of bronies, while new fans *do* continue to join the community, the story seems to primarily be one of fans who get on-board and stick with the show over time, rather than being replaced every few years by new fans.

Perhaps not surprisingly, bronies also seem to put the "bro" in the term brony[9]: the fandom consistently reports being primarily male. As we've previously stated, this does *not* mean that all bronies are male (despite the label itself having masculine connotations),[10] but it does show that the fan community in our sample tends to be resoundingly male.[11] This predominantly-male composition has likely led to the perception of the community as "invading" a domain originally intended for younger girls.

Sex data such as this can allow us to test hypotheses regarding potential differences between male and female fans in the brony community (we elaborate on these differences in greater detail, along with issues pertaining to gender, in Chapter 6). Among male fans, being a brony is often their first fan community, something not as likely to be the case for female fans, who tend to be older (having likely grown up with earlier generations of the show) and who have belonged to more fandoms. This sex difference in the way male and female fans behave, coupled with the fact that the fandom is predominantly male, may explain why the fandom has a tendency to discover the show and stick with it over time. It could also be the case that this collection of younger, mostly male fans were the ones most likely to embrace the show and spend a large amount of time on message boards and websites where we typically recruit participants for our studies.

As a last short comment, our surveys have evolved over time, thanks in no small part to members of the LGBTQ+ community who have correctly pointed out the shortcomings in our past measures of sex and gender. We have, in response to this well-deserved criticism, aimed to better understand both the distinction between sex and gender and the broad diversity of gender identification within the fandom. While our analyses here primarily look at male/female sex differences,[12] we have, in recent years, begun looking at members of the brony community who identify as transgender, genderfluid, and with identities across the broad spectrum of gender.[13]

Speaking to this point, in Figure 4.3 we've compiled some information concerning gender identity as collected from one of our most recent surveys. Based on our most up-to-date data, around 3–5 percent of the brony community identifies outside of a binary gender spectrum, either as genderfluid or explicitly non-binary. In our 2016 study, we asked about gender identification in an even more nuanced manner and found that 5.4 percent of bronies identify as transgender and 3.6 percent as non-binary or genderqueer. These are far higher proportions than is typically seen the general population. Whether this is due to the fandom's fairly young and more progressive demographics relative to the general population or due to the community's norms of acceptance and inclusion remains to be seen. And while not every study has looked as thoroughly at gender identity as our most recent studies, a small percentage of participants in every study *did* report either no answer or no identification as male or female, suggesting that they have always been a part of the fandom, but were simply not being properly identified due to limitations in the way we were asking our questions.[14]

Fandom Membership

Over the past few years researchers and bronies alike have been asking questions about whether people are joining or leaving the fandom and, if so, who's doing so. Overall it seems that most fans currently in the brony

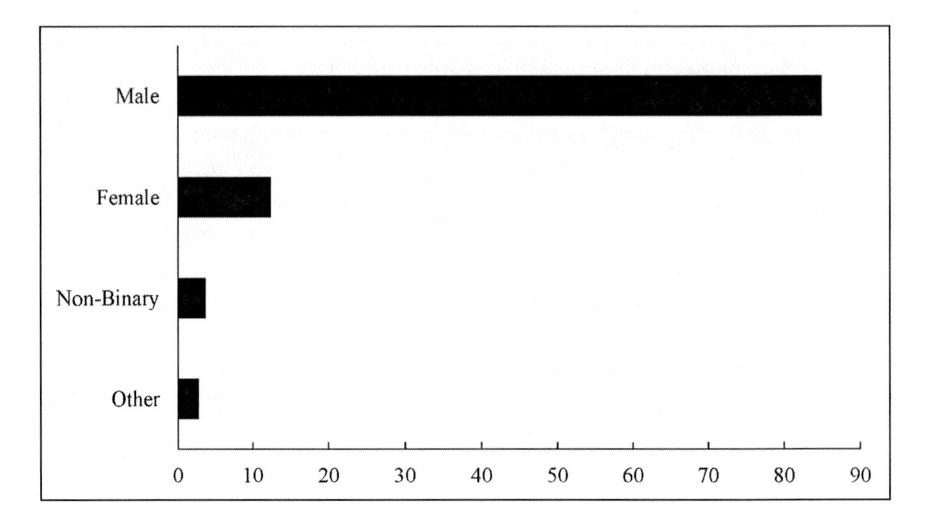

Figure 4.3. **Gender identity in the brony fandom, 2017 study. (*Note:* Participants who marked "other" were given space to write in their own response, yielding responses such as agender, genderfluid, non-gender, human, and "I'm not sure, male enough to get by." It is also important to note that in addition to being asked about their sex and gender, participants were also asked whether they identified as transgender specifically.)**

community joined early, with a small group of fans joining and leaving throughout the show's run for various reasons. We'll discuss the future of the fandom in greater detail in Chapter 20.

As of 2016, when explicitly asked whether they used the label "Brony" to describe themselves, 93.4 percent of fans identified as such. Reflecting our earlier discussion about the male connotation of the term, 95 percent of male fans used the term to describe themselves, while 79.3 percent of females did so.

When did you become a fan? Most bronies reported joining the fandom around the second/third season. After season 3, there seemed to be a steady trickle of new fans joining during each additional season, with about a 5–10 percent increase each season. As of 2016, our data has shown that most fans have been in the community for an average of 3.7 years, with the highest proportion indicating they had been a fan for 5 years (see Figures 4.4 and 4.5).

These results reveal that the brony fandom is far from stagnant. While some may spread doom and gloom about the fandom's future, these data suggest that the fandom, which solidified its core by season 2 and 3, continues to pick up new fans. Follow-up analyses also seem to show that fans stick around in this fandom. Overall, this means that bronies tend to join early and bring in the occasional new fan to replace those that happen to leave.

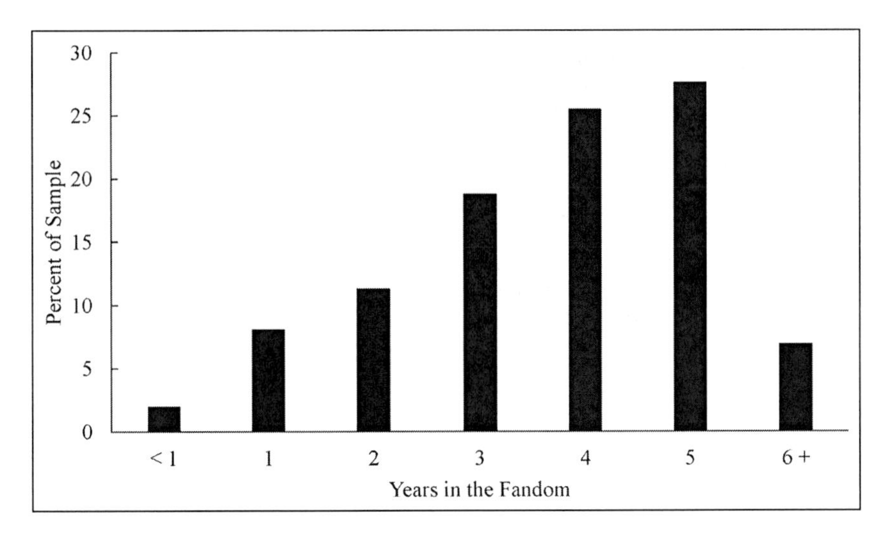

Figure 4.4. **Years spent in *MLP* fandom.**

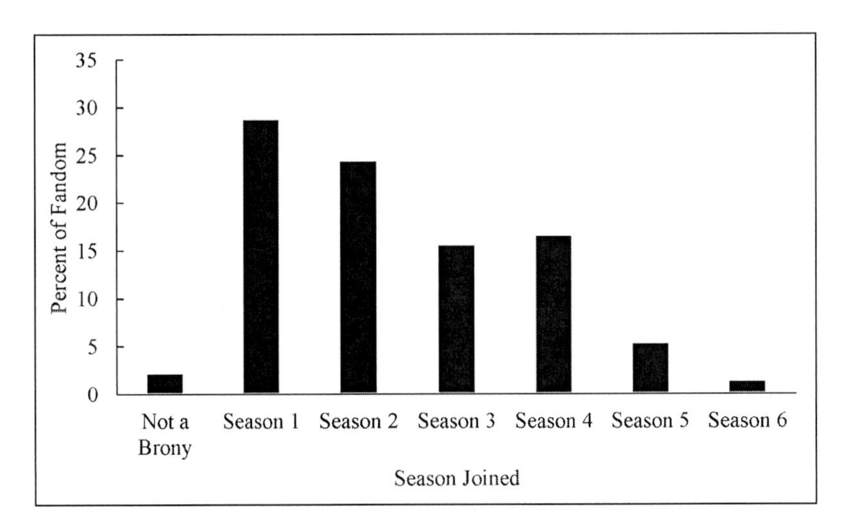

Figure 4.5. **When did bronies first call themselves a brony (post season 6)?**

While some people undoubtedly grow tired or bored of the show or the fandom itself, many seem content to stick around for each new season.[15]

Fandom membership beyond MLP. In our earliest studies we wanted to examine some of the *other* interests bronies may have had outside of *MLP*. While many reported having a variety of such interests, male bronies were especially likely to say that brony community was their first real fandom.[16]

Figure 4.6 outlines some of the other interests that *MLP* fans have beyond

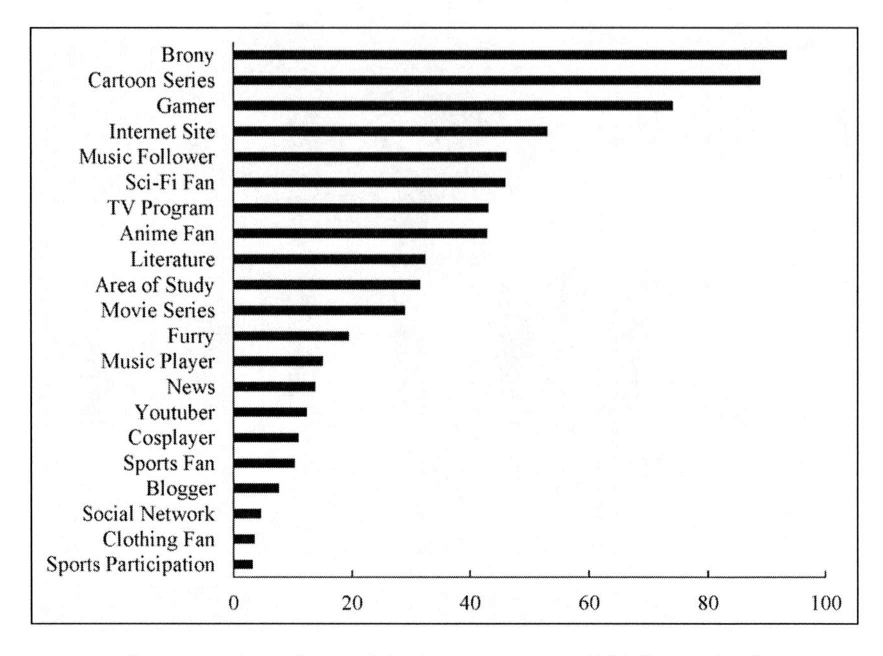

Figure 4.6. **Prevalence of fan interests among *MLP* fans in 2016.**

the show itself. As fans of an animated television show, it is perhaps unsurprising that many bronies are also fans of other cartoon series. Many are also likely to be gamers.[17] Other popular interests tend to revolve around those typically seen in "nerd" culture, including science fiction, anime, and the Internet. It's also worth noting that about one in five bronies self-identified as a furry: a number comparable to the number of furries who identify as bronies. This overlap is far from surprising, given that *MLP* is essentially a piece of media featuring anthropomorphized animal characters, something that furries, by definition, are a fan of.

In follow-up analyses, when bronies were compared to non-fans, the biggest differences were that bronies were about *half* as likely to be sport fans (9 vs. 19 percent) and were far *more* likely to be into video games (76 vs. 48 percent). Beyond these differences, however, it was surprising to see that bronies didn't differ very much from non-bronies with respect to their other interests. If anything, the differences which *do* exist may be chalked up to age differences between bronies and non-bronies or bronies' general preference for interests traditionally associated with "nerd" culture.

Finally, when looking at the brony community over time, the biggest changes in their interests from 2012 to 2016 seems to be an increase in their interest in cartoons in general (40 percent to 89 percent) and interest in news sites (5 percent to 14 percent).[18]

Sexual Orientation

One of the earliest media-perpetuated stereotypes about bronies was that they were a bunch of males who enjoyed a show made for girls because of their own insecurity about their heterosexuality and were simply expressing effeminate behavior stereotypically associated with being gay. Our studies have shown these stereotypes to be largely unfounded. In our first studies, 70 percent of bronies identified themselves as heterosexual, 10 percent as bisexual, 2 percent as homosexual, 9 percent as asexual or not interested, and 3 percent as unsure. This is obviously a far cry from the characterization of bronies as being a group of "gay men who watch a show for girls." Far from a one-time fluke, our findings have been fairly consistent over time (see Figure 4.7). While bronies *are* about twice as likely to identify as lesbian, gay, or bisexual than others of a comparable age, it is grossly inaccurate to characterize the brony fandom as being predominantly gay.

Additional analyses have shown another reason why the characterization of bronies as gay men falls flat: Within the brony community, female fans are *far* more likely than male fans to identify as non-heterosexual. Indeed, while most males identify as heterosexual, only around half of female bronies do so. These findings are generally in line with studies of the general population showing that women are more likely than men to report being non-heterosexual.

As a final note, when compared to national averages from the United States, the brony fandom seems to be more inclusive and diverse with respect

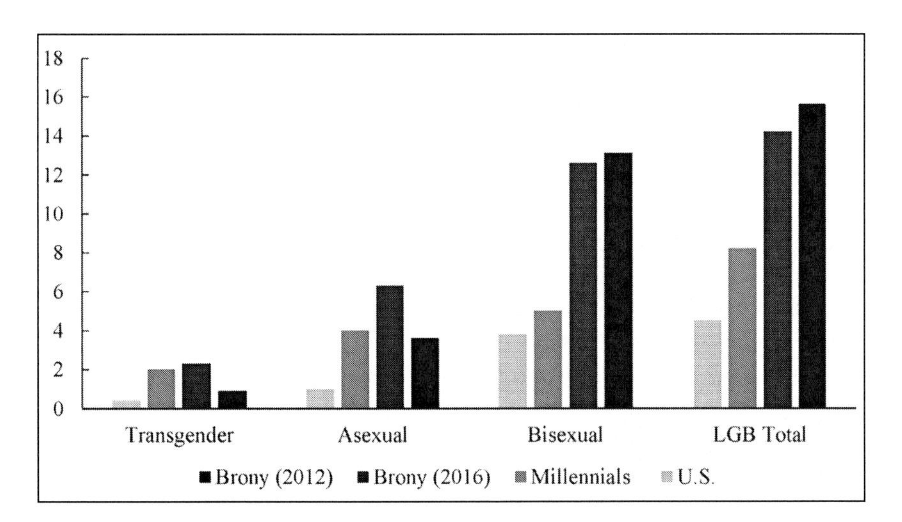

Figure 4.7. **LGBT+ identity in bronies, millennials, and U.S. comparison (*sources:* Gates, 2017; GLADD, 2017; Meerwijk & Sevelius, 2017; Storrs, 2016).**

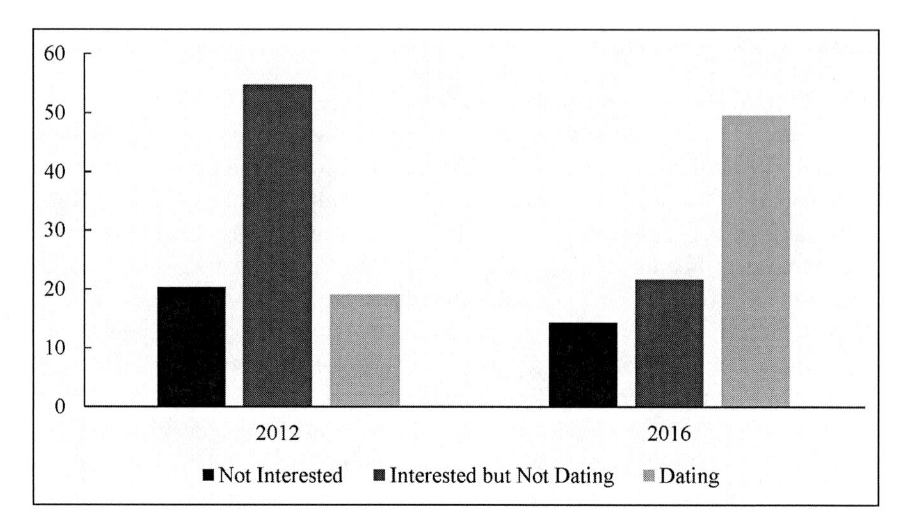

Figure 4.8. **Relationship status of bronies across two studies.**

to not only their sex, but also with respect to their gender identity.[19] The reasons for this may be tied to bronies being both younger than the general population and being part of a fandom with norms of acceptance and inclusion (Oskamp & Jones, 2000; Taschler & West, 2017).

Dating Life

In addition to sexual orientation, we also looked at whether bronies differed from others with respect to their dating and romantic life—something which again speaks to the stereotype of bronies as socially awkward, socially undesirable, and perpetually single.

In general, bronies were unlikely to be married (94 percent reported being "unmarried")—not surprising when you consider the average brony is in their early to mid twenties at a time when millennials are placing college and financial security before early marriage (Levenson, 2010).

But what about non-married dating relationships? In our earlier studies, there seemed to be *some* truth to the stereotypes of the "lonely brony": A majority of bronies were *interested* in dating but currently not in a relationship. This seems to be a product of age rather than anything inherent about being a brony, however. By 2016 this pattern of results had completely reversed, with most bronies currently in a dating relationship (see Figure 4.8). As is the case with many of our demographic results, it would seem that many of the characteristics often attributed to "being a brony" are, in all likelihood, a product of bronies being a fairly young group.

The Brony Typology

If you haven't noticed, ore research has revealed a theme that represents bronies as being much like their peers, but that even amongst millennials or any generation we should also be wary in terms of generalizing the entire group. One of the ways this concept of "not all fans are alike" is tied into the history of our own research is through our earliest attempts at understanding the fandom. The fruits of these early explorations was the development of a brony typology, which was based on the different motivations for bring a fan the individual bronies had experienced and their willingness to identify as a brony to others.[20] This typology, like the fandom itself, evolved over time, officially first showing up (outside of brainstorming and early discussions) in the 2013 documentary *Bronies: The Extremely Unexpected Adult Fans of My Little Pony*, which described hipster, moderate, and creative bronies which were based upon their initial reaction to the fandom.[21] Taking this as a starting point, our initial analysis led to four "types" based on two main factors: (1) the fans' sense of meaning and direction received from watching the show and taking part in the fandom and (2) the level and degree of disclosure which they displayed in their starting interest (Edwards, Griffin, Chadborn, & Redden, 2014).[22] This original survey assessing fan types along with reexamining it again and again until the end of the wave one surveys, resulted in five "types" of bronies.[23]

1. Social Bronies: high in meaning derived from the show and group as well as open about their identity as a brony. They represent the most visible, dedicated, and engaged fans of the show. 25–30 percent of the fandom identify as social brony.
2. Secret Bronies: They share the meaning seen in the social bronies, but not the disclosure. They, for several reasons (i.e., parental and peer acceptance), do not disclose their identity as it can lead to rejection, bullying, etc. 20–25 percent of the fandom identify as a secret brony.
3. Hipster Bronies: Low in meaning and direction, but high in identification, these fans were most likely to enjoy the shock value or identity in a small exclusive group, but as the fandom grew and the shock wore off became less interested and shrunk as a percentage of the fandom. 10–15 percent of the fandom identify as a hipster brony.
4. Hidden Bronies: low in both meaning and disclosure, this label represented individuals who were members of the fandom because of some personal function the groups gives them rather than the show or social aspect of the fandom itself. Only about 5 percent of the fandom identifies as a hidden brony.

5. Mixed Bronies: Individuals who found themselves not quite in one group, arguing that the typology did not quite fit their motivations, labels, and interests within the community and through the show itself. Some meaning, some direction, and able to share with some friends and family, but not others. 25–30 percent of the fandom identifies as a mixed brony.

These types, while not a strict label to be applied to any fan, especially with nearly ⅓ of fans identifying somewhere in between, does represent a way to understand and investigate fandom, especially in our early approaches to investigating the brony fandom in relation to itself rather than the broader psychological theories we have moved on to. There are also two important lessons to take from these labels. First, as with personality (see Chapter 16) one factor or type may represent several other individual traits and processes, like social and secret bronies also representing individuals high in fandom and fanship identification (see Chapter 13). And second, as Dr. Edwards puts in when discussing brony typology, is that it can help to demonstrate that not everyone in a group is alike in their views and approaches to shared activity (Edwards, Griffin, Langley, Redden, & Chadborn, 2015). Expanding this to other fan communities as well could also pose an issue as each fandom may have its own distinct set of factors "typing" their fans. While for bronies it seems to be meaning and disclosure for another fan community, the core factors that separate different types of fans may be different. Regardless of this, we can say that while not all bronies seek guidance, meaning, or direction from the show it is an important factor for a subset of fans and that importance, like with many other factors has influence on how those fans interact with others and the world around them (see Chapter 9 for more).[24]

Conclusion

So what can we take from this initial foray into the demographic composition of the brony fandom? Well, bronies are a group of fairly young, mostly male fans of the television show *My Little Pony: Friendship Is Magic.* While there are *some* notable differences between fans and non-fans and between male and female fans, these differences are more the exception than the rule. As it turns out, bronies aren't all that much different from similarly-aged groups of non-bronies. In contrast to media-driven stereotypes, most bronies are straight, although there is a higher LGBTQ+ presence in the brony fandom than one typically finds in the U.S. general population. And while fans early on may have had some difficulties finding a dating partner, this tendency seems to have all but disappeared over time. Additionally, we can also see a wide spectrum of motivations, labels, and differences even when looking within the community as well.

But this is still only a partial snapshot of the brony community—an incomplete picture. If you're like other social scientists, a stream of questions is coming to mind: What about their home life? Education? What else do bronies have in common with the average person, and is there anything about them that makes them stand out?

We'll turn to the answers to these questions in the next two chapters.

Chapter 5

From Ponyville to Manehattan: The Background and Family Life of Bronies

"I wasn't raised in a barn. My family just happens to have a barn. Where I was born. And ... spent most of my formative years...."
—*Applejack* (My Little Pony: The Movie, *2017*)

In the last chapter we started developing a picture of who bronies are. In this chapter, we'll dive a bit deeper into other facets of their lives and paint a fuller picture of the average brony, including their families and day-to-day experiences as students and employees. Armed with this additional demographic information, we can better test some of the additional stereotypes the brony community has faced.[1]

As we discussed in the previous chapter, bronies are a group of relatively young people—late teens and early to mid 20s. It will be important to keep that in mind as we go through this chapter. While it might be unusual for a 40-year-old to be unemployed and live in their parent's basement, this is not so out of the ordinary for recent high school graduates and college students, especially in the wake of America's 2007–2008 financial crisis. Our data allow us to track these demographics and how they've changed as the fandom matures.

This chapter, coupled with the previous chapter, will also lay the groundwork for the next chapter, which discusses both differences between the brony fandom and the general population and differences *within* the fandom, including the question of whether there are differences between male and female fans.

For now, let's start off broad and work our way toward more specific questions about bronies' lives. That means starting with the question of where you can find bronies in the first place.

Where the Herd Roams

Our survey-based research tends to recruit participants from popular brony websites such as Equestria Daily. While this might seem like a trivial detail, it has important implications for our conclusions. Nearly all of the sites we recruited participants from were English-speaking—a necessity, given that all of the researchers' first language is English. This means that the surveys primarily recruit English-speaking fans and is largely inaccessible to fans who don't speak English.

As such, it should come as no surprise that the majority of our participants come primarily from English-speaking countries.[2] Our samples likely overrepresent English-speaking countries (e.g., the U.S. and Canada) and underrepresent other countries, although this hasn't stopped us from recruiting fans from around the world. Speaking to this point, you can see in Figure 5.1 that while most of our sample lives in North America, about 20–30 percent of any given sample comes from Europe, Australia and New Zealand, South America, Russia, and throughout Asia and Africa. For the purposes of being as representative as possible, unless otherwise stated, our analyses involve *all* of the bronies sampled, regardless of where they come from.

Zooming in from country of residence, we've long been interested in looking at the communities from which bronies hail—namely whether there

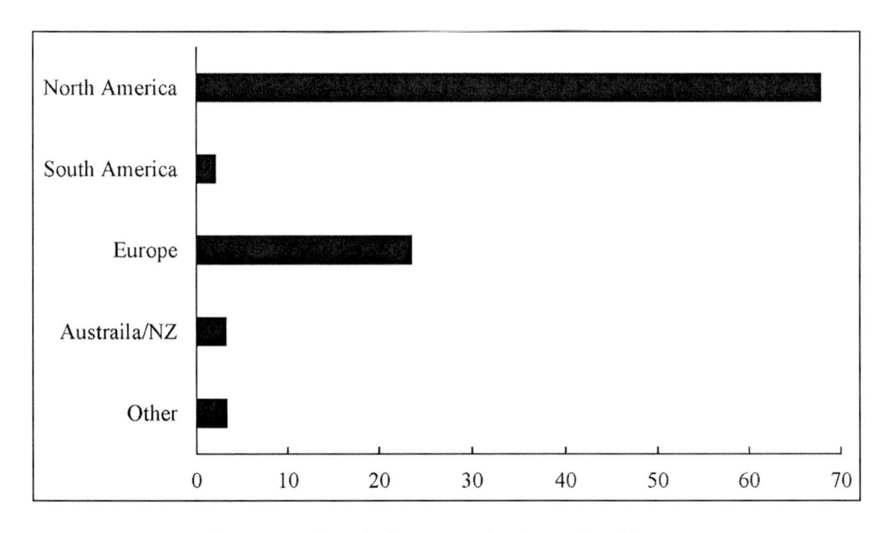

Figure 5.1. **Bronies' country/region of residence.**

***Figure* 5.2. Population size of bronies' home community.**

are differences between bronies living in urban regions and those living in more rural regions. After all, one can imagine that laving in an urban area increases the likelihood of bumping into a brony on the street or casually learning about the fandom in the first place! It may also increase the likelihood of there being a local gathering of bronies near you.

Most of our participants report coming from larger cities (population over 500,000 people), although there is a fairly good mix of bronies across all types of regions (see Figure 5.2). The smallest, least-represented region is small, rural areas, where only about 8 percent of bronies dwell. This may be driven by the fact that fewer people tend to live in such rural areas than in more urban areas in general. It may also be that rural areas are less likely to have access to the Internet and reduce the likelihood of meeting and engaging with other bronies.

In addition to being able to find other fans, living in urban areas also seems to be linked to different "types" of bronies being more likely in certain regions (for more on these types, see Chapter 4 and 8).[3] Those from urban areas were more likely to be open about being a brony with their peers and parents. This may have something to do with the political makeup of bronies' communities, with large, urban areas tending to be more liberal than rural areas.

Let's zoom in further still and take a look at bronies' living accommodations—that is, where they currently reside. As a group, bronies tend to be pretty evenly split between living at home with a parent or relative and living on their own, with roommates, or with a spouse (see Figure 5.3). At first glance this might seem to lend credibility to the perception of bronies as people

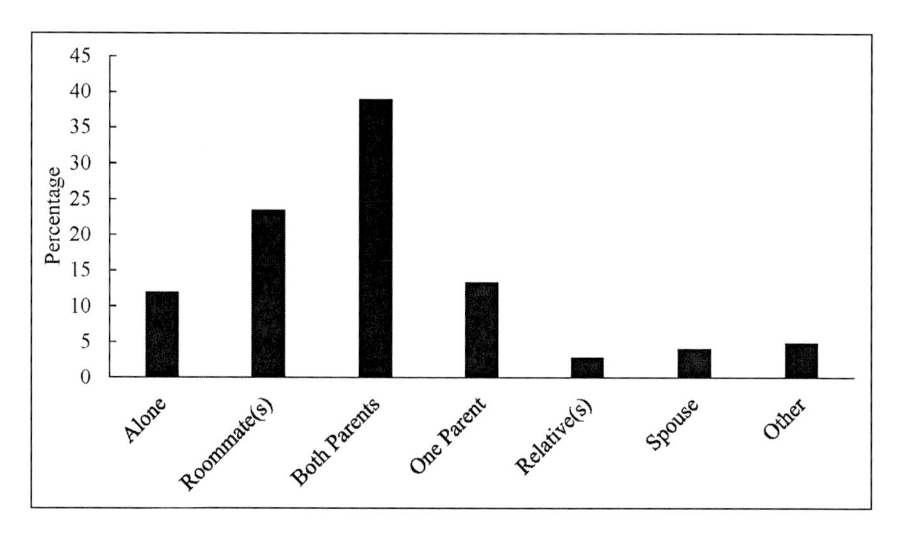

Figure 5.3. **Living arrangements of the brony community, 2012.**

who live in their parents' basements. The results become less surprising, however, when you contextualize them with what we know about young people in general. In the general population, 36 percent of 18- to 34-year-olds still live at home or have had to move back home (Fry, 2016).[4] This tendency for people to reside with their parents at increasingly later ages can be attributed to recent economic downturns, increased time spent in college, and a larger number of millennials waiting later to settle down and start a family of their own (Levenson, 2010).

In fact, within our own data we can see evidence of this. Participants living at home were, on average, about 20–21 years old, while those living alone were an average of 25 years old. Those living with a spouse were an average of 29 years old. It should also be noted that "living with a relative" could mean a lot of things, including living with an older relative to help take care of them.[5]

To help us shed some light on these findings and paint a clearer picture of bronies' living situations, we next turn to data looking at bronies' work and educational history.

Suited for Success

For those of us on the team who've chosen Twilight Sparkle as our favorite character, part of the reason for this (outside of her love for science and reason) comes from her journey as a scholar. Over the seasons, Twilight started out as a student, graduated and went on to advanced studies under a mentor, and finally spread her wings and found a job and a sense of purpose in teaching.[6] In the show, many characters discover their calling fairly early, literally having it emblazoned on their flank as a "cutie mark." Unfortunately, the real world is rarely so simple. With so many bronies in the 18–25 age range, where one tends to find most college students, it makes sense that many are still attending college and struggling to discover what it is they want to do with their lives.

Education

Figure 5.4 lays out bronies' current educational pursuits over time, starting with the average from our earliest studies and proceeding chronologically to our latest studies. Across all samples we find evidence that a considerable number of bronies are currently attending college at some level (30–70 percent).[7] Follow-up analyses reveals that among those bronies pursuing education, many were doing so as full-time students (40–60 percent).[8] A careful look at the figure reveals a curious trend: It would seem that, over time, bronies are *less* likely to be attending college (e.g., undergraduate education). Taken at its face value, one might conclude that bronies were simply dropping out or becoming less interested in college over time.

Additional data reveals an alternative explanation, however. As seen in Figure 5.5, many bronies end up completing their degrees (15–30 percent), a number that largely increases over time, and does so almost perfectly in step with the decline of bronies currently attending college. This suggests a *matur-*

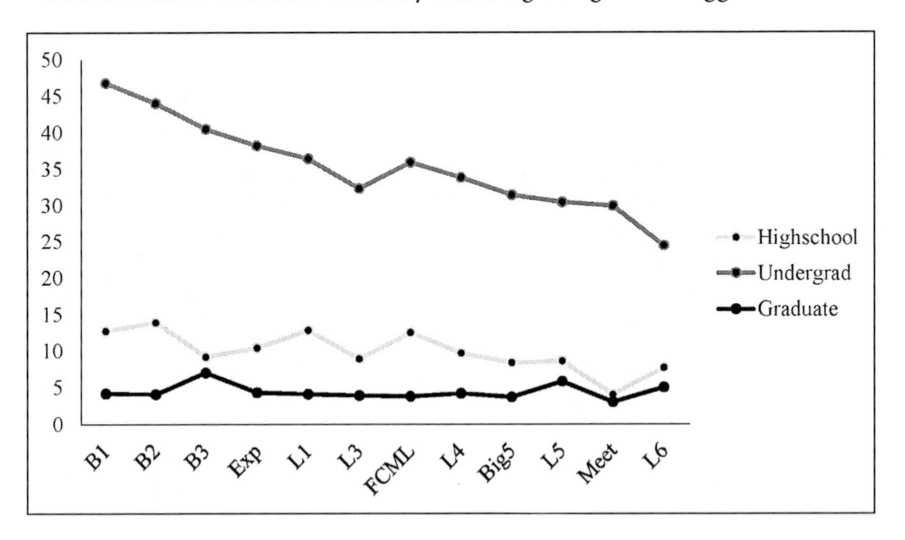

***Figure 5.4*. Education changes in the brony fandom over time: current school attendance.**

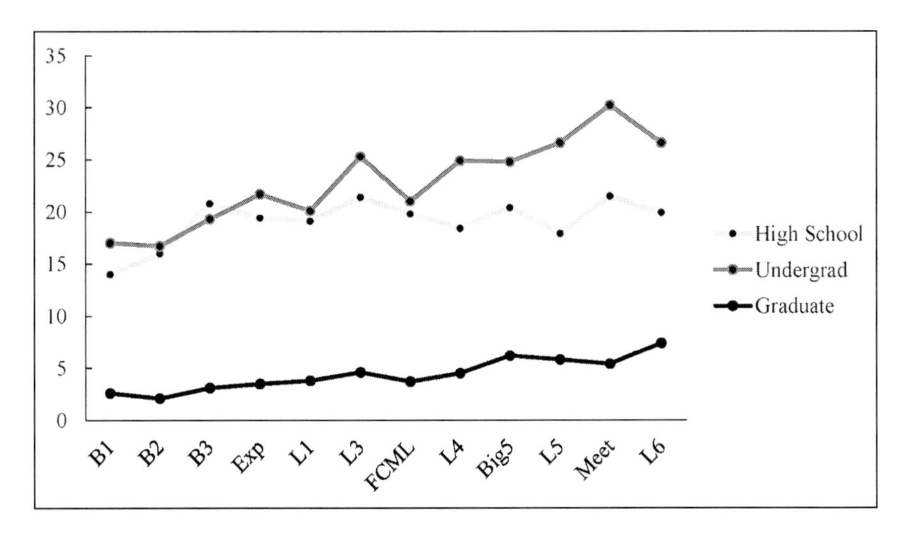

***Figure 5.5.* Education changes in the brony fandom over time: percent having graduated.**

ing brony community, one of bronies attending and eventually graduating from college. It would seem then that many bronies spend a fair portion of their day in school—something we would *expect* to see in a group of young adults belonging to the millennial and post-millennial generation.

Employment

There's more to life than the classroom: Sooner or later, classes come to an end and we have to find a job. As Figure 5.6 reveals, however, a considerable number of bronies are not currently working: 15–30 percent work full-time, while 20–25 percent work part-time and 18–20 percent remain unemployed.[9] While, at first glance, this may seem alarmingly low, this needs to be contextualized against the high number of bronies currently enrolled in college. Speaking to this point, the U.S. Bureau of Labor Statistics reported that only about 30 percent of four-year college-enrolled students were currently participating in the labor force—a number that's in the same ballpark as what we find in our brony samples.

The results presented in Figure 5.6 also lend credibility to the idea that bronies are, over time, graduating from college and going on to find jobs. Alongside the decline in student status is a gradual increase in employment status. Despite this, however, it's worth noting that there *is* a fairly high rate of unemployment in the fandom, a number around 6–8 percent higher than the 12.6 percent average for millennials in 2016 (Beaton, 2016; U.S. Chamber of Commerce Foundation, 2012; Bureau of Labor Statistics, 2018). Likewise,

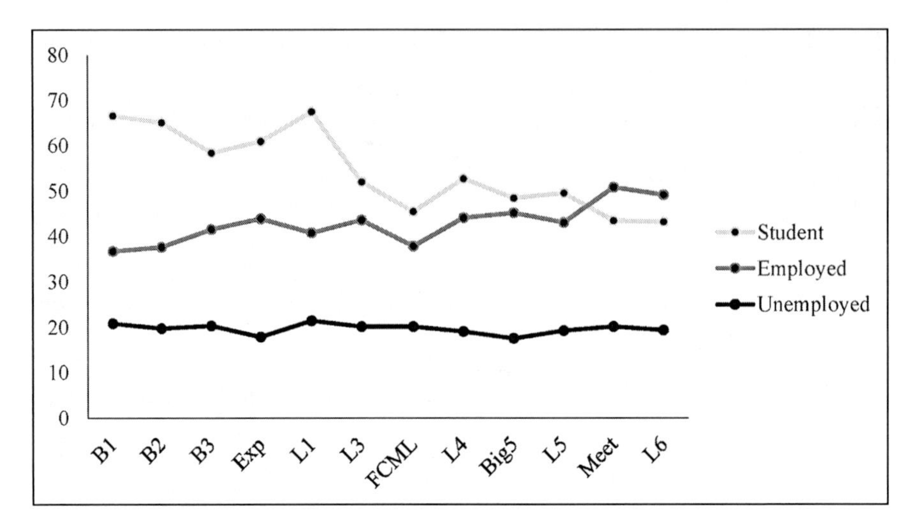

Figure 5.6. **Bronies' employment status (2012–2016).**

the rate in which student enrollment is declining is somewhat faster than the rate in which employment is increasing. This could be explained by the fact that millennials in general are struggling to find employment in their respective fields after graduating from college.

Wrapping up this section on employment, it would seem that bronies, as a largely millennial group, have many of the same educational and employment statistics we find on other samples of millennials. While it may be tempting to fall back on simple stereotypes about "basement-dwelling nerds" or "gamers who live in their parent's basement," the data suggest that these are largely inaccurate. As it turns out, like with many of our demographic findings comparing bronies to non-bronies, the real story is that, at least when it comes to work and education, bronies are not all that different from the average millennial.

Being a Pear in a Family of Apples: Brony Parents and Acceptance

Given that the impetus for much of our original research was the negative stereotypes floating around about the brony fandom, one of the main focuses of our first surveys had to do with bronies disclosing their brony identity to others. We quickly discovered that while some bronies are ardent and outspoken fans who love to preach to others about their love for all things *MLP*, many were quite the opposite, hiding their interests from those around them. We found plenty of examples of bronies attending brony conventions without their parents knowing that they were at a *My Little Pony* conventions.

Of course, this wasn't the case for *everyone* in our studies. We had the pleasure of interviewing many parents who drove hundreds of miles to take their kids to the convention, knowing full well what the convention was for. But it *does* raise questions about how or whether parents and peers affect how bronies experience the brony fandom and come to terms with their brony identity. Unlike the background information we've discussed up to this point, this is our first real look into the family and community lives of bronies.

Common sense (and a mountain of psychological research) tells us that our caregivers have a tremendous impact on our lives (Harlow, 1958, Radetzki, 2018; Yip, Ehrhardt, Black, & Walker, 2018). While we're not *entirely* defined by our parents and the people we grew up around, their support or rejection *can* have a profound impact on our interests.[10] As such, parental involvement—and particularly parental acceptance—plays an important role in how bronies enjoy and participate with their fandom. This is, of course, far more likely to be an issue in younger bronies than in older ones. Nevertheless, the more bronies feel a sense of acceptance from their parents, the more likely they are to identify strongly as a brony, to be open about being a brony to others, and to consume show-related content. As it turns out, it's easier to engage with your fan interest when you don't have to hide it from your friends and family.[11]

Data on acceptance also seem to suggest that bronies feel a greater sense of acceptance from their parents and peers than do non-bronies. These results allow us to conclude that while not *every* parent may be open and accepting of their son or daughter's love of *MLP*, bronies seem to disproportionately come from households with parents who *do* seem more open and accepting. The same can be said for bronies' non-brony friends and peers, who also seem to be fairly open and accepting on average.

Praise the Sun and Rock the Vote: Bronies, Spirituality and Politics

It's said there are three things you shouldn't talk about around the dinner table: politics, sex, and religion. As psychologists, however, we have no such reservations, and regularly study all three. As you've already seen, we're more than happy to talk about sex, as we did in the previous chapter (and will do again in Chapter 6 and Chapter 11). So what say we go for the other two and make it a perfect trifecta of taboo?

In a 2017 study, bronies were compared to a sample of university students

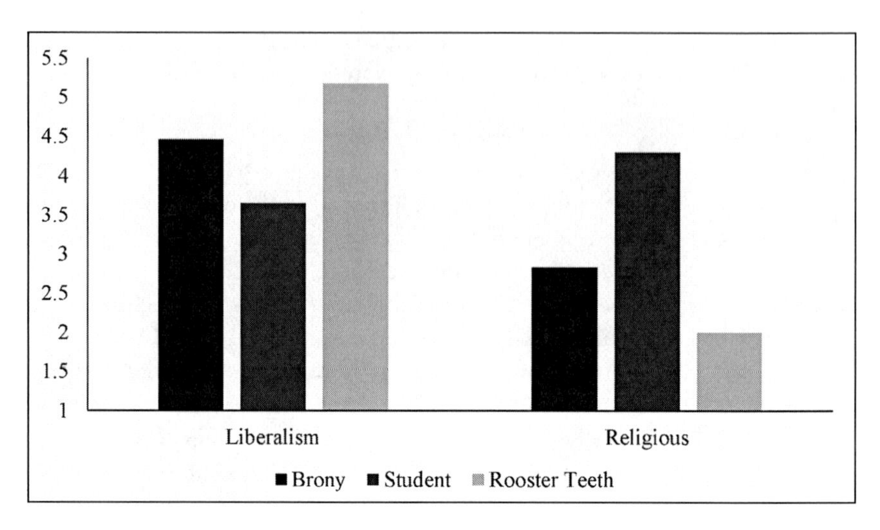

Figure 5.7. **Political liberalism and religious identification between bronies, university students, and Rooster Teeth fans.**

and a sample of Rooster Teeth fans.[12] Participants were asked about their political orientation on a 7-point scale ranging from conservative to liberal.[13] The results can be seen in Figure 5.7. Bronies tended to fall somewhere between being more liberal than the average university student but more conservative than another Internet-based fan community.[14] Bronies' average on the 7-point scale reveals that, as a group, bronies do score somewhat liberal, but only moderately so (i.e., not extremely liberal). In future studies, it will be necessary to use a more refined measure of political orientation to tease out the meaning of these results.[15]

If we didn't scare you away with that political discussion, let's delve further into the taboo rabbit hole and discuss religion. For the characters in the show there isn't much religion to speak of outside of reverence for the Princesses, who may be seen as the embodiment of old pagan gods with their respective domains. Celestia, after all, controls the sun, while Luna controls the moon (and peoples' dreams).[16]

In humans, however, religion is a far messier concept.

As seen in Figure 5.7, bronies, as a group, did not consider themselves to be all that religious when rating themselves on a 7-point scale—falling well below the scale's midpoint. Another piece of evidence speaks to this conclusion that bronies are not, as a group, a terribly religious bunch. In another study looking at church attendance, most bronies either didn't attend church at all or only attended for special occasions (Christmas, Easter, etc.; see Figure 5.8). The results were quite different for their parents, who were *much* more likely to attend church.[17]

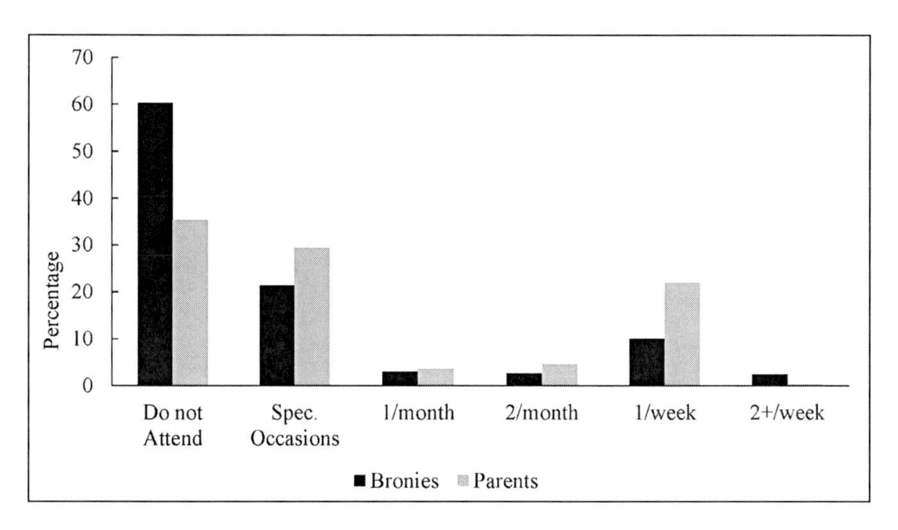

Figure 5.8. **Church attendance among bronies.**

These findings raise the obvious question: Why should bronies be less likely than anyone else to be religious? One possible explanation has to do with the fact that many mainstream religions have rules or norms governing what is moral or appropriate behavior—including expectations regarding traditional gender norms. Norms which many bronies—being male—routinely eschew. Additionally, we found in some previous analyses that while religious bronies vary in the level their religious teachings conflict or merge with the messages in the show, most, religious or not, also reported the show's message easier to understand.

This may well explain why people who are *highly* religious may not be drawn to the show and to the fandom, but another way to approach the question is to ask why *less*-religious people might be *more* drawn to *MLP* and to the brony fandom itself. For those who are not religious or have moved away for more strict religious practice, one of the things they may be lacking is the sense of purpose or meaning in life and a feeling of community that churches often provide their congregation. As we'll discuss in later chapters (e.g., Chapter 9, Chapter 14) the brony fandom provides both of these for at least some bronies. Speaking to this point, the same study also found that bronies, as compared to non-bronies, tend to have a higher need for guidance and be more likely to seek out meaning in their life. In short, some less-religious bronies may be using their fan interest as a way of providing the sense of meaning and community that church otherwise fulfills for others.

It should also be noted that, like with many of our other demographic variables, bronies need to be considered within the context of the millennial generation. In 2016, 39 percent of Americans aged 18–29 reported having no religious affiliation, a number which had increased from 10 percent in 1986 (Cooper, Cox, Lienesch, & Jones, 2016). In short, the U.S. is rapidly becoming a less-religious, increasingly secular country. As a relatively young group, bronies fall well within what we would expect to find in terms of religiosity among young adults. As such, it would be inaccurate to *define* bronies by their relative lack of religiosity.

Conclusion

Our ongoing story of the brony fandom is one that, at least demographically speaking, seems to reflect the story of the millennial generation. Any attempt to explain what makes bronies different from non-bronies probably has less to do with where they live, their family lives, or their political and religious beliefs, and likely has more to do with their personality, specific beliefs and values, or their worldview.[18]

We will continue this discussion about what makes bronies distinct as a community in later chapters, delving into their thoughts, feelings, and behavior and how they compare to other groups. Along the way, we should make sure to keep in mind what we've learned from this chapter: Any differences likely owe themselves to the brony fandom and to the show itself, rather than to demographic differences between bronies and non-bronies, factors that were in place long before they even sat down to watch their first episode of *MLP*.

Chapter 6

Equestria Girls and Pony Boys: A Few Final Demographic Comparisons

"Time to put our differences behind us. We were meant to rule together...."
—*Princess Celestia* (*Season 1, Episode 2,* Friendship Is Magic: Part 2)

As we've seen in the past couple of chapters, the differences between bronies and non-bronies can mostly be explained by the fact that bronies largely belong to the millennial generation. Later in this book, we'll look to finer, more nuanced psychological factors that may distinguish bronies from non-bronies.

But for now, it's worth taking a look at our assumption up until now that bronies, as a group, are fairly similar to one another. Is this an assumption we can safely make? Are the important subgroups within the brony fandom, and do they differ significantly from one another?

Think about it this way: In the episode "Too Many Pinkie Pies," the titular character clones herself many times, resulting in a group of Pinkie Pies that terrorize Ponyville. Without a doubt, as a group, we could say that this group of Pinkie Pies differs meaningfully from the rest of the ponies in Ponyville. But the Pinkie Pies are not perfect clones of one another: Somewhere within that group is the "Real" Pinkie Pie, who differs meaningfully from the imposters, many of whom also differ from one another. In other words, we can look at variation *within* the group as well as considering differences *between* the group and other groups.

So what are some of the likely differences *within* the brony fandom? One of which involves the question of sex differences between male and female bronies. As it turns out, this is a bit of a touchy subject for bronies.

At the first Baltimore BronyCon in 2013 we presented our data on the topic to a mixed response from the crowd. Since then, not a whole lot has changed with response to the pattern of results, but we may be able to offer a bit more *nuance* on the subject with the aid of additional data and time to reflect. As such, a considerable portion of this chapter will be devoted to the non-male side of this predominantly male fandom to discuss some of the differences that may make these female bronies (for those who eschew the term pegasister) unique.

We will also spend some time discussing two related topics, both of which are also oft-dreaded: the "-isms" of feminism and sexism within the fandom. Feminism has been a hot-button issue on the Internet for years now, ranging in focus and tone from a reasoned discussion about the definition and relevance of feminism in today's society to decrying the "Feminazis" and "SJWs" who are ruining society.[1] It's in part because of these discussions, but also because of the stereotypes that exist about males (and their seemingly "out-of-place" nature in what people consider to be a "feminine" fan interest) that we sought to examine sexism and feminism within the community.[2]

In short, we're aiming to move beyond the Internet flame wars and accusations of social justice ideology.[3] Our primary goal is to have a respectful, data-driven conversation about sex and gender within the brony fandom.[4] Our approach was born out of the hypothesis that fans of a show predominantly populated by female characters, created by a woman and self-proclaimed feminist, and which preaches love, tolerance, and equality, might be more likely than the average person to care about issues like sexism, feminism, and gender.

And to make sure we don't lose you completely—especially if you *are* a little squeamish about these topics, we'll also be looking at other differences between bronies and non-bronies with respect to factors that were likely in place before they became bronies.

Into the minefield we go!

Sex Differences in the Brony Fandom

As we have discussed previously, we've mainly studied the topics of sex and gender in the overly-simplified context of whether bronies called themselves male or female. To be crystal-clear: In this chapter, when we discuss differences between male and female bronies, we're not intentionally leaving anyone out. This oversimplification is the product of our early studies using overly simplistic questions to address the more complex question of sex and gender identity. As we've seen in earlier chapters, once we received feedback from the community and improved our sex and gender measures, other interesting findings emerged. But rather than throwing out all of our original data, it's at least worth looking at whether they had *something* interesting to tell us.

One pattern that emerges from this early male/female fan data is that, for the most part, male and female fans have a lot more in common than they have differences. Among the few differences which did emerge were that female bronies tend to have more experience with prior fan communities than did males. In general, male and female fans have similar interests in other, related fandoms (with the exception of gaming, where males were far more represented than females). Despite this, female fans out-represented males in most of these other interests. The brony fandom is hardly unique in this regard: Many studies of early fan cultures have found that these communities were typically started by older female fans. For example, *Star Trek*'s fan following began with groups of women meeting and writing fanfiction about characters from the show (Coppa, 2008; Jindra, 1994; Tosenburger, 2008).

These findings may help to explain why, for example, male bronies are less likely to split their identity among multiple fan interests than female bronies are. We can also speculate that, to some degree, some of the early conflicts between male and female bronies may have stemmed from these differences in prior experience with fandoms. In general, male bronies were more likely to be first-time fans than female bronies. This may also explain other data showing that, compared to male fans, female fans are far more likely to react negatively to changes in the fandom and to drama and criticism from within the fan community (as we will discuss more in Chapter 20). For fans who have more experience and know what to expect when it comes to fan communities, it would make sense that they would be more likely to be frustrated by immature or inexperienced fans, especially if they incur backlash and criticism from others outside the fandom as a result of these fans' poor behavior.

Demographic and Personality Differences

Early on, we found evidence of small demographic differences between male and female fans, with females being slightly older, more likely to be in college, more likely to be married, and more likely to live outside of the home. These differences largely boil down to female fans being older than male fans.

But what about personality: Do male and female fans have dramatically different personality make-ups? In a word—no. While small, statistically significant differences *have* been found (see Figure 6.1 below), these differences tend to be small differences in magnitude or degree, rather than categorical differences.[5] These results have been fairly consistent over time, with females being, on average, more open to experience, agreeable, and extraverted than

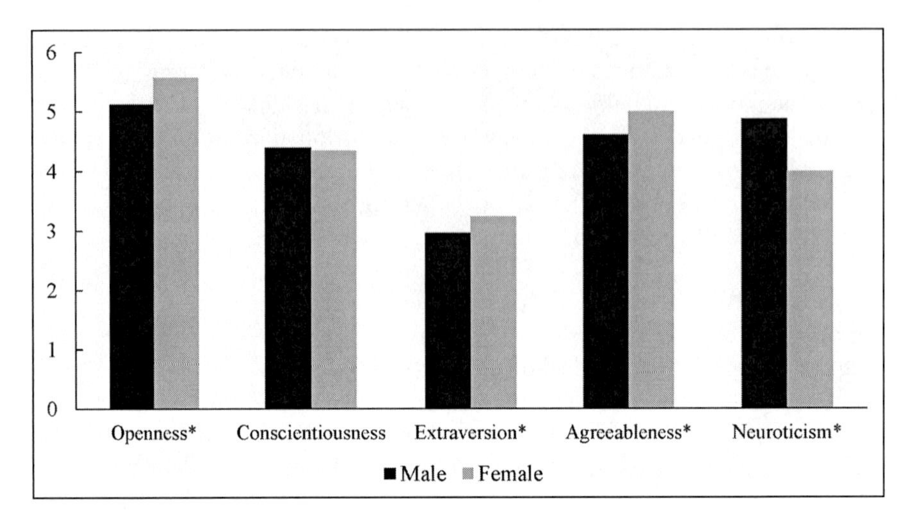

Figure 6.1. **Personality traits of male and female bronies. (**These differences are statistically significant.*)**

their male counterparts and males being somewhat more neurotic (e.g., emotionally unstable). That said, as we'll discuss in Chapter 16, these differences are fairly small compared to differences between bronies and non-bronies as a whole. In short, male and female bronies are more similar personality-wise than they are different.

In Chapter 4 we explained another difference between male and female bronies: Males were *far* more likely to be heterosexual than were females (79.5 percent compared to 47.9 percent), a trend mirroring the trend generally found in non-fan populations as well. This may be due to the lack of stigma historically associated with female homosexuality and bisexuality as compared to males.

As it turns out, these stigma differences between males and females may also extend to other domains as well. For example, while male and female fans don't differ with respect to how much their parents accepted their *MLP* interest, females reported having far more accepting peers than males (see Figure 6.3).

Motivations and Exposure

Early on in our research we, like many others, wanted to know what motivated bronies to join and stick with the fandom. While much of the previous research on fan culture has focused on the importance of belonging to a larger community (Obst, Zinkiewicz, & Smith, 2002a; Reysen, Plante, Roberts, & Gerbasi, 2016) and entertainment (Pearson, 2010; Tsay-Vogel & Sanders,

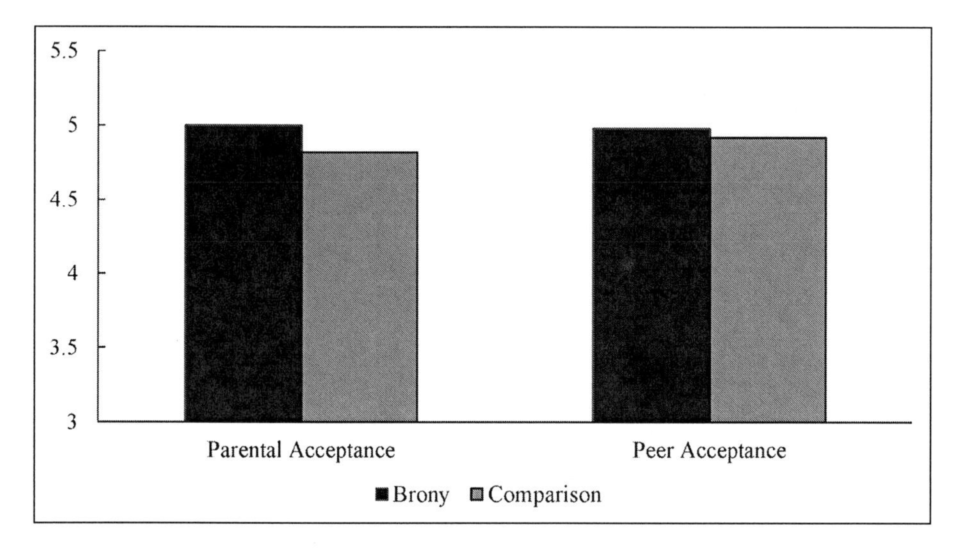

Figure 6.2. **Parental and peer acceptance of bronies and non-bronies across studies.**

2017), we also believed that at least *some* fans use the show and the fandom as a way to find meaning and purpose in their lives. This seems especially likely, given that many bronies are in their early adulthood, where one commonly finds themselves wondering where they're going and what they're meant to do with their life.

To this end, we've often asked bronies whether they had or were seeking a sense of meaning and purpose in their life. Male and female fans didn't seem to differ with respect to how much meaning and purpose they felt in their lives, or with how much the brony fandom provided them with this sense of meaning. Likewise, male and female fans didn't seem to differ with respect to how much they were driven to the brony fandom seeking a community to belong to (see Figure 6.3).

That said, female fans *were* more likely to use *MLP* and the fandom as a source of entertainment. We can also see this difference in the ways male and female fans consume show-related content: In general, female bronies show greater appreciation for the show's features (i.e., animation, colors, etc.) and in their emotional response to the show (i.e., feelings it creates, identifying with the characters). This isn't to say that males *don't* appreciate these things in the show, of course—simply that they don't do so to the same extent on average![6]

One important difference in the experience of male and female fans has to do with exposure to previous versions of the show: Female fans are *far* more likely than male fans to have watched earlier generations of the *MLP* TV show and films and to have played with *MLP* toys. Despite this, however,

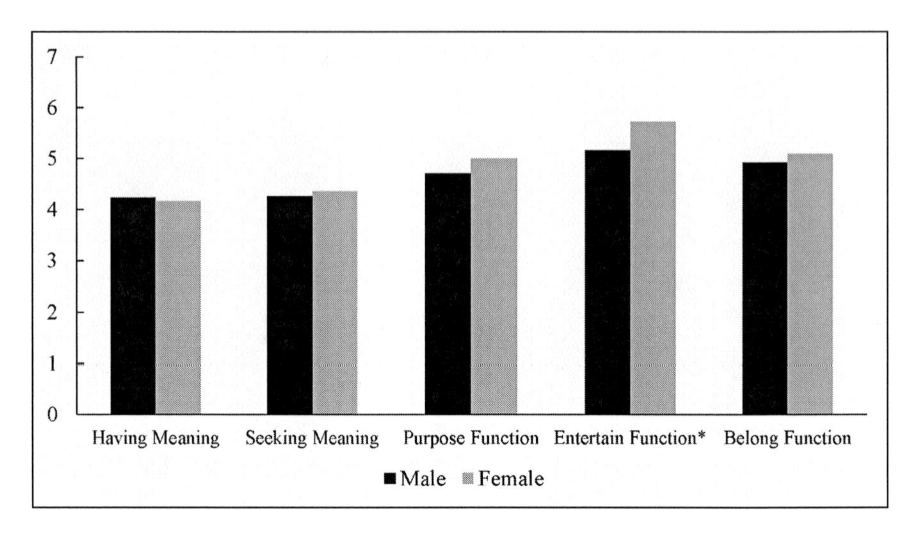

Figure* 6.3. Meaning and motivation of male and female bronies.** (*These differences are statistically significant.***)

female fans did take slightly longer on average to join the fandom after watching *MLP:FIM* specifically, though we're talking about a matter of weeks after their first viewing of the show, rather than months- or years-long differences.

Feminism

Presently, we define feminism as an ideology (with a wide range of political and social movements) aimed at seeking equality between sexes.[7] As a whole, bronies do not identify as feminists. That said, this is largely driven by the fact that the brony fandom is predominantly male. When you compare male and female bronies separately, female bronies are about four times as likely (43.9 percent) as male bronies (11.9 percent) to adopt the label of "feminist."

While this number might seem low for fans of a show created by Lauren Faust, a self-described feminist (Faust, 2010), one which espouses strong feminist messages, this is not entirely surprising if you consider why people shy away from using the label "feminist." Some may believe, for example, that equality *already* exists, and thus there is nothing left to fight for. Others may actively oppose changing societal norms as they are. Still others may agree with feminist ideals but avoid using the label due to the backlash associated with it.

We find it interesting that the message espoused in feminism that women can like traditionally male things is also the same message that men and boys can like a show with colorful ponies that was originally intended for girls.

While we had expected to find more fans of the show endorsing feminism, these results make sense considering how controversial the label of feminist has become in recent years. Speaking to the idea that it's more about the label than the ideas themselves, analyses have shown that bronies *are* less likely to endorse traditional gender roles than non-bronies—a sign that they *do* support at least some feminist ideals, if not the label itself!

To wrap up this section on sex differences within the brony fandom, it seems like we've looked at a lot of things that either didn't differ between males and females or which only amounted to small differences when compared to the differences between bronies and non-bronies. And that's kind of the point. There's no "one true fan" or any one person who perfectly embodies the entirety of the brony fandom. Bronies are a diverse group from all walks of life, but who also share a lot in common.

So just what is it that bronies have in common that make them unlike other groups?

Comparing Bronies to Non-Bronies

In many of the analyses we presented earlier we found that bronies differed from the general population with respect to variables like age, sex and gender composition. But what if we statistically "control" for these factors? Do bronies and non-bronies differ from one another after we take into account these sorts of age, sex, or other demographic factors? The analyses below, which were compiled by "yoking" bronies to non-bronies, show some of the answers to these questions.[8]

One possible difference between bronies and non-bronies that may explain who does or does not become a brony has to do with how they respond to seeing the show itself. To test this, in one of our studies we exposed several groups of undergraduates to an episode of *My Little Pony: Friendship Is Magic.*[9] The short version of the results is that nothing we found really predicted who would be "converted" into liking the show versus who would not.[10] And while bronies *do* seem to have more accepting peers and parents than non-bronies, as shown earlier in this chapter, this alone isn't enough to explain why some people might get into the show while others do not.

We also mentioned previously that part of our interest in fans of *MLP* was whether or not they would differ from non-bronies in their perception of gender and if, over time, their views would change once they watched more of the show. In line with this hypothesis, we *did* find evidence to support this idea: Bronies were *less* likely to endorse gender stereotypes and sexist attitudes than were non-brony university students—a group one would typically associate with progressive beliefs with respect to gender issues (see

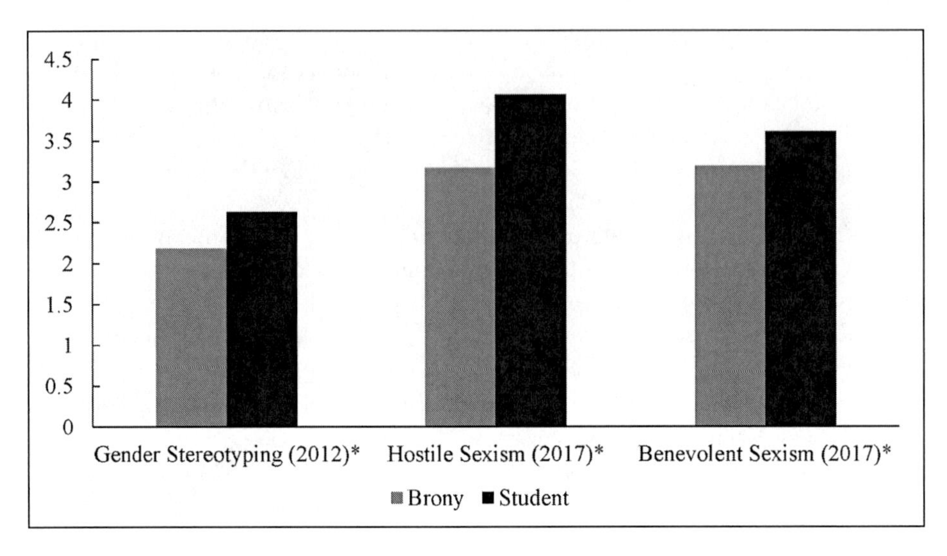

***Figure 6.4.* Sexism and gender perceptions in bronies and non-brony university students. (**These differences are statistically significant.*)**

Figure 6.4). Bronies *also* scored significantly lower in measures of both hostile and benevolent sexism,[11] showing that bronies have a greater concern for equality when it came to stereotypes and traditional gender roles.

What we can conclude from this is that bronies, either through their exposure to the show or through their general greater acceptance of more equal gender norms, show *less* sexist views and gender stereotyping compared to non-bronies. While the show itself may not be creating a new generation of self-identified feminists, we *do* see an increased number of people who endorse feminism-consistent ideals among fans of the show.

Conclusion

Our goal in the preceding chapters has been to show that bronies, when you get down to it, are a group of fairly typical people who just happen to like a cartoon about friendship and magic. There are, to be sure, some differences between bronies and the general population, and while anyone can become a brony, there *may* be certain traits or variables that draw certain individuals to the show or, at least, make it easier for them to enjoy the show. Such characteristics may include beliefs and norms regarding the acceptance of others, no matter who they are (e.g., LGBTQ+ people), or less adherence or support of traditional gender norms.

In the next section of the book we'll shift our focus to questions specific to the brony community, examining the relationship between bronies and the show (fanship) and between bronies and the fan community (fandom). Additionally, we'll discuss how watching a show about cartoon horses and taking part in the fan community that sprung up around the show can have a profound impact on the bronies who do so.

Chapter 7

Welcome to Equestria: The Making of a Brony

"I can't believe you two are going on a friendship quest! This is amazing!"
—Twilight Sparkle (Season 8, Episode 23, Sounds of Silence)

When we talk to our friends, family, and research colleagues about our research on the brony fandom, we're usually hit with two questions[1]:

1. Why would a group of grown adults watch a children's show like *My Little Pony*? We're talking about the same show, right—the one with all the pretty pink horse princesses, butterflies, and tea parties?
2. How does a person realize that they like a show like this? Do they just wake up one morning and decide. "Today I really want to watch a show about pretty pink horse princesses, butterflies, and tea parties?"

We'll touch more on the first question at the end of this chapter and in depth in Chapter 8. For now, let's start with the second question, which asks about the path into *MLP* fanship.

It actually makes a surprising amount of sense to be curious about the pathway into fanship. After all, fans—regardless of what they're a fan of—are defined as people with an *unusually* strong interest in something. Whether we're talking about fans of sports, science fiction, or colorful friendship equines, the average person doesn't show the same level of passion for the topic as fans do. As such, it's natural human curiosity to speculate on how people might have come to be such ardent supporters of something. As we'll discuss in the first section of this chapter, stereotypes and common misconceptions make it far too easy for people to assume that the pathway to fanship is paved with deviance or dysfunction—an abnormal explanation for abnormal behavior.

In the sections which follow, we shed some light on some of the *actual* ways bronies stumble into their love of *MLP*—and, as you'll see, the use of the word "stumble" is quite deliberate here. We'll discuss the critical role that the Internet played for many bronies—though it's something not altogether unique to the brony fandom. We'll also discuss the surprising role that pure happenstance plays in the discovery of one's interest in *MLP*. We'll then mention the importance for many bronies of having a friend or family member lead them into their discovery of the show. Finally, we'll finish up by discussing how the question of "What got you into *MLP*" is an *entirely* different question from "Yeah, but why *MLP specifically*?"

How People *Think* Bronies Come to Be

Nearly a century of combined experience and concerted studying of human psychology has taught psychologists a pair of important lessons. First, people are amateur psychologists (Lilienfeld, 2011). Whether we realize it or not, we spend a great deal of mental energy trying to understand human behavior. Whether it's trying to understand why your partner's upset with you, what your boss is thinking when he calls you into his office, or whether to count on your friends to show up on-time for your party, you're doing psychology.

The second lesson is that people like simple, straightforward explanations. As it turns out, the world's a pretty complex place, and dwelling on this fact is enough to make anyone feel an overwhelming sense of unpredictability and powerlessness. To avoid this, we look for ways to make the world make sense—simple explanations and intuitive rules that help us get a grasp on what would otherwise be a meaningless and impossible-to-navigate existence (Heider, 1958; Heine, Proulx, & Vohs, 2006).[2]

When you put these two lessons together, the result is a tendency for people to come up with overly simplistic explanations for human behavior. For example, why did that customer shout angrily at the cashier? The easiest explanation is to say it's because the customer is an angry person. This is a phenomenon known as the *fundamental attribution error*, a tendency for people to explain behavior in terms of someone's assumed traits, rather than considering more complex situational or systemic explanations (Jones & Harris, 1967). Because of the fundamental attribution error, people largely assume that behavior is the result of someone's race, gender, nationality, personality, or something about *them*—especially if there are already existing stereotypes to support those assumptions.

Enter bronies, stage left. Here we have a group of people engaging in a fairly unusual behavior. To see just why it was unusual, let's return to our discussion of the history of *My Little Pony* from Chapter 1 for a bit of context.

Since the 1980s, the *My Little Pony* franchise was a cultural touchstone for all things schlocky and girly (Connelly, 2017). As such, a simple and intuitive explanation for why anyone would be a fan of the show in the 2010s would be that they simply *like* things that are schlocky and girly.

But there's a problem with this explanation: Most bronies are adult males, a group not typically associated with either schlocky children's toys or with largely-female stereotypes. Kids are supposed to like schlocky things, and girls are supposed to like girly things! Indeed, as Connelly points out in her book about the history of *MLP*, people had to find a way to square this particular circle. They often did so by assuming that these were simply effeminate or gay men, an assumption which continues to this day (e.g., Martin, 2015). Others are far less charitable in their explanations, pointing to developmental difficulties or divergent brain functioning (e.g., autism) as a means of explaining how an adult could possibly like a show aimed toward a child.

Of course, as you'll see in later chapters of this book, these explanations are gross oversimplifications grounded in misconceptions and stereotypes. Moreover, these explanations actually do very little to explain *how* anyone became a fan of the show. After all, even if it *were* true that gay men were more likely to watch the show, it wouldn't explain *how* they came to discover that they liked the show in the first place (nor would it explain why most gay men *do not* watch the show—if it were simply a matter of "being gay," we would expect being a fan of the show to be fairly universal among gay men).

In short, despite the fact that lay explanations for what caused bronies to discover the show and become interested in it are overly simplistic and grounded in misconceptions, it *does* nicely illustrate the fact that people *do* feel a need to explain the phenomenon. In the hopes of addressing this need with data, rather than idle speculation and relying on stereotypes, let's ask bronies themselves about their gateway into the world of *MLP*.

Common Paths to *MLP* Discovery

MLP:FIM is a television show, first and foremost. As such, it's helpful to think about it in much the same way we think about any fan base which has sprung up around a piece of media (e.g., anime fans; Reysen et al., 2017). Since we can take it as a given that you probably have to watch at least one episode of a show *before* you can know if you like it, it's work asking *how* anyone discovers a new television show in the first place.

We can imagine at least a few common ways people get introduced to a new television show. One way is through exposure to online advertising and word-of-mouth discussion through social media websites. After all, billions are spent every year on Internet-based advertising. For many of us, our first impressions about a show or film are through these advertisements, comments, and reviews posted on social media websites.

Another way we're exposed to new media is through direct suggestions from our friends and family. Most of us can probably recall a time when we handed the remote control (or, in today's age, the Netflix account) to someone else in the room and said, "Here, you choose what to watch." Or perhaps you've had the experience of a friend or family member who excitedly told you that you simply *had* to watch this new show because they enjoyed it so much.[3] As such, it seems conceivable that at least *some* bronies would have stumbled upon the show in this manner.

And, of course, one has to take into account the role of pure dumb luck in discovering something you like. You might recognize this from your own experience: Maybe you were sitting in the waiting room at the dentist's office or walking through the mall when you overheard a song that you liked. Or perhaps you found yourself stopping to watch a particularly interesting scene from a film or show playing on the display screen at an electronics store. Or—though this is less likely to occur today in the age of digital television and Netflix—perhaps you simply found yourself channel-surfing one idle evening and discovered a show that caught your attention.

All of these possibilities were assessed in a 2014 survey we conducted on nearly 1,900 bronies. Specifically, bronies were given a list of different ways they could have discovered *MLP* or the brony fandom itself and were asked to choose which one best fit their own experience. They were also permitted, if none of the answers matched, to choose an "Other" category. The responses are summarized in Figure 7.1.

As you can see from the figure, there is no one singular gateway into the brony fandom. Social media emerged as the largest single point of entry, but it applied to fewer than half of bronies. Accidental discovery was the second-most popular entry point, but only if the categories "friends" and "family" are kept separate. If they are combined as a single category of "others trying to get you to watch the show," they may be just as big an influence, if not a bigger influence than stumbling into the fandom by accident. Finally, the figure indicates that these reasons tend to account for the vast majority of bronies' entrance into the fandom: Only 3.7 percent of bronies indicated that some other factor was responsible for their discovery of the show.

Let's take a look at each of these routes to discovery in a bit more detail.

The Role of Social Media and the Internet

The biggest gateway into bronies' interest in *MLP* was the Internet, with social media websites being of particular prominence (Edwards, Scher,

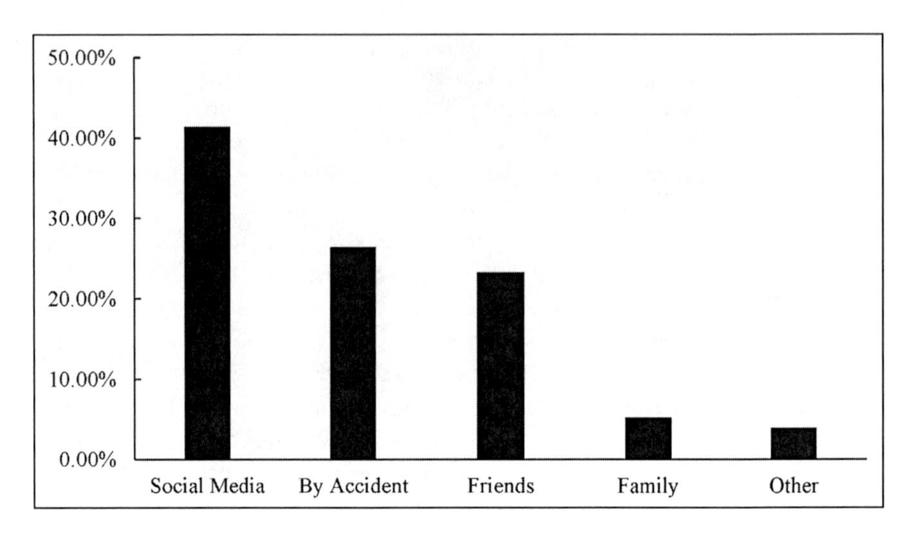

Figure 7.1. **Brony responses to the question "Which of the following circumstances best fit the situation regarding your discovery of MLP: FIM and the Brony fandom?"**

& Griffin, 2016). This is hardly surprising to researchers, for at least two different reasons.

The first reason is historical. As we discussed in Chapter 1, the brony fandom owes its existence (and, indeed, the term "brony" itself) to online forums such as 4chan's "Comics & Cartoons" board.[4] It was here that like-minded fans of related content (e.g., comic books, animated shows) first noticed the show's revival and began discussing it amongst one another. As such, it makes sense that many people who did not fall within Hasbro's target audience demographic (and were thus unlikely to hear about the show through advertising during children's programming) would learn about the show through forums focused on cartoons and animation.

The second, and perhaps more interesting reason why social media may have been such a draw to the brony fandom has to do with how small and niche the interest is—at least for adults. Research on other fan and interest groups has shown that when it comes to fairly non-mainstream or relatively rare interests, the Internet, social media, and interest-specific forums play an important role in helping people with similar interests find one another and congregate.

For a particularly relevant example, we turn once again to the furry fandom—people who are fans of media featuring anthropomorphized animal characters (e.g., animals that walk, talk, and act like humans do). Originating as an offshoot of the science fiction fandom in the 1970s and 1980s, the furry fandom was small and existed largely outside mainstream attention. Furries existed in regional pockets where small gatherings and conventions occurred.

During this period, furries communicated with one another largely through mail (e.g., zines and mailing lists). While it was a very active community, it remained fairly small, mostly owing to the fact that most people had no idea that it even existed. As such, if you were a person who was interested in art and writing featuring anthropomorphic animal characters, but you didn't directly encounter one of these mailing lists or conventions, you had no reason to believe that anyone else shared their interest.

The prolific spread of the Internet in the 1990s changed all of this, however. Most furries credit the Internet with their discovery of the fandom through the mass-sharing of art, stories, and other furry-themed media. Where once a furry artist or writer might have their work seen by a few dozen people who received a zine by mail, thousands could now see their work online. Likewise, furries in geographically remote areas where there were no other furries around were now able to find and stay in communication with other furries. This increased their ability to interact and organize and also led to a massive increase in both the number of, and size of, conventions.

Similar stories exist for numerous other niche communities, many of which went from small, isolated pockets of fans to globe-spanning international communities with thousands of members. Within this context, the role of the Internet in both the discovery of *MLP* and the spread of the brony fandom makes a lot of sense. Without the Internet, it's entirely likely that most potential bronies would skip over *MLP* without a second thought simply because they were outside the target demographic or because they had no information about it. By allowing them to hear from others who had watched the show, especially in forums with people who shared their interest in comics or animation, any reluctance or hesitation they may have had dissipated. If nothing else, hearing about *MLP* more frequently in the forums one frequents might have simply piqued the curiosity of at least a few people, if only to see what all the fuss was about.

"I just don't know what went wrong": Accidental Fans

Very much in line with the role of the Internet in the discovery of *MLP*, more than a quarter of bronies describe their discovery of the fandom as purely accidental—in the sense that they were not actively seeking to become fans of the show.

There are a myriad of different ways this could potentially happen. One way, as we've discussed, is through the rapid propagation of both awareness of and interest in the show online. Simply put, a person who might otherwise not have heard about the show could stumble upon writing, fanfiction, artwork, or discussions of the show online while browsing for other content. For instance, it's unlikely that most of the people who frequented the /co/ board of 4chan *expected* to see a thread about *MLP*. As such, their discovery of it was unplanned, a matter of being in the right place at the right time. And, as word of the show increased online and bronies became increasingly active in their creation and dispersal of fan-made content, it became increasingly likely that some would have such a chance encounter.[5]

There are other, non–Internet ways to have chance encounters with the show, of course. As we've previously mentioned, daily life presents us with numerous opportunities to be incidentally exposed to media. A person sitting in the waiting room at a dentist's office might see the show on the screen. With nothing else to do while they wait, they may find themselves watching the show and unexpectedly liking it.

The role of such unexpected, unplanned, chance encounters with the show cannot be understated. For example, while it's easy to imagine a person getting into the show because a brony friend of theirs introduced them to the show, more than a third (34.9 percent) of bronies in the 2014 study mentioned earlier had never heard the term "brony" prior to watching the show. This means that for at least one-third of bronies, their interest in the show had *nothing* to do with their knowledge of an existing fan community. For these fans, their interest was far more likely to be driven by other situation-specific circumstances or simply by their own genuine interest in the show's content.

Friends, Family and the Power of Word of Mouth

As any advertising professional can tell you, one of the biggest hurdles to persuasion is the fact that people reflexively respond with doubt or mistrust when they realize someone is actively trying to persuade them.[6] This is why companies have, in recent years, begun actively pursuing word-of-mouth marketing—that is, getting customers to do the "advertising" for them (King, Racherla, & Bush, 2014). After all, you may believe that a company telling you that their product is great has an underhanded reason for doing so, but there's little reason to believe that your *best friend* has a reason to deceive you. As such, people are easily persuaded to try out a restaurant, buy a product, or watch a show if someone they care about has suggested it to them.

This might explain one particular route to discovering *MLP*: being persuaded by a friend or family member. In the same 2014 survey described above,

19.8 percent of bronies indicated that they personally *knew* someone who was a brony prior to watching the show themselves, and 25 percent said that they had a family member who, while probably not a brony, watched *MLP*.[7] Of course, without directly asking whether this person was the *specific* reason they chose to watch the show, there is no way to know for sure whether this person was the *main* reason soon-to-be-bronies decided to watch the show for themselves. Nevertheless, knowing someone who is a brony *dramatically* increases your likelihood of watching the show for at least two reasons—one direct and one indirect.

The direct reason is the obvious one: If your friend is a brony, they may attempt to convince you to check out the show for yourself. Whereas advertising campaigns and the word of strangers on the Internet may have failed to persuade you to watch the show, having a friend or family member vouch for the show personally can make it seem more appealing. After all, if you share other things in common with them (e.g., you have similar tastes in computer games or music), it makes sense that you may like a show that they like. And, of course, there's something to be said for having someone close to you harp on you repeatedly to try something!

But there's a subtler, indirect reason why knowing a brony could increase your chance of watching the show yourself. Let's assume for a moment that you knew your friend was a brony, but they never once tried to push it on your or discuss it with you. If you value your friend and think positive things about them, you're also likely to value their judgment. After all, we tend to surround ourselves with sound, level-headed people whose opinions we trust and respect. As such, if given the opportunity to watch *MLP* one day (e.g., while channel surfing), you might find yourself stopping to watch the show precisely because you *know* that your friend watches it. Whether they tried to persuade you or not, their stamp of approval *does* lend some credibility to the show and your willingness to watch it. If nothing else, you want to know what they see in it![8]

And, of course, even if your little sister isn't actively trying to coax you to watch the show with her, if you're in the house while she's watching it, you're likely to have an accidental encounter with the show, whether it's while co-viewing with her (e.g., babysitting) or simply having your attention caught by the show as you walk past.[9]

Before we move on, it's worth making a final note about the role of friends and family when it comes to sparking interest in *MLP*. In a 2012 study of nearly 14,000 bronies, researchers asked participants whether they found out about *MLP* through a male or a female friend. The results, showing in Figure 7.2 below, found that while male and female bronies were *both* more likely to have been introduced to the show by a *male* friend, female bronies were *far* more likely than male bronies to have been introduced to the show

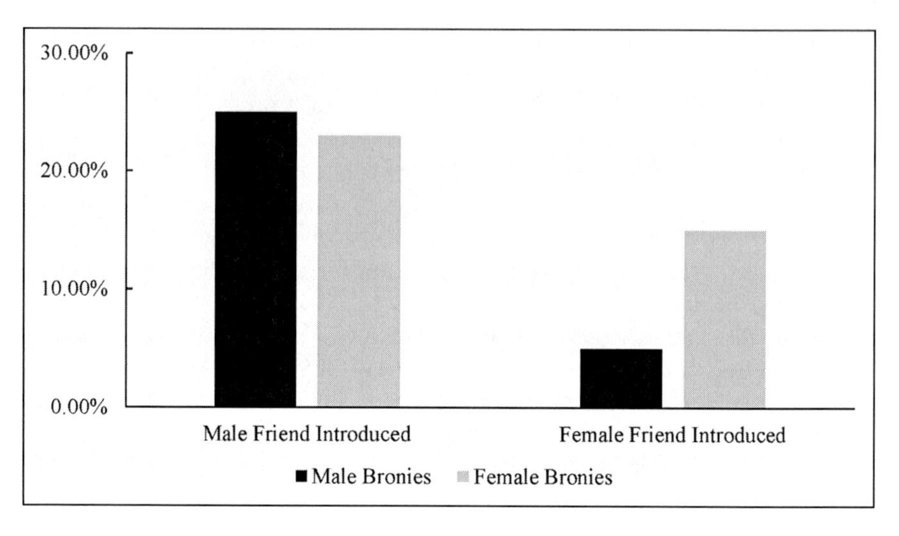

Figure 7.2. **Frequency of male and female bronies indicating that a male or female friend first introduced them to *MLP*.**

by a female friend. One possibility is that male bronies may simply have fewer female friends than female bronies do. Another possibility might be that, given the stereotypes of *MLP* as a show for girls, males may not be as persuaded to watch the show by a female fan than they are by a male fan—hearing about it from a male might "make it okay" for them to watch a show stereotypically thought to be for girls.

Why Did It Have to Be Ponies?

To this point, we've looked at various "gateways" into the brony fandom, specifically looking at the factors that contributed to people sitting down to watch *MLP* for the first time.

This, however, is far from the only question worth asking on the subject. For instance, the question "What got you to watch the show in the first place?" is *very* different from "Why did you *keep* watching after the first episode?" To use an analogy, I could get a person to try chocolate for the time in a lot of ways: I could sneak it into their food, I could bribe them to try it, I could persuade them that they'll like it—the list is as extensive as you are creative.[10] But saying you've *tried* chocolate is different from saying you *like* it: Regardless of how you initially came to try chocolate, your sense of taste will determine whether you like it and continue to eat it on your own or not.

The same holds true for bronies and *MLP*. We've only just scratched the surface when it comes to understanding what it is about the show that people come back for more. To be sure, that question is, in and of itself, somewhat difficult to answer. Returning to our chocolate example, what reason can a person give for liking or disliking chocolate other than "it tastes good" or "it tastes bad"? Is there anything particularly special about the show or the fandom that keeps bronies coming back for more, or which makes it categorically different from other television shows that developed a fan following?

In Chapters 8 through 15 we address these questions, looking at different facets of the show, the franchise, and the fandom itself to move beyond the question of the first "taste" of *MLP* to the far more psychologically interesting questions of "Why *MLP* and not something else?" and "Why do you keep coming back?"

Chapter 8

Come for the Show, Stay for the Swag

"You know, Rainbow Dash was right. Eavesdropping on your own fan club isn't weird at all."

—*Scootaloo (Season 8, Episode 20,* The Washouts)

Nothing is more alienating than being an outsider looking into a fandom to which you don't belong. Let's imagine, for example, that your friend, a sport fan, dragged you to a football game, even though you know nothing about the sport itself. You might reasonably expect to sit in a crowded stadium with a beer and some fried food in hand while watching some grown men throw a ball around and smash into each other while a crowd of people cheer them on.

What you *wouldn't* expect to see at this football game is 10,000 fans around you wearing giant foam blocks in the shape of yellow cheese on their head. And yet, if the game is being played at Lambeau Field in Green Bay, Wisconsin, this is *precisely* what you'd find.

As another example, imagine a different friend of yours was a huge fan of the 1975 film *The Rocky Horror Picture Show*. You know nothing of the film yourself, but figure it must be good if people are still talking about it more than 40 years after its release. You're dragged along to a screening of the film, where you might expect to grab some popcorn and a drink and watch a classic film among excited fans.

What you *wouldn't* expect is to have a greeter at the door put a giant "V" on your forehead in lipstick. You also probably wouldn't expect to *not* hear the film over the audience continually shouting out comments in response to almost every line of dialogue. Nor would you expect to have to dodge flying rice, toast, and toilet paper while holding a newspaper over your head and waving around a flashlight. And yet, this is a fairly regular occurrence at screenings of the film.

For a final example, let's imagine a friend of yours is a huge fan of the musical group Insane Clown Posse.[1] They managed to score two tickets to an upcoming concert, and you agree to accompany them. You brush up on some of the band's songs and expect the concert to involve what most concerts involve: loud music, thousands of screaming fans, and some impressive light displays.

What you probably *weren't* expecting was to see thousands of fans wearing face paint. You're probably going to be even more caught off-guard when the band starts spraying liters of Faygo-brand soda into the front row of the audience. And yet, this is a regular occurrence at an Insane Clown Posse concert.

These examples all illustrate the complexity of fan-related behavior. On its surface, fan behavior seems like it should be simple and straightforward. If a fan is a person with a strong interest in something, it's easy to think of behaviors consistent with that interest: Television fans probably watch their favorite shows a lot, music fans probably listen to their favorite bands a lot, and hobbyists probably spend a lot of time doing their hobby. And yet, as you dive deep into specific fandoms, it becomes apparent that each one is a unique subculture with its own distinct behaviors, memes, values, and language.

It's for this reason that we're devoting a chapter to better understanding what, exactly, bronies *do*. After all, if it were simply a matter of "they watch *MLP* a lot," there wouldn't be a lot to write about. Nor, as we argue, would the brony fandom be all that interesting. In fact, one of the things that makes the fandom *so* interesting to study is the myriad of different behaviors bronies engage in above and beyond simply watching the show. After all, plenty of children grew up watching *MLP* in the 1980s and 1990s. Few people felt this was unusual or noteworthy enough to conduct studies on or write news stories about. What makes bronies interesting is the culture and wide range of fan behaviors that have developed among adult fans of the show.

We begin this chapter by first focusing on watching the show itself, looking at the frequency with which bronies watch the show, their attitudes and interest toward it, and the *way* in which they watch the show. We then move beyond the show itself to other fan-related activities, including the creation and consumption of fan-related content and attending conventions with other fans. Finally, we finish up with a discussion of "brony swag"—*MLP*-themed merchandise and some of the underlying motivations driving bronies to buy and display it to fans and non-fans alike.

Watching *MLP*

Perhaps unsurprisingly, most bronies watch *MLP*. This is the core around which the brony fandom has formed—the central pillar of the fandom. The show serves as the primary source of "official" content for the fandom. The show's writers and animators are the only ones who get to officially create new characters, settings, and story arcs within the *MLP* universe—referred to by fans as the official "canon." The show is the touchstone of the fandom, serving as a common well of material from which all fans can draw inspiration for discussions and the creation of their own fan content.

As such, it makes sense that most bronies have at least some passing familiarity with the show, since failing to do so would mean lacking important information about the show's universe. In this regard, the layperson's intuition that most bronies probably watch the show with at least some regularity is supported by the data. In a 2016 study of more than 1,000 bronies, participants overwhelmingly indicated that they watched the show at *least* a few times per week—more than 80 percent of bronies indicated that this was the case (see Figure 8.1). This is particularly noteworthy for at least two reasons. First, new episodes of the show only air for a portion of any given year—it's not uncommon for the show to have a several-month hiatus in any given year, meaning there are months when no new episodes air. Second, even when new episodes of the show *are* being aired, there is only typically *one* new episode per week. With most fans watching several episodes per week on average, this means that most fans aren't just keeping up with new episodes of the show, they're watching and re-watching old episodes. A lot.

In another study of more than 500 bronies taken shortly after the end of the show's fifth season, participants were asked about the number of episodes of the most recent season of the show they had seen. As it turns out, 94.5 percent of participants said that they had watched all or nearly all of the new episodes, with only 0.8 percent of participants saying that they hadn't seen a single episode from the recent season. This suggests that bronies aren't *just* re-watching their favorite past episodes of the show, but also tend to keep current on the show's recent developments. It also makes sense when one considers that the fandom has its origins in online forums where people discuss their favorite comic books and cartoons (Connelly, 2017). If a brony were to fall behind in the newest episodes, they run the risk of not only being unable to participate in these discussions, but also the risk of having plot twists or surprising outcomes spoiled for them.[2]

In fact, this interest in the show itself seems to drive not only future watching of the show, but future involvement in the fandom itself. This was discovered in a longitudinal study which tracked more than a thousand bronies across multiple seasons of the show. Participants who were the *most* interested

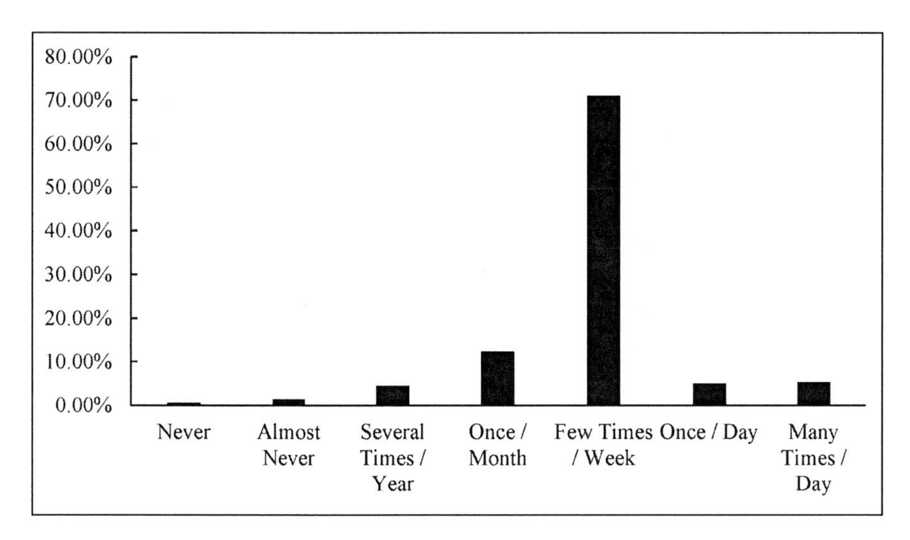

Figure 8.1. **Frequency with which bronies watched the show *My Little Pony: Friendship Is Magic.***

in the show at an earlier point in time were the most likely to also show an *increase* in their interest in the show and were more likely to participate in the fandom in the future. Or, to put it another way: Watching the show seems to create its own "hype," driving fans to want to see more of it and increasing their interest in interacting with others who also watch the show.

How Bronies Watch: Immersion

So far the results we've discussed seem pretty straightforward: Bronies, defined as adult fans of the television show *MLP:FIM*, unsurprisingly watch the show a lot. But if you're a fan of anything, you know that there's more to an interest than merely consuming the media. There's something specific about the *way* in which fans consume their preferred media.

To see what we mean, consider this: *Anyone* can put on a jazz record or look at a piece of modern art. But there's a *world* of difference between the way a jazz aficionado listens to jazz and the way most of the rest of the world listens to jazz. Whereas many of us might hear arrhythmic saxophone squeaking[3] and a lack of any coherent structure or melody, the trained ear hears something the untrained one cannot and appreciates it on an entirely different level. The same holds true for modern art, which, to most people, often seems nonsensical and silly. But to a person with a true appreciation for the subtlety, nuance, and context of the piece, it can be an incredibly stirring experience.[4]

The same almost certainly holds true for bronies, who likely appreciate *MLP* in an entirely different way than those who are not fans of the show. One way is the extent to which they become immersed or engaged with the show. Terms like "immersion" and "presence" are somewhat fuzzy in the psychological literature, but generally refer to people allowing themselves to be brought into the world of a piece of media. It may include the extent to which people feel like they're "really there," the extent to which their mind responds as though the story were real, or simply the feeling of "losing oneself" in the moment and losing track of the real world (e.g., Brockmyer et al., 2009; Busselle & Bilandzic, 2009; Green & Brock, 2000; Jin & Park, 2009; Ryan, Rigby, & Przybylski, 2006; Skalski, Tamborini, Shelton, Buncher, & Lindmark, 2011).

To a non-fan watching *MLP*, there may be numerous barriers preventing them from becoming immersed. For example, a person might dismiss the idea of anthropomorphized animals outright, finding it impossible to accept the show's premise of sentient, talking horses. Others may dislike the aesthetics of the show, finding the multicolored pastels or the animation style unpleasant to focus on. Still others may be put off by pre-existing beliefs about the show as being for little girls. With these issues looming large in the viewer's mind, it seems unlikely that they could allow themselves to be transported completely into the story, which also means they're less likely to be emotionally affected by it or to see the characters as people they could identify with.

In contrast, bronies, who have little problem accepting many of the shows premises (e.g., Equestria is a world where magic exists, the characters are horses who can talk like humans), seem to be *far* better able to immerse themselves into the show, allowing them to get more out of it. In our recent 2018 study, for example, it was found that the more strongly a person identifies as a brony, the more likely they are to report feeling a greater sense of immersion and presence into the show itself. They got more wrapped up in the moment while watching. Much like the jazz fan or the fine arts student, bronies seem to be appreciating the show on an entirely different level than non-fans. Where fans feel genuine emotion, identify with the show's characters, and feel their imagination soar in a world of boundless magic, non-fans sees a bunch of obnoxiously-colored cartoon horses moving around on a screen.

It should come as no surprise, then, that the same people who experience the show in a more vivid and immersive way are also the same people who watch the show more often. Our 2017 study revealed this to be the case, showing that the extent to which a person was a brony and the extent to which they were motivated by the entertainment the show provided were both positively associated with watching the show more. Of course, as a correlational study, the directionality of this effect is not yet clear. Though it seems plausible that a bidirectional effect is occurring: People who get more immersed into the show enjoy it more, causing them to become bigger fans of the show which, in turn, causes them to become even *more* immersed in and engaged with the show itself.

This is what's missing from many laypeople's understanding of bronies and the flood of questions about how bronies seem to get so much gratification out of watching a show that they, themselves, find underwhelming (or outright annoying). A non-fan simply doesn't understand that bronies are getting far more out of the show than they are.

Watching Fan-Made Content

One might assume that the story of what bronies do would be finished now that we've talked about watching the show itself. But the show itself is really just scratching the surface of what bronies do. It's very much akin to the perplexed outsider we discussed at the start of the chapter, watching a football game, a screening of *The Rocky Horror Picture Show*, or an Insane Clown Posse concert, all the while wondering, "I thought we were all just here to watch a football game/film/concert?"

Like with many other media-based fandoms, the canon universe is just a jumping off point for fans. The original creators of the show create worlds that spur the imagination of fans who, highly immersed in these worlds, want to infuse them with their own ideas.

The prevalence of fan-made content is hardly novel to the *MLP* fandom. *Star Wars* fans spent decades creating non-canon content inspired by the films after *Return of the Jedi*. With the *Star Wars* franchise seemingly finished, fans found themselves craving additional stories from the universe they had come to love, and so they took it upon themselves to tie up any loose threads, come up with backstories for their favorite background characters or spaceships, and write both sequels and prequels explaining what had come before and what was to come next for the Rebel Alliance.[5]

The best-known examples of fan-created content comes not from the *Star Wars* universe, but its "rival," the *Star Trek* universe. In the years following the end of the iconic science fiction show *Star Trek*, fans who found themselves enamored with the show's utopian and futuristic setting began generating their own content in the form of fan-fiction. A great deal of academic work has focused specifically on female fans of the show, who often wrote character-driven fan-fiction involving Captain Kirk and Mr. Spock, which delved into aspects of their relationship (e.g., romance or sexual tension) or other topics that were not addressed in the show itself (Bacon-Smith, 1992; Jenkins, 1992).

Given the prevalence of fan-made content in other fandoms, it should come as no surprise that fan-made content can be found in the brony fandom as well. But whereas fandoms such as the *Star Trek* fandom existed at a time prior to the Internet, where fanfiction and artwork was primarily exchanged in person at conventions or via fan-created, independently-published zines, the brony fandom was a product of the Internet itself. As such, fan-made content is far more prevalent, distributed far more widely, and can take many more forms than the fan content of yesteryear.

Non-bronies can probably guess at least some of the more obvious forms of fan-made content. Fan-created artwork abounds, with sites such as DeviantArt, Tumblr, and Derpibooru making it easy for fans to share their own visual portrayals of the show's characters—as well as characters of their own creation—with other fans. Speaking to this point, Derpibooru alone contains more than 1.6 million unique images as of the time of this writing. And while some artists attempt to closely emulate the show's trademark style, others imbue their work with their own style. Others still eschew two-dimensional images altogether in favor of animation or 3D graphics. Bronies often collaborate with one another in the process, sharing assets and knowledge to create 3D animated movies featuring the show's characters, complete with voice actors from within the fandom itself.[6]

Also popular in the brony fandom is fan-fiction—stories written by fans of the show. These often include new stories involving official characters, including non-canon backstories, the formation of relationships between two canon characters (referred to as "shipping"), or the crossing over of the *MLP* universe with other fictional universes. One particularly notable example of the latter is *Fallout Equestria*, a fan-created spin-off universe that mixes the bright and cheerful world and characters of *MLP* with the dark, post-apocalyptic setting of the *Fallout* computer game franchise. The titular first book of what has become an extended universe is more than 600,000 words long and has been downloaded by thousands of fans. In fact, the book itself has been released as both an audiobook and in hardcover format.[7] Illustrating the sheer volume of *MLP* fanfiction generated by fans, the website Fimfiction—a popular brony fanfiction website—features more than 100,000 unique fan-created stories.

But the creativity and expression of fans is not limited to the written word or fan-made drawing and animation. Many fans cosplay as their favorite characters, ranging from donning outfits or hairstyles worn by their favorite characters to full-body, mascot-style suits that cost thousands of dollars and hundreds of hours of work. The fandom is also home to a large number of talented musicians who range in genre from classic guitar to rock to electronica and everything in between. Several of these musicians have followings of millions of subscribers on YouTube, with many more having more than 100,000 subscribers.

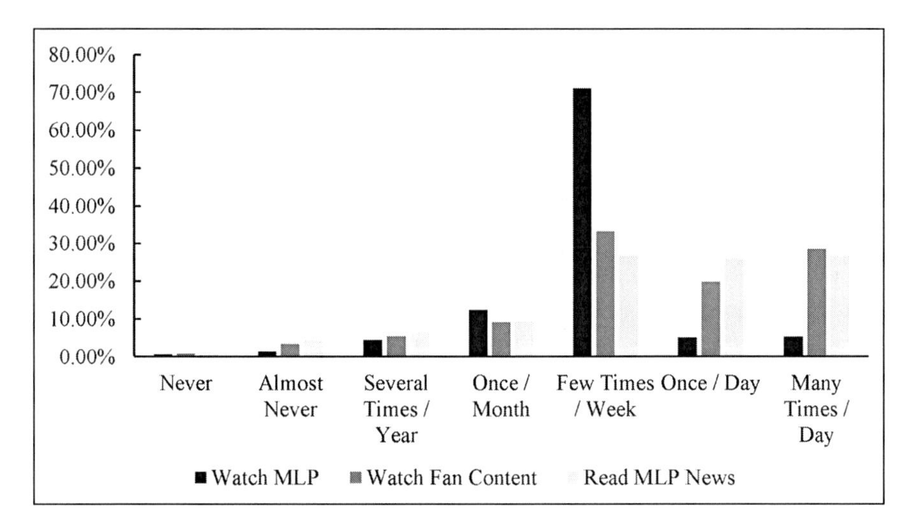

Figure 8.2. **Frequency with which bronies watched the *My Little Pony* and consumed fan-made content and news related to the show.**

Beyond artistic endeavors, many bronies create a wide range of content for the fandom, doing so using online platforms such as YouTube. These include a whole host of analysts and critics who break down, discuss, and debate new episodes. Others create "reaction" videos, allowing viewers to co-view episodes of the show with others.[8] Content aggregators and brony news sites also serve an important function in the fandom, helping draw attention to up-and-coming creators, popular trends, or important updates in the world of the brony fandom.

It should be clear by now that bronies consume far more *MLP*-themed content than simply the show itself. In fact, as popular and universal as viewing *MLP:FIM* is among bronies, it turns out fan-related content may be just as important, if not *more* important to bronies. In the same 2016 study which found that most bronies watched the show at least a few times a week, participants were also asked about the frequency with which they viewed *fan-made* content and read up on fan-made news (from websites like *Equestria Daily*, which have millions of pageviews). As Figure 8.2 shows, fans consume both fan-related content and read *MLP*-related news with greater frequency than they watch the show itself. In other words, while bronies are unarguably fans of *MLP*, it would seem that they're just as big a fan of the content produced by the brony fandom itself. This is a point often overlooked by outsiders scratching their heads and wondering what a grown adult sees in a television show for little kids.

Convention Attendance

As the previous section makes clear, bronies are far from passive viewers of a television show. In addition to being avid content creators themselves, the fandom involves a great deal of social interaction. We'll discuss this point in greater detail in Chapters 13 and 14, but for now it's worth noting the importance of fan conventions as an important part of the brony experience. Since 2011 there have been nearly 200 brony conventions worldwide, with the largest one, BronyCon 2015, having more than 10,000 attendees. The popularity of these conventions may be driven by the fact that the brony fandom itself is geographically diverse. Bronies typically interact with one another online through forums, websites, and social media. Outside of small, local gatherings (typically in larger cities) it can be difficult for bronies (especially those in rural areas) to meet other bronies in person. Conventions afford them that opportunity, which is why they're often an important part of bronies' fandom experience.

In Chapter 1 we introduced the distinction between fanship—the extent to which one considers themselves to be a fan of something—and fandom—the extent to which one identifies with a community of like-minded fans. As it turns out, this distinction is not a nitpicky pedantic one, as there are considerable differences between bronies who are primarily driven by fanship and those primarily driven by fandom. In our 2017 study, for example, it was found that higher scores on measures of fandom were associated with attending more conventions; in contrast, fanship was unrelated to the number of conventions a brony had attended. Of course, the direction of the relationship between fandom and convention attendance is not yet clear—it may well be the case that bronies develop stronger feelings of fandom *as a result* of going to brony conventions. The possibility also exists that the link is bidirectional—that caring more about the fandom leads to a greater desire to attend conventions which, in turn, strengthens one's feelings of connection to the brony fandom. Regardless of the direction of this relationship, the evidence suggests that convention attendance and being a part of the brony community go hand in hand, a social element of the fandom that is also often goes overlooked by outsiders who erroneously assume that bronies simply like to watch a television show.

Of course, there's more to convention attendance than simply going because you like the show. Most people attend fan conventions to have fun. The opportunity to interact with other bronies, to talk about content one is passionate about, and to meet voice actors, writers, musicians, and animators who work on your favorite show is undoubtedly a good time for most fans. Speaking to his point, the same 2017 survey also found that bronies whose interest in the fandom was driven both by a need to belong and by its entertainment value were also the *most* likely to attend fan conventions.

As it turns out, bronies who are in it for a good time tend to go to more conventions, where they have a good time. Who knew?

Brony Swag

In the final section of this chapter we'll be looking at one of the most visibly recognizable aspects of the brony fandom: merchandise. Whether you call it swag, collecting, or an expression of your fan interest, owning brony-themed stuff seems to be important for many bronies. This is hardly surprising, given that the *MLP* franchise was, at its core, designed first and foremost to sell toys to kids. It's also not surprising that this is not unique to the brony fandom. In the same manner, *Star Wars* fans are often depicted as people wearing stormtrooper outfits and waving around plastic lightsabers and *Doctor Who* fans all seem to all have *something* emblazoned with a TARDIS (the iconic blue police phone box which doubles as an interdimensional vessel for the show's titular character).

In our 2018 study, we discovered just how *much* brony "swag" (merchandise) bronies had. The 221 bronies in the study had an average estimated value of just under $1,050 worth of *MLP* merchandise. While that seems like a lot (and it's certainly not a trivial amount), it includes clothing (e.g., t-shirts, socks, backpacks), commissioned artwork, posters, figures, plushies, accessories (e.g., mousepads, glassware), lunchboxes, stickers, DVDs and Blu-ray discs, and games—just to name a *few* things. For bronies who have been fans for years, this amounts to a couple of hundred dollars per year.[9]

Which raises the important question of why. Why do bronies—and indeed, fans in general—devote so much time and effort to collecting and displaying objects related to their hobby? Interestingly, we might find an answer in existing theories about consumer devotion. These theories suggest, in a somewhat religious theme, that devotees often engage in rituals as a way of sustaining their devotion (Pimentel & Reynolds, 2004). After all, fans *themselves* often use of religious terms/metaphors when describing their fandom activities.[10] It was this precise devotion to the *Star Trek* universe and its characters that led researchers to studying them as a sort of "religious phenomenon" in the first place (Jindra, 1994)!

These "sustaining rituals" are a behavioral manifestation of a fan's devotion, something we can categorize and look at based on the possible functions they serve. For our purposes, we've grouped these rituals into five categories:

1. Display Behaviors—Using fan objects as a symbol of your level of interest and commitment to the fandom.

   EXAMPLES: wearing a brony t-shirt, *MLP* bumper stickers on one's car, cosplaying as your favorite character, profile pictures featuring your favorite pony or *MLP* in general on your social media profile

2. Sharing Knowledge—Talking with others about the fandom, espousing its "virtues," attempts to recruit new members.

   EXAMPLES: talking about the show, sharing stories about brony activities, explaining who the "best pony" is, using fan speak (e.g., "20% cooler"), posting opinions on brony sites

3. Ritual Activities—Active routines involving the fandom. May also involve pilgrimages to important places.

   EXAMPLES: regularity watching new episodes of *MLP*, meeting with bronies regularly, waiting in line for the *MLP* movie on release day

4. Collecting—Searching for and securing objects that have significance with respect to *MLP*. May include the construction of a "shrine" (special place) to hold fan items.

   EXAMPLES: collecting figurines, autographs, show memorabilia, posters, fan artwork, DVDs, displaying your valued collection items in a special location

5. Sacrifices—Using resources in a way that puts fan needs over family or work demands. Risking taunts or bullying to prove your devotion.

   EXAMPLES: Scheduling weekend life around a new episode, giving up family time to attend a convention, spending money you don't have on merchandise, losing friendships because of the show

It should be noted that many common expressions of devotion likely serve more than just one of these motivational needs. For example, wearing an *MLP* t-shirt can act as means of display, a way of sharing knowledge (e.g., if it says who the "best pony" is), a form of collecting, and a way to sacrifice (e.g., risking enduring bullying).

With respect to display behaviors in the brony fandom, participants in our study were asked about the extent to which they wore *MLP* themed clothing (e.g., t-shirts—18.7 percent said frequently/daily), whether they "ponytized" various items in their lives (e.g., named their car after a pony, etc.—26.2 percent said yes), whether they used the "lingo" associated with the show characters (e.g., "20% Cooler," "praise Celestia," "brohoof"—40.2 percent frequently did), whether they have, or would like to have, a drawing of themselves as a *MLP* pony character (49.3 percent said yes), how frequently they attended brony meet up groups or conventions (16 percent said frequently or occasionally), and whether they had received a *MLP* themed tattoo (1.1 percent had). In short, it appears that a significant minority of bronies *do* display their fan interest in very visible ways (e.g., wearing MLP clothing) by wearing clothing. Many more, however, participated in more low key display behaviors like ponytizing items and using the "lingo" associated with the fandom, as such behaviors can more easily be hidden or suppressed if the social environment (family, friends, or strangers) could be threatening.

With respect to sharing behaviors, we asked how frequently bronies read and posted to brony themed thread/sites (45 percent do so almost daily), whether they frequently create fanfiction (8.6 percent), fan artwork (12 percent) or fan collectables (5 percent), whether they have "recruited" others to become fans of *MLP* (22 percent have recruited a family member, 46 percent have recruited a male friend, and 28 percent have recruited a female friend), whether they viewed themselves as a brony recruiter (15 percent said yes), and whether they expected to be friends with someone they heard using *MLP* phases or wearing *MLP* themed clothing (33.8 percent said yes, with 57.2 percent saying it, at very least, helps them form a positive impression of the person). While only a small subset of the brony fandom actively creates artwork, fanfiction, and collectable objects, a sizable proportion of fans go online to read and post to brony-themed sites or social media. The active recruitment of new fans is common, especially for male fans, although a much smaller proportion of fans would label themselves as "active recruiters" or what some have called "evangelical bronies."

With respect to ritual behaviors, we asked how frequently participants watched brony-made videos (73 percent said almost daily), how frequently they listened to brony-themed music (70 percent said almost daily), how frequently they read brony fanfiction (39 percent said almost daily), how frequently they watched reruns of the show between seasons (42 percent said frequently), and whether they searched toy stores looking for *MLP* merchandise (37.2 percent said yes). Compared to the previously mentioned and more visible display behaviors and sharing knowledge activities, the ritualistic activities of viewing the show and other (fan-produced) content was undertaken on a regular basis by a sizable proportion of the fans. This is possible, of course, because of the vast volume of brony-produced content, as mentioned earlier regarding the sharing and consumption of "fan produced" materials (artwork, fanfiction, music and videos). These ritualistic actions clearly represent what are called "consumer behaviors" and point to an important aspect of the brony (and, indeed, any Internet-based) fandom.

With respect to collecting behaviors, we asked bronies whether they have ever purchased DVDs of the show (7 percent said yes), Hasbro-produced *MLP* figurines (28 percent said yes), brony-themed clothing (29 percent said yes), fan-produced merchandise (11 percent said yes), a poster or a wall hanging (14.2 percent said yes), and if they had a "special place" or shrine where they displayed their *MLP* items (36.1 percent said yes). Additionally, 49 percent reported that they had never purchased *MLP*-related merchandise, while 33 percent reported they had made less than six and 18 percent reported that they had made more than six purchases. Purchasing for the sake of collecting was undertaken by nearly half of bronies, though extremely dedicated (over 6 purchases) purchasers made up a smaller (less than one in five) segment of the fandom.

Finally, with respect to the sacrifices bronies make for the fandom, we asked about the degree to which they built their weekly schedule around the *MLP* episodes even if it means missing out on events (6.3 percent regularly do), sacrificed spending time with family and friends so they could be involved with *MLP* (7.3 percent do), and whether they had lost friendships because of their interest in *MLP* (1.8 percent had). These data suggest that while some fans apparently shape their lives to conform to the show and the fandom (less than 10 percent) the vast majority of bronies cherish and celebrate their fan interest without apparent adverse effect. This seems to suggest something we'll revisit in Chapter 18: Despite the assumption among many that bronies are dysfunctional in their fanaticism for the show, the fandom seems to, if anything, have a profoundly positive effect on its members.

Chapter 9

"Yes, but *why*?" Brony Motivation

"But are you sure you feel content? ... Not even a tingle of dissatisfaction? ... Not even the slightest naggin' sensation that you don't really know what your purpose is in life...."

—*Applebloom* (*Season 6, Episode 4,* On Your Marks)

What comes to mind when you hear the word "motivation"?

Maybe the word conjures up an image of a sentiment-laced poster telling you to "Hang in there!" when times are tough. Or perhaps you find yourself thinking about a related term, "inspiration," causing you to recall people or media that have inspired you to achieve something. Alternatively, you might think about what a *lack* of motivation looks like: a listless, lethargic person sitting on the couch doing nothing.

All of these thoughts are related to, albeit not perfect definitions of, the psychological concept of motivation. In a nutshell, psychologists define motivation as "a driving force that initiates and directs behavior" (Stangor, 2010, p. 521). In other words, motivation is an impulse or impetus originating from somewhere within us that (a) compels us to act, and (b) guides our actions in service of a particular goal. Any time we do something to fulfill a need or satisfy a goal—everything from scratching an itch to going to college—we're engaging in motivated behavior.

So what motivates us? Some sources of motivation seem pretty obvious, like those rooted in biology. Imagine a person walking to the store to buy a slice of pizza. This person's behavior is likely motivated by a universal biological need—food. Other biologically-driven motivational states like hunger, thirst, and oxygen deprivation guide us toward specific behaviors (i.e., eating, drinking, seeking air) in order to survive. Piece of cake so far![1]

But life-or-death contingencies aren't the *only* things that motivate our behavior. After all, politicians, storytellers, and advertisers alike have known for ages that sex is an incredibly powerful motivator, and nobody has ever died as a direct result of a lack of sex. Despite this, people and animals alike often go to great lengths in the pursuit of sex. This nicely demonstrates another principle of motivation: We can be powerfully motivated by factors beyond basic biological needs.

This fact has been long recognized by psychologists like Abraham Maslow (1943), who suggested that behavior involves balancing a hierarchy of needs that include biological needs, but also broader, more abstract needs like safety (e.g., shelter), love/and belongingness (e.g., friends), esteem (e.g., respect from others), and self-actualization (e.g., improving ourselves and becoming the best version of ourselves that we can possibly become). Other theorists propose alternative models of motivation, like self-determination theory (Deci & Ryan, 2000), which argues that self-chosen behavior involves a combination of three different motivations: the need to be autonomous (free to choose one's own experiences), the need for competence (to feel like we're capable and knowledgeable), and the need for relatedness (to feel connected with others).

So what does all of this have to do with bronies and *MLP*? Well, if the goal is to understand the seemingly unusual behavior of bronies, it's helpful to understand what motivates them. After all, let's return to our example of sex as a motivator of animal behavior. Without understanding that sex motivates behavior, cosmetics, attractive clothing, and spending vast amounts of resources on a potential mate makes absolutely no sense. Only when you understood the need driving this behavior can you truly get a full understanding of *why* people do it.

With this goal in mind, the present chapter discusses the motivations driving fans from all walks of life to pursue their interests—whether we're talking about sport fans, anime fans, or bronies. What motivates fans to become fans in the first place? Why do they feel the need to consume fan-related content, to buy fan merchandise, or to create fandom-related content? What drives them to seek out and meet with fellow fans at conventions or meet-ups? We'll begin to answer these questions by briefly reviewing some of the first psychological research ever done on fans, research which focused primarily on the motivations of sport fans. We'll argue that many of these same motivations may explain other types of fan interests, including bronies. Next, we'll explore how different bronies can be driven by different motivations and see how these differences can affect the way bronies experience the show and the fandom. We'll then finish the chapter by examining how three motivational factors in particular play a powerful role in determining what individual bronies' thoughts, feelings, and behaviors.

Early Studies of Fans: What Motivates Sport Fans?

Our look into the motivations driving fan behavior begins with a psychology researcher named Daniel Wann. Wann extensively studied the psychology of sport fans. Indeed, it's nearly impossible to study the psychology of fans *without* building upon Wann's work on sports fans in one way or another.

So what makes Wann's work so important? In 1995, he created one of the first scales designed *specifically* to measure the motivations underlying sport fan behavior. He suggested that sport fans are driven by a combination of eight different motivational factors. They actually make a lot of sense if you know (or can imagine) a typical sport fan:

1. Eustress: Seeking positive stress or arousal associated with sport-related activities.

   e.g., Watching the big game and not knowing if your team will win or lose.

2. Self-esteem: Seeking positive feelings about yourself through sport-related activities.

   e.g., Feeling a sense of pride when your team wins the championship or from your knowledge of sport-related trivia.

3. Escapism: Seeking a distraction from boring or undesirable real-world events.

   e.g., Watching the game to distract you from work or relationship problems.

4. Entertainment: Seeking sport-related activities because they're enjoyable in and of themselves.

   e.g., Enjoying the act of playing or watching a particular sport being played.

5. Economics: Seeking profit from the pursuit of sport-related activities.

   e.g., People in a hockey pool or fantasy football league winning money for choosing a winning team or players.

6. Aesthetics: Appreciating beauty, quality, skill, or artistry in sport-related activities.

   e.g., Marveling at an expertly-crafted play or a professional player's skills.

7. Group affiliation: Seeking to belonging to a group of others who share your interest.

e.g., Going to a stadium to be part of a crowd of 40,000 people cheering for your team.

8. Family: Seeking sport-related activities as a way of bringing your family closer together.

   e.g., Having a tradition of watching the game with your siblings or parents every Sunday.

In his initial study, Wann measured each of these eight motivations in a sample of sport fans. He found that that the highest-rated reasons for being a sport fan were, in order, entertainment, eustress, group affiliation, and self-esteem. These same factors were also strongly correlated with the strength of one's identification with a particular sport team. In other words, the more a sport fan said they were motivated by entertainment or eustress, the more likely they were to *also* be a bigger fan of a particular team. In contrast, the extent to which fans profited from a hockey pool or used sport as a convenient way to interact with their family had little to do with how strongly they identified with their favorite team. Later research reinforced these findings (Wann, Schrader, & Wilson, 1999).

In the years since Wann's model of sport fan motivation, others have come up with their own models. For example, Kahle, Kambara, and Rose (1996) proposed that sport fans were motivated by a combination social factors (e.g., feeling camaraderie or obligation toward fellow fans), a deep bond with a particular sport or team, and being able to define and express themselves through a team. In another example, Milne and McDonald (1999) listed 13 different motivations, some of which differed from Wann's model (e.g., physical fitness, risk-taking, stress reduction) and others which were covered by his model (e.g., belongingness, self-esteem, aesthetics). Still others have proposed even *more* motivations in more recent research (e.g., Gau, 2013; Funk, Ridinger, & Moorman, 2004; Trail & James, 2001). But let's not turn this into a needlessly complicated chapter about sport fans. For now, it's enough to say that there's been considerable research done on what motivates sport fans and this research can help us learn a thing or two about non-sport fans. If you're a brony yourself or know a friend or family member who's a brony, you may have noticed that many of the same motivations driving sport fans could also be said about bronies.

Explaining Fan Motivations in Non-Sport Fans

Given the popularity of sports worldwide, it should come as no surprise that researchers studying fans have historically focused on sport fans as the lowest-hanging fruit. They are, after all, an easily-available that can be studied pretty much anywhere.[2] Because of this, up until recently, most psychological research on fans has focused on sport fans (Reysen & Branscombe, 2010). Recently, researchers have begun to branch out, looking at what motivates *other* fans, including fans of film (Oliver & Bartsch, 2010), furries (Reysen, Plante, Roberts, & Gerbasi, 2017a), and celebrities (McCutcheon, Lange, & Houran, 2002), to name just a few.

One of the major focuses of this work has been to test whether it's fair to use sport fans as a model for *all* fans. On the one hand, it makes intuitive sense why sport fans could serve as a model for all fans: If a fan is a person driven by their enjoyment of a particular activity, does it really matter whether that activity is? Is a chocolate-lover *really* all that different from a vanilla-lover if they both eat their preferred sweet because they like the taste of it?

On the other hand, however, fan activities come in all shapes and sizes, including music fans, television or film fans, and fans of crafts or hobbies (e.g., model train enthusiasts). Given how broad and distinct these different activities are (e.g., building a model train in one's basement vs. cheering for your team amidst 40,000 other screaming fans), can we *really* just assume that the differences between fan groups are *only* a matter of preference? Is there *any* evidence showing that fans of different activities differ in what motivates them?[3]

To examine such similarities and differences in fan motivation, Schroy, Plante, Reysen, Roberts, and Gerbasi (2016) surveyed anime fans, furries, and fantasy sport fans. Each group completed Wann's scale assessing the (1995) eight different motivations for sport fans, along with two additional motivations for good measure (i.e., doing it for attention and feelings of sexual attraction). The results found that, despite the differences between the three fan groups, all three rated entertainment and escape as their top two rated choices. This suggests that there's some truth to the idea that fans are fans, regardless of what they're fans of. Despite superficial differences in the content of these fan activities, most fans are motivated by the fact that they enjoy the activity and it gives them a break from their day-to-day lives.

But that's not the whole story. In the same study, the researchers found that while the groups were *similar* in terms of which factors were the most important, they *did* differ with respect to how much each of these factors linked to their identification as a fan.[4] For example, how strongly a person identified as a furry was driven by their need for belongingness, entertainment, and family (in order of strength). For anime fans, identification was driven by belongingness and entertainment, like with furries, but *also* by eustress, escape, self-esteem, and even family. This means that the motivational profile of an anime fan differs from that of a furry—what makes a furry feel like part of the furry community differs from what makes an anime fan feel like part of the anime community. The same held true for fantasy sport fans, whose identification with other fantasy sport fans was driven by belongingness and family. In short, while there *are* some similarities in what motivates fans of all kinds, not all fans are motivated to the same extent by the same things.

The results of studies like this one highlight two important points. First, regardless of which fan group we're talking about, belongingness seems to be an important motivator for fans. Indeed, a concept very similar to belongingness is found in almost every model of human motivation, including Maslow's (1943) hierarchy of needs and self-determination theory (Deci & Ryan, 2000), described earlier in this chapter. Whether we're striving to fit in with our fandoms or our families, workplaces, church groups, or countries, we're motivated to do so by a powerful need to belong to groups.

Second, despite the similarities in motivation across fan groups, there are also *differences* in what motivates members of different fan groups. Riketta (2008) suggests that different groups provide members with different benefits, helping them meet different sets of needs. As such, people should identify more strongly with the groups that best fulfill their unique set of needs.

With all of this in mind, let's turn our attention, at last, to the question of what motivates bronies. What needs might *MLP* and the surrounding fandom be providing for bronies?

The Multi-Dimensional Motivation of Bronies

Following in the footsteps of numerous fan researchers before them, Plante, Reysen, and Chadborn (2018) sought to better understand differences between different fan interests. To do this, they came up with a set of 20 factors that allowed them to differentiate the profiles of fans of pretty much anything—from sport fans to model train enthusiasts.

The scale itself, developed in studies using a variety of different fan groups, was then given to a sample of bronies. So what does it say about the factors underlying the brony fandom? In Figure 9.1, bronies' average score for each of the 20 facets are listed, with higher numbers indicating that more bronies rated that facet as an important component of their involvement in the brony fandom. The figure reveals that five of the top-rated, most important facets of being a brony include (1) identification with other members of the brony community, (2) finding the show and fan-created content aesthetically pleasing, (3) being exposed to novel experiences, (4) getting to escape from the routine of day-to-day life, and (5) experiencing a sense of personal growth.

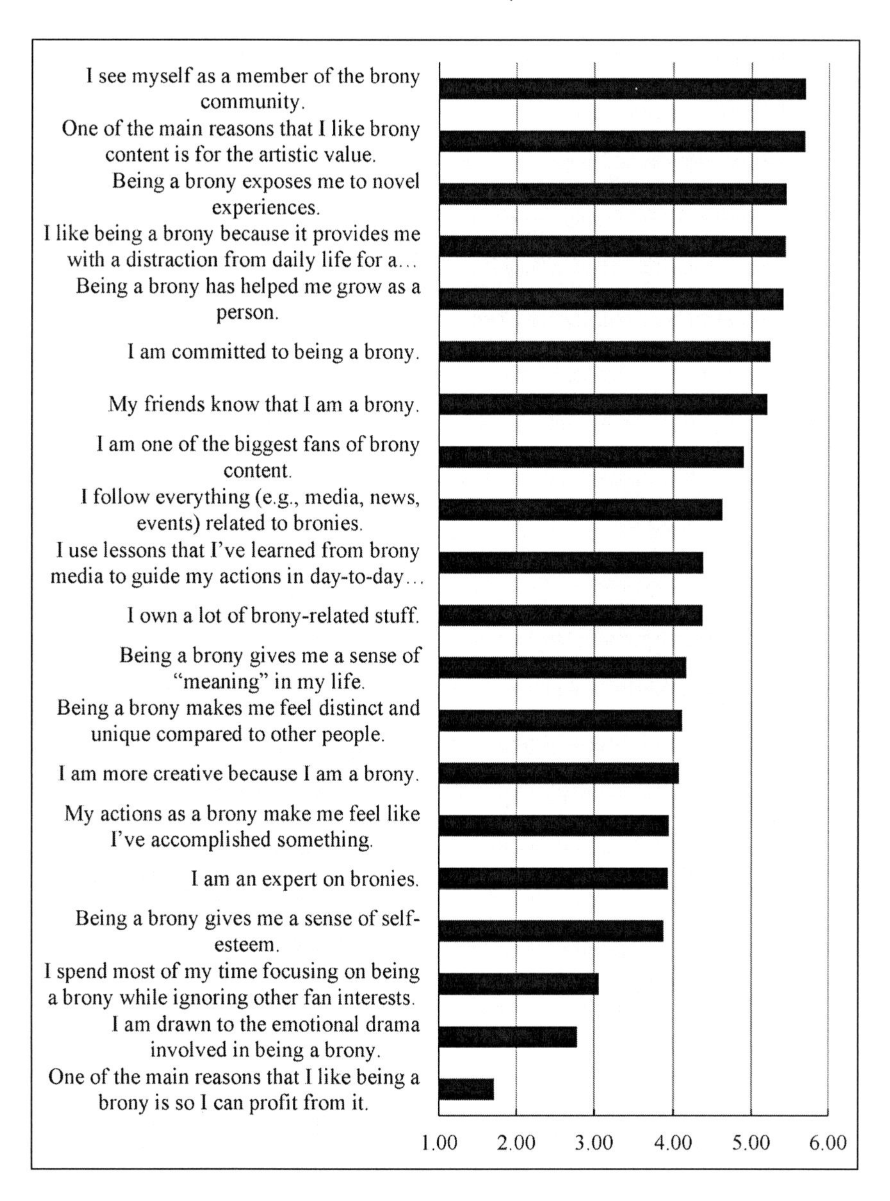

***Figure 9.1.* Average scores for items on the fan dimensions scale (with 4 as the mid-point of the scale).**

It's worth noting that some of these components are not unique to the brony fandom. Identifying with other bronies sounds a lot like "belongingness"—something important to members of other fan groups (e.g., furries, anime fans, and sport fans). Likewise, a sense of aesthetic enjoyment and escapism also underlies numerous other media-based fan activities. In short, that these facets may not, in and of themselves, make bronies unique in their fan profile.

It's also informative, however, to look at the items which were *least* popular among bronies. For example, the three lowest rated items among bronies were those reflecting (1) economic benefits to being a brony, (2) eustress and drama, and (3) focusing exclusively on one's interest in the show (to the exclusion of other fan interests). Unlike fantasy sport fans, for whom financial benefits were one of the biggest incentives, few bronies can say the same for their interest in *MLP*.[5] Likewise, while the anxiousness and drama of not knowing whether your team will win the big game is a driving force for many sport fans, there doesn't seem to be anything analogous in the brony fandom: If anything, bronies would prefer to avoid drama and stress and simply be left to enjoy their show in a relatively drama-free environment.

In short, while there seem to be some similarities in the profiles of bronies and other fan groups, there also seem to be at least a few noteworthy idiosyncrasies or quirks of bronies in particular.

While these findings are certainly interesting in and of themselves, allowing us to debate whether bronies, as a group, are different from other fans as a matter of kind (i.e., categorically different) or a matter of degree (i.e., scoring slightly higher or lower on the same scale), as skeptical scientists, we must always ask ourselves the million-dollar question: "So what?" So what if we can show that bronies score higher or lower than other fan groups on one dimension or another. If these differences don't amount to anything important (e.g., differences in how they behave, differences in values or opinions), is there any reason to care about them at all? Ultimately, we're asking whether these are *differences that make a difference.*

So what *can* we learn about bronies based on these results? To answer this question, Plante and colleagues (2018) conducted what's called a "factor analysis" on each of the 20 scale items, which let them condense the items into a set of four different "dimensions" of fandom.[6] These four dimensions were (a) commitment to the fandom (e.g., identification with fandom, extent of participation), (b) significance of the fandom to you (e.g., growth as person, sense of meaning in life), (c) benefits obtained from the fan interest (e.g., sense of accomplishment, self-esteem), and (d) escapism (e.g., eustress, escape).

When it comes to the dimensions of commitment, significance, and escapism, bronies score above the midpoint of a 7-point scale, as seen in Figure 9.2. But when it comes to the tangible benefits of the fan interest itself, bronies actually scored *below* the midpoint. What this means, in a nutshell, is that bronies, on average, devote considerable amounts of time and resources to their interest, find it personally significant, and see it as a way of escaping

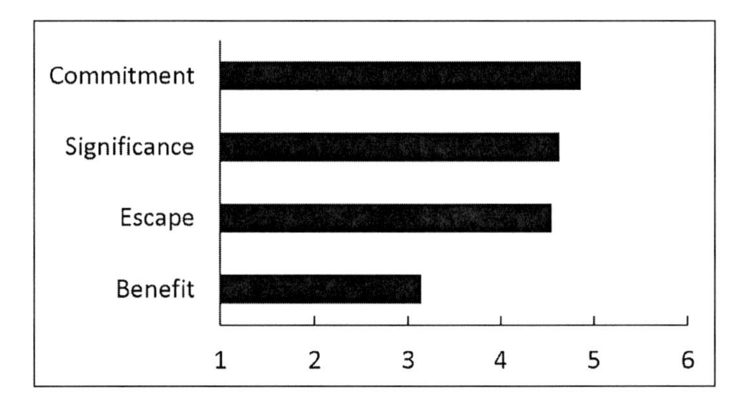

***Figure 9.2.* Average of bronies' scores on four different dimensions of being a fan.**

the drudgery of day-to-day life.[7] Their engagement with the show doesn't seem to be strongly tied to any direct, tangible benefits.[8]

The authors then went one step further, testing whether these dimensions could tell us anything about the beliefs or behaviors of bronies. To understand how, keep in mind that the scores in Figure 9.2 represent *average* scores for the bronies in the sample. As such, individual bronies will vary from this average profile: Some will score lower than average in commitment or higher than average in terms of tangible benefits they gain from the fandom itself. So what can these differences *within* the brony fandom tell us about each of these dimensions and how they pertain to fan behavior?

A type of analysis called regression analysis allowed the researchers to test exactly that, shown in Table 9.2.[9] When it comes to fanship—how much you consider yourself to be a fan of the show, scoring higher in commitment to the show and find the show personally significant was related to being a more committed fan. In contrast, benefiting from the show or using the show for escapism was unrelated to how much you considered yourself to be a fan. Along these same lines, we can see that fan commitment was *also* related to greater identification with other fans (fandom), more engagement with content (e.g., watching the show), giving more help to people in need, becoming more immersed in the show itself, having more friends who were bronies, and having a greater self-esteem.

Bronies for whom the show was personally significant were also more likely to be bigger fans of the show, to identify more strongly with other bronies, and to become more immersed in the show—findings similar to that of commitment. Personal significance differed, however, in that it was *negatively* associated with engaging with the show—that is, those for whom the show was more personally significant actually watched the show *less* frequently. It also differed from commitment in the sense that those for whom the show

Table 9.1. Fan Dimensions Predicting Bronies' Opinions and Behaviors

Variable	Commitment	Significance
Fanship	.55*	.22*
Fandom	.32*	.21*
Engagement	.59*	–.17*
Status	–.02	.30*
Empathy	.10	.33*
Give Help	.31*	.00
Immersion	.19*	.22*
Percent Friends	.21*	–.08
Self-Esteem	.21*	.04

*This effect is statistically significant.

was more personally significant also showed greater empathy toward those who were suffering or in need (but, interestingly, were no more likely to actually give help to those in need).

Finally, the extent to which one received tangible benefits from watching the show and the extent to which the show provides one with a sense of escapism are largely unrelated to most behaviors and opinions. The only exceptions to this rule are that those who receive tangible benefits from the show are actually *less* likely to show empathy toward those in need and those who watch the show for escapism are slightly more likely to engage more frequently with *MLP*-related content.

Taken together, these results illustrate several important points. First, bronies share a lot in common with other fandoms, but are also distinct in several important ways. Far from being trivial distinctions, these differences have a measurable impact on fan-related behavior. Specifically, the extent to which bronies are personally committed to the show and to the fandom and the extent to which the show itself is personally significant and meaningful to them is strongly tied to their fan-related attitudes and behaviors. In contrast, while escapism might be a popular reason for many bronies to watch the show, it, along with tangible benefits that only a few bronies seem to get from being a fan, say relatively little about the attitudes or behaviors of individual bronies.

With all of this said, it's worth keeping in mind that this approach to understanding bronies—that is, measuring the different factors associated with being a fan—is just *one way* to measure and test the underlying motivations that make bronies tick. In the next section, we'll consider a second way we've studied the motivation of bronies.

Fandom Functions: What Does Being a Brony Do for You?

Chadborn, Edwards, and Reysen (2017) took an alternative approach to measuring the motivation of fans—one that involved assessing the needs that the fandom fulfilled for bronies. Or, to put it another way: What itches did being a fan scratch for them?

To do this, the researchers constructed the fandom functions scale, which measured three categories of needs. These needs included the need for purpose (e.g., “My involvement with this fandom provides me with a focus or sense of purpose”), the need for escapism (e.g., “My involvement with this fandom provides me with a break from life’s stresses”), and the need for social connection (e.g., “My involvement with this fandom provides me with an activity to share with my existing friends/ways to stay connected”).[10] In this particular line of research, the authors were interested in testing specifically whether these different motivations could explain the link between feeling connected to one’s fan interest (i.e., fanship) and displaying symbols of one’s fan interest (e.g., wearing/displaying items related to the fandom). They found precisely that: People who were bigger fans were more likely to display symbols of their fan interest—something they did precisely *because* of the social connections associated with being a fan. Or, to put it another way, fans who love their fan interest are interested in making friends who share the same interest, and so they wear symbols of their fandom.

So what happened when the same measures were used in studies of the brony community? As shown in Figure 9.3, bronies were primarily motivated to escape the daily hassles of life, while fulfilling a sense of purpose and satisfying social needs seemed to be somewhat less important by comparison (Edwards, Chadborn, Griffin, & Redden, 2014).

As was done in the previous section, the three potential functions of the fandom were tested for their ability to predict important fan-related attitudes and behaviors. Since individual bronies differed in the extent to which they were motivated by the sense of purpose, escapism, or belonging to *MLP* and the surrounding fandom provided them with, the researchers were able to test whether these differences translated into differences in attitudes and behavior among different bronies.

Table 9.2 illustrates some of the implications of being motivated to be a brony for different reasons. For example, when it comes to watching the show itself, both purpose and social factors seem to be associated with more watching of the show, while escapism was unrelated to how frequently one watches the show. In contrast, when it comes to actually interacting with other bronies, a sense of purpose was strongly associated with more interaction with other

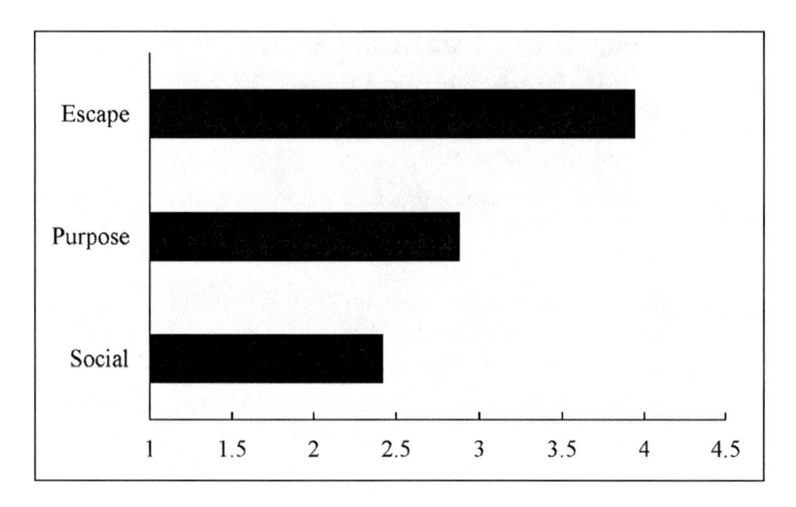

Figure 9.3. **Average score of bronies on dimensions of fandom functions.**

bronies (both in person and online), while social motivation was unrelated to the extent to which bronies interacted with other bronies. If anything, escapism was associated with *less* online interaction. Or, to put it another way, those who watch the show simply to escape the drudgery of day-to-day life may not be as interested in interacting with other bronies.

When it comes to the creation and consumption of content, these different motivational factors also play an important role. Social connections were once again positively associated with buying *MLP* products. In contrast,

Table 9.2. Fandom Functions Predicting Bronies' Opinions and Behaviors

Variable	Purpose	Escape	Social
Watch MLP	.27*	.03	.13*
Interact Online	.44*	–.22*	.10
Interact in Person	.49*	–.14	–.07
Buy MLP Products	.04	.04	.24*
Create MLP Content	.35*	–.15*	.10*
Number Meetups	.10	–.13*	.27*
Fanship	.32*	.28*	.04
Fandom	.54*	.11	.03
Empathy	.07	.33*	.04
Charitable Giving	.20*	–.03	.13*
Wishful ID	.33*	.17*	.02

*This effect is statistically significant.

bronies motivated by purpose and escapism were no more likely to spend money purchasing *MLP* merchandise. But when it comes to creating content, the pattern of results is very different: Those motivated by purpose and social interaction are more likely to *produce* content, while those motivated by escapism are actually *less* likely to produce fan-made content.

We can see some of these same patterns reflected in the data on fanship and fandom: A sense of purpose provided by the fandom is associated with both being a bigger fan (fanship) and with a greater sense of connection to the brony community (fandom). In contrast, escapism is only tied to being a bigger fan of the show—not with feeling a sense of connection with the fandom itself. Surprisingly, being motivated for social reasons was unrelated to either the extent to which one called themselves a brony or the extent to which they considered themselves to be a member of the brony community.

When it comes to empathy, only escapism was positively associated with greater feelings of empathy. Strangely, however, while escapism was more strongly tied to feelings of empathy for others, it was the extent to which the show provided bronies with a sense of purpose and social interaction that drove *actual* charitable behavior (e.g., donating blood, giving to charities).

As a final measure of interest, the researchers looked at the extent to which participants experienced wishful identification, defined by Hoffner and Buchanan (2005, p. 325) as a "desire to be like or act like the character"—in this case, their favorite character from the show. The results showed again that the factors motivating individual bronies influenced the extent to which they desired to be like their favorite character from the show. Those who found the show to be personally significant and those who sought escapism from the show were the most likely to experience a sense of desire to be like their favorite character, while those using the show as a way to meet friends were no more likely to have the same desire.

Together, these results illustrate that the brony fandom provides some bronies with a sense of purpose in one's life and a much-needed escapism from the real world. These functions are, in turn, are associated with a variety of different attitudes and behaviors. It's worth noting that "providing a sense of purpose" is not a motivation found or measured in the early sport fan motivation literature. As such, this research illustrates one of the important ways that studying the brony fandom can help inform research about other fandoms: It might be necessary to see whether sport fans are similarly motivated by the extent to which their favorite teams or sports provide them with a sense of purpose or significance in the way that *MLP* does for many bronies.

It should also be noted that the present findings should not be taken to mean that social connections are unimportant to bronies. Indeed, marketers and convention organizers will be interested to know that this social component of the fandom plays an important role in creating and consuming content, as well as in getting bronies to come out to meet-ups and conventions. Likewise, as we'll see in upcoming chapters, even if social factors are not the *biggest* draw of bronies to their interest in *MLP*, the social component of the fandom has incredibly important consequences.

Conclusion

In the present chapter we reviewed prior research on the motivations of fans. Within psychology, the bulk of research has tended to focus on sport fans while neglecting the experiences of fans of other interests. It's important to note that there is no single profile of a fan: People are motivated to engage with their fan groups for myriad of reasons, which may differ both between different fan groups and even within the same fan group. We can understand why people belong to fan groups by understanding the needs that different fan groups fulfill, whether it's the need to be entertained, the need to make lasting friendships, or simply the need to be distracted from the humdrum of everyday life. While bronies show *some* similarities with sport fans (e.g., being motivated by the need for entertainment and escape), bronies also show unique motivations, including finding purpose and meaning in the show itself. These differences matter when it comes to explaining some of the ways bronies experience the show and the fandom itself.

Chapter 10

The Pony I Want to Be

"Being the best should never come at the expense of our fellow ponies."
—*Spitfire* (*Season 3, Episode 7,* Wonderbolts Academy)

If you spend enough time around bronies, sooner or later *the* age-old question comes up, the one that's plagued bronies for as long as the fandom itself has existed.

"Who is best pony?"

The question itself is a funny one when you think about it. The *MLP* franchise was initially created as a way to sell toys to little girls (Connelly, 2017). Decisions about how many different ponies to create or what colors they should be were a matter of marketing and focus groups, not artistry or world-building. In fact, in early generations it didn't make sense to talk about "characters" at all: The original figures were just carbon copies of one another with different hair and a different color. The decision about whether you preferred Blossom, Snuzzle, or Minty boiled down to whether you preferred lavender, grey, or green and whether you preferred *your* pony to have eleven *flowers*, eleven *hearts*, or eleven *clovers* adorning her flank.

To the extent that onlookers watching the fandom from the outside believe this to be the current state of *MLP*, it's no surprise that they think it's weird that anyone would feel *attachment* or *prefer* any of these characters. In this chapter we'll push back against this conceptualization, beginning with a closer look at how the characters in *MLP:FIM* have evolved into far more compelling, fleshed-out entities that are actually at the core of what makes the show appealing for most bronies. We'll then delve into fan opinions regarding favorite characters and the distinction between the "Mane 6" and the background characters who fill out the world of Equestria. We'll then dive into the heart of the debate, seeing whether preferences for one character over another are simply a matter of superficial aesthetic or whether they tell us something deep a brony's psyche. Finally, we'll finish up by differentiating between liking a character for their traits and outright identifying *as* a character in this fictional universe—an important distinction if we want to determine whether bronies are out-of-touch with reality, as misconceptions suggest.

The Allure of Interesting Characters

If you asked the kids who played with the original G1 *MLP* toys why they liked them, the answers they would give would refer to the toys themselves—you can brush their hair, they're very pretty (they were designed by a team of market researchers to be aesthetically appealing to little girls), and you can play with them alongside your friends, who own *different* ponies from yours. Until the show *My Little Pony 'n' Friends* came along, there was very little else to base your enjoyment on, since the toys were not themselves "characters." In fact, the only real "characterization" the toys had was a sentence or two written on the back of the box (e.g., "On sunny days, Snuzzle likes to take a leisurely nap under the rainbow").[1]

While earlier generations of the show added a bit of characterization to the toys, there was still little opportunity to get to "know" the characters in any deep or meaningful way. They were largely recognizable by their appearance or by the activities they engaged in. The show was just a vehicle to display the different characters (especially as the roster of available ponies increased) with little attention on creating distinct personalities, motivations, or backstories for them.

This lack of attention to character development was precisely what Lauren Faust sought to overcome with *MLP:FIM*. There was a concerted effort to narrow the focus of the show to a "Mane 6" ensemble of characters: Applejack, Fluttershy, Pinkie Pie, Rainbow Dash, Rarity, and Twilight Sparkle. Importantly, each character was given a distinct personality, their own ambitions, and a unique set of strengths and flaws. Twilight Sparkle, for example, begins the series as bookish and organized, but standoffish. She aspires to learn, not only for knowledge's sake, but to gain the approval of her mentor, Princess Celestia. In contrast, Applejack begins the series as friendly and down to earth, but stubborn at times. She cares deeply for her family and aspires to help the family's apple farm to grow and become successful. The differences between these characters are established in the show's first episode, *Friendship Is Magic, Part 1*, through each character's very different interaction with Twilight Sparkle as they meet her for the first time. To hammer the distinctiveness of each character home, each is imbued with a unique "element of harmony" based on a facet of their personality: Honesty, Kindness, Laughter, Loyalty, Generosity, and Magic. In short, from the very first episode, viewers are encouraged to see each character as distinct.

Just as important as the *distinctiveness* of each Mane 6 character, however, is their *dynamic* nature. Each character changes as the show progresses. As an illustrative example, take the character Rainbow Dash. In early seasons, Rainbow Dash mocks Twilight Sparkle for her bookishness, brags about her own athletic prowess, and is single-mindedly focused on her dream of getting into the Wonderbolts—an elite aerial acrobatic team. As the show progresses, Rainbow Dash evolves with respect to each of these characteristics. In the season two episode *Read It and Weep*, Twilight Sparkle helps Rainbow Dash discover her love of reading through the action-packed *Daring Do* series of books. In the season three episode *Wonderbolts Academy*, Rainbow Dash is confronted with a rival, Lightning Dust, and learns through competing with Lightning Dust that being the best flyer doesn't matter if it means being reckless and endangering others. And in the season eight episode *The Washouts*, Rainbow Dash—now a wonderbolt herself—reveals her own insecurity about being a wonderbolt when she loses the admiration of Scootaloo, a young filly who is like a little sister to Rainbow Dash. Each of these instances reflects a significant change in Rainbow Dash's character as the series progresses, making her feel less like a cardboard cutout and more like a person with a distinct and nuanced personality.

But are these dynamic and nuanced characters appealing to bronies? Perhaps be best way to answer this question is to observe their responses to the show itself, in particular the backlash and criticisms they level at the show when a character is seen as acting out of character or is seen to be backsliding—that is, engaging in undesirable behavior that they have previously overcome in an earlier episode. We can see this point illustrated in the comments of bronies on a forum listing their least-favorite episodes of the show (rainbowdashrules, 2018). With respect to the season four episode *Somepony to Watch Over Me*:

- "Applejack was disgracefully out-of-character, I mean, the way she treats Apple Bloom is unbelievable ridiculous and against her nature! This episode contradicts the other episodes in the past involving the relationship of these sisters."

- "Applejack is supposed to be the practical one in the group, not some freaky stalker.... I could buy Applejack being a little bit apprehensive, but nowhere near this level.... This is paranoia I would expect from Twilight, not Applejack."

- "Applejack was SO out of character in this episode ... it contradicts everything that has happened between AJ and Apple Bloom."

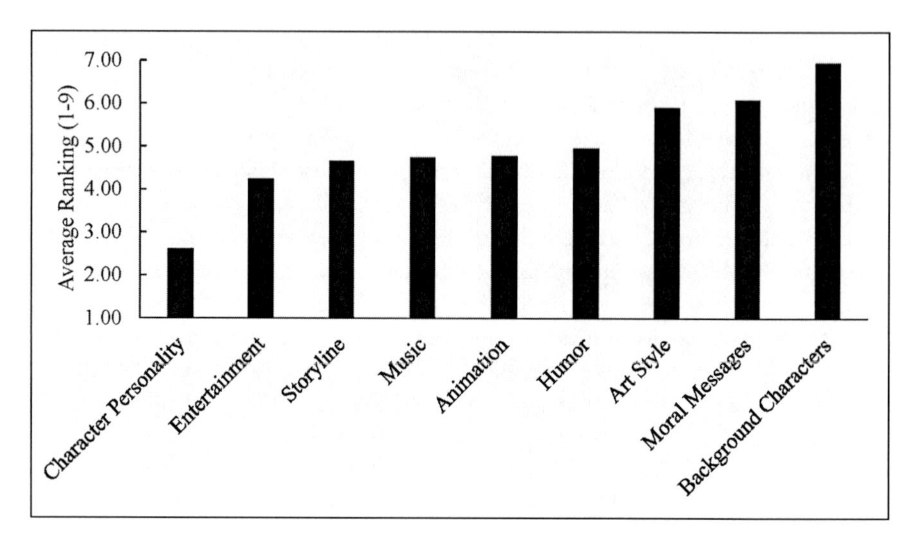

Figure 10.1. **Bronies' ranking of the influence of different facets of *My Little Pony: Friendship Is Magic* on their enjoyment of the show.**

The fact that someone acting out-of-character can ruin an episode of the show for bronies reveals just how central a role the characters themselves play in bronies' interest toward the show. The results of two of our studies drive this point home. In a 2014 survey, 1,716 bronies were asked to rank, from 1 being the most important and 9 being the least important, which facets influenced their interest in the show. As Figure 10.1 reveals, the personalities of the main characters were hands-down the most important feature of the show for bronies.

A later study, conducted in 2015 during the show's fifth season, similarly asked more than 500 bronies which of the same features listed in the 2014 study was the number one reason for their liking of the show. Figure 10.2 reveals almost the exact same trend: The personality of the characters are the driving force behind bronies' interest in the show. It would seem *MLP* has come a long way from the days when the most likeable feature of the brand was the ability to brush the characters' hair.

No, Really, Who Is "Best Pony"?

Given how central the characters are to many bronies' enjoyment of the show and given that each character is fairly unique in their personality and motivation, it should come as no surprise that fans will endlessly debate with one another about which character is the best. This is especially likely when

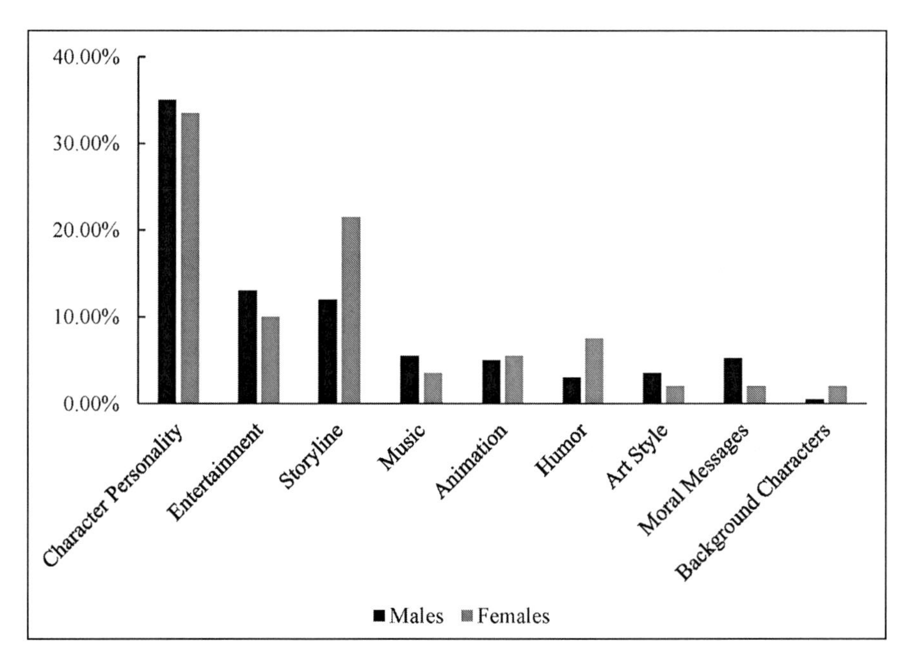

Figure 10.2. **Frequency of male and female bronies' choice of different facets of *My Little Pony: Friendship Is Magic* as the most influential on their enjoyment of the show.**

you consider that bronies themselves are a diverse bunch who come from a myriad of backgrounds and who differ in their own personalities. In fact, this topic is *so* hotly debated that it has been studied by the fandom itself through many informal polls on brony forums and websites.

In a 2016 study of more than one thousand bronies, we asked participants to list their favorite characters from the show. Then, they were asked to choose their favorite from the list and to indicate whether that character could be considered to be a main character. The results showed that 75 percent of bronies chose a favorite character who also happened to be a main character from the show. This isn't altogether surprising. After all, a character who has more screen time is more likely to catch the attention of fans and has more time to have their personality and motivations fleshed out. It also means they're more likely to do something that may endear them to the audience.

In an earlier study (the aforementioned 2014 study) our focus was a bit more narrow. We asked participants to choose which of the Mane 6 characters specifically was their favorite. As Figure 10.3 shows, there was a fairly clear winner: Twilight Sparkle,[2] though it was by no means a blowout. As a testament to how well-written and relatable the show's characters are, there was only a 15-point spread between the most-popular and least-popular character

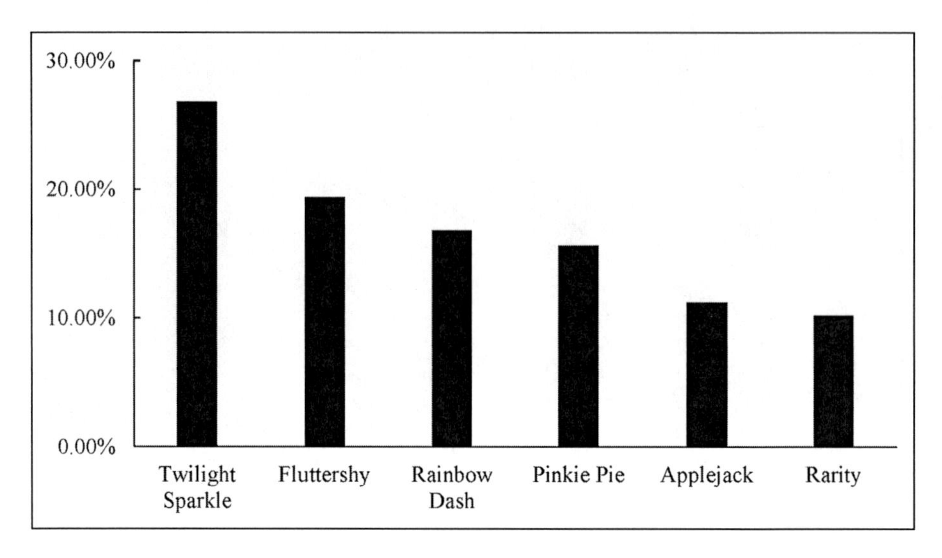

***Figure 10.3.* Percentage of bronies' choosing each Mane 6 character as their favorite.**

of the Mane 6. The favoriting of Twilight Sparkle may owe itself to the fact that she gets more screen time than any other character in the show (My Little Pony Friendship Is Magic Wiki, 2018) and to the fact that she is generally considered to be the show's "main character"—at least based on the structure of the first episode of the show, where the audience follows Twilight as she first comes to Ponyville and meets the rest of the characters.

To this point, we've primarily focused on the show's Mane 6 characters. Our earlier results mentioned, however, that while 75 percent of bronies chose favorite characters from the Mane 6, fully 25 percent chose other characters as their favorites. These characters include important secondary characters like villains (e.g., Discord), location-specific characters (Mrs. Cake), characters related to the main characters (e.g., Apple Bloom), or background characters who frequently fill out the background of a scene but who rarely, if ever, have spoken lines or interact with the Mane 6 (e.g., Lyra).[3]

By far the post popular of the non–Mane 6 characters, as indicated in Figure 10.4, was Princess Luna, the reformed villain from the first episode of the show and the oft-ignored younger sister to Princess Celestia, the deity figure in the show's lore. We'll speculate in the last section of this chapter about how that may be driven, in part, by bronies' tendency to identify with Luna's character. Interestingly, the second, fifth, and sixth spots were also claimed by reformed villains, suggesting that the complexity or dynamic nature of these characters make them particularly interesting to fans. Muffins, the character known to the fandom as "Derpy Hooves," was the third-most popular, owing in part to the great deal of attention she received from the

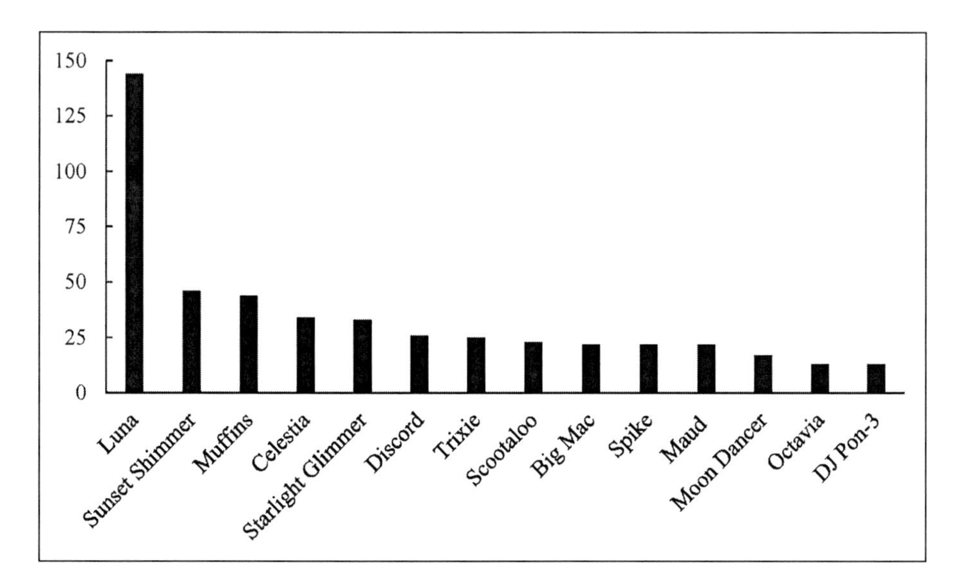

Figure 10.4. **Frequency of bronies' choice of favorite non-Mane 6 character.**

brony fandom early on in the show's history and her symbolizing the show's staff recognition of the brony fandom. It is also noteworthy that a character like DJ Pon-3/Vinyl Scratch, a character without a single spoken line and who has almost exclusively existed a character in the background of scenes, was among the more popular of the fandom's non–Mane 6 characters.

Illustrating the importance of the non–Mane 6 characters to fans of the show, we also combined data on the relative popularity of the Mane 6 characters and the non–Mane 6 characters, allowing participants to write in as many characters as they liked. As Figure 10.5 reveals, Twilight Sparkle, while still the most common among most fans' favorites, is nearly usurped by Princess Luna, a non–Mane 6 character.

Just as characters in the show change, so too do fans of the show and their preferences. In a 2017 study of nearly 600 bronies, participants were asked whether they had ever changed their favorite character. A sizable minority of bronies, 33.1 percent, had. The most popular reason for changing one's favorite character was changes in the character's personality over time, a reason cited by 61.5 percent of participants who changed their favorite (e.g., "I used to really enjoy watching Twilight, especially when she was snarky or freaking out.... Now she doesn't snark, and she rarely freaks out"). A second reason, changes in the plot of the show which introduced new characters or changed the roles of existing characters, was also cited by 15.4 percent of participants.

As a final note, we looked at whether there were differences between bronies who had changed their favorite character over time compared to

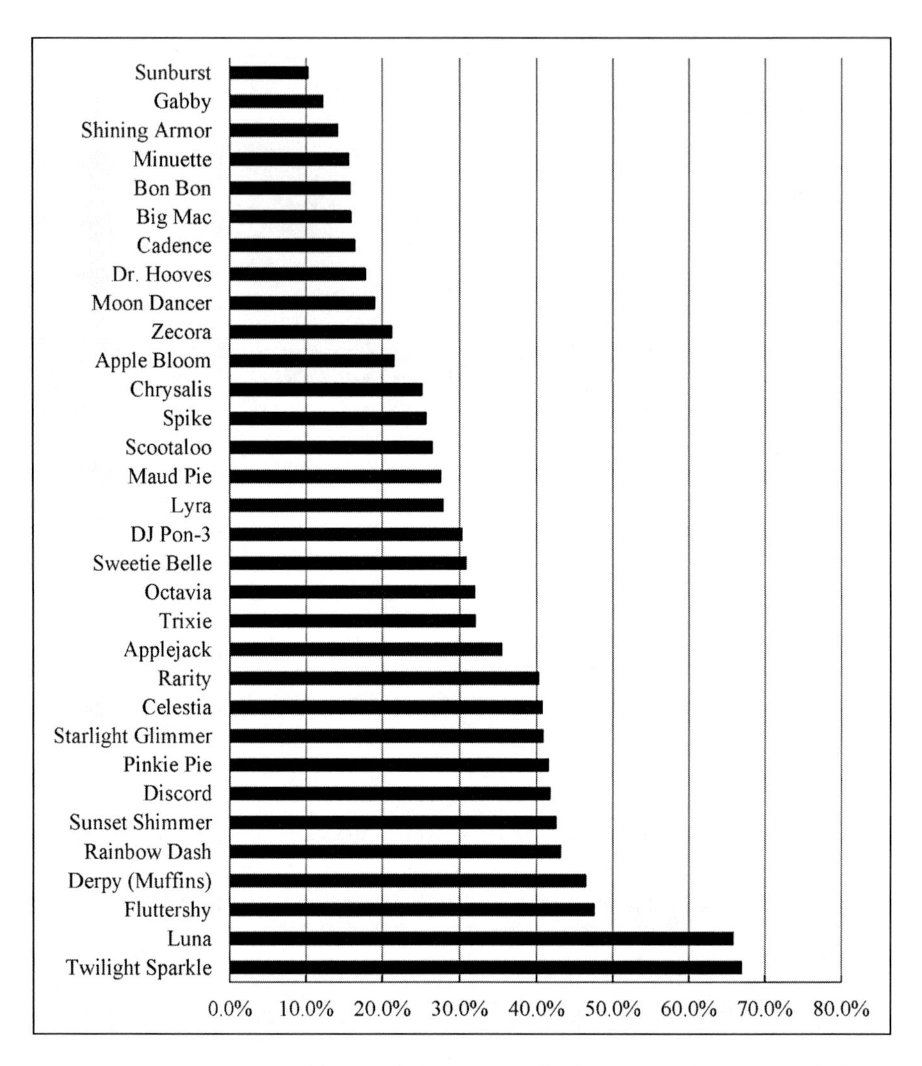

***Figure 10.5*. Percentage of bronies' choosing each character as being among their favorites.**

bronies who had kept the same favorite character over time. Analyses revealed that those who had never changed their favorite character were more inspired by the character, felt a greater sense of similarity to the character, and identified more strongly with the character than those who had changed their favorite character over time. We will return to the issue of what it means to identify with a fictional character at the end of this chapter. But for now, let's move beyond which characters bronies choose as their favorites to instead ask what, if anything, a brony's favorite characters can tell us about them.

What Your Favorite Pony Says About You

On an intuitive level, it makes sense that different bronies would find different characters from *MLP* appealing for a variety of reasons. On a purely aesthetic level, bronies may like a character because of their appearance—a unique feature (e.g., Tempest Shadow/Fizzlepop Berrytwist's broken horn), a unique character model (e.g., Discord, the one-of-a-kind Draconequus), or have a unique accessory that makes them stand out from other characters (e.g., Trixie's great and powerful hat, DJ Pon-3's rocking sunglasses). But bronies may also be drawn to particular characters because of their perceived similarity to the character, be it a similarity of personality traits (a fun-loving brony loving Pinkie Pie's fun-loving personality) or a similarity of ambitions (a university student feeling a sense of camaraderie with Twilight Sparkle over long hours spent studying).[4]

If it's true that certain people may be drawn to particular characters from the show because of perceived similarities to the characters (Reysen, Plante, Roberts, & Gerbasi, 2018a), it should also mean that there are measurable similarities between people who choose the same ponies as their favorite. This was precisely what we tested in our 2016 study: We used statistical analyses to look at whether bronies who favorited particular characters differed significantly from those who did *not* favor those characters on a myriad of personality measures. Based on these measures, we've come up with some basic profiles of bronies who chose different characters as their favorites. Of course, it goes without saying that these are only *average* tendencies. These differences turn out to be fairly small, only barely detectable due to our having the power of more than a thousand bronies' responses to work with in our analyses. Keep this in mind for the next section: We don't intend to paint all fans of a particular character with the same broad brush!

Twilight Sparkle. People who chose Twilight Sparkle among their favorites were the most likely of the bunch to be writers themselves. Among bronies, they were more likely to both write and to consume fanfiction. Twilight Sparkle fans were likely to say that their favorite character (in this case, Twilight) represents the sort of person they wished they could be more like. They were also more likely to say that their favorite character was a source of support for them in difficult times. Twilight Sparkle fans also tend to be more anxious than the average brony, but also more mature. Finally, they also identify more strongly as a brony than the average brony does.

Princess Luna. People who chose Princess Luna among their favorite characters were among those in the brony fandom who watched the show the least frequently. They were also the least likely to disclose their interest in *MLP* to others, preferring to keep it a secret. They scored among the highest of the bronies on measures of depression and anxiety (though not quite to the same extent as Fluttershy fans) and scored among the lowest on narcissism (the tendency to be self-absorbed and have a fragile self-esteem). They were also more likely than average to also be members of the furry fandom (for more on furries, see Chapter 12).

Fluttershy. People who chose Fluttershy among their favorites scored the highest on fanship—that is, they considered themselves to be the biggest fans of the show itself. Despite being the biggest fans, however, they were also the least likely of the bronies to experience stigma or discrimination for being a brony (for more on this stigma, see Chapter 17). Fluttershy fans were less likely than the average brony to cosplay. Like Twilight Sparkle fans, they were more likely than average to turn to their favorite character (Fluttershy) as a source of support during difficult times, though not quite to the same extent as Twilight fans. Fluttershy fans scored the lowest on measures of psychopathy and Machiavellianism (i.e., a tendency to manipulate others), but they also scored the lowest on measures of self-esteem and the highest on measures of anxiety and social anxiety and among the highest on depression (behind only Rarity fans). Fluttershy fans were also less likely than the average brony to view pornography.

Rainbow Dash. People who chose Rainbow Dash among their favorite characters were more likely to be writers (though not to the same extent as Twilight Sparkle fans) and musicians. They watched *MLP* more frequently than any other group of bronies and were among the biggest fans of the show (behind only Fluttershy). They scored higher than average on fandom (being part of the brony community), second only to Pinkie Pie fans. Like their favorite character, Rainbow Dash fans scored higher than average on measures of narcissism (but lower than Rarity fans did). They were also more likely than average to have personally experienced discrimination for being a brony.

Applejack. People who chose Applejack among their favorite characters were more likely to be male than the average brony. Applejack fans were the least likely to be artistic, though they did identify more strongly as a brony than the average brony. Applejack fans scored the highest on every measure of well-being: They scored the highest on self-esteem and the lowest on depression and anxiety, and among the lowest on social anxiety (second only to Pinkie Pie fans).

Rarity. People who chose Rarity among their favorites were the most likely to identify as both artists and cosplayers. Among the different groups, Rarity fans scored the lowest on both fanship (being a fan of the show) and fandom (being part of the fan community). Rarity fans were the most likely to openly tell others around them about their interest in *MLP* and were also more likely to have personally experienced discrimination for being a brony. Rarity fans scored highest on measures of depression, narcissism, and Machiavellianism.

Pinkie Pie. People who chose Pinkie Pie among their favorite characters were more likely than average to cosplay, though not to the same extent as Rarity fans. They scored the highest on fandom (being part of the brony community), and the lowest on social anxiety. They were also more likely than average to be open about their interest in *MLP*. Pinkie Pie fans were also more narcissistic than the average brony.

Villains. Those who chose a villain among their favorite characters were more likely than the average brony to cosplay. They also scored higher than average on narcissism and Machiavellianism and were more depressed than the average brony. Otherwise, they were not dramatically different from other bronies.

Male characters. Those who chose a male character among their favorites (e.g., Spike, Big Mac) were, like Applejack fans, significantly more likely to be male themselves. They were less likely than average to be artistic. Fans of male characters tended to be bigger fans of the show and felt closer to the fandom itself than the average brony.

Identifying with Characters

In the previous section we saw that, far from being a completely arbitrary aesthetic preference (e.g., I like purple hair versus pink hair), bronies' choice of favorite characters from the show tend to be rooted in some fairly significant aspects of the characters' personality. As we've alluded to throughout this chapter, it may not be a coincidence that people with particular personalities or interests may be drawn to specific characters from the show. In this final section, we'll ask whether bronies not only *like* the characters from the show, but identify with the characters in some way.

The research upon which this section is based comes from two different studies of bronies: An early 2013 brony survey looking at general patterns in fan behavior in more than 4,200 bronies and a more focused 2017 survey directly testing the nature of almost 600 bronies felt relationship with the characters in the show.

One of the first findings in this area found that the bigger a fan of the show a brony was, the more likely it was that they strongly identified with a character from *MLP*. Of course, the direction of this relationship is not yet clear, and could conceivably happen in both directions. For example, a person who watched the show and strongly identified with the character of Fluttershy (e.g., her shy personality and love for animals resonated with their own), might find themselves becoming an increasingly big fan of the show precisely because it gives them the opportunity to see more Fluttershy. Alternatively, a person who's already a big fan of the show might watch it more frequently, pay more attention to it, and think more about it, which could lead them to think more about a particular character and feel a greater sense of connection to them, something in line with what psychologists know as the mere exposure effect (Zajonc, 1968).

Other analyses show that beyond simply "being a bigger fan of the show," the *reasons* driving your interest in the show may play a potential role in the extent to which bronies identify with characters from the show. As we discussed in Chapter 8, bronies differ in the motivational factors driving their interest in the show: Sometimes it's for the entertainment it provides, sometimes for the sense of belongingness the community affords, and still other times for the sense of purpose it provides for bronies. This last motivation is particularly relevant, because analyses suggest that it is the most strongly tied to bronies' tendency to identify with characters from the show. Or, to put it another way: Bronies who feel that the show provides them with a sense of guidance, direction, or purpose, feel a greater sense of connection to the characters in the show.

As it turns out, it also matters both who you are and who your favorite character is when it comes to how much you identify with the character. For example, female bronies tend to, on average, identify more strongly with the (predominantly female) characters in the show than do male bronies. But it also matters who your favorite character is: Those whose favorite characters were among the Mane 6 identified more strongly with their favorite character than those whose favorite characters were not among the Mane 6. This may, as previously mentioned, simply be due to the fact that characters who get more screen time may reveal more complex or nuanced personalities that may resonate more with viewers.

Of course, all of this raises questions about what, precisely, it means to "identify with" these fictional characters. Are bronies who identify strongly with these characters simply stating a desire to be more like the characters? Do they feel a sense of companionship with them? A romantic interest in them?[5] Do they consider themselves to *literally be* the ponies on the screen? When these different facets of identification were compared, the strongest component by far was a sense of parasocial friendship—the idea of being friends with a fictional or media characters (see Figure 10.6). To be clear, this doesn't mean that bronies are delusional or actually think they are making friends with fictional characters. Instead, they experience a *hypothetical*

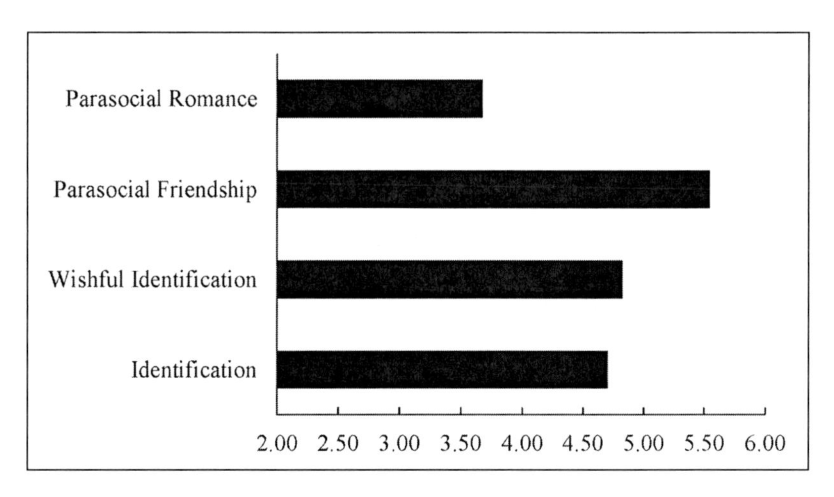

***Figure 10.6*. Relative strength of the different facets of bronies' felt connection to their favorite character from *MLP*.**

friendship—that their favorite character from the show is someone they *could* be friends with in person, or with whom they *could* talk about what's on their mind with. On the other end of the spectrum, far fewer bronies agreed (only about 3.7 on a 7-point scale) that their favorite character from the show is physically attractive or that they longed to have a romantic relationship with them.

It is worth mentioning the "wishful identification" and "identification" components of some bronies' felt connection to their favorite character. These suggest that for many bronies, their favorite characters are people they see aspects of themselves in—or at the very least aspects of the person they *want* to be. As an illustrative example, look at the sheer number of bronies who identified Princess Luna as their favorite character. Given the relative lack of screen time Princess Luna gets compared to the other Mane 6 characters, it's likely that her popularity reflects the fact that her character resonates with how many bronies feel. Luna's character is one who was often ignored, neglected, and who was ultimately ostracized from society. Given that many bronies experience considerable stigma and bullying themselves (see Chapter 17), they may feel a sense of empathy with Luna for the suffering she's endured and identify with her as such.

With respect to wishful identification, many characters in the *MLP* universe may serve as role models for viewers. Rainbow Dash, for example, spends several seasons pursuing her lifelong dream of becoming a Wonderbolt, where she will be recognized for her physical prowess. Likewise, Twilight Sparkle aspires to be recognized by her mentor Princess Celestia and is driven by her thirst for knowledge. Both of these are very admirable goals to be pursuing.

Insofar as fans of the show are pursuing similar goals themselves, they may find it inspiring to look up to fictional characters who are achieving those very same goals.[6]

To this end, some of our analyses have looked at whether there are differences between the Mane 6 characters with respect to whether fans see themselves reflected in the characters, whether they see the characters as someone they would *like* to be, or both. When it comes to the Mane 6 characters, bronies, for the most part, see themselves reflected in the characters and aspire to be like them, with a couple of notable exceptions: Rarity was the character fans *least* felt like they presently identified with, while Rainbow Dash was the character fans felt the biggest discrepancy with, but wanted to be like the most.

We'll finish this chapter with one final comment. As you might imagine, liking, identifying with, and feeling inspired by fictional characters living in a fictional word requires a tremendous amount of imagination. After all, if you can't get past the fact that you're looking at drawings on a screen, you'll never be able to immerse yourself in the fictional world and see the characters as actual characters. Speaking to this point, a final analysis found that the extent to which bronies had an active imagination likely plays a role not only in the extent to which they identify with the characters themselves, but even the extent to which they could imagine *themselves* as a character in the show. That said, there's a fairly clear line between an active imagination and delusion, and while bronies may find it fun to imagine themselves transported to the whimsical land of Equestria, there's no evidence to suggest that they lose track of the line between fantasy and reality.

Chapter 11

Rule 34: Ponies, Pornography and Perceptions of the Fandom

"I'm not evil, princess. I'm chaotic. Not the same thing. I oppose order, not good."
—*Discord* (Friends Forever, *Issue #20*)

We began discussing this book back in 2015. As part of those discussions, we wondered what bronies wanted to know about their fandom. To find out, we added several questions to the end of each of our next few surveys asking bronies to tell us what they wanted us to study and what they would prefer that we left out.

Among the top contenders for "things bronies would prefer we *didn't* study" was the topic that would become the chapter you're reading.[1]

So why did we go against the wishes of so many bronies and (a) study the topic of pornography in the brony fandom and (b) decide to put it in this book? In our minds, there are at least two good reasons.[2] First, this topic is an inescapable part of both Internet culture and fan culture—including the fact that pornography isn't openly discussed (or is, at very least, treated as a "dirty little secret"). Second, the topic is a heated and particularly divisive one that reverberated throughout the brony fandom early on, with fans trying to balance, on the one hand, an Internet culture which caters to adults (who have adult thoughts, feelings, and desires) and, on the other hand, a show that was originally created for kids. It's because of how many bronies were talking about this subject that it *became* so important to study.[3]

All of this said, we're not insensitive to the fact that this is a sensitive topic for bronies. As it is, sex is considered a taboo subject in polite company.

But when you combine that with the fact that bronies, as a group, are already stigmatized by a plethora of stereotypes and misconceptions, it might seem like we're playing with fire here.

Let's be clear: Our goal in this chapter is to broadly discuss the topic of pornography, not just in the brony fandom, but in fandoms *in general.* By putting our research within this broader context of *all* fandoms, we hope to help bronies and non-bronies alike understand both the inevitability of pornography in an Internet-based culture and the ways the brony fandom has been unique in dealing with this issue. And if we can take some of the "ick" factor out of any discussion of bronies by showing that the existence of pornography is neither unique to the brony fandom nor a defining feature of it, then we feel this chapter will have been worth it.

That Which Shall Not Be Named: The History of "Rule 34"

While this chapter focuses on pornography within the brony fandom in particular, we can't have a proper discussion about the subject without first acknowledging the presence of adult-themed content in virtually all fandoms and communities on the Internet.[4] To be sure, its creation is not always approved of, wanted, or even produced by members of the fandom. Nevertheless, pornographic content exists *everywhere.*

Not that there's anything inherently *wrong* with enjoying pornography or sexually explicit material in most contexts. One can certainly discuss research on the potential benefits or harmful effects of pornography in general. But the question of whether pornography is a net good or a net bad for consumers is *very* different from the far more common question of whether it's morally right or wrong. Philosophers like St. Thomas Aquinas have argued that the excess of pleasure is, in and of itself, a sin (Milhaven, 1977), while early psychologists like Freud saw sexual pleasure as a fundamental drive in all humans (Freud, 1955). Instead of getting bogged down in either of these conversations, however, we'll strive to take a fairly neutral approach to the subject: neither endorsing pornography nor condemning it. No judgment here for those who consume pornography nor condemnation for those who reject the sexualization of media characters.[5]

What follows is a brief discussion of the history of pornography and its relation to fandom. We'll then shed light on what our own data have revealed about the approval, acceptance, and consumption of pornography among bronies.

Rule 34

Many have described the Internet as a wild, lawless frontier. As it turns out, this couldn't be further from the truth: The Internet itself has a set of rules. And, to be clear, when we talk about rules, we're *not* talking about formalized, government-imposed rules, like laws governing copyright and online harassment.

No, when we talk about the rules of the Internet, we're talking about *The Rules*, the closest thing such a diverse group of people online will ever get to a formally-recognized acknowledgment of what the Internet is like. Or, put another way, they're a set of norms that an entire generation of Internet users have largely agreed upon.

The rules first appeared online in late 2006 and were archived for posterity on January 10, 2007 (FY & Lolrus, 2018). Different references put the number of rules from as few as 18 to as many as 100. The rules themselves originated in message boards like 4chan, although they have become widely accepted across the Internet due to the fact that they resonate with users from all regions of cyberspace.

Some of the rules are, themselves, silly and grounded in media-based memes, such as Rule 1 and 2: Do not talk about /b/ (a reference to the film *Fight Club*, adapted her to refer to the 4chan's most infamous "random" forum).[6] Others are taken far more serious, including Rules 3–5, which were taken up as the mantra of the online activist group Anonymous: (3) We are Anonymous, (4) Anonymous is legion, (5) Anonymous never forgives.[7]

Most relevant to the current discussion are the rules pertaining to fandoms and media specifically. Rule 63, for example, states that "for every given male character, there is a female version of that character" and vice versa.[8] But undoubtedly, the most infamous of these media-related rules is Rule 34, which states that "there is porn of it, no exception."[9]

Again, to emphasize, we acknowledge that no formal governing body has laid out these rules.[10] Nor is any organization actively monitoring their enforcement. Nevertheless, if we take these rules as a recognition of nearly-universal experiences among Internet users, we can see the rules themselves as recognized norms of the Internet. In the case of Rule 34, the easy accessibility of media coupled with the inexhaustible creativity of Internet users creates a "perfect storm" that almost guarantees that someone out there has thought to create explicit material of any piece of media you can imagine.[11]

To be clear: The existence of Rule 34 art does *not* mean that most Internet users want or approve of all of this explicit content.[12] Instead, it's a recognition that, given the sheer size of the Internet, there *will* be some people who engage in behavior that the general population will find distasteful. What's more, given the shocking or unusual nature of this behavior, it will be disproportionately discussed and shared, often making it seem larger or more prevalent than it actually is.

Pornography, Art and History

While the musical *Avenue Q* may have been onto something when it sang "The Internet is for porn," the concept of explicit material featuring real or fictional people is hardly new. In fact, pornography itself is as old as civilization itself and can be seen throughout the millennia in works of art from around the globe. Vases, coins, sculptures and frescoes of many cultures depict a variety of sexual positions and acts. One in particular, the Turin Erotic Papyrus, dates back to 1150 BCE and contains a series of erotic pictures of animals engaging in human tasks—possibly in a satirical light—which has been dubbed the "world's first men's magazine" (Shokeir & Hussein, 2004).[13] For Greeks and Romans, much of their pornography represented everyday encounters, although some included the gods themselves (Clarke, 1998). The Romans saw these depictions as works of art worth displaying in their homes, while poets like Sappho depicted love and relations between every combination of people imaginable.[14] Medieval history continued this trend with etchings, paintings, and books containing depictions of sexual activity (Smith, 2009). Of course, this content really wasn't always seen as obscene or explicit.[15] In fact, the condemnation of erotic art or art featuring nude characters owes much of its influence to the Victoria era and the decades of sexual repression that would follow.

In the 20th century, we can see ties between erotic content and fan culture made more explicit. For example, from the 1920s until the beginning of the 1960s, the widely popular Tijuana bibles (named because people thought these erotic mini-comics were being smuggled into the U.S. from Tijuana) depicted famous media icons of the time such as Dick Tracy, Blondie, Popeye, and Little Orphan Annie[16] in a sexual context (Paasonen, 2017; Williams & Lyons, 2010). These magazines also featured characters clearly inspired by the day's movie stars and athletes, something one could consider to be an early version of Rule 34.

The Tijuana bibles may well have been the inspiration for an entire genre of pornographic films: porn-themed spoofs and parodies. Prevalent in the late 80s and early 90s, such parodies left no story untouched, including classics such as *It's a Wonderful Life*, *A Tale of Two Cities*, and *The Honeymooners*.[17] As with the Internet's Rule 34, nothing was sacred or safe from this sort of transformation. Someone asking "Why would anyone *need* a porn parody of *that*?" would be missing the point entirely: It existed precisely *because* someone wondered whether anyone had ever made an *Everybody Loves Ray-*

mond porn spoof.[18] And it all happened decades before the age of the Internet and its oft-decried Rule 34.

Pornography and Fandom

Many of the examples we provided in the previous section were spoofs or parodies of popular media—designed to get a chuckle but otherwise not to be taken seriously. Fandom itself, however, has had a long history of incorporating erotic or explicit themes into a person's hobby or interest.

With respect to modern media fandoms, the origins of erotic fanfiction can be traced back to at least the original fans of *Star Trek*. Early fans, most of whom were female, would collaborate and share their own fiction based on the characters from the show. These stories often explored topics, themes, and relationships that were not featured in the show itself, adding depth and extra dimensions to the characters that were not—and often could not be—in the show itself (Jenkins, 1992).

The result of these fan-created stories would become what we today call fanfiction.[19] Making clear the fact that these stories often involved erotic elements, the term "slash fiction" was born out of the *Star Trek* fandom in the 1970s, derived from the slash in the term "Kirk/Spock," which represented a story featuring a romantic or sexual relationship between the characters (Dhaenens, Van Bauwel, & Biltereyst, 2008; Salmon & Symons, 2004). Other fandoms would later show the same tendency toward fanfiction, varying from fandom to fandom with respect to norms about how love and sex were depicted and the openness with which erotic material was discussed. As a general rule, erotic works of fiction were not universally accepted in most fandoms and, in some cases, were actively admonished. But they were almost always present.

With the advent of the Internet, distribution and access of fan-created content became far easier. Instead of putting oneself on a mailing list to receive a fan-created independent publication (e.g., zines), one could instead immediately (and privately) access any fan-made content they could possibly want online. Likewise, fans could anonymously post their stories online without fear of repercussion due to their erotic content. The result was an increase in both the overall quantity of fan-made material and a gradual acceptance of the existence of a non-trivial amount of erotic-themed content within any fandom.

It's within this historical context—after nearly two decades of fans sharing their fanfictions and artwork online—that the rules of the Internet in the mid 2000s should be understood. Porn exists of everything because there are fans of almost everything, and those fans, like most people, have a biologically-driven interest in sex. As it turns out, what we consider to be a rule of the

Internet is actually a rule of civilization itself, no more or less lewd or prevalent now than it was for the ancient Greeks.

So what, if anything, makes Internet-based fandoms different from the fandoms of the 70s and 80s?

One of key differences is exposure. In the early 70s and 80s, it was difficult for non-fans to stumble upon erotic fanfiction or art by accident. Unless you were interacting with other fans or on a mailing list, you weren't about to stumble into a spicy Kirk/Spock "forbidden love" story. With the Internet, however, a clumsy image search can lead to the accidental—and often unwanted—discovery of such material.[20] Moreover, the ubiquity of the Internet has meant that increasingly younger audiences—those who may be less diligent in the way they browse the Internet—can be exposed to this material.[21]

This may explain why bronies—and indeed many modern fandoms—may be taking flak for being a supposedly corrupting force. Bronies may be especially likely to find themselves in the crosshairs because their fandom centers around a show intended for a younger, female audience. The existence of *MLP*-themed erotic content may be perceived as the corrupting influence of adult male fans on an otherwise "pure and untainted" show—despite the fact that, historically, there has been almost no media that hasn't, at one time or another, been subjected to Rule 34.

To be fair, modern fan cultures are also very much aware of the problems associated with the existence of erotic content for a show which has such a broad demographic. Many have taken steps to address this concern, aiming to protect against the possibility of younger fans inadvertently stumbling upon age-inappropriate content, such as the Safe Search Roundup.[22]

Often, however, complaints about pornography in fandoms such as the brony fandom are less about the actual show-themed explicit content, and more about an attack on pornography in general. Or they simply represent an attack against the brony fandom in general, using the existence of pornography as just another excuse to decry bronies as "degenerates" or deviants. Either way, the positions seem ignorant (either innocuously or willingly so) to the fact that there is certainly explicit material within all fan content—including whatever interest is the person crying foul happens to be a fan of.

So where do we go from here? As we delve into our own research on pornographic content within the brony fandom we urge readers to contextualize these findings within the history of pornography in general and the history of fandoms specifically. Let's not pretend that Rule 34 only pertains to *MLP*. Nor should we sweep the existence of this content under the rug and pretend it doesn't exist: It exists because *someone* is creating it and *someone* is consuming it. Some produce the content because there's a market for it. Some do it because they enjoy the content or because it adds extra dimensions and a sense of maturity to characters they love from the show.[23] Others, like Rule 34 artists we have interviewed, do it for money, if people commission "elf porn" that's what they draw, and when people ask for ponies, "ponies it is." And some do it simply to troll people, making them uncomfortable by showing them content that offends or disgusts them.

With this in mind, let's look at what we've found when we've polled bronies about their thoughts on Rule 34, their level of consumption of explicit material, and their acceptance of this content as part of the fandom.

Pornography and the Brony Fandom

By our third survey on the fandom, we decided to dive feet-first into the topic of pornography in the brony fandom. We have since continued to ask a variety of questions related to the topic. The questions presented here illustrate the wide range of topics we've covered on the subject over the years.

First, we'll go over some data regarding bronies' willingness to discuss pornographic content and perceptions of it within the fandom. Next, we'll ask who supports the material and how it relates to non-pornographic art within the community. Finally, we'll expand our discussion to include questions about the consumption, production, and sharing of content. We'll finish with the question "What, if anything, should the fandom do about it?"

As we'll see throughout this section, there is often a disconnect between what someone perceives to be real and what is real. For fans, the perceptions of their own communities impacts what behaviors they condone, reject, or engage in themselves. This is why our data focuses not only what the reality is, but also on what fans *perceive* the reality to be. For example, bronies perceive brony community to be somewhat unwilling to openly discuss pornography (average 3.27 on a 1–7 scale). This is somewhat comparable to reality, with most fans being fairly opposed to openly discussing their attitudes about *MLP*-related pornography (average 2.5 on a 1–7 scale; see Figure 11.1). That said, fans seem to *overestimate* how open the average brony is to these sorts of discussions. One can imagine how this might affect their own behavior (e.g., feeling pressured to be "more okay" with pornographic content than they actually are).

Support

The previous findings show that, as a community, there is a reluctance to openly discuss the topic of Rule 34. Within this absence of discussion, however, misconceptions and erroneous assumptions thrive. As such, it's important to assess how bronies feel and act with respect to *MLP*-themed

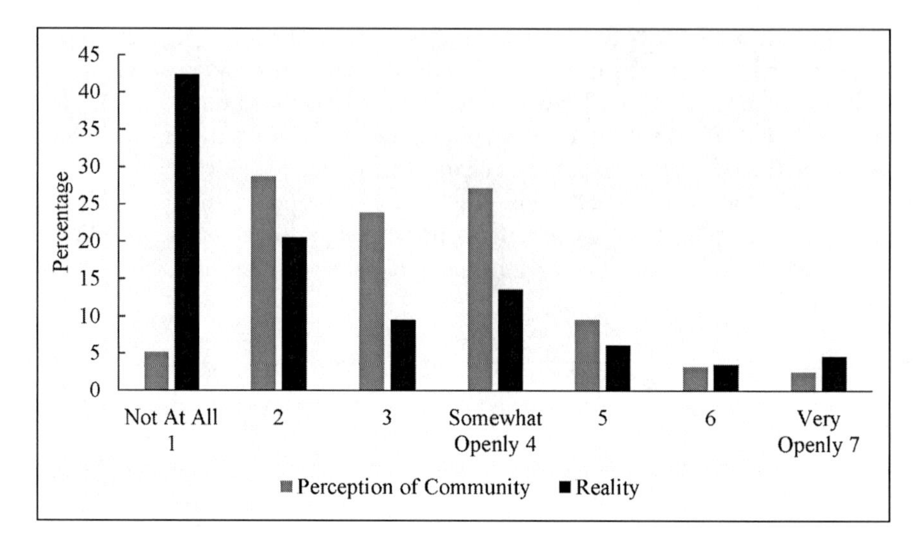

Figure 11.1. **Bronies' perceived and actual willingness to discuss *MLP*-themed pornography.**

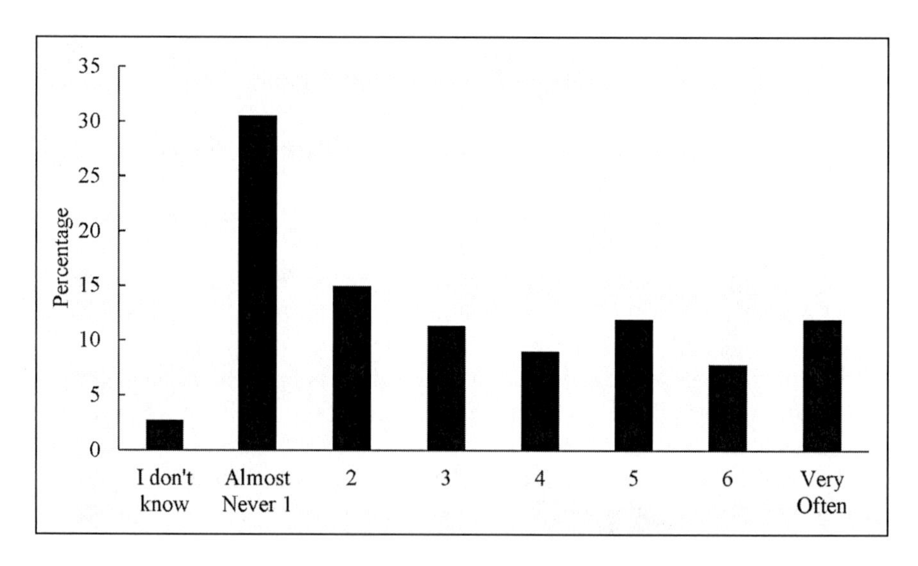

Figure 11.2. **Bronies' consumption of Rule 34 material.**

pornography when they're able to answer anonymously—as they're able to do in our surveys.

First, let's look directly at the question of whether bronies *actually* view Rule 34 material. As we can see from Figure 11.2, bronies are all over the board. About one third of bronies almost never consume *MLP*-themed pornography, another third rarely or somewhat consume it, while the remaining third frequently consume it.

Given this breakdown of how often bronies consume Rule 34 content, we might expect to see almost identical results when it comes to how bronies *feel* about Rule 34 content. But, as we can see in Figure 11.2, consumption and support are not one and the same: The majority of bronies seem to be either ambivalent about pornography in the fandom or, if anything, skew toward more favorable than non-favorable attitudes toward it than not. Despite the fact that nearly one-third of bronies almost never consume Rule 34 *MLP* content, only about 13 percent hold very negative views toward it. This suggests that bronies may recognize a distinction between their own private or personal behaviors and the question of what is acceptable (so long as it doesn't hurt anyone). Many bronies may not personally consume explicit *MLP* content, but may not be strongly opposed to others doing so. At very least, the spike at the midpoint of the scale suggests that for most bronies, the issue is, at best, a mixed bag. It gets even more complex when you realize that, despite only a small proportion of bronies being strongly negative toward the topic, most bronies nevertheless feel negative about *discussing* the issue.

Other analyses we've done have suggested that how bronies feel about *MLP*-themed pornography may differ, in part, by how strongly they identify with other bronies. Put simply, those who more strongly identified with other bronies were also less negative toward pornography in the fandom. One possible explanation for this relationship is that those who consume more explicit *MLP* content *develop* a stronger attachment to the brony fandom over time. Alternatively, it may be the case that only people who strongly identify with the fandom may even seek out or consider looking at Rule 34 content.

We offer another argument: Perhaps being a member of the brony community involves understanding and accepting the norms of that community. Being a member of any modern fandom likely means understanding that Rule 34 exists and that at least some members of the group will be drawn to it. It may thus be the case that a strongly-identified brony would be more willing to accept Rule 34 content and those who consume it, rather than outright denying their existence or opposing their presence in the fandom. Whether this explanation holds more water than the others remains a topic for future research to test.

A last analysis on the subject of how bronies feel toward pornography looks specifically at whether bronies see *MLP*-themed explicit content as a form of self-expression and/or whether it should be tolerated (see Figure 11.4). The findings suggest quite clearly that while not every brony may like or consume pornography in the fandom, for the most part, the community sees it as a valid form of self-expression. In fact, less than 20 percent of the community wishes to see the material limited or outright banned.

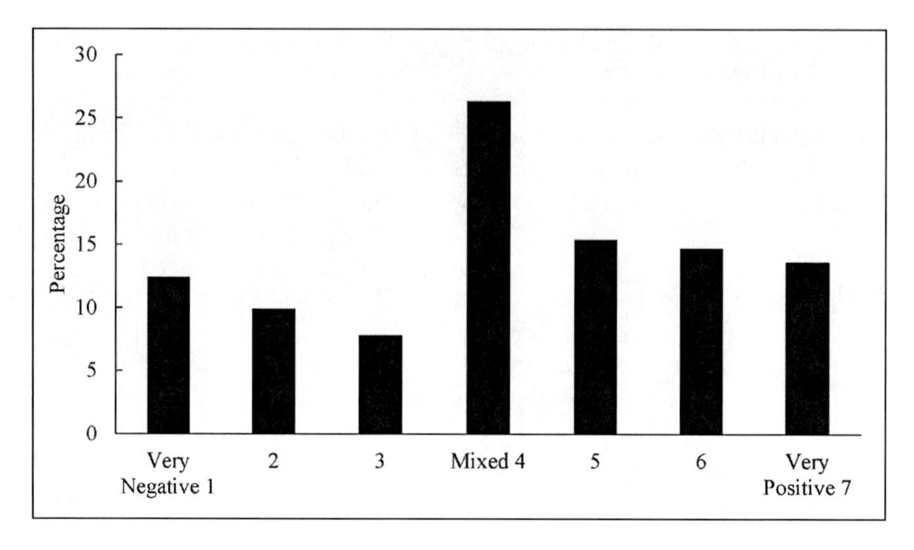

***Figure 11.3.* Bronies' attitudes towards *MLP*-themed pornography.**

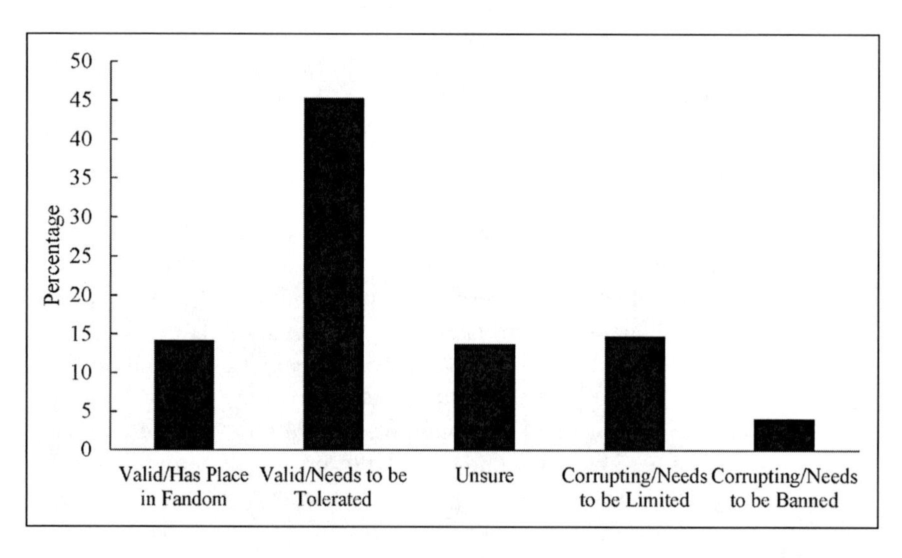

***Figure 11.4.* Bronies' attitudes toward pornographic content as a form of self expression.**

This first look at bronies' attitudes toward pornography seems to suggest that while bronies may not entirely agree on whether Rule 34 content is positive or negative, regardless of if they consume it or not, most bronies agree that they should at very least tolerate it and those who create it—even if they're not particularly willing to openly discuss it.

Exposure

Beyond asking bronies how they felt about explicit material in the fandom, we also asked whether they actively sought the material out and how likely they were to actually encounter it—since it's entirely possible that most pornography-viewing was accidental or unintended. We also wanted to address the stereotype that most bronies were driven to the show solely by the existence of explicit material—which might suggest that being a brony may be more of a fetish than an actual fan interest.

Speaking to this last point first, we asked bronies to what extent the existence of *MLP*-themed porn drove their entrance into the fandom and whether they believed this was the case for the average brony. The results of Figure 11.5 are clear: The overwhelming majority of bronies were *not* drawn to the show by porn, suggesting that it makes little sense to characterize bronies as people seeking to satisfy some kind of *MLP*-themed fetish.[24] Interestingly, despite this fact, it would seem that bronies *overestimated* how many other bronies might have been drawn to the fandom by porn. Few suggested that most bronies were drawn to the porn, but most bronies assumed that the average brony was at least a *little* bit drawn to the fandom by porn. The data, as we can see, would seem to suggest that bronies themselves are not immune to this stereotype about bronies.

But how often are bronies *actually* seeing explicit content? As it turns out, they see it a lot—most bronies report being occasionally or frequently exposed to the content (see Figure 11.6). This seems to be a product of the

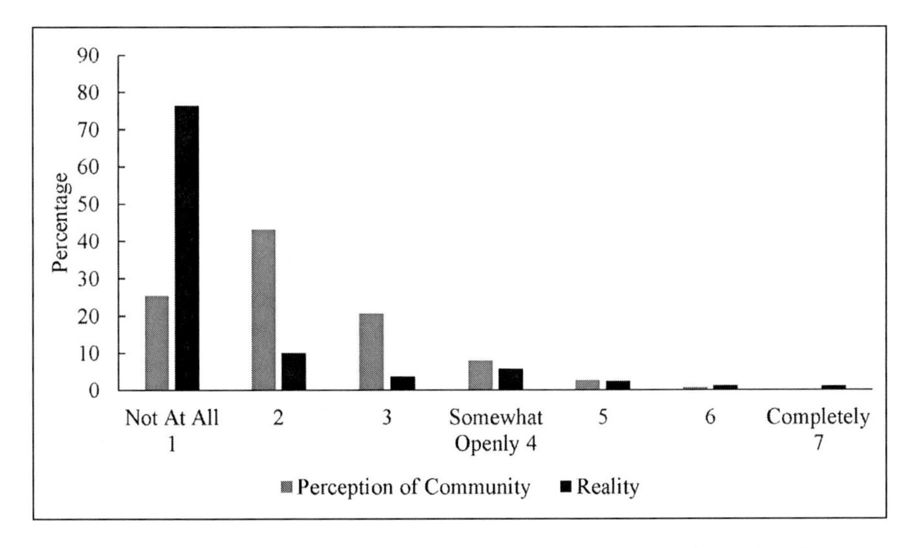

Figure 11.5. **Extent to which bronies were drawn to the fandom through Rule 34—perception and reality.**

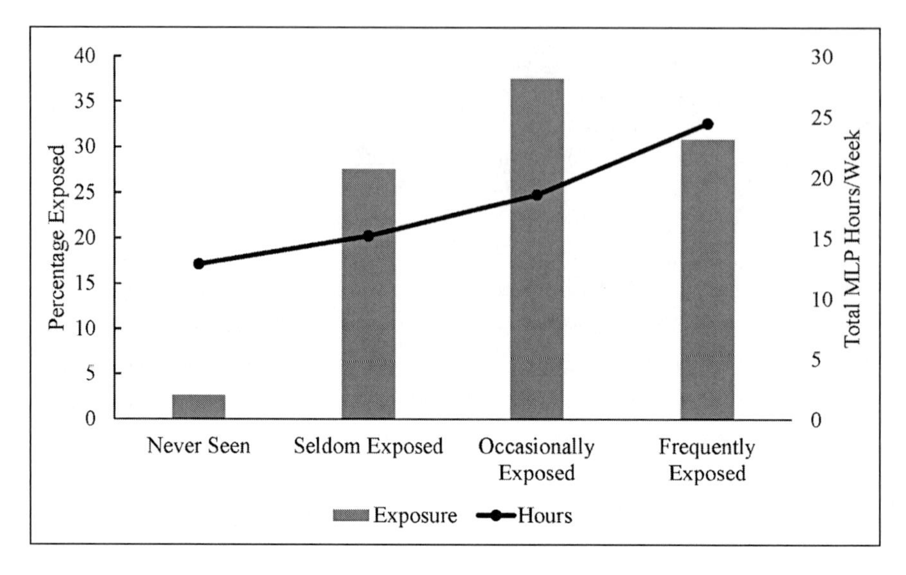

Figure 11.6. **Bronies' exposure to Rule 34 content and hours of general content consumption.**

frequency with which bronies consume *MLP* content in general: Those who spend more time on forums interacting with other bronies and seeking out *MLP* art and images will be more likely to stumble into Rule 34 content.

Speaking to this point, when we asked bronies how they were exposed to Rule 34 content, the results suggest that, more often than not, it was an unintended exposure (see Figure 11.7). In other words, the data seem to suggest that, most of the time, bronies' exposure of explicit content is incidental—something they encounter while trying to find something else related to the show. Given how closely the numbers for choosing to view explicit content overlap with the number of bronies who frequently encounter erotic material and the number of bronies who have a positive attitude toward adult material, it would seem that a *lot* of these views are coming from bronies who are actively seeking it out—at least for about a third of the fandom.

General Consumption

While most bronies do not appear to be actively seeking out *MLP*-related pornography, questions about consuming explicit content in the brony fandom remain. For example, while a third of bronies may actively seek out explicit content, does that mean they *prefer* explicit content over non-explicit content?

The answer seems to be no. As seen in Figure 11.8, most bronies (56 per-

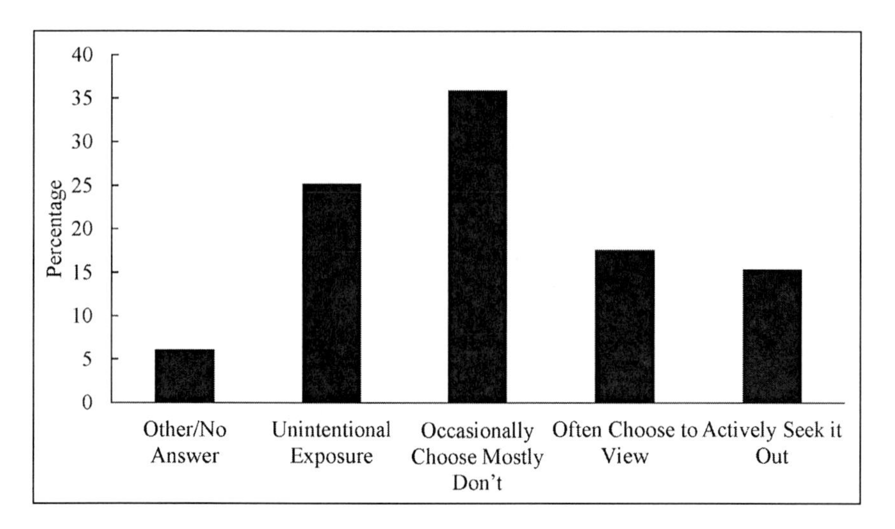

Figure 11.7. **Bronies' Rule 34 exposure-seeking and viewing.**

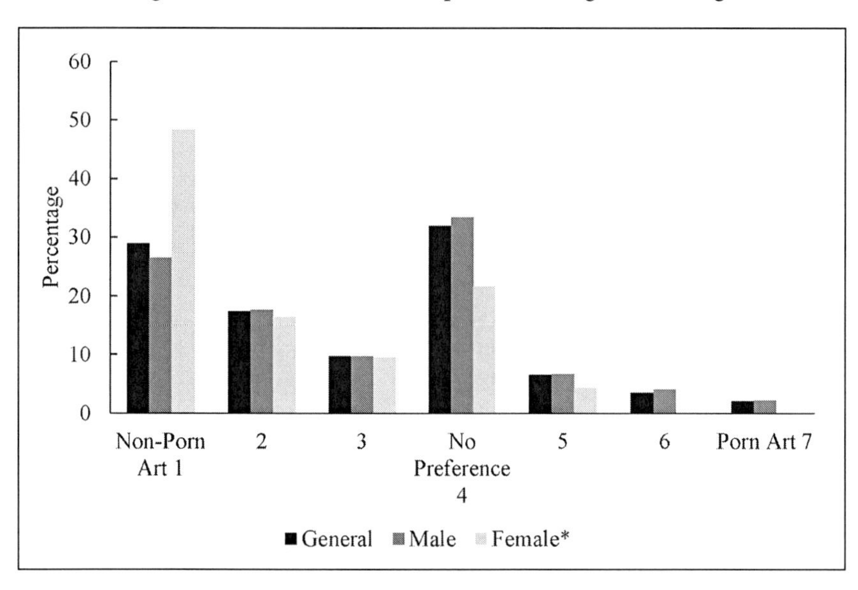

Figure 11.8. **Bronies' Preferences for Rule 34 or non-pornographic *MLP* art. (**No female participants marked a 6 or 7.*)**

cent), if anything, prefer non-pornographic *MLP* art over pornographic *MLP* art. A further 32 percent of bronies have no strong preference one way or another. Only a small minority of the community (12 percent) have a preference for explicit material over non-explicit material. Or, looking at it another way 29 percent of bronies very strongly prefer non-pornographic art, while only 2 percent very strongly prefer explicit art. This paints a picture of a community that, contrary to stereotypes, is not defined by sexualizing the characters of an animated show, but which instead simply enjoys art and content from the show in general—even if it is a bit lewd on occasion. This, in fact, is largely in line with how most people would describe fan art in other fandoms (e.g., anime).

It's also worth pointing out an important difference between male and female fans in this regard: Female fans are *far* more likely than male fans to prefer non-explicit artwork. While the reasons for this remain to be seen, one possible explanation may boil down to the motivations driving male and female bronies' fandom involvement or the factors which got them into the fandom, which may differ by sex. For example, whereas the vast majority of male bronies likely became interested in *MLP* as a teenager or adult, female fans are more likely to have been interested in the franchise from a younger age. As such, given the show's nostalgic ties, they may be less likely, or even more uncomfortable with, seeing the show portrayed in an explicit manner.

In addition to looking specifically at *MLP*-themed pornography, it may be informative to look at porn use in general (*MLP* and otherwise). As seen in Figure 11.9, male bronies consume considerably more pornography than do female fans in an average week, with female bronies being nearly four times more likely to report not watching porn at all in any given week. We can also see, in Figure 11.10, that when bronies *do* consume pornography, it is not frequently *MLP*-themed—especially among female fans. This again counters the stereotype of bronies as defined solely by a sexual attraction to *MLP* characters. At most, this could perhaps be said to characterize the about approximately 10 percent of the fandom for whom *MLP*-themed pornography is exclusively (or almost exclusively) the only pornography they consume.[25]

Even after dissecting bronies' explicit content consumption as thoroughly as we have, there are still a multitude of questions that remain to be asked about in future research. Such questions include how the disparity between perceptions and stereotypes of the fandom's pornography use and reality come to be and how they affect the public's perception of groups based around an animated show for kids.[26] It will also be necessary, in future research, to further clarify where bronies draw the line between what constitutes art and what constitutes erotica or porn. While we have, to this point, allowed fans make their own distinction, it's worth noting that at least some of the discrepancy between perceptions and reported behavior may boil down to differences in what fans may consider to be porn.[27] And, lest you think these problems are limited to the psychological study of pornography within fandoms, remember that society at large has, for ages, continued to grapple with this very same issue.[28]

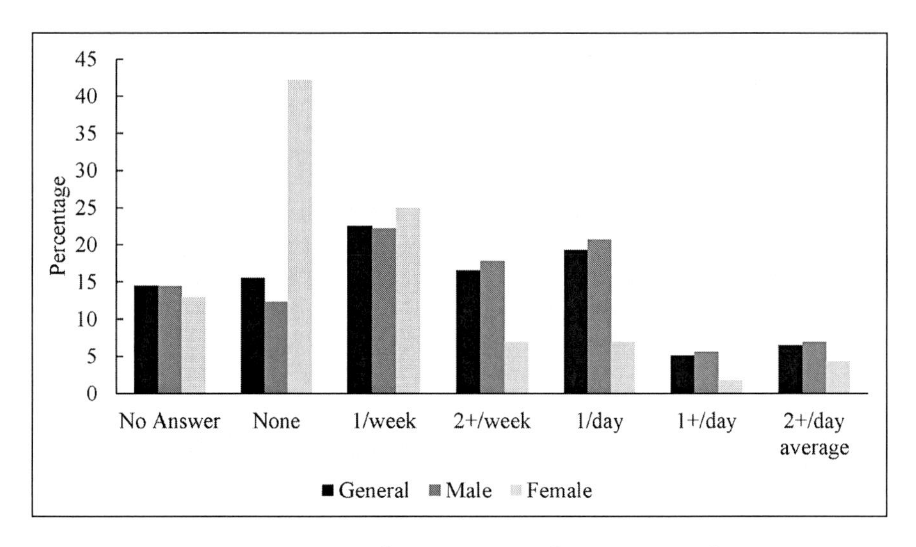

Figure 11.9. **Bronies' consumption of porn in general.**

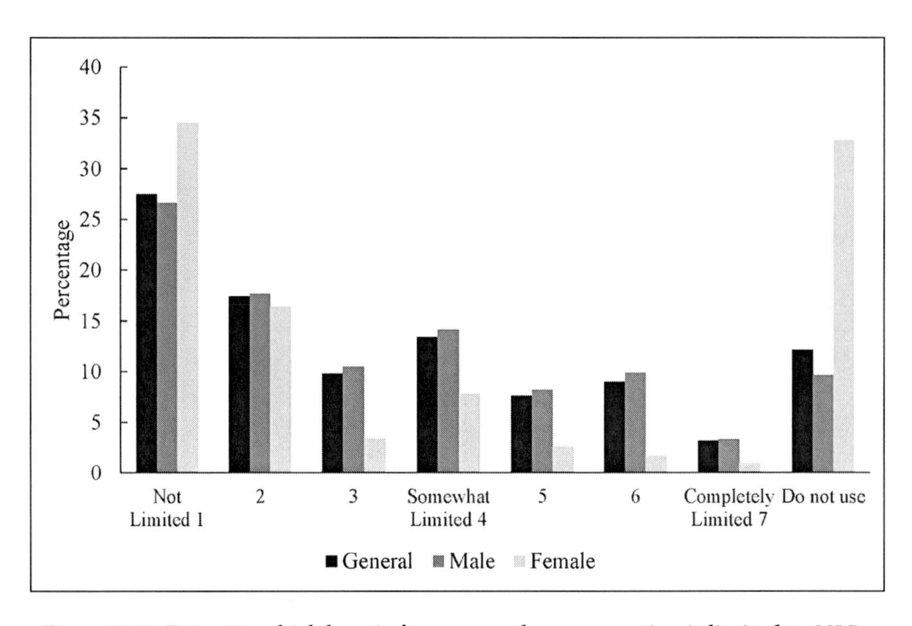

Figure 11.10. **Extent to which bronies' pornography consumption is limited to *MLP*-themed content.**

Who *Consumes?*

To this point, we've looked at the nature of bronies' pornography use and have even shown that male and female bronies differ with respect to who is more likely to seek out and view Rule 34 artwork. But we can look at other factors related to consumption that go beyond mere demographics of consumers and look at questions about the reaction to sex and explicit materials. As one example, we can look at feelings of guilt associated with sex and pornography.

To begin, we should point out that most bronies, in general, didn't feel guilty viewing *MLP* related porn. On average, the fandom scored 3.39 out of 7—below the mid-point of the 7-point scale we used. One way of interpreting these scores is to say that fans generally don't consume a lot of *MLP*-themed porn, and thus have little to feel guilty about. Alternatively, they may also reveal a progressive, modern fandom, wherein fans, whether they look at it or not, at least consider fandom-related porn to be acceptable.

Figure 11.11 shows a breakdown of the five items which made up the scale of sex-related guilt that we used. In general, scores were low across the board, with one exception: Regardless of how bronies felt about their own consumption of Rule 34 content, most agreed that their parents would be disappointed if they found out about it.[29] Whether this reflects shame at their parents being made aware of *anything* pertaining to their sexuality in general or a general feeling of embarrassment about anyone in general discovering *MLP*-themed porn consumption remains to be seen, but may help us to better understand the role that stigma toward the brony fandom may play in specific brony behaviors like hiding their interest.

Production and Sharing of Explicit Content

The controversial issue of pornography in the brony fandom wouldn't exist were it not for the efforts of those who create the explicit content in the first place. To better understand this issue, as well as the issue of who helps to *share* content once it's been produced, we asked bronies whether they produced explicit *MLP* content and whether they had ever shared the material with others in the fandom.

As figure 11.12 shows, only a very small fraction of the brony fandom—4.9 percent—had produced *MLP*-themed pornographic images, fanfiction, or videos. Among those who had, more than half reported that the shared this content with other bronies. This means that the majority of fans consume explicit content produced by a very small minority of fans—although at least 20 percent of bronies couldn't rule out the possibility of creating explicit artwork themselves in the future. Whether this is being done out of their own interest in the content or driven by demand for such content remains to be seen. What this *does* tell us, taken together with our previous findings, is that despite stereotypes to the contrary, producing, sharing, and consuming explicit material, while present in the brony fandom, is far from the

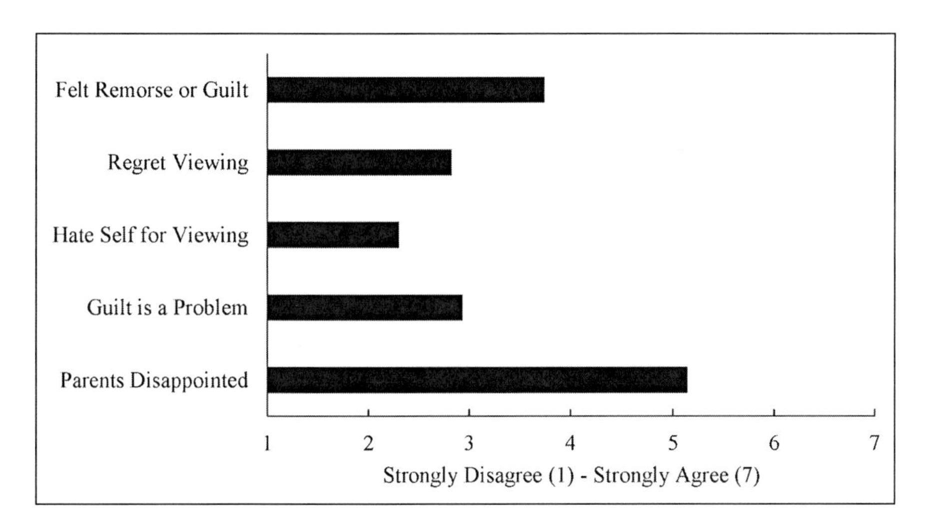

Figure 11.11. **Bronies' trait sex guilt inventory scores, Rule 34 edition.**

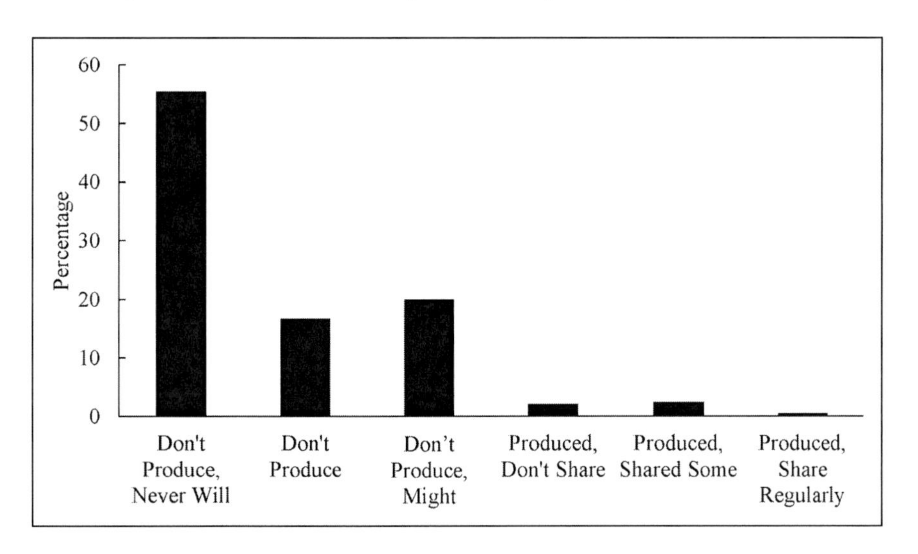

Figure 11.12. **Bronies' creating and sharing of Rule 34 content.**

fandom's main purpose, nor does it comprise the main fan-related behavior of most bronies.

What Should the Fandom Do?

Let's wrap this section up by asking a "bigger picture" question—what, if anything, should be done about the issue of pornography in the brony

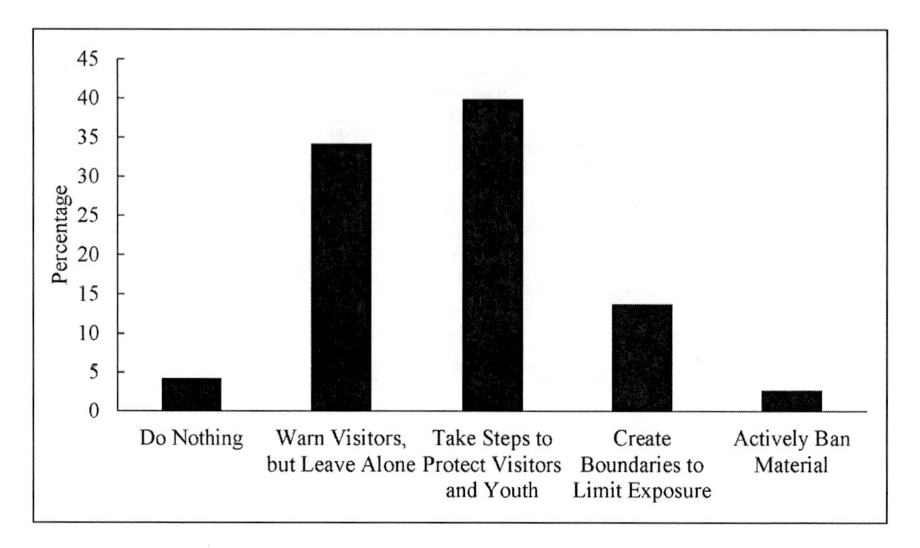

Figure 11.13. **Bronies' beliefs about what should be done about Rule 34 content.**

fandom? After all, talking about statistics regarding how bronies feel about pornography and their own consumption of explicit material is one thing. But none of these statistics makes it clear what, if anything, *should* be done. In light of the stigma facing the brony fandom, often stemming from the existence of Rule 34 content, do bronies believe that the fandom would be better if something were done to limit or outright bar erotic material?

Figure 11.13 reveals the results of this question when asked to bronies—who were given a choice of several different responses. To begin, it's worth noting that, in line with their relatively moderate attitudes about Rule 34 content, *very* few Bronies took to the extremes and suggested doing absolutely nothing with respect to explicit content—leaving it as a sort of free-for-all with no rules or policies to govern its use or distribution—or actively censoring the material itself.[30]

Some fans seem to support creating boundaries, perhaps relegating explicit artwork to a cordoned-off part of the web or setting in place rules limiting what sorts of content can be displayed. But by far the most popular suggestions involved warning visitors and others about potentially offensive or explicit material and taking steps as a community to protect visitors and youth from being exposed. These steps could include the implementation of safe-search options on brony-themed art websites and flagging or tagging images to ease the task of keeping people who don't want to be exposed to such material (or who ought not to be exposed) from being inadvertently exposed to it.

We bring this topic up because, despite anything we or anyone else could possibly say about the subject, history has shown us that explicit material will inevitably be produced. Nearly every fan community has to acknowledge this reality in their fandom. Many have dealt with it by avoiding the topic or engaging ceaselessly in back-and-forth arguing with little action one way or another.

Interestingly, bronies stand out as a fairly distinct example of a fan group that went out of its way to address their own concerns regarding explicit content. In 2014, the Tumblr blog "Bronies Against Bullshit" set out to promote #SafeSearchWrapUp. Their goal was to organize bronies, twice a month, to seek out offensive, inappropriate, or adult content on Google and other sites and flag it. The idea was to ensure that a little girl who was searching for pictures of Pinkie Pie to stick on her locker at school wouldn't be upset, shocked, or otherwise traumatized by what she saw.[31] The same group also suggested expanding their efforts to include other fandoms, including *Avatar: The Last Airbender*, *Young Justice*, *Steven Universe*, and more. As we watched this movement unfold—ever the curious social scientists—we were struck by how this movement inspired other fandoms to take similar action. Like the 40 percent of Bronies who agreed that some measures should be taken to protect children, fandoms of others shows with a large base of younger viewers saw a need to be more responsible than fans of shows geared at an entirely adult audience.

Regardless of your own stance on the appropriateness or moral "rightness" of pornography in the fandom, you've got to give bronies credit: While people often decry them as immature, this collective action was arguably one of the more mature, thoughtful, and considerate things we've heard of a fandom doing. Instead of offloading responsibility for the issue to parents or to content creators, they took it upon themselves to actively improve the perception of their fandom and to make it a more inviting place for *all* of its members—young and old.

Conclusion

So what can we take from an entire chapter written about one of the most controversial subjects in the brony fandom? Well, for starters, we hope that learning a bit about the history of pornography and its existence across all fandoms puts the subject into perspective. Rule 34 is neither new to the brony fandom, nor is it a defining feature of what makes a brony a brony, as we've seen from our own data. Second, a lot can be gained from having a reasonable, data-driven conversation about these topics in one's fandom. You certainly don't have to beat people over the head with the topic to the point of making them feel uncomfortable with it, but there's also no need to pretend that it doesn't exist either. Regardless of your own stance about the appropriateness or inappropriateness of explicit material in the brony fandom, we can, if nothing else, say that bronies have done more than most fandoms to maturely and responsibly work to improve some of the stereotypes they have been unfairly saddled with.[32]

And what can we say about bronies from the data itself? Well, the fandom is somewhat lukewarm about explicit content in general. While only some bronies consume it with any regularity, most bronies recognize it as an acceptable form of self-expression—in line with the show's own espoused values of tolerance. Given enough time, most fans are eventually going to encounter the material, although it's not something most will end up seeking out for themselves. And despite the fact that Rule 34 content is often seen as a hot-button, controversial subject within the fandom, our own work suggests that it's not nearly as big an issue as it's made out to be—either by outsiders looking in or by bronies themselves.

Sometimes the most interesting story is the lack of story in the first place!

Chapter 12

The World Outside *MLP*

"I wish the other changelings could meet you all. You're not really as strange as the stories say."

—*Ocellus* (*Season 8, Episode 2,* School Daze—Part 2)

When studying a unique group of fans like bronies it's easy to develop tunnel vision. We often forget that there's more to these peoples' lives than the unusual television show that they and their friends enjoy watching. It's also helpful to maintain a sense of cultural perspective, remembering that the brony phenomenon didn't arise within a cultural vacuum. After all, if the brony fandom arose on Internet forums such as 4chan (Connelly, 2017), it stands to reason that many bronies were active users of these Internet forums *before* they were bronies—and many probably continue to do so! This means they had an active interest in cartoons and comics that predated their interest in a show about colorful friendship horses.

In this chapter we're going to finish up our discussion of fanship and the specific behaviors of bronies by taking a step back and looking at some of the other interests they have. We'll begin by looking at some of the more popular subgroups *within* the brony community, revealing how, despite being a single fandom, the activities and interests of individual bronies often vary considerably. Next we'll zoom out a bit further and consider the brony fandom in relation to *other* fandoms, some very similar in content to *MLP* and others distinctly dissimilar. Lastly, we finish up this chapter by situating the brony fandom within the broader context of Internet culture.

Subgroups Within the Brony Fandom

Let's imagine, for a moment, that you're just now learning about bronies for the first time. You've been told that the children's television show *MLP:FIM* has an avid adult fanbase. With only this information to go on and nothing else, try to imagine what you might expect to happen at a convention like BronyCon, where several thousand bronies get together for a weekend.

For many laypersons, their expectations probably look something like this: Everyone at the convention gathers together in a large hall to watch episodes of *MLP* together.[1] Maybe there's a merchandise room where that they can all file in after watching to pick up some DVDs (so they can watch the show at home), along with some posters, t-shirts, and knickknacks branded with the show's logo and characters. And perhaps a few of the voice actors or writers show up to sign autographs.

If you've ever *been* to a brony convention, you probably realize that this notion of what goes on at a brony convention is almost painfully simplistic—but also not wholly inaccurate. After all, it's not uncommon for brony conventions to involve screenings of new or fan favorite episodes. There almost always *is* a vendor's hall where merchandise (both official and unofficial) can be purchased. And there often *are* opportunities at these conventions to meet cast and crew members from the show.

But a quick glance at any convention schedule reveals a *lot* more going on than just these activities. Art, writing, music, video production, and costume-building tutorials are common staples of many brony conventions, as are meet-and-greets for bronies who create content for the fandom. Competitions are also a common occurrence, including video and card game competitions and trivia contests. News and discussion sessions take place alongside meet-ups for people with interests in specific facets of the show or for people from particular areas, helping bronies introduce themselves to other bronies in their area.

In short, despite the fact that bronies love *MLP*, they do a *lot* more than just sit around and passively watch the show. And while a myriad of unique interests exist within the brony fandom—everything from people interested in drawing pony-plane hybrids to people who create life-sized plushies—a few fairly common subgroups do emerge upon study. In a 2016 study of over a thousand bronies, we asked them to check off from a list which of several different subgroups within the brony fandom they considered themselves to be a part of.

One of the most popular of these subgroups was "artists"—approximately 55 percent of female bronies and 22.5 percent of male bronies checked this particular box. It should come as no surprise that a fandom based around an animated television show has a tremendous interest in artwork. Many of the fandom's largest websites are, themselves, repositories for artwork (e.g., derpibooru) or regularly feature fanart (e.g., Equestria Daily). Likewise, some of the most popular brony-related YouTube videos are fan-created animations (e.g., WarpOut's *Lullaby for a Princess* or Duo Cartoonist's *Children of the*

Night, both of which have tens of millions of views). And, dispelling the notion that bronies are simply passive consumers of content, these data suggest that many bronies actively *contribute* art to the fandom.

Similar to the results for artists, it turns out that many in the brony community also write: 32.5 percent of female bronies and 22.5 percent of male bronies consider themselves to be writers. Of course, this doesn't mean that every single one of them has written a book or published a popular and critically-acclaimed story. But many bronies *do* end up trying their hand at writing show-inspired fanfiction. This is reflected in the popularity of sites like Fimfiction, a repository of more than 100,000 different fan-created stories.

Of course, not every brony chooses to express their interest in *MLP* through the creation of *MLP*-themed content. Some prefer to bring the characters to life through cosplay—something that 30 percent of female bronies and 7.5 percent of male bronies engage in. Such cosplays typically involve dressing up as one's favorite character from the show (or, albeit less commonly, as one's own original character[2] inspired by the *MLP* universe), typically with the intent of being seen by the fandom at large.[3] And for those who have little interest in spending time and money to dress up as a character, there's the option to express your interest by collecting merchandise related to the show: vinyl figures, lunchboxes, cards, plushies, toys, clothing, stickers, and a myriad of other products.[4] In fact, collecting may arguably have been the first subgroup to have formed around the *MLP* fandom, with its origins in conventions like the My Little Pony Collector's Convention, which began in 2004—years before *MLP:FIM* and the brony fandom even existed! And collecting is alive and well within the brony fandom, with 50 percent of female bronies and 30 percent of male bronies considering themselves to be collectors of some type.

Before we finish this section on subgroups within the brony community, we'd be remiss if we didn't point out one particularly interesting trend in the data: Female bronies are significantly more likely to belong to these subgroups than are male bronies. Or, to put it another way, male bronies appear to be more likely than female bronies to express their fanship by simply sitting back and watching the show.

One possibility for this may have to do with norms surrounding the brony fandom—in particular its being a predominantly male fandom (see Chapter 4 for more on the demographic composition of the brony fandom). Put simply, when an adult female fan of *MLP* approaches the brony fandom, they may be confronted with an image of the fandom as being mostly male—a sort of "boy's club." While there are no explicit rules or active attempts to dissuade women from entering the fandom, the fact that it's predominantly male may discourage more casual female fans from calling themselves bronies—if only out of fear of standing out or not belonging.[5] Evidence speaking to this point specifically is discussed in greater detail in Chapter 13.

This is where being a member of a subgroup may come in handy for female bronies. To counteract the feeling of "maybe I don't belong here," female bronies may be able to reassure themselves of their belongingness to this group by pointing to one of these subgroups. For example, a female brony could say, "Of course I belong here, I'm an artist who draws *MLP* characters!" These subgroups may serve as a way to get their "foot in the door," so to speak, validating their belonging in the fandom should their "credentials" be challenged (see Chapter 15 for more on gatekeeping within the fandom). In other words, while it may be enough for a male brony to simply say, "I'm a brony because I like the show," a female brony may feel like she has to have something to *prove* that she belongs in the fandom—which may explain why female bronies are far more likely to belong to specific subgroups in the fandom than male bronies—a trend which has been observed in other predominantly-male fandoms as well (e.g., the furry fandom; Plante, Reysen, Roberts, & Gerbasi, 2016).

Interest in Other Fandoms

If I were to ask you what sort of food you enjoyed, you could probably rattle off a list of interests: Perhaps you like sushi, curry, and pizza in particular.[6] If someone gave you this list, you probably wouldn't think twice. After all, it makes perfect sense that a person could enjoy all of those different things. It would be silly, in fact, to expect a person to *only* be a fan of one particular style of cuisine, since aesthetic preferences are not often mutually exclusive—liking one thing doesn't mean you can't also like something else.

The same can be said for fan groups as well. Laypersons and researchers alike are guilty of conceptualizing fans in overly-simplistic ways. We might say, "Tom over there is a brony" and find ourselves imagining Tom spending all or most of his spare time on *MLP*-related pursuits. In reality, the brony fandom is likely only one of Tom's *many* groups representing a variety of Tom's different interests.[7] To be sure, being a brony could very well represent Tom's *strongest* or *favorite* fan interest. But we shouldn't assume that he doesn't have other interests that matter as well.

There're several important reasons why we should consider additional fan interests when trying to understand the brony fandom. For one thing, doing so can help us better understand the relationships different fandoms have with one another. If, for example, there was a considerable overlap between two fandoms, it would make sense to hypothesize that members of those two fandoms probably get along pretty well with one another. Understanding additional fan interests also matters because it can help us to better understand the apparent crossover or bleeding of one fandom into another fandom. This is especially likely to be the case when two fandoms share something in common (e.g., they both involve animated media).

So what sorts of other fandoms do bronies participate in? We asked this question in at least two different studies—our initial 2011 study of more than 3,600 bronies and in our more recent 2016 study. The results revealed that one of the most common fandoms bronies participate in is the gaming fandom: 75 percent of male bronies and 60 percent of female bronies consider themselves to be gamers. Of course, what constitutes a "game" varies from person to person. Gaming culture can include tabletop board and card games, the influence of which can be seen in the popularity of gaming panels and events at brony conventions and the popularity of *MLP*-themed games (e.g., the *My Little Pony* collectable card game, Twilight Sparkle's Secret Shipfic Folder).

But gaming can also include computer and video games, which themselves represent fairly large fandoms with subgroups of their own. Our study found that bronies played significantly more hours of video games on average than non-bronies and we can see the influence of this computer and video game culture in the *MLP* fandom. For example, the fan-made game *Them's Fightin' Herds* began as an *MLP*-themed 2D fighting game.[8] Likewise, references to computer games can be found littered throughout brony YouTube videos, including references to games like *Portal* and *Team Fortress 2* in fan-made 3D animations created using Source Filmmaker.[9] Other references to gaming can be found in the popular series "Two Best Sisters Play," which features Princesses Celestia and Luna playing video games together, as well in the YouTube channel Fire Team Harmony, which features bronies donning *MLP*-themed power armor from the *Halo* series of computer games.

There is also considerable overlap between the brony fandom and the anime fandom, with 55 percent of female bronies and 40 percent of male bronies considering themselves to be anime fans. Anime—animated cartoons and comics typically originating in (or heavily influenced by) Japan—overlaps conceptually with *MLP* insofar as both of them are essentially cartoons. In fact, the same study found that bronies were twice as likely to watch cartoons as non-bronies were. As such, it makes sense that a person who can enjoy a slightly strange cartoon about animated horses would also probably enjoy the often-eccentric or exaggerated stylings of anime. The influence of anime culture on the brony fandom can be observed through the popularity of anime memes (e.g., the use of the term "pony-waifu" borrows from the anime fandom and fans' having a "waifu" character) and the integration of anime tropes into fan-created works.[10]

Another fandom whose content conceptually overlaps with that of the brony fandom is the furry fandom. Furries are people who are fans of media featuring anthropomorphized animals—that is, characters who are animals imbued with human traits, such as the ability to talk or walk in a bipedal fashion. Given that *MLP* is a show about horses that can talk and which have human-like personalities, it's not much of a stretch to argue that bronies and furries share a lot of common ground. In fact, our studies suggest that 19.4 percent of bronies also call themselves furries, a number mirrored in the furry fandom, where approximately 20 percent of furries consider themselves to be bronies (Plante et al., 2016). This raises interesting questions about whether the overlap between the two fandoms represents furries who became bronies because they discovered the liking of the show (among other furry-themed media) or whether it represents bronies who were fans of *MLP* and then, because of this interests, sought out similar media featuring anthropomorphic animal characters. The data suggest that the latter case is more than twice as prevalent as the former: People who are both bronies and furries tend to be bronies first and then become furries later on down the road.[11]

Another overlapping fan interest can be found in the science fiction fandom: 47.5 percent of male bronies are science fiction fans, as are 35 percent of female bronies. Conceptually, the link between these two fandoms isn't nearly as clear as it is between the brony and furry or brony and anime fandoms. One possibility is that bronies tend to be part of a broader "nerd" culture, which includes an interest in gaming, cartoons and comics, the Internet and computers (as we'll see in the next section), and science fiction. One can see elements of science fiction infused in brony fanart and fanfiction, including cyberpunk and post-apocalyptic themes (e.g., *Fallout Equestria*, a crossover of *My Little Pony* and the popular science-fiction themed *Fallout* computer game franchise).

As a final note, in addition to studying the overlap between different fandoms, our studies have also looked at the sheer *number* of different fan groups bronies belong to. The results suggest that bronies actually belong to *fewer* fan groups than a non-brony control group. A further analysis suggests that for many bronies, the brony fandom was their first major fan community, suggesting that the brony fandom may be a sort of "gateway" into other fandoms—at least for male bronies. This does not mean, of course, that bronies might not also be fans of various other interests (e.g., video games) prior to becoming bronies. It does suggest, however, that while bronies may have been fans of various things, the brony community was, for many of them, the first time their interest in something led to their involvement in a *community* of fans.

Bronies and Internet Culture

With the brony fandom arising almost entirely as a result of Internet culture, it makes sense that, in addition to overlapping with various other fandoms, bronies may be part of a broader "Internet culture." We tested this possibility in study comparing a sample of approximately 600 bronies to a matched control group of non-bronies. Each group was given a questionnaire assessing various aspects of being part of the "net generation" or Internet culture (Edwards et al., 2016).

The results found that, in general, bronies scored higher on traits associated with being part of an Internet-based culture. For example, bronies were more likely to endorse items about having a fundamental right to access information and express opinions—something characteristic of Internet culture. Bronies also expressed greater comfort with new technology and a general tendency toward being tech savvy. Finally, bronies reported feeling less inhibited on the Internet—finding it easier to express themselves online (e.g., through social media).

When it comes to the reasons for using computer technology and the Internet, bronies again show signs of being more involved in an Internet culture than the typical non-brony. Bronies were more likely to use the Internet for entertainment and stress relief purposes. Given that the brony fandom itself originated in a recreational Internet forum (4chan), these results make a lot of sense. Likewise, given that much of the brony fandom is geographically diverse and, as such, communicates with one another online, it would seem to follow that a brony would have to be fairly well-versed with the Internet and fairly comfortable with using it to be able to keep up with and contribute meaningfully to the brony fandom.

That said, there is little evidence suggesting that bronies, despite their more frequent use of the Internet and computers, are addicted to them. These findings are analogous to the conclusions we drew from Chapter 9, which suggested that while bronies have particularly active imaginations, they rarely step over the line into delusion. As such, while bronies spend a great deal of their recreational time interacting with the fandom online, all evidence seems to suggest that they do so in moderation and know how to set appropriate boundaries so that their fan interests don't interfere with their real-world obligations. We'll return to this theme of bronies as surprisingly well-adjusted (despite misconceptions to the contrary) in Chapters 17 and 18.

Chapter 13

"One of us": Bronies as a Fandom

"In our town!/In our town/We don't have to wait/To find out that our destiny/Is just to emulate!"

—*Villagers (Season 5, Episode 1,* The Cutie Map—Part 1)

Humans are a social species—it's in our nature to organize ourselves into tribes, to see the world in terms of "us vs. them," and to think of ourselves and others in terms of the groups we belong to. For decades, social psychologists have studied these social identities, reaching the conclusion that, for the most part, a group is a group. In other words, whether we're talking about racial groups, national identities, or the sport team you happen to be a fan of, many of these groups are interchangeable for the purpose of understanding their underlying psychology. As such, while non-bronies might consider being a fan of *MLP* to be abnormal (Reysen & Shaw, 2016), we argue that the brony fandom is, at least from a psychological perspective, no different from any other group that people belong to.

In the present chapter we briefly delve into the theories explaining why bronies, despite being superficially different from other groups, should nevertheless be governed by the same psychological processes as any other group. We start by describing the two main theories psychologists use to understand the psychology of groups. Next, we'll review research showing that we can apply these theories to our understanding of fans and fan communities. We'll then describe some of our own research showing how the concepts of fanship and fandom can help us better understand bronies as a whole. Finally, we'll show how this work can be applied to a practical question: How can we predict whether a brony will or will not attend conventions and gatherings?

Understanding Group Psychology: The Social Identity Perspective

One of the ways psychologists understand groups is through a lens known as the social identity perspective. This perspective is actually a combination of two related sub-theories, called social identity theory (Tajfel & Turner, 1979) and self-categorization theory (Turner, Hogg, Oakes, Reicher, & Wetherell, 1987). While it sounds like a lot of jargon at first, they're actually pretty simple and intuitive once you hear what they have to say.

We begin with social identity theory, which was developed in the 1970s (Hogg, Terry, & White, 1995). Henri Tajfel was trying to understand stereotyping and prejudice (Hogg & Williams, 2000) along with his graduate student, John Turner (Turner & Reynolds, 2012). The two began with the proposition that people often think of themselves in terms of the groups they do or do not belong to. There are, according to Tajfel (1972), three components to this group identification.

First, people are aware that they are part of a group and self-categorize as a member (e.g., "I am a brony."). Second, people compare their ingroup's status with relevant out-groups (e.g., "Bronies seem to be lower in social status than sport fans."). Third, people feel an emotional tie or attachment to their group (e.g., "I am proud to be a brony."). Various researchers over the years have proposed different ways of measuring this ingroup identification, sometimes using these three dimensions, sometimes using the simpler question of how much connection you feel to a group (Ashmore, Deaux, & McLaughlin-Volpe, 2004; Reysen, Katzasrska-Miller, Nesbit, & Pierce, 2013).

In short, you can think of yourself as an individual compared to other individuals (e.g., "I'm more introverted than the person sitting next to me") or you can think of yourself in terms of a group you belong to (e.g., "I'm an anime fan, and anime fans are more introverted than sport fans.") We're quite capable of doing both, and often switch between the two when it's convenient or beneficial for us to do so. For example, research shows that sport fans are seen as higher in status than less-mainstream fan groups, like bronies (e.g., Reysen & Shaw, 2016). We, as members of groups, are keenly aware of these sorts of status differences. And since, according to social identity theory (Tajfel & Turner, 1979), we strive to belong to positive and distinct groups, we may choose whether we want to think of ourselves as members of a group if it's going to reflect well or poorly on us (e.g., choosing not to identify as a brony if it's going to make you look bad to others.)

Understanding Group Psychology: Self-Categorization Theory

After Tajfel's death in 1982 (Hogg & Williams, 2000), Turner continued working on social identity, eventually proposing a second theory known as self-categorization theory (Turner et al., 1986). According to the theory, identities can be categorized at different levels of abstraction: (1) personal identity (me vs. you), (2) intermediate identity (e.g., bronies vs. sport fans), and (3) superordinate identity (e.g., humans vs. insects). Greater levels of abstraction reflect greater inclusiveness. For example, a brony can think of themselves as a brony compared to sport fans, or they can move to a higher level of abstraction and think of themselves as a fan in general, which makes them part of the same, bigger group as sport fans.

As we go about our day-to-day lives we seamlessly transition between various identities. For example, we may think of ourselves in terms of our brony identity while talking with other bronies online, but when we log off, we may switch identities and take on our role within our family (e.g., a brother or sister) or workplace (e.g., an employee getting ready for work). Which identity happens to be on our minds at any given time will depend on both the person (e.g., how meaningful is a particular identity to us) and on our situation (are we in a situation where a particular identity is relevant?). For example, we might think of ourselves as a brony if we find ourselves in a room full of anime fans (e.g., "I'm different from them"), but if a bunch of sport fans walked into the room, we might start thinking of ourselves as media fans more generally (e.g., "I'm just like these anime fans—we're both fans of cartoons, unlike these sport fans").

At this point, you might be thinking, "Who cares whether we're thinking about ourselves as bronies, cartoon fans, or fans in general?"[1] As it turns out, which identity is on our mind matters: Once an identity is on our minds, we automatically apply group-relevant stereotypes to ourselves: We start to think and act in accordance with the stereotypes that exist about that particular group. For example, the authors of this book are all professors. In our day-to-day lives, we don't typically think of ourselves this way. But when we're standing in front of a classroom full of students, our membership in the group "professor" is very much on our minds. And, as such, we find ourselves acting in ways stereotypical of professors: We might use less profanity, dress more professionally, and speak more confidently about a topic than we might do otherwise.

In fact, this tendency to take on the stereotype of one's own group becomes even *stronger* if you strongly identify as a member of that particular group. For example, lets assume that there's a stereotype about bronies being introverted (more on personality in Chapter 16). In situations where people are reminded about being a brony (e.g., at a brony convention), highly identified bronies will be more likely to act in an introverted manner than people who only somewhat identify as bronies.

Together, social identity and self-categorization theories can help us explain why people behave the way they do in groups and why they are influenced by groups as they are. And, since these processes are thought to operate regardless of the *type* of group we're talking about, we can apply these principles to fan groups to gain a better understanding of fans.

Applying Group Psychology Theories to Fan Groups

In their 2010 paper, Reysen and Branscombe make a somewhat counterintuitive argument. Put simply, they argue that despite all of the differences that exist between different fan groups (e.g., think fans of the Insane Clown Posse compared to *My Little Pony* fans), they should nevertheless all be susceptible to the same behavioral tendencies and patterns of thought predicted by the social identity perspective. This means that, regardless of the fan group you belong to, we should still see predictable tendencies according to a social identity perspective, like the tendency to treat members of your own fandom better than members of other fandoms or the tendency to act in ways stereotypical of your fandom when you highly identify with that fandom.[2]

We can find evidence for this by looking at research on sport fans. For example, sport fans are found to bolster their self-esteem by attaching themselves to winning teams and to protect their self-esteem by distancing themselves from losing teams (Bizman & Yinon, 2002). And just like other groups, sport fans show ingroup bias, favoring other fans of their team over fans of other teams (Markman & Hirt, 2002; Wann & Dolan, 1994).[3] Additionally, highly identified sport fans are more likely to think, feel, and behave in stereotype-consistent ways (Yoshida, Gordon, here, & James, 2015). As an example, in a sample of basketball fans, Toder-Alon, Icekson, and Shuv-Ami (2018) found that highly identified sport fans were more likely to rate themselves as more aggressive and considered aggression more appropriate—both supporting the stereotype of sport fans as hypermasculine and aggressive.

These outcomes aren't limited to sport fans either. Those who more strongly identify with the Harry Potter fan community are more likely to consume the books/films, appreciate the series more, and report having a greater desire to purchase show-related products compared to less identified fans (Tsay-Vogel & Sanders, 2017). In short, the bulk of the research suggests that fan groups operate like any other group when it comes to social identity processes, with predictable effects on group members' interest in the topic, emotions, enjoyment, normative behavior, treatment of other fans, and spreading of their fan interest to others.

Up to this point, we've spoken about fans as groups of people sharing a similar interest. However, psychologists make an important distinction between *fandom* (identifying with a community of other fans) and *fanship* (identifying as a person with a particular interest; see Chapter 1 for examples of the distinction between the two). Although fandom and fanship often go hand in hand (i.e., people who identify with a fan interest also tend to identify with other fans), the two concepts do differ in important, if subtle, ways (Reysen & Branscombe, 2010). The social identity processes we've discussed so far are related to measures of *fandom*, not necessarily to *fanship*. For example, in a longitudinal study of Japanese soccer fans, Yoshida, Heere, and Gordon (2015) found that identifying with the soccer fan community (fandom) was more strongly associated with frequency of game attendance than simply identifying as a fan of a particular team (fanship).[4]

With this in mind, let's briefly review what fanship is and how fanship is related to important fan-related thoughts, feelings, and behaviors.

Fanship

Daniel Wann and Nyla Branscombe (1993) published the most often used measure of fan identification. In their initial paper, they found that highly (vs. low) identified fans attended games frequently, were willing to wait longer in line for tickets, and have more friends who were also fans of the team. Subsequent research has shown associations between team identification and variables such as customer satisfaction, intention to attend games (Bodet & Bernache-Assollant, 2011), responding more emotionally to the outcome of a game (Wann, Royalty, & Rochelle, 2002), aggression (Wann, Carlson, & Schrader, 1999), and psychological well-being (Wann, 2006).

Unfortunately, the measure itself was worded in a way that really only makes it useful for studying sport fans (e.g., asking questions about rivalries between competing teams—something that doesn't happen among, say, music fans or fans of television shows).[5] For psychologists who wanted to study fanship among non-sport fans, Reysen and Branscombe (2010) created a new measure of fanship that could be used on fans of *any* interest.[6] In this study, which looked at a myriad of different fans, they found that fanship was positively correlated with frequency of consumption and being willing to drive further to participate in their interest. Later studies have since found that fanship is related to displaying symbols of fan group membership (Chadborn et al., 2017), word-of-mouth evangelizing about one's fan interest (Plante, Chadborn, & Reysen, 2018), feelings of entitlement as a fan (Shaw, Plante, Reysen, Roberts, & Gerbasi, 2016), and well-being in furries (Mock, Plante, Reysen, & Gerbasi, 2013) and in anime fans (Reysen, Plante, Roberts, & Gerbasi, 2017b).

Now that we've reviewed some of the theoretical background surrounding the concepts of fandom and fanship, let's turn our attention to studies of the brony fandom specifically.

Fanship, Fandom and Engagement with *MLP* and the Brony Community

In our own study of bronies, we assessed bronies' fanship ("I strongly identify with being a brony") and fandom ("I strongly identify with other bronies in the brony community"), along with measures of different ways of engaging with the show and with the fan community. The results are shown in Table 13.1.

The table shows, first and foremost, that fandom appears to be more strongly associated with a variety of fan-related behavior than is fanship. Specifically, while neither fanship nor fandom were positively associated with frequency of watching *MLP* specifically, fandom was much more strongly associated with consuming or creating fan-made content or purchasing fan-made products. Fanship—that is, being a fan of the show itself, was associated with more purchasing of official merchandise and with wearing or displaying

Table 13.1. Fanship and Fandom Predicting Bronies' Fan Behavior

Variable	Fanship	Fandom
Watch MLP	.06	.13
Watch MLP Fan Content	.07	.21*
Talk to Friends about MLP	.07	.33*
Purchase Official Merchandise	.22*	.04
Purchase Fan Made Products	.13	.21*
Display Fan Symbols	.20*	.12
Talked to Non-Fans	.10	.17*
Created Content	−.01	.29*
Attended Convention/Meetup	−.08	.30*
Watched Re-Runs	−.06	.30*

*This effect is statistically significant.

that content, a finding in line with previous work by Chadborn and colleagues (2017) showing that for fans of any interest, fanship is associated with displaying fan symbols as a way to find new friends who share the same interest. Ultimately, one's felt connection to the fan community (fandom) predicts interacting with other fans (e.g., attending conventions or meet-ups) and talking to friends and non-fans about the show. Simply being a fan of the show itself is largely unassociated with fan-related social activities.

We also examined the associations between fanship and fandom on various psychologically-relevant variables (see Table 13.2). Fandom, but not fanship, was associated with greater feelings of intragroup status (that is, feeling higher in status relative to other bronies) and with stronger feelings of empathy toward others. The result regarding status is understandable, as fans who are heavily connected to the fandom are likely to put more thought into their ranking within the group, while fans who simply love *MLP* may not think about their status relative to other fans. Likewise, those who are engaged with the fandom pick up on the fandom's norms of understanding, tolerance, and acceptance in the group. Interestingly, despite this difference, fandom and fanship were equally likely to be associated with becoming more immersed in the show. In other words, while both fanship and fandom are tied to "getting into" the show more, fandom may be uniquely associated with applying the show's themes of acceptance and understanding to one's social interactions.

Fandom, but not fanship, was associated with perceived stigma toward oneself. This may be due to members of the brony fandom being exposed to more stories of bullying or being more visible as a brony and, as such, being more likely to experience bullying first-hand.

Fanship was positively related to both identifying with characters from the show and with wanting to be more like a character from the show, some-

Table 13.2. Fanship and Fandom Predicting Bronies' Scores on Psychological Constructs

Variable	Fanship	Fandom
Intragroup Status	.11	.19**
Empathy	.06	.14*
Immersion	.29**	.29**
Perceived Stigma	.03	.35**
Character Identification	.45**	.05
Wishful Identification	.32**	.05
Disclose Identity	.16**	.10
Fan Entitlement	.33**	–.11

*This effect is statistically significant.

thing that was not associated with fandom. This may reflect feelings of connection with the show itself, rather than with other fans of the show.

Unexpectedly, fanship, not fandom, was significantly associated with disclosing one's brony identity to others. We are not entirely sure how to interpret this result. In the previous findings we found that fanship predicted more buying of official merchandise and displaying symbols of one's fan identity, presumably as a way of soliciting friends. This finding may reflect that relationship, but future research is needed to explain this particular finding.

Finally, fanship, but not fandom, was associated with fan entitlement. This is in line with past research (Shaw et al., 2016) showing that fanship in anime and fantasy sport fans was associated with greater feelings of entitlement among fans (e.g., feeling like one is owed special treatment from content creators in exchange for their loyalty or devotion).

Fanship, Fandom and Sense of Brony Community

As mentioned in Chapter 9, in one of our studies we looked at bronies' feeling of community—that is, both their local neighborhood community and the brony community. Prior research has found that fans tend to rate their fan community *higher* than their local community on dimensions such as belongingness and a shared sense of community (Chadborn, Edwards, & Reysen, 2016; Obst et al., 2002a, 2002b). In Figure 13.1 we show the response of bronies to these same measures, broken down by sex.[7]

In line with prior research, the present findings show that bronies do, in fact, rate the brony community higher across all measures of community than their local neighborhood community—regardless of participants' sex. This provides evidence that bronies, like other fans, feel a strong sense of connection to their fandoms. That said, within ratings of the brony community, female participants scored the brony fandom slightly lower than male participants did across all of the dimensions. This suggests there may be merit to the idea that female bronies may feel slightly less connected to the brony fandom than their male counterparts.

Within this sense of community measure is a dimension called conscious identification, which can be thought of as another way to measure "fandom." In three separate sets of analyses, we examined whether this conscious identification with one's fan community was related to three other variables of interest related to the production, consumption, and purchasing of fan-related content.[8] In the first of these analyses, bronies rated their own creativity (from 1 = *not at all creative* to 5 = *highly creative*) and the frequency with which

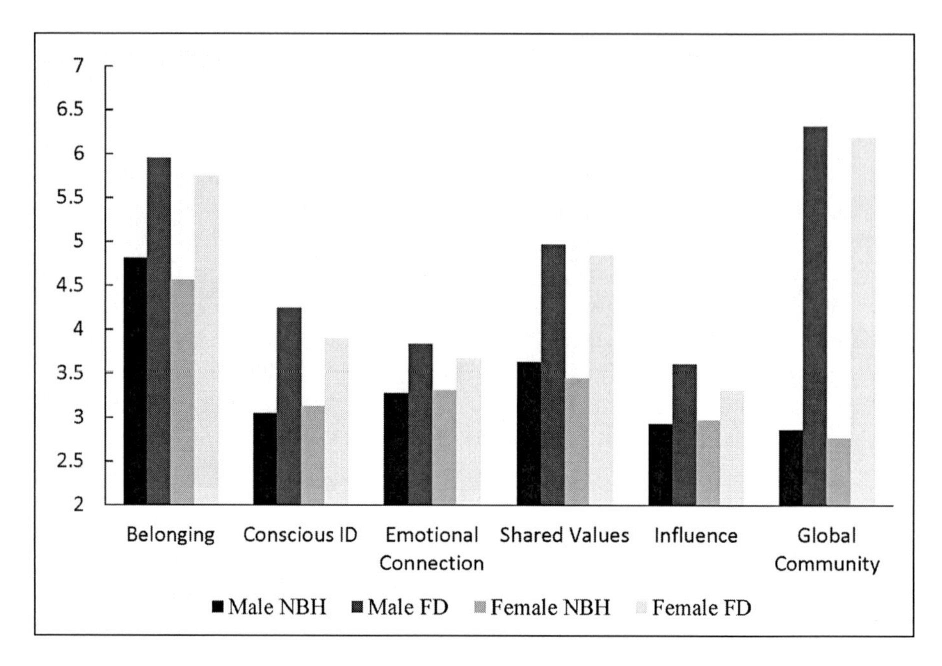

Figure 13.1. **Mean responses of male and female bronies regarding neighborhood (NBH) and brony fandom (FD) sense of community.**

they produce *MLP* related things (i.e., YouTube videos, music, fanfiction, fan artwork, and collectibles like plushies and buttons). As shown in Figure 13.2, highly identified bronies who saw themselves as creative created the most *MLP*-related content, suggesting that artists and writers in the fandom may not simply be there to make money, but rather consider themselves to be strongly connected to others in the community.

In another analysis, we examined the functions of the brony fandom (purpose, escape, social connections; see Chapter 9) and the extent to which they could explain the link, commonly found among sport fans, between identifying with a fan community and content consumption (e.g., watch videos, read fanfiction, view art). As shown in Figure 13.3, the relationship between identifying with the community and content consumption held for bronies as well (top pathway in Figure 13.3.) More importantly, purpose and escape motivation seemed to explain the relationship, but social motivation did not (due to the lack of a significant link between social functions and content consumption).

Finally, we examined whether the same fandom functions could explain the link between identifying as a brony and purchasing content (e.g., purchasing official and fan made products, wearing *MLP* related clothing). Like in the previous analysis and in line with existing research on sport fans (e.g.,

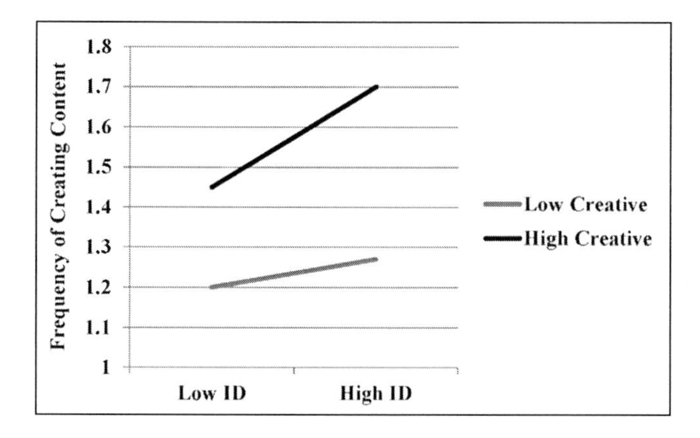

Figure 13.2. **Interaction between sense of community conscious identification and self-rated creativity predicting fan content production.**

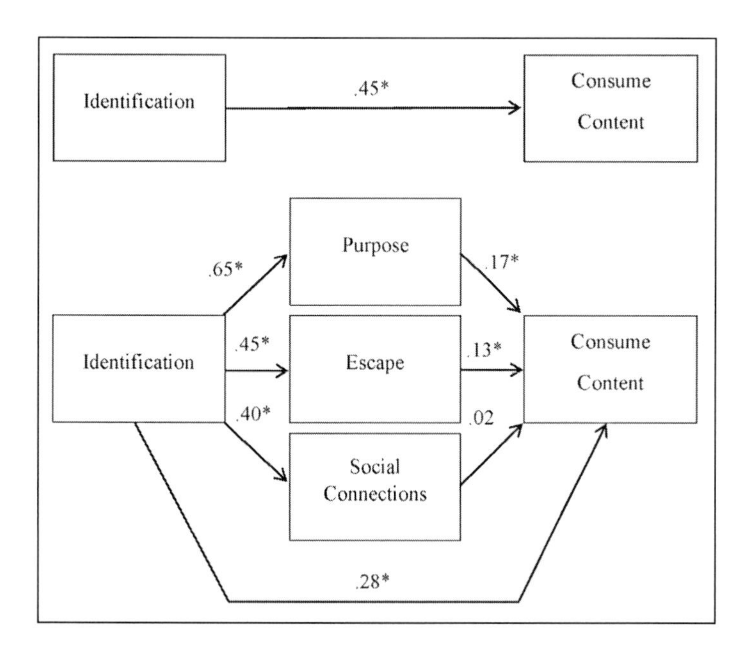

Figure 13.3. **Fandom functions explaining the relationship between identifying with the brony community and consumption of MLP related content. (*This effect is statistically significant.*)**

Gwinner & Swanson, 2003), identification with the brony community was related to the purchase and display of *MLP* related products (top pathway in Figure 13.4). This relationship was also explained by the functions that the brony fandom fulfilled for individual bronies. Specifically, the significant

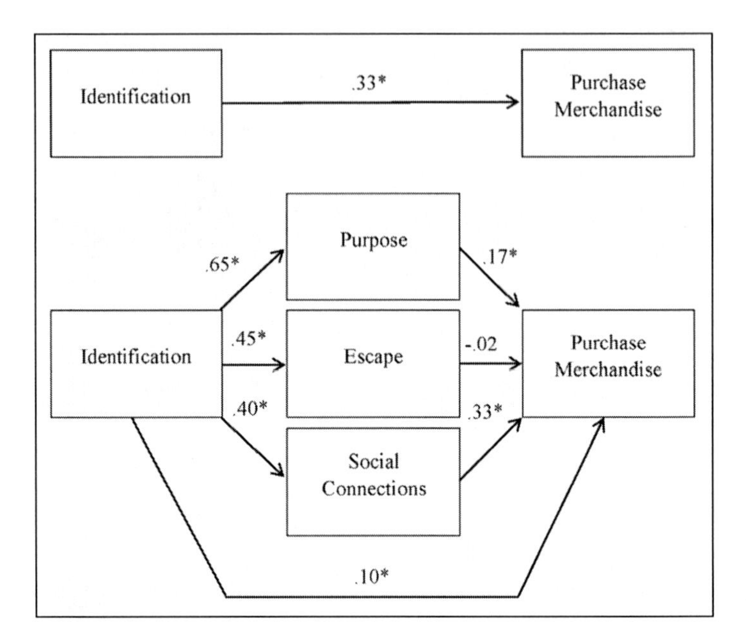

Figure 13.4. **Fandom functions explaining the relationship between identifying with the brony community and purchasing of MLP related products. (**This effect is statistically significant.*)**

pathway through "Social Connections" would seem to suggest that bronies are buying and displaying group symbols in part to advertise that they are a fan and to form and maintain friendships with others, something we've found in research with other fan groups (Chadborn et al., 2017).

Fanship, Fandom and Brony Meet-Ups and Conventions

For many bronies, the cost and time to travel to a convention is a burden. For those seeking to connect with bronies locally, there are often meet-ups where bronies can meet others in the area who share their interest in *MLP*. Interestingly, despite the importance of the social aspect of the fandom to many bronies, most do not attend face-to-face meet-ups (78.5 percent) or conventions (75.8 percent). In this last section we asked bronies to pick the aspect of the fandom they most appreciate, along with the reasons why they do not go to meet-ups, why they stopped attending meet-ups if they have stopped and, if they continue to attend, why they continue to attend.

Speaking to our first question, Figure 13.5 reveals the aspects of the brony

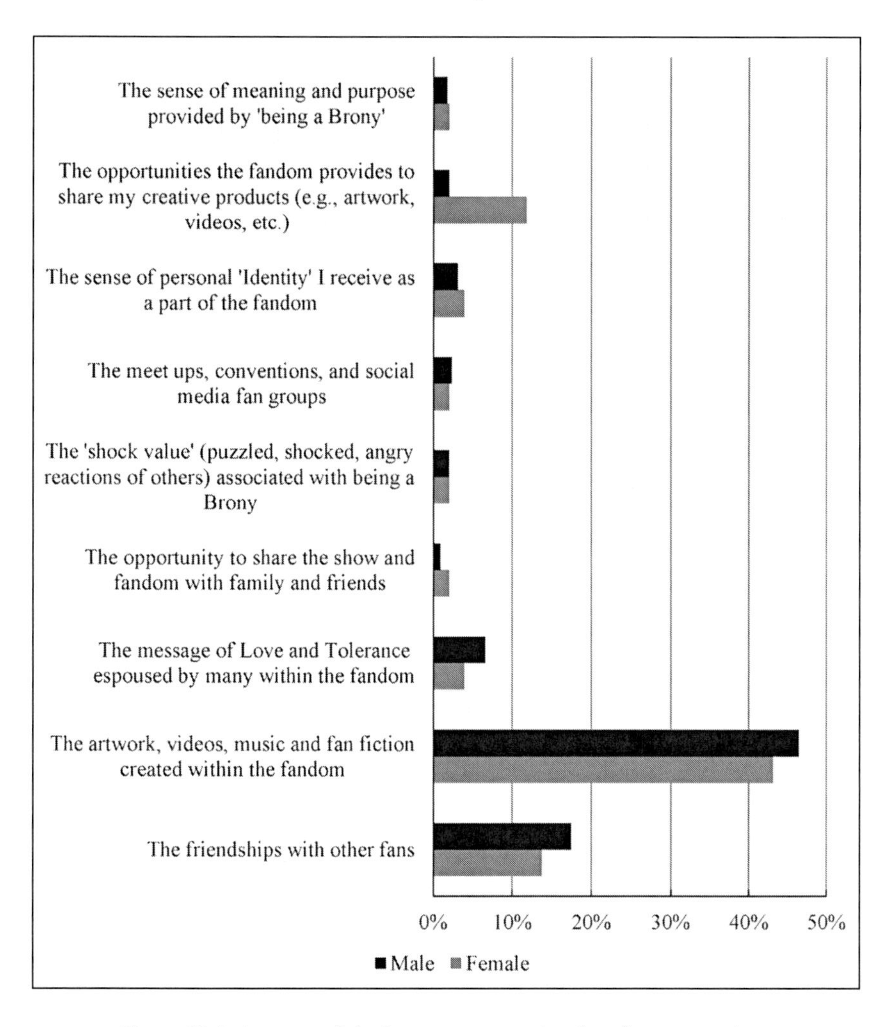

***Figure 13.5.* Aspects of the brony community that fans appreciate.**

fandom that are most appreciated by bronies: the artwork and friends. For the most part, there is little difference between male and female bronies in this regard. The one exception is that female bronies seem more likely to appreciate the opportunity to produce and share their artwork. This is understandable, given that female bronies are more likely to be artists and writers than male bronies.

Speaking to the final three questions, we first asked participants who had never attended a meetup or convention why they had not. Two primary reasons stood out: They were simply too far away to attend or participants were unaware of any meet-ups in their area. Among participants who *had* attended meet-ups but chose to stop, the top reasons were a lack of time or scheduling difficulties and feeling like one did not fit in—although it should be pointed out that these reasons were rated well below the mid-point of the scale. Finally, among the top reasons for those who continued to attend meet-ups, the main reasons for doing so included enjoyment of socializing and feeling a sense of belonging.

Conclusion

Psychologists have largely studied fan groups (particularly sport fans) within the framework of social identity and self-categorization theories. With respect to these psychological processes, fan groups resemble any other group, with few predicted differences between different fan groups regardless of the specific interest. Put another way, fans of all types should show similar tendencies toward ingroup favoritism and stronger tendencies to think, feel, and behave in stereotypical ways if they strongly identify with their fan groups. We found that fanship and fandom, despite being conceptually related to one another, predict different outcomes: Fanship predicts purchasing and displaying of group symbols, presumably to make friends, as well as connection to one's favorite character. Fandom, on the other hand, is associated with greater engagement with fan-made content, more interaction with other fans, more empathy, more felt stigma, and greater concern with status. In general, bronies feel a greater psychological sense of community with the brony fandom than their local neighborhood, and this sense of identification, in turn, is associated with the production, consumption, and purchasing of fan related content. We also examined reasons why bronies do (and do not) attend local meet-ups, which may prove invaluable for those attempting to host such meet-ups themselves while trying to avoid common pitfalls.

Chapter 14

"Where I belong": Other Motivations for Fandom Participation

"I never felt joy like that before. It felt so good I just wanted to keep smiling forever."
—*Pinkie Pie (Season 1, Episode 23,* The Cutie Mark Chronicles)

"Believin' in somethin' can help you do amazin' things."
—*Applejack (Season 4, Episode 20,* Leap of Faith)

In Chapter 9 we discussed some of the motivations driving bronies to watch *MLP* (e.g., escapism, provides a sense of meaning or purpose). Let's return for a moment to the question of motivation, having just discussed the topic of social identity in the previous chapter. In this chapter, we'll look at the extent to which issues pertaining to social and personal identity may motivate bronies to participate in the brony fandom itself.

We'll begin by discussing some additional motivational factors that may explain why bronies engage with the fandom. This includes examining the extent to which bronies seek help from their family, friends, and peers and the extent to which bronies use the fandom as a means of gaining social support. Next, we review a popular psychological theory called optimal distinctiveness theory which suggests that people constantly struggle to balance the need to stand out and be distinct with the need to fit in and belong to a group. Viewed from this theory, bronies may find the fandom to be an appealing place precisely because it allows them to maintain an optimal level of these two needs. Following this discussion, we switch gears and discuss another very different motivation underlying some bronies' participation in the fandom: a desire to become like a character from the show. In particular, we will test several models looking at whether the different motivations driving brony behavior can explain why highly-identified bronies often wish to become more like a character from the show. Finally, we wrap up the chapter by looking at whether bronies and non-bronies alike feel a sense of purpose in their lives and, if so, where they gain that sense of purpose.

"I'll be there for you": Where Bronies Seek Social Support

Take a moment to think about a bad day you've had.[1] What sorts of things improved your mood? Perhaps you treated yourself to something you enjoyed—a bowl of ice cream or binge-watching a show you enjoyed while sitting in a pair of comfy pajamas. Or maybe you found solace through physical activity, going for a run or doing some calisthenics to work the frustration out or feel the bliss of a runner's high.

Chances are pretty good, however, that on your last bad day you sought comfort and support from a co-worker, friend, partner, or family member. Seeking others for comfort or assistance in times of need is referred to as social support. It can take the form of a shoulder to cry on, a small loan to help you get back on your feet, or simply a couch to crash on for the night. According to Kahn and Antonucci (1980), social support can include affective support (e.g., providing a person with a feeling of respect or a source of positive emotions), affirmation (e.g., confirming for someone that they are correct), or aid (e.g., good advice, a ride to the hospital).

As it turns out, social support is more than just a convenient leg-up in a bad situation: Social support has been found time and time again to be a critical part of our well-being. As a social species, we've evolved to depend on those around us to get us through the occasional rough patch. Research has consistently found that having people who are there for you when life is tough is linked better well-being, including everything from better quality of sleep (de Grey, Uchino, Trettevik, Cronan, & Hogan, 2018) to better overall mental health (Harandi, Taghinasab, & Nayeri, 2017). As a general rule, people who have more social support can rely on (i.e., more people who are able to give support) tend to be better off than those who have fewer people around (Abbey, Abramis, & Caplan, 1985).

Okay, so social support is good for us. But who do we turn to in our hour of need? To answer this, take a moment and ask yourself who *you* would turn to if, for example, your house burned down and you needed a place to stay for a few days? Who would you call if you found yourself bed-ridden and needed someone to bring you food? Who could you count on to listen to you or give you advice if you broke up with your partner or had a rough argument with your best friend? Studies show that people tend to answer questions like these in fairly predictable ways: We seek support from those who are close to us. In a study of Belgian adults, for example Agneessens, Waege, and Lievens (2006) asked participants to indicate whether they could count on different people in their lives for social support. The results showed that most people relied on their partner (74.6 percent), their friends (61.7 percent), and their family (58 percent) when they needed help.

So what about bronies—are they any different when it comes to who they turn to when life gets them down? To examine this, we surveyed bronies and compared them to a control sample of average adults from the surrounding community. Participants all completed a scale measuring the frequency with which they discussed their problems or sought advice from their family, friends, and peers (i.e., people at work or school). As shown in Figure 14.1, while bronies tend to turn to the same sources of social support as everyone else does, they tend to do so at a *lower* rate than the average person does. While it would be incorrect to say bronies have *no one* to turn to in times of trouble, the results *do* suggest that bronies may have fewer sources of social support than non-bronies do. Or, to put it another way, when times are tough, bronies may not be able to rely on friends or family to the same extent that others can.

So what does this mean—are bronies simply doomed to suffer in silence and fend for themselves?

Not exactly. In addition to our friends, family, or co-workers, people have other resources they can tap for support. In particular, the groups we belong

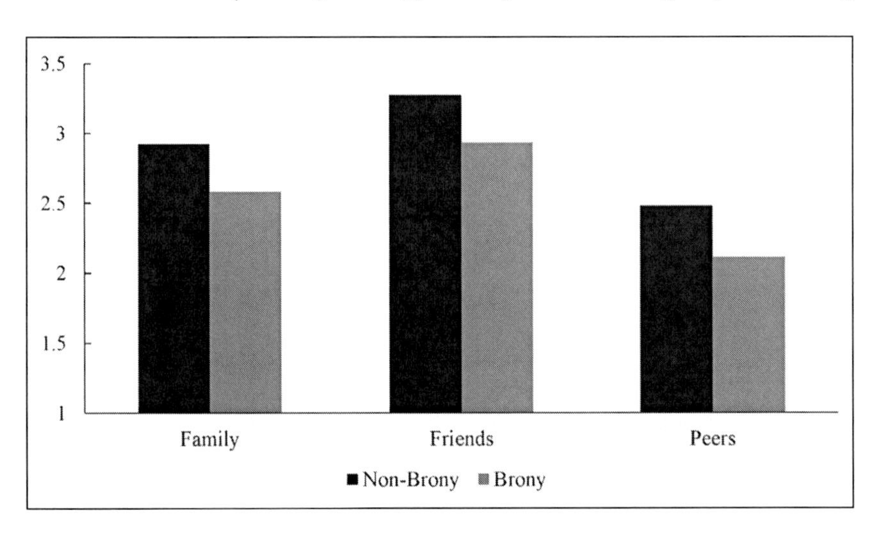

Figure 14.1. **How often bronies and non-bronies shared problems and sought advice from family, friends, and peers.**

to can also be an important source of social support (Haslam, Jetten, Postmes, & Haslam, 2009). As a fairly common example, a family struggling to make ends meet around Christmas or who is threatened with homelessness after an emergency may find support from their church community, who bands together to help them out. These sorts of organizations, both formal and informal, may prove essential in times of need, given that they can offer the combined efforts of numerous people, rather than a single person.

While it makes sense that traditional organizations like churches can provide social support, it may surprise people to learn that even seemingly trivial or superficial groups can be counted upon. Most presently relevant, researchers shown that fan groups, despite seeming to exist solely for the purpose of recreation, can often be counted upon to provide people with social support in times of need (Wann, 2006). As such, it might not be a stretch to suggest that bronies, who may be lacking other sources of social support, may find help from fellow fans to be a considerable draw to the fandom. In fact, as we discussed in Chapter 9, many sport fans reported being motivated to engage in their fandom precisely because of the value of belonging to a community of like-minded fans.

The same can be said for non-sport fans. O'Connor, Longman, White, and Obst (2015) interviewed Australian World of Warcraft players and found that they did, indeed, form online communities in which they both gave and received social support. Speaking to this point, we showed in Chapter 13 that bronies feel a greater psychological sense of community with their fan group than they do from their local neighborhood. In other words, whereas earlier generations may have turned to their neighbors or church groups for help, newer generations, including bronies, may be taking to their fandom for social support. We'll discuss helping behavior within the fandom in greater detail in Chapter 19. For now, though, it's enough to suggest that bronies may want to belong to the brony community precisely because of the comfort of knowing they're surrounded by others who have their back in times of need.

As we'll see in the next section, however, belongingness is only one half of a delicate balance of social factors people strive to maintain in groups.

Optimal Distinctiveness Theory

Let's return for a moment to the social identity perspective introduced in Chapter 13. In a nutshell, this perspective argues that our identity is inextricably tied to the groups we belong to. In order to maintain a healthy sense of self-esteem, people are motivated to belong to groups that make them look and feel good about themselves (Tajfel & Turner, 1979; Turner et al., 1987).

Building on this approach, Brewer (1991) proposed a theory about a concept called "optimal distinctiveness." According to this perspective, people find themselves caught between two opposing desires. On the one hand, we have the need to feel similar to others and to fit into a group (i.e., belongingness).[2] On the other hand, we also have the need to feel unique and stand out as an individual (i.e., distinctiveness).[3] Being part of a group puts these two needs into direct conflict with one another: The better we fit into a group by becoming similar to other members of the group, the more we satisfy that need to belong, but the less we feel like unique individuals. The more we distance ourselves from groups, the more we feel like unique individuals, but the more vulnerable and alone we feel.

Brewer argued that people strive to reach an optimal level of these two opposing needs. Ultimately, we don't want to disappear into large, faceless masses (lacking distinctiveness), but we don't want to stand out painfully or be a notable minority (lacking belongingness). Of course, where we find balance between the need for belongingness and distinctiveness will differ from person to person: Most of us can think about someone we know who is quite high in their need for distinctiveness and others who are quite high in the need to fit into a group.

In the end, the groups we find most appealing and will want to identify with are those that provide us with our optimal level of distinctiveness and belongingness (Leonardelli, Pickett, & Brewer, 2010). To this end, fans of different interests will often be drawn to teams, music, and other interests which provide them with this optimal distinctiveness. A person with a higher need to stand out may find themselves drawn to bands, teams, or genres which stand out (e.g., punk music, unpopular teams, indie games), while a person with a higher need to fit in may be drawn to more popular, mainstream interests (e.g., pop music, the league's most popular teams, AAA games).

Illustrating this point, Andrijiw and Hyatt (2009) interviewed Canadian hockey fans who chose to identify with a non-local team. Fans' responses indicated that the fans felt like they belonged to a group (i.e., fans of this non-local team), but also noted that within their local community they felt a sense of distinctiveness (i.e., they felt different from fans of the local team, which made up the majority of people around them). In this way, these fans gained both a sense of belongingness and a sense of distinctiveness from their team affiliation. Similar results were found for rugby fans in South Africa (Goldman, Chadwick, Funk, & Wocke, 2016).

In a similar vein, a 2009 study by Abrams analyzed data from UK youth (ages 18–21) regarding their preferred music and fan-related behaviors. Participants bought more records, attended more concerts, bought clothes and had a hairstyle consistent with other fans when it came to moderately popular music as compared to the most popular and least popular music styles. To put it simply, these young adults showed more consumption and involvement with music that was in the butter zone between being "too popular" and "too unpopular." In effect, they chose the music that provided them with the greatest degree of optimal distinctiveness. The same can be said for both furries (Reysen, Plante, Roberts, & Gerbasi, 2016) and anime fans (Reysen, Plante, Roberts, & Gerbasi, 2017c), studies of which have found that high belongingness needs and high distinctiveness needs both predict the strongest feelings of ingroup identification.

With this in mind, it makes sense to ask whether bronies derive the same balance of needing to be distinct while also needing to belong from their participation in the brony community. To do this, we examined whether the satisfaction of these two needs predicted the extent to which individual bronies identified with the brony fandom. Specifically, we asked bronies about the extent to which the fandom provided them with a sense of belongingness ("I feel included and well-integrated into the brony community," "I feel a strong sense of belongingness within the brony community") and a sense of distinctiveness ("The brony community is very unique when compared with non-brony groups," "The brony community is different and distinct compared to non-brony groups"). We also asked them about the extent to which they identified with the brony fandom ("I strongly identify with bronies in the brony community," "I am glad to be a member of the brony community," "I see myself as a member of the brony community"). Analyses showed that bronies who said that the fandom provided them with *both* belongingness and distinctiveness reported the highest degree of identification with the brony fandom (see Figure 14.2).

In short, it would seem that yet another reason why bronies are moti-

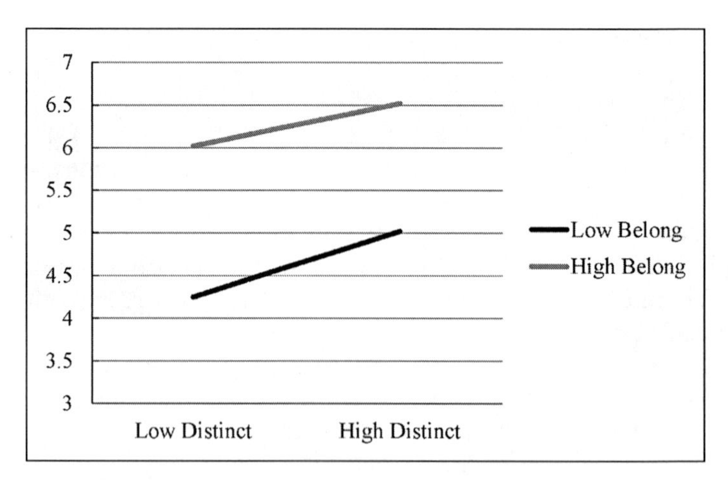

Figure 14.2. **Belongingness and distinctiveness needs being satisfied by the fandom predicting bronies' degree of identification with the brony community.**

vated to be part of the fandom is the fact that the brony community satisfies their competing needs to both fit into a group and to stand out as an individual.

Me or Somepony Like Me

As we noted in Chapter 10, bronies feel a fairly strong connection to their favorite character from *MLP*. In addition to those questions asking about the extent to which they *wished* they could be like their favorite character, we *also* examined bronies' connection to *MLP* by examining the extent to which they felt like they *were* essentially a character from the show.[4] These concepts (i.e., being or becoming a character) are consistent with research by communications and media scholars regarding identification with fictional characters. For example, Cohen (2001) defines identification as "an imaginative process through which an audience member assumes the identity, goals, and perspective of a character" (p. 261). Indeed, Igartua and Barrios' (2012) measure of identification includes a dimension about the sensation of becoming the character. In effect, what happens to the character is experienced empathically as though it were happening to oneself. This is similar to, but not quite the same as, the concept of wishful identification—"the desire to be like or act like the character" (Hoffner & Buchanan, 2005, p. 325); research with anime fans has found that these two constructs, identification and wishful identification, are closely related to one another, but not quite the same as one another (Reysen, Plante, Roberts, & Gerbasi, in press).

Let's first look at what this phenomenon looks like in a non–*MLP* context. In one study, participants' degree of identification with their favorite character in a reality television program was found to be related to the perceived realism of the show, with paying greater attention to show, with feeling a greater sense of cognitive and emotional involvement in the show, and ultimately greater satisfaction with the show and more post-show online activities (Godlewski & Perse, 2010). Identification with one's favorite media characters has been found in other studies to be correlated with feelings of being in a sort of "parasocial relationship" with the character, a greater sense of similarity, and more liking and imitation of the character (Dibble, Hartmann, & Rosaen, 2016; Kistler, Rodgers, Power, Austin, & Hill, 2010; Shen, 2009). Wishful identification has also been found to predict becoming more transported into a piece of fictional media (Cuesta, Martinez, & Cuesta, 2017).

Okay, so it appears that fans of all sorts often find themselves wishing to be like a fictional media character and, in some cases, even feel a sense of similarity or identification with these characters. And, for the most part, these experiences can powerfully affect how fans experience the media itself, leading to more immersive viewing experiences and greater participation in fan-related activities.

But does this happen among bronies—are some bronies motivated by this felt connection to their favorite pony character from the show? In the present research, we tested exactly that, measuring bronies' desire to become one of the characters from the show with three items ("I feel/believe I have a special kinship with the ponies on *MLP:FIM*," "I feel/believe that I really could 'fit in with' the ponies on *MLP:FIM*," "I feel that if I could I would not hesitate to become an actual pony on *MLP:FIM*"). We went one step further and measured the extent to which bronies actually felt like one of the characters from the show with four items ("I feel/believe that I am NOT 100% human, but in fact truly 'part' pony," "I feel/believe that I share personality characteristics with the ponies on *MLP:FIM*," "I feel/believe that I have a mystical/spiritual connection with the ponies on MLP:*FIM*," "If I 'cosplay' (dress as a *MLP:FIM* character) I feel/believe that I have a stronger connection to the ponies on *MLP:FIM*").[5] We also examined some of the functions that the fandom fulfills for bronies (see Chapter 9) to see whether they might help to explain why there might be a link between identifying as a brony and feeling a connection to a character from the show.

Our first finding was that those who identified more strongly with the brony fandom also showed a greater desire to become like a character from the show (see top pathway in Figure 14.3). This link seems to be driven by those for whom the show provides a sense of purpose or meaning and, to a lesser extent, those who seek to escape the hassles of everyday life. In other words, for at least some bronies, a character from the show may be a source of guidance for them or allow them to think about ways they could otherwise transcend their normal lives.[6]

In Figure 14.4 we ran the same analyses, this time replacing "wanting to become a character" with *actually* feeling similar to a character from the show. Once again we found that highly identified fans were more likely to report feeling a greater sense of identification with a character from the show. In addition, this connection seemed to be present for all three motivations (the fandom provides a sense of purpose, a sense of escape, and a chance for social interaction). That said, as with the previous question, the largest predictor by far was the extent to which the fandom provided bronies with a sense of purpose or meaning in life.

Taken together, these results suggest that at least some in the brony fandom may be motivated by the desire to become like a character from the show, or even by a felt sense of similarity to a character from the show. This may be especially likely for those for whom the show and the fandom provides them with a sense of purpose or meaning in their life.

Since the present findings seem to suggest that it's important to know

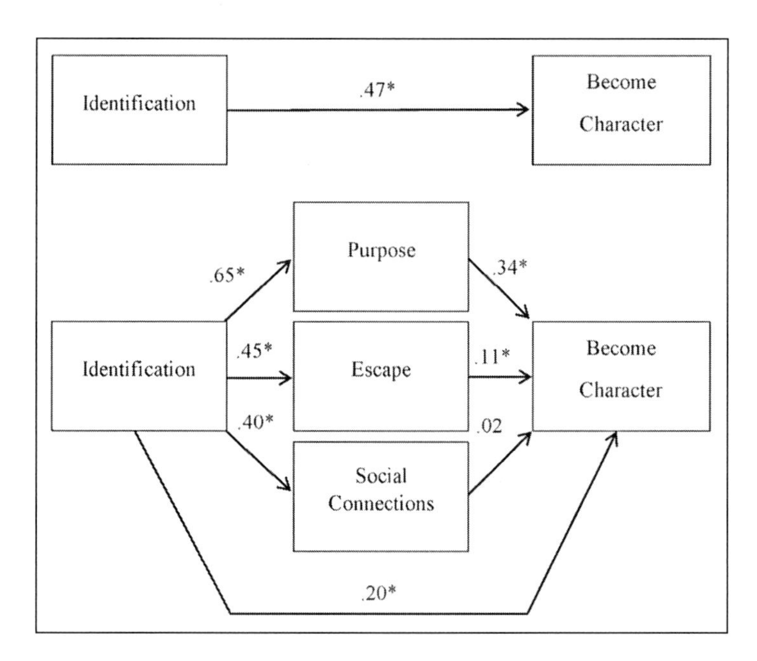

Figure 14.3. **Fandom functions explaining the relationship between identifying with the brony fandom and desire to become a pony character from the show *MLP*. (**This effect is statistically significant.*)**

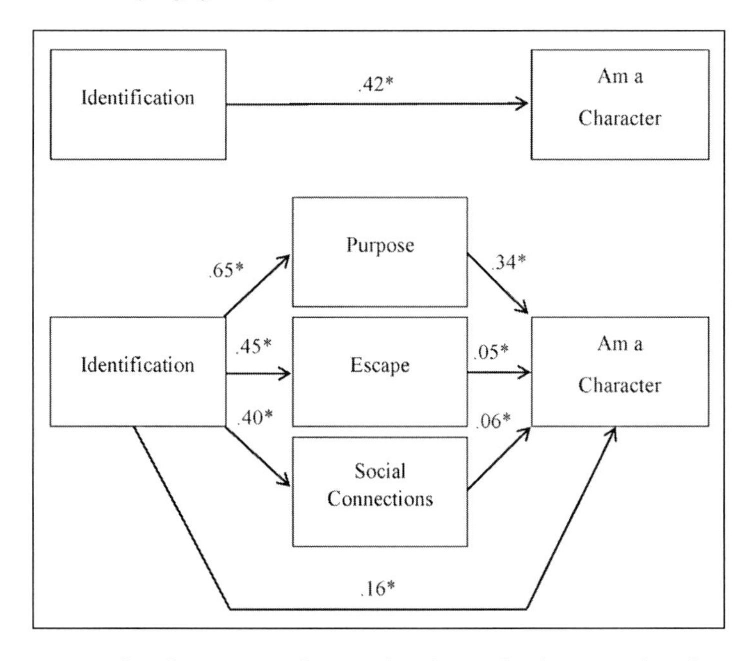

Figure 14.4. **Fandom functions explaining the relationship between identifying with the brony fandom and feeling like a character from the show. (**This effect is statistically significant.*)**

whether a brony is getting a sense of purpose or meaning from the show, it's also worth knowing whether bronies, as a group, tend to feel a sense of purpose in their lives in general. We examined this question in the following section, comparing bronies to a non-brony community sample.

"Who am I and why am I here?" Purpose in Life

McKnight and Kashdan (2009) define purpose in life as "a central, self-organizing life aim that organizes and stimulates goals, manages behaviors, and provides a sense of meaning" (p. 242).[7] At first glance, it might seem trite or trivial to ask about this topic: Does it *really* matter if someone feels like their life has a sense of significance or meaning, especially since none of us can really know for sure *why* we're here?

As it turns out, however, having a sense of purpose in one's life is actually quite important from a psychological perspective. Researchers have shown, for example, that those who have a sense of purpose or meaning in their lives tend to report greater psychological well-being than those who lack a feeling of purpose or meaning (Scheier et al., 2006). Indeed, Ryff (1995) argues that having purpose in one's life should be considered a core component of one's psychological well-being.

And while it's easy to trivialize leisure activities as "that silly thing we do for fun" or time-wasting and frivolous, studies suggest that taking time for enjoyable leisure activities is related to having a greater sense of purpose in one's life (Pressman et al., 2009). To see how, it's useful to look at studies on how people spend their leisure time, including, for example, consuming screen media.[8] In their studies of media use, Oliver and Bartsch (2010, 2011) make a distinction between *enjoying* media and *appreciating* media. Enjoyment is associated with hedonism (e.g., pleasure-seeking), while appreciation is more closely tied to seeking a meaningful experience.[9] In general, appreciation, rather than mere enjoyment, tends to inspire the audience to think about important questions such as their purpose in life. Chadborn and colleagues (2017) argue that fandom can often be a source of inspiration and answers about life, with many fans being motivated to participate in their fandom by the fact that it provides them with this sense of meaning and significance.

To this end, we examined whether bronies report gaining more purpose in life from their fan groups (including *MLP*) than non-brony college students get from their respective fan interests (e.g., music, film, sport). Participants (bronies and non-bronies) were asked to rate the extent that they find purpose

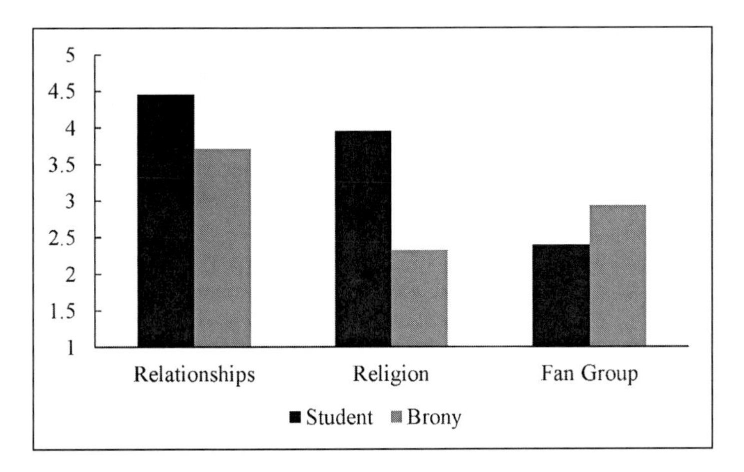

Figure 14.5. **Comparing bronies and non-bronies on where they find purpose in life.**

and meaning in life from their personal relationships (e.g., friends, family), religion or spiritual beliefs, and their fan communities (1 = *provide no purpose* to 5 = *provide essential purpose*).

As shown in Figure 14.5, students and bronies alike both said that the biggest source of meaning and purpose in their life came from their relationships. That said, bronies did score lower than non-bronies in this tendency. The same was true for religion, where non-bronies were significantly more likely to say that they got a sense of meaning from their religion. In contrast, bronies were more likely than non-bronies to say that their fandom provided them with a sense of meaning and purpose. In short, while bronies do not seek the fandom as their primary source of purpose or meaning in life, they are *more* likely to do so than other fans are, suggesting that the brony community may provide some purpose and meaning for some bronies which motivates them to engage with the fandom.

Conclusion

Across several chapters (e.g., Chapter 9, Chapter 13) we've looked at possible motivations driving bronies to become part of the fandom. The present chapter adds additional motivations to that list: Bronies were more likely than others to gain social support from their fan community, identify more strongly with the fandom when it satisfies their combined need for belongingness and distinctiveness, gives them characters to aspire to become like, and can even provide them with a sense of meaning and purpose in their lives. This list should not be seen as an exhaustive list of all of the potential reasons a brony can be a brony: Indeed, every brony is likely motivated by a unique combination of many of these factors and more. If nothing else, however, these chapters do suggest that a complete story of what makes *MLP* and the brony fandom so compelling for bronies will need to be complex and nuanced in its recognition of a myriad of motivational factors. In the same way that no two ponies are exactly alike, no two bronies are in the fandom for the exact same reasons.

Chapter 15

Inter- and Intra-Fandom Dynamics

"I motion that Rainbow Dash be declared the most awesome pony in Ponyville."
—Scootaloo (Season 2, Episode 8, The Mysterious Mare Do Well)

As a general rule, people tend to believe that the groups they belong to are better than the groups they *don't* belong to—something called *ingroup favoritism*.[1] This makes a certain amount of sense. After all, if you didn't think the group you belonged to was awesome, why would you waste the time and effort to join it in the first place?[2] But while this ingroup favoritism might apply to the groups that are considered "important" to society—the school we attend or the career we work in—can the same be said for more "trivial" groups, like the sports teams we're fans of or the people we hang out with to watch a particular television show? Does a brony *really* give preferential treatment toward another brony simply because they both happen to like the same show about magical friendship equines?

In this chapter we'll consider data from our studies showing that bronies may well consider other bronies to be "better than average" as compared to members of the non-brony general population. We'll then look at what happens when bronies turn a critical eye inward, toward their own fandom: Is there such a thing as status and elitism in the brony community and, if so, what makes a person, as Rarity puts it, "the type of pony every pony should know?" We'll finish up by turning our attention once more to the outside world, not with a critical eye, but with a focus on how bronies grow the fandom: How and why do they seek out new recruits for the brony fandom?

"My fandom's better than yours!"

According to social identity theory, people have a need to feel good about themselves—something they do, in part, by strategically managing the groups they belong to (Tajfel & Turner, 1979; Turner, Hogg, Oakes, Reicher, & Wetherell, 1987). As an example of this, in a classic psychological study, researchers found that university students were *more* likely to wear clothing featuring their university's athletics teams the day after there team had *won*, but were *less* likely to do so the day after their team had *lost* (Cialdini et al., 1976). Why? Because being associated with a winning team boosted their self-esteem, while being associated with a losing team was bad for their self-esteem.

In the same vein, people also tend to strategically compare themselves to *other* groups to make themselves look better by comparison—a phenomenon known as making downward social comparisons. Traditionally, this has been studied within the context of racial or sexual minorities, where members of one group compare themselves to members of other groups who are doing worse off than they are, allowing them to see themselves as superior by comparison. Anecdotally speaking, we have witnessed this first-hand in our own research on members of fan groups. For example, while studying members of mainstream fan groups, it is not uncommon to see them derogate members of other, less-mainstream fan groups, like anime fans (Reysen & Shaw, 2016). After all, if someone's going to make fun of you for wearing the jersey of your favorite player or painting your face to show team spirit, what easier way to deflect that criticism and protect your self-esteem than by pointing to a group of people who are even *weirder* than you, like those people who cosplay as their favorite animated characters?[3]

So we strategically juggle our group identities and compare them to others in ways that make us look good. As it turns out, another way we manage our self-esteem is with a healthy dose of bias, something called ingroup favoritism (Brewer, 1999). In short, one of the assumptions inherent in many of these strategies (or perhaps as a by-product of using these ego-boosting strategies) is a tendency for us to believe that members of our group are simply *better* than members of other groups. For example, in a series of studies, researchers found that people assigned to completely arbitrary groups (e.g., people who overestimate the number of dots on a screen vs. people who underestimate the number of dots on a screen) tended to give preferential treatment to those in their own group and to treat members of the other group worse (Tajfel, Billig, Bundy, & Flament, 1971).

So can we find evidence that bronies do the same thing? In short, yes. Bronies, and indeed members of pretty much any fan group we've studied (e.g., furries, anime fans, sport fans), tend to think more positively about members of their own fan group than they do about members of other groups or even the average person. In a 2011 study of more than 3,600 bronies, we went one step further, looking at the factors which predicted the *extent* to which bronies showed this tendency to view bronies more positively. Specifically, participants were asked to indicate the extent to which they agreed with statements like "If I see someone wearing an *MLP* shirt I immediately look more positively at that person." Participants largely agreed with this statement, a sentiment reflected personally by at least one of the self-described bronies authoring this book.[4]

Participants who scored higher on this measure of ingroup favoritism also tended to score higher on two other measures. The first was the extent to which they strongly belonged to the brony fandom (e.g., "I feel like I am not alone in this world because of the presence of other bronies"). In other words, bronies who feel a stronger sense of belonging to the brony community exhibit stronger tendencies toward ingroup preference for bronies. The other measure was the extent to which people had a high need for uniqueness (e.g., "I need to feel distinctly different from the majority of people"). This means that people who have a strong need to stand out and be different are also more prone to this tendency to see other bronies in a more favorable light, simply for being brony.

In a 2013 follow-up study of nearly 4,300 bronies, we again asked participants to indicate the extent to which they both identified as a brony (whether the label of "brony" was important to them) and the extent to which they showed favoritism toward bronies. This time, however, we asked an additional set of questions about participants' morality, including questions about the importance of being loyal to one's group. Sure enough, in a finding that Rainbow Dash herself would approve of, participants who identified more strongly as bronies also stated that it was more important to be loyal to one's groups which, in turn, was associated with a greater tendency to see other bronies in a favorable light.

These findings make a certain amount of sense, especially when you consider that bronies themselves are a fairly stigmatized fan group (see Chapter 17 for more on this). Bronies, like other stigmatized minority groups, often suffer because of their stigmatized group identity, often finding themselves the subject of ridicule or hostility (Meyer, 2003; Mock, Plante, Reysen, & Gerbasi, 2010; Roberts, Plante, Gerbasi, & Reysen, 2015a). What they may gain from this identity, however, is a strong sense of community and a willingness to help one another; after all, if the world isn't going to be kind to them, they need to be kind to each other. For this reason, it makes perfect sense why, all else equal, a brony might prefer to have a brony for a roommate, to hire a brony over another job candidate, or to help a brony in need when they might decide they simply don't have the time or money to help someone else.

"Real" vs. "Fake" Bronies: Gatekeeping, Status and Entitlement

It's clear from the research up to this point that bronies, like any group, readily compare themselves to outsiders. But do they ever turn their focus inward on the fandom itself? After all, if you can make yourself feel better by comparing yourself to someone worse off who's outside of your group, you can probably do the same to a member of your own group if you're in a pinch (e.g., if there's no one else around to compare yourself to).

Anecdotally speaking, there's plenty of evidence to suggest that such intra-fandom comparisons occur within fan groups, and that they can be a source of problems. For example, the issue of status, elitism, and gatekeeping frequently rears its ugly head in the comic book fandom, where newer members of the fandom may find themselves intimidated by the knowledge or outright snobbery of long-time, die-hard fans. The stereotype was even made into a recurring character in the long-running television show *The Simpsons*: Comic Book Guy. The character, an owner of a comic book shop, could be regularly found berating customers for not knowing trivial facts about a particular series, something that could very well drive newer fans away from these fandoms.

This elitism or snobbery may be tied to two related phenomena—entitlement and gatekeeping. Entitlement focuses on the tendency for some fans to feel that they deserve special treatment as a result of their devotion to a subject. The issue of fan entitlement has arisen in numerous high-profile series, perhaps most prominently in recent history with respect to the *Star Wars* prequel trilogy. Despite the fact that George Lucas was, at the time, both the creator of *Star Wars* and the owner of the *Star Wars* franchise, it could safely be said that Lucas was entitled to be the final arbiter of what was part of the "official" *Star Wars* universe. Nevertheless, there was considerable backlash from long-time fans of the franchise regarding many of Lucas' decisions, including many fans vehemently insisting that Lucas bend to the will of fans regarding how characters should act, what was accepted canon, and the tone and style of the films themselves.[5] Similar examples of entitlement can be found in other fandoms, such as the anime and furry fandoms, where long-time fans of artists may feel entitled to special treatment from their favorite content creators (Plante, Reysen, Roberts, & Gebrasi, 2017; Shaw, Plante, Reysen, Roberts, & Gerbasi, 2016).

The second related phenomenon, gatekeeping, is the idea that someone's expertise in an area qualifies them to judge whether another person qualifies as a "real" fan or not. For example, someone may determine that a player of video games doesn't get to call themselves a "gamer" because they don't play enough games, the right genre of games, or know enough about the history of a game series. At best, gatekeeping may be irritating to those who fall victim to it, and at worst it may be a deterrent to future fans, who may find such criticism discouraging or give the impression that the fandom itself is a hostile place they would prefer to avoid.

So what does research on the brony fandom show? Do bronies take after Fluttershy—full of compassion, kindness, and understanding—or are they more like Rarity—do they crave status and whine when they don't get their way?

At least one study suggests that there *is* a link between greater identification with the brony fandom and a sense of having more status than other bronies. In a recent 2018 survey of 221 bronies, participants were asked about the extent to which they identified with the brony fandom and, more importantly, to indicate how much they agreed with statements about their relative status in the fandom like "Status-wise, I would say that I am probably in a higher standing in the fandom than the average brony" and "Other bronies look up to me as an example of what a brony should be." While bronies, as a whole, tended to score reasonably low in their agreement with these items, those who more strongly identified with the fandom were more likely to agree with these sorts of statements. This suggests there may be at least *some* truth to the idea that those who consider themselves to be "more brony" also tend to see themselves as someone to be looked up to and admired in the fandom. In fact, it may be illuminating to note that in a 2016 study, bronies who identified more strongly with the fandom were also the least shy about being bronies—possibly because it was a particular point of pride for them.

That same 2016 study also provided evidence of entitlement within the brony fandom. Specifically, those who more strongly identified as a brony were significantly more likely to agree with statements suggesting that they were entitled to special treatment: "Artists are obligated to go above and beyond expectations to fulfill their fans' requests" and "If I email an artist, I expect them to email me back." If you find yourself thinking that such entitlement is uncouth or rude, you'll also find it validating to hear that the same study also found that these same people also agreed "It's acceptable for other bronies to act immaturely" or "It's acceptable for other bronies to swear or use explicit language when younger fans are around." In future studies it might be worth testing whether a lack of self-criticism or lack of social skills explains some of these findings.

Returning to the 2018 study, we do find evidence that gatekeeping is present in the brony fandom. Bronies were asked to indicate the extent to which they personally engaged with the franchise, including watching the show, purchasing merchandise, and creating fan content themselves. This allowed us to compare highly-engaged fans (those who spent a lot of time and resources on the show) to those who were lower in engagement. We then asked them to indicate the extent to which they agreed with a number of beliefs related to gatekeeping, including "You can't call yourself a brony unless you've been in the fandom for awhile" and "Some people who call themselves bronies aren't 'true' bronies." Like with entitlement, most bronies strongly disagreed with these opinions. However, bronies who engaged with the franchise the most were also the highest-scoring on this measure of gatekeeping.

In sum, there does seem to be some evidence that a minority of bronies are comparing themselves to other bronies, possibly as a means of attaining status or because of a felt sense of entitlement. While it can't be stated enough that these behaviors are by no means the norm for the brony fandom, they do illustrate that *some* undesirable behaviors exist within the brony community because of this sense of elitism, which can have the unintended effect of driving away content creators (entitlement) or new fans to the series (gatekeeping).[6]

Speaking of new bronies in the fandom, let's change gears for a moment and look at the opposite of gatekeeping—bringing new members into the fandom's ranks.

"Join the herd!" New Brony Recruitment

When you consider that the origin of the brony fandom was an online message board for cartoon and comic fans, it becomes apparent just how important word-of-mouth advertising was for the initial growth of the brony community (Connelly, 2017). After all, the show itself was not intended for an adult audience and, as such, its advertising was primarily directed at a young audience and not intended to appeal to adults. This chapter's author can attest to the fact that his own interest in the show was a direct result of a brony friend of his asking him to sit down and give the show a try.[7]

While it's certainly not uncommon for fans to proselytize about their hobbies—after all, they are, by definition, people who are passionate about the things they love—bronies have earned a particular reputation for being persistent when it comes to trying to win over new fans to the show.[8] Whether it's because many early fans were drawn to the show by word of mouth themselves or because fans believe that the community can't grow on its own without recruitment, bronies soon earned this reputation. So much so, in fact, that expressions like "Join the herd!" became popular memes among the brony community.

So just how many bronies actively seek out new recruits for the fandom? The question may be a time-sensitive one, based in part on the changing dynamics of the fandom itself. In its earliest years, the brony community was a small, fledging one—an unlikely group of people who had collectively stumbled upon a gem of a show they were never intended to discover. But, as seasons passed and the fandom grew—both in size and in mainstream media recognition—it likely became less necessary for fans to spread word of the show via word of mouth. As we prepare to enter the show's ninth season, it's unlikely that fans are spreading word of the show with the same vehemence that they did in its early seasons. By this point, most of society has heard about the show and the fact that some adults enjoy watching it. It's likely that most people have made up their mind about whether or not they're going to watch the show. For this reason alone, it's unlikely that any of our future studies will look at attempts to recruit new bronies into the fandom.

When we first assessed attempts to convince people to "join the herd," we did so a bit late in the game—in a 2014 study of nearly 1900 bronies. While far from the show's latest season, it was also well into the show's fourth season, so it was hardly catching bronies in the midst of the fandom's most rapid period of growth. Nevertheless, undeterred, we asked participants about the extent to which they had actively attempted to bring others into the brony fandom. Specifically, we asked people whether they had never bothered to try, whether they had not actively tried (but talked to others about it), whether they had actively tried (with no success), or whether they had tried and succeeded in recruiting people into the brony fandom.

The results in Figure 15.1 make it clear that, despite the popular belief that all bronies incessantly and aggressively try to recruit new fans of the show, only about one in four bronies (26.8 percent) have actively tried to convince people to watch the show. That said, a couple of points are worth noting here. First, because this data was collected during the show's fourth season, it's entirely possible that many of our participants were not "first-adopter" fans, and thus lacked the same passion to actively recruit others. Alternatively, it may also be the case that by the fourth season, interest in growing the fandom had diminished, since the fandom had already grown about as much as it was going to.

The second point worth noting is that while most bronies were not actively trying to recruit new bronies, most bronies *did* nevertheless talk about the show with others. While bronies may not have considered this to be "actively recruiting," outsiders may consider this passionate discussion of the show to be an *attempt* to persuade them to watch it. Thus, even if it were the case that most bronies were not actively recruiting new fans, seeing the passion with which bronies spoke about the show may have led to the public's perception that bronies were going out of their way to convince others to watch the show.

In a final set of analyses, we can look at the factors which predict which bronies will actively attempt to recruit others into the fandom. Perhaps unsur-

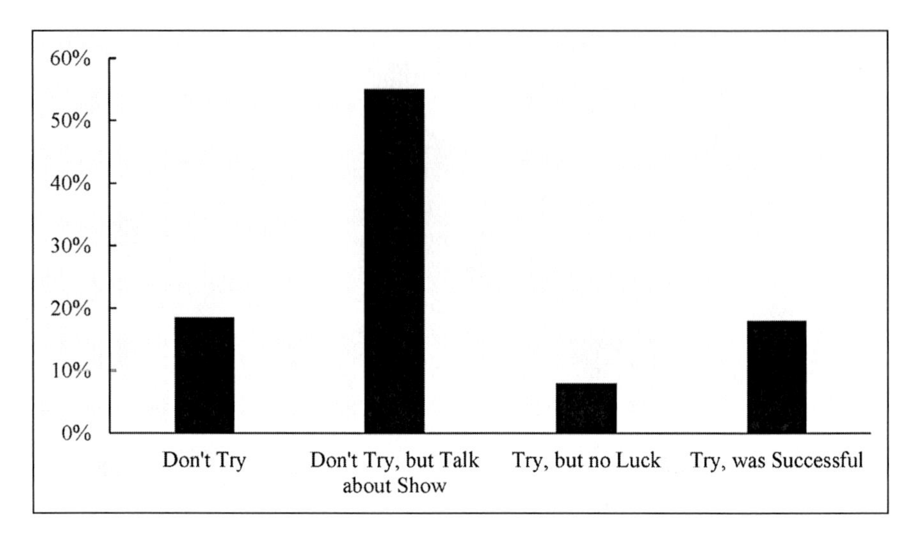

Figure 15.1. **Percentage of bronies engaging in the recruitment of new bronies.**

prising to some readers, those who consider themselves to be the biggest fans of the show (e.g., the ones most likely to agree with statements like "I have rescheduled work to accommodate my brony interests" and "I want everyone to know I am connected to my fan interest") were the most likely to actively recruit new bronies. What's more interesting, however, are two motivational factors that may explain this link. Specifically, to the extent that being a fan of the show gave fans a sense of purpose and to the extent that it afforded them the opportunity to belong to a group of friends, being a fan was more likely to lead to active recruitment of new fans. In other words, simply being a fan of the show might not be enough or fully explain why bronies would try to get others to watch their show. Only to the extent that the show was meaningful to them or provided them with a sense of community did bronies decide to try and pull others into the fandom. Those who "merely liked" the show as a source of recreation but nothing more were not the ones trying to pull others into the fandom.

Despite the fact that some people may have been annoyed with bronies' persistence in trying to recruit them into watching a show, it may well be the case that bronies who try to recruit others to watch the show may have thought they were doing them a favor, not just introducing them to an enjoyable television show, but helping them find a deeper sense of meaning in their life or a community they could belong to. Perhaps, in a very literal way, they were trying to follow in the hoofprints of Twilight Sparkle and spread the magic of friendship themselves.

Chapter 16

Personality Profiles of People Who Prefer Ponies

"But now I realize that who I am is not the same as what I am. I may have been born a dragon, but Equestria and my pony friends have taught me how to be kind, loyal, and true!"

—*Spike* (*Season 2, Episode 21,* Dragon Quest)

"Personality" is one of those words that people throw around in day-to-day conversations, usually as a way to describe someone. But have you ever stopped to think what the term *actually* means? Your friend might describe someone as being "*full* of personality," causing you to form a mental image of a quirky, eccentric person. Conversely, if they told you that someone "lacks personality" this likely conjures up a picture of someone who's boring, drab, and generally uninteresting. We don't stop there, of course. We have all sorts of words to describe *different* personalities: shy, outgoing, cranky, happy go lucky, nerdy, kind, competitive, risk-seeking, cheap, polite, brash—to name just a few! But talking about whether someone *has* personality or not, or different *kinds* of personalities doesn't answer our original question. Just what are we talking about when we talk about someone's personality?

Psychologists, as it turns out, spend a great deal of time thinking about such things, and can shed some light on this question. In short, personality is a person's "characteristic patterns of thought, emotion, and behavior," along with "the psychological mechanisms—hidden or not—behind those patterns" (Funder, 2007, pp. 1–2). In other words, your personality is any consistency in the way you think, feel, or act that distinguishes you from others. So if, day after day, you go out of your way to chat with people around you, one could say this tendency is part of who you are—your personality. In contrast, if having one bad day where you act grumpy and off-putting is uncharacteristic of you, we would not consider this to be part of your personality.

So how do psychologists *study* something as broad as personality? After all, there are hundreds, even thousands of things we could consider characteristic about the way each of us thinks, feels, and behaves. It seems like psychologists have given themselves an impossible task! And even if they *could* make sense of it all, so what? What's the big deal if one person has a shy personality while another person has an outgoing personality. Isn't this just applying labels to people? Does it actually tell us anything *meaningful*?

These are questions psychologists who study personality have devoted their careers to answering. They make sense of this chaos by recognizing that, despite the uniqueness of every person on the planet, some common traits do emerge across situations, cultures, and over a person's lifespan (Costa & McCrae, 1997; Stangor, 2010).[1] These traits, in turn, are more than mere labels: They tend to be fairly good predictors of peoples' behavior. For example, if I told you that two friends were coming a party, one who was outgoing and one who was shy, you could probably guess which friend would be more likely to strike up a conversation with you and which would be more likely to stand in the corner.

Across decades of studying personality, researchers have come up with a variety of models for categorizing all of the different personality traits people can express. In the present chapter we'll focus on the best-known and most frequently-used model, known as the "Big Five" model. First, we'll review what these "Big Five" dimensions of personality are and what they can tell us about a person's behavior. Then we'll review the little research which *does* exist looking at these big five personality traits in fan groups. Next, we'll report the findings of our research, which compares bronies and non-bronies on these personality traits and looks at what these traits tell us about how individual bronies experience the fandom. We finish with a warning about relying too much on personality to understand people and the question of whether personality is something people are stuck with or whether it's something that can change.

The Big Five Dimensions of Personality

The big five personality dimensions began with researchers trying to compile and organize lists of all the different ways people differ from one another (John, 1990). To get an idea of the scope of this task, the earliest personality psychologists stared by scouring the dictionary for *every* word that could be used to describe people.[2] The result was a list of more than 18,000 different adjectives! Researchers (e.g., Cattell) worked on whittling this list down by trimming away words that were essentially the same as other words in the list.[3] Next, they gave their trimmed-down list of words to participants in studies to rate each word on numerous dimensions. This allowed researchers to put numbers to each word and compare them to one another mathematically (McAdams, 1997). Analyses repeatedly found that the different words tended to fall into five fairly distinct dimensions. As repeated studies found these same five dimensions emerging over and over again, researchers began referring to them as the big five, and they eventually became the most widely-used and researched model of personality (Gosling, Rentfrow, & Swann, 2003).

Each of these five dimensions can be thought of as a bipolar continuum: Everyone falls somewhere between two extreme ends of each one. As such, someone's overall personality can be summarized as their scores on each of these five dimensions (John & Srivastava, 2008). The five dimensions themselves can be easily remembered with the acronym OCEAN, with each letter reflecting one of the five dimensions:

1. Openness to new experiences (e.g., adventurous, curious) versus closedness to experience (e.g., conservative, risk-avoiding)
2. Conscientiousness (e.g., organized, responsible) versus lack of direction (e.g., careless, disorderly)
3. Extraversion (e.g., talkative, outgoing) versus introversion (e.g., quiet, shy)
4. Agreeableness (e.g., kind, warm) versus antagonism (e.g., unfriendly, cold)
5. Neuroticism (e.g., anxious, tense) versus emotional stability (e.g., calm, stable)

Far from being trivial labels, researchers later discovered that where a person scores on each of these dimensions tells you a *lot* about their behavior—at an individual level, at an interpersonal level, and at an institutional level (Ozer & Benet-Martínez, 2006). We'll spare you the hassle of reading hundreds of articles on the subject and provide you with a very brief summary of some of just *some* of the outcomes associated with each of the different dimensions:

1. Openness: People who score more toward the openness end of this dimension tend to worry more about existential concerns, become more readily inspired, pursue more artistic interests, and tend to be more politically liberal.
2. Conscientiousness: People who score more toward the conscientiousness end of this dimension tend to be more religious, take fewer risks

and live longer, do better at their jobs, are more satisfied with their families, and engage in less criminal behavior.

3. Extraversion: People who score more toward the extraversion end of this dimension tend to score higher on measures of psychological well-being, be happier with their relationships, volunteer more, and tend to be more satisfied with their jobs.
4. Agreeableness: People who score more toward the agreeableness end of this dimension tend to be more religious, are more satisfied in their relationships, and engage in less criminal behavior.
5. Neuroticism: People who score more toward the neuroticism end of this dimension tend to be lower in psychological well-being, have more problems coping, experience more anxiety and depression and have more problems in their interpersonal relationships and at their jobs.

Personality and Fans

To date, there has been a considerable amount of research on personality, especially when it comes to these big five dimensions. In contrast, there has been comparatively *little* research focusing specifically on the personality traits of fans. This is due in no small part to the fact that there's been little psychological research on fans in general. In this section we'll review what little research *has* been done on the subject and look at what personality traits tell us about fans and fan behavior.

In one study, researchers measured U.S. college students' big five personality trait scores, along with their tendency to experience parasocial interactions with a favorite athlete[4] (Sun, 2010). The study showed that fans who scored higher on neuroticism, openness, and conscientiousness were more likely to experience parasocial interactions with their favorite athlete. In another study of sport fans, Aiken, Bee, and Walker (2018) found that extraversion and emotional stability were associated with more obsessive consumption of sport-related media (but being closed to experience was not). A third study found that sport fans who scored higher on extraversion, agreeableness, and openness spent more time on social media and were more likely, at least for those who were high in extraversion, to use social media to seek out recognition from others (Kim, Kim, & Kim, 2017). Taken together, studies such as these make it clear that a sport fan's personality can tell us a few things about how their interest in sport can manifest itself.

In recent years researchers have begun looking at less-popular categories of fans, including fans of geek culture, furries, and anime. For example, McCain, Gentile, and Campbell (2015) found that members of geek culture who scored higher in neuroticism, extraversion, and openness were more active in their engagement and consumption of fandom-related material (e.g., watching more shows, cosplaying more). Openness is also relevant to members of the furry fandom: Furries who score higher in openness experience a greater sense of connection to their fursonas (i.e., anthropomorphic animal representations of themselves; Reysen, Plante, Roberts, & Gerbasi, 2019). And among anime fans, cosplayers were more likely than non-cosplaying fans to score higher not only in openness, but also in extraversion, agreeableness, conscientiousness, and neuroticism (Reysen, Plante, Roberts, & Gerbasi, 2018b). Other studies of cosplayers have found that neuroticism is a particularly important trait to study, as cosplayers who score higher in neuroticism also tend to blur the lines between fantasy and reality and are more at risk of becoming disconnected from reality altogether (Reyes et al., 2017).

Studies such as these have shown that personality helps us to predict differences between fans within a particular fan group. But at least one study has also suggested that members of different fandoms differ in their average scores on these personality dimensions (Reysen, Plante, Roberts, Gerbasi, & Shaw, 2016). In this study, researchers measured the personality scores of anime fans, furries, fantasy sport fans, and a group of random college students. They found that anime fans were the most introverted, least conscientious, and least agreeable of the groups. Fantasy sport fans, in contrast, scored the lowest in neuroticism, while furries scored the highest on openness to new experiences. Put simply, these findings illustrate that studying personality can help us better understand fans—both specific fan behaviors but also differences between fandoms.

With this in mind, it's worth asking whether there's anything about the personality of bronies that makes them stand out.

Bronies versus Non-Bronies

To examine whether bronies' personalities differed from that of college students and members of the general public, we asked members of each of these groups to complete a short measure of the big five personality dimensions (Gosling et al., 2003). As shown in Figure 16.1, bronies tended to be more introverted (less extroverted) and less conscientious than the other two samples. Bolstering the argument we'll make in Chapter 18 that the brony fandom tends to be good for bronies' well-being, bronies also scored slightly higher on emotional stability (i.e., lower neuroticism) than the other two groups. Interestingly, this personality profile of bronies is strikingly similar to that of anime fans (Reysen, Plante, Roberts, Gerbasi, & Shaw, 2016). And while bronies may be more considerably more introverted than the comparison groups, for

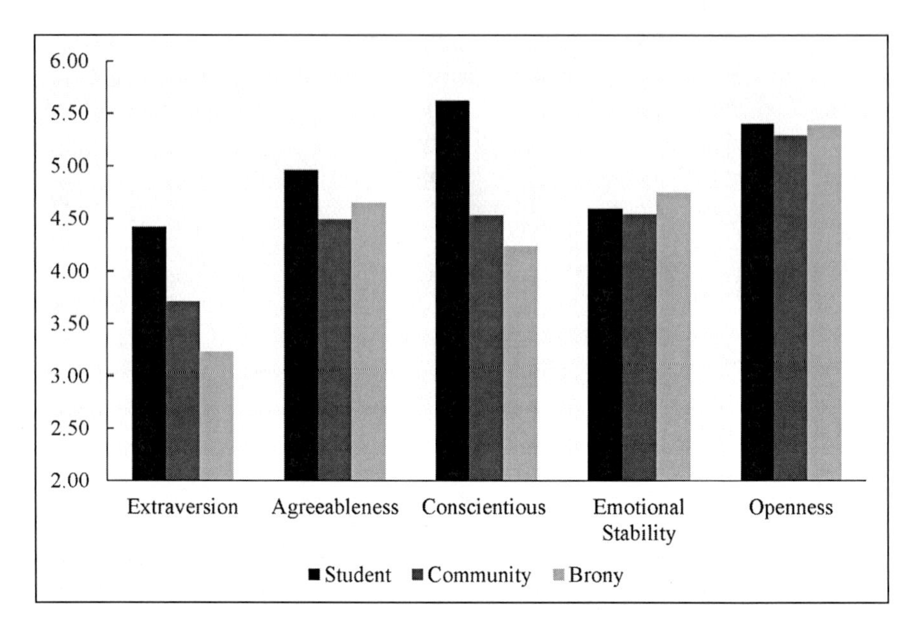

***Figure 16.1.* Big five personality dimensions of students, community members, and bronies.**

the most part, the differences between bronies and the other groups were not dramatic. This suggests that where bronies *do* differ from non-bronies in terms of personality, the difference is a matter of degree and not a matter of being *categorically* different.

As a quick aside: For the introverts reading this book, it may be worth picking up a copy of Susan Cain's 2012 book *Quiet: The Power of Introverts in a World That Can't Stop Talking*. In her work, Cain outlines how Western cultures tend to be set up in ways that benefit extroverts. Illustrating this point, a study of non-anime-fans found that, to the extent non-fans perceived anime fans as introverted, they also tended to want to distance themselves from anime fans (Reysen, Plante, Roberts, Gerbasi, Mohebpour, & Gamboa, 2016). On its face, this might seem to suggest that it's a bad thing to be an introvert, and indeed, some work suggests that, to the extent introverts think this is the case, they may experience lower psychological well-being (Lawn, Slemp, & Vella-Brodrick, 2018). But don't despair! Cain's work also reveals that there are numerous *positive* aspects to introversion too, including greater empathy, creativity, and academic achievement (Cain, 2012). If nothing else, the detriments of introversion may not be as devastating as they seem at first glance. In a later study by Reysen and colleagues, the researchers found no evidence of prejudice toward anime fans due to their introversion (Reysen et al., 2016). In fact, anime fans, as introverts, were considered to be more nerdy, but this

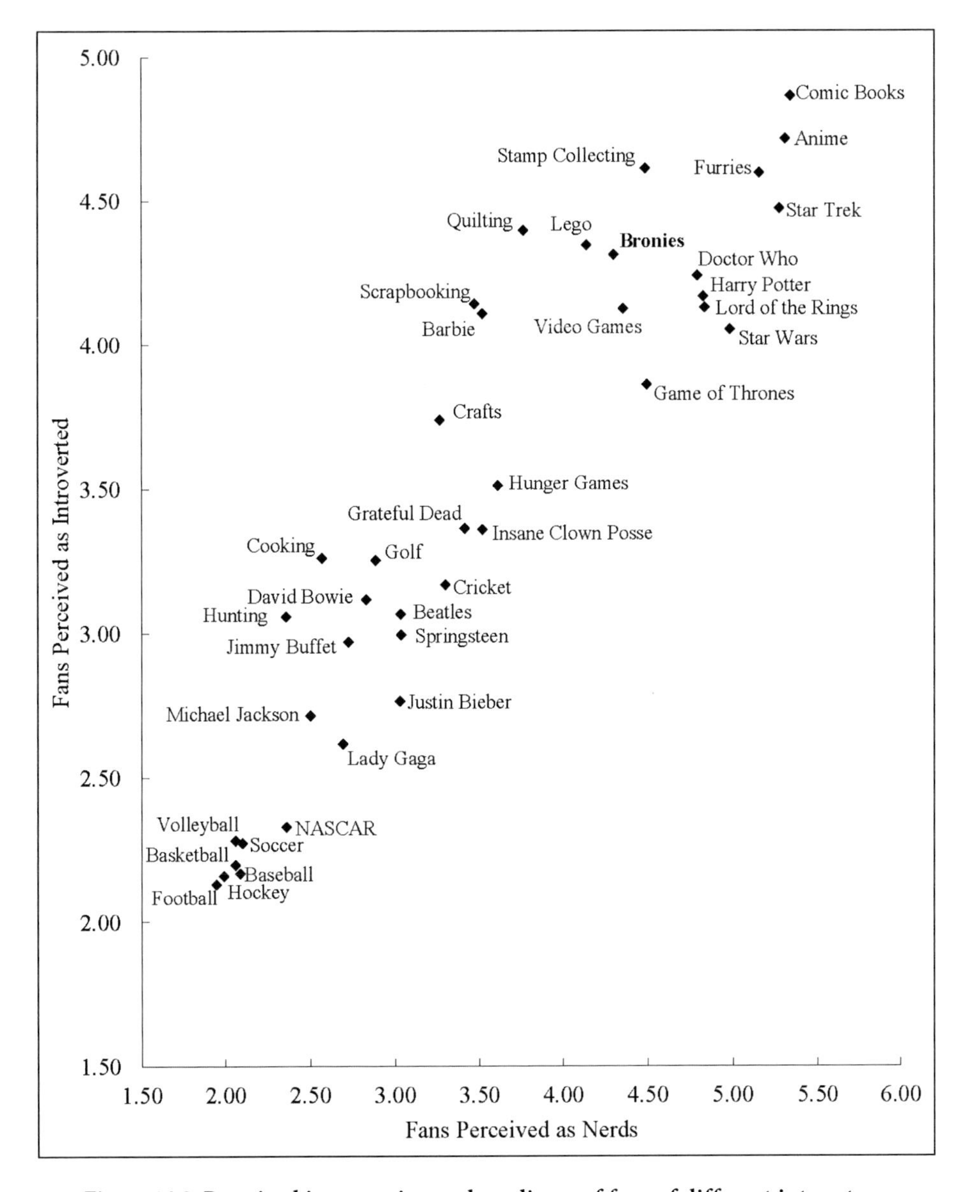

***Figure 16.2.* Perceived introversion and nerdiness of fans of different interests.**

wasn't, in and of itself, a bad thing. As shown in Figure 16.2, bronies were similarly seen to be both nerds and introverted, moreso than a more mainstream fan group like sport fans.

In short, while bronies and other atypical fan groups may be perceived to be introverts and, as the data suggest, probably *are* more likely to be introverts, this is a far cry from the stereotypically asocial loner (for more on stigma and stereotypes, see Chapter 17).

Correlations of the Big Five Dimensions in Bronies

To examine the association between the big five dimensions and brony-specific variables, we tested a series of correlations (see Table 16.1). Before we delve into what they mean, it's important to note that most of these correlations are quite small. This means that while there are small relationships between personality and the various outcomes, personality is just one small factor among *many* that predicts the way bronies think, feel, and behave.[5]

When it comes to the number of hours per week bronies spend engaging in brony-related activities (e.g., watching *MLP*, interacting with other bronies, viewing artwork), only agreeableness was found to be correlated—and only very weakly so. More agreeable bronies tended to engage with the show and fandom-related activities more than less-agreeable bronies. In contrast, how extraverted, conscientious, neurotic or open to experience a brony is tells us nothing about how much they engage in brony-related activities.

Since fan engagement is such a broad category, we also looked at other, more specific aspects of fan behavior. For example, openness to experience was

Table 16.1. Correlations of Outcomes with Big Five Personality Dimensions in Bronies

Variable	O	C	E	A	N
Hours Engaged	.02	−.01	.01	.06*	.02
Create Fan Content	.23*	.04*	.10*	.07*	.03
Collect MLP Artifacts	.10*	.06*	.08*	.08*	.05*
Display Symbols	.14*	.07*	.15*	.08*	.01
Public Identity	.18*	.02	.25*	.05*	< −.01
Recruit	.20*	.05*	.24*	.09*	−.06*
Viewing with Others	.17*	.08*	.22*	.15*	−.03*
Purpose Function	.24*	.06*	.13*	.18*	.04*
Escape Function	.09*	< .01	< .01	.10*	.11*
Social Function	.16*	.07*	.27*	.13*	−.01
Become a Pony	.12*	.08*	.08*	.17*	< −.01
Belonging	.18*	.09*	.14*	.19*	−.13*

*This effect is statistically significant. O = openness to new experiences, C = conscientious, E = extraversion, A = agreeableness, N = neurotic.

the personality trait most strongly associated with creating fan content (e.g., art, stories), such that fans higher in openness to experience were more likely to create fan-made content. This was also the case, albeit to a lesser extent, for the collection of *MLP*-themed artifacts (e.g., figurines, merchandise). When it comes to displaying symbols of one's brony identification publicly, however, both extraversion and openness to experience were about equally influential.

This raises interesting questions about more social aspects of the fandom, including the question of whether one publicly identifies as a brony to others. While openness to experience is related to this tendency, extraversion plays a considerably larger role: More extraverted bronies are more likely to be public about their involvement in the brony fandom and, perhaps unsurprisingly, are also more likely to recruit other bronies into the fandom. In a related vein, this finding may also explain why more extraverted bronies are also more likely to view the show with others.

We can speculate on two points when it comes to the link between brony behavior and the big five personality dimensions. First, extraversion and, to a lesser extent openness, is associated with fandom-related interactions with others. For bronies who are more extraverted, their interest and engagement with the show may be a more social one than is the case for more introverted bronies, for whom the show may be a solitary hobby they'd prefer to keep to themselves. Speaking to this point, extraversion was the most closely tied personality trait to the display of brony symbols. As noted in Chapter 9, research by Chadborn et al. (2017) has argued that fans display symbols of their fan group, in part, to make friends with like-minded others. This suggests that extraverted bronies may be especially likely to want their fan interest to be a social activity.

A second point worth making before we move on is the fact that fan content is most strongly correlated with the personality trait of openness. Openness has been found in other psychological research to be associated with intellectualism and creativity (Maslej, Oatley, & Mar, 2017; Nettle, 2006). As such, these findings are in line with existing research and suggest at least one reason why the bronies most open to experience may also be the most likely to create content.

We also examined the motivations underlying bronies' participation in the fandom (see Chapter 9 for descriptions of the various functions that the fandom can fulfill for bronies). Speaking to this point, openness, agreeableness, and extraversion were all associated with feeling like the fandom provides one with a sense of purpose or meaning in life, although openness was the strongest of these relationships. This suggests that the bronies most open to new experiences were also the most willing to see the show and the fandom as being personally significant and meaningful to them—a finding consistent with past research showing that people who are more open to experience are also more likely to search for meaning in their lives (Steger, Kashdan, Sullivan, & Lorentz, 2008).

With respect to using *MLP* as a means of escaping the daily hassles of life, this was associated with openness, acceptance, and, most importantly, with neuroticism. This point is particularly important to note, as it ties into research on how people cope with problems in their lives. In general, people higher in neuroticism tend to cope with stress in less adaptive ways—by withdrawing from or avoiding problems rather than tackling them head-on (Connor-Smith & Flachsbart, 2007). For most people, this might include escaping into Facebook or other social media (Marison et al., 2016) or into video games (Plante, Gentile, Groves, Modlin, & Blaco-Herrera, 2018). Here, we see evidence that, at least for bronies higher in neuroticism, the show itself is a source of escapism for them—a way of maladaptively coping with problems in their lives.[6]

When it comes to using the fandom for social purposes (e.g., as a way of making and maintaining social connections) the results are fairly straightforward: Extraversion was the personality trait most strongly associated with using the fandom for this purpose. This result supports our earlier position that extraverted bronies are especially likely to engage with the show in ways that encourage social interaction with like-minded others.

We next examined whether the big five personality traits were associated with bronies wanting to become more like a character from the show (see Chapter 14 for a review of this idea). Agreeableness and openness were the variables most strongly associated with this desire. As we noted earlier in this chapter, these findings are not unlike what's been found with furries, who identify more strongly with their fursonas as they become more open to experience (Reysen et al., 2019). Similarly, openness to experience is associated with identifying more strongly with a video game character (Soutter & Hitchens, 2016). Since openness has been found to be related to creativity and fantasy (Reyes et al., 2017), it might simply be the case that more open-minded bronies lead more active fantasy lives and, as such, are more likely to think about wanting to become a character from the show. When it comes to agreeableness, it helps to recall that the show itself has strong themes of friendship, kindness, and helping behavior. The characters themselves strongly express these virtues.[7] As such, it would make sense that a highly-agreeable person would be more likely than a less-agreeable person to want to become more like the highly-agreeable characters in the show.

Finally, we examined whether personality traits were associated with the sense of community bronies reported feeling (see Chapter 13 for further elaboration about sense of community). While all of the traits were associated with a sense of community, the strongest connections were between agreeableness and openness and feelings of belongingness. Agreeableness, in particular, makes sense, as friendlier people seem like they would be the most likely to seek out and belong to groups. Interestingly, greater neuroticism was associated with *reduced* feelings of belongingness. This suggests, in line with our earlier findings regarding escapism, that bronies higher in neuroticism are not using the show for social purposes, but rather as a means of distraction from reminders of their day-to-day life.

A Word of Caution: A Social Identity Perspective of the Big Five Personality Dimensions

If you're not a psychologist, it's easy to lump all psychologists together in the same category. After all, without knowing the history of the field or all of the subtle distinctions between different perspectives or theories, it's easy to assume that psychologists largely agree on the interpretation of data. After all, they all have the same goal: to understand, predict, and explain human behavior using data collected from studies.

That said, there are divisions within the field itself. These disagreements stem in part from the different perspectives or theories different psychologists use to understand behavior. Presently relevant, there is a bit of a rift between psychologists who fall into two different camps: personality psychologists and social psychologists. As noted by Funder and Fast (2010), some social psychologists think that personality theories focus too much on individual differences between people and don't focus enough on the impact of situations on behavior. In contrast, personality psychologists argue that there are meaningful differences between people, and that different people will consistently act different across all situations.

At the heart of the debate is the question of just how stable personality is across situations and whether personality *changes* depending on one's situation. While this may seem like a philosophical question with no practical implications, think about what this means for bronies as a group. We found, in our studies, that bronies are more introverted than non-brony samples. If you are an introverted brony, does this mean that you're stuck this way for life? Is there any chance for you to become more extraverted, or should you resign yourself to your fate of leaving parties early and avoiding large groups of people?

Social psychologists, arguing from the social identity perspective (Tajfel & Turner, 1979; Turner et al., 1987) would say that context matters more than personality.[8] In Chapter 13, for example, we discussed how some situations can make people act in ways that are consistent with stereotypes about their group. So what if the stereotypes of the brony fandom say that it's chock full of introverts?

We can see how important it is to consider this possibility by looking at the results of a study on the furry fandom—a group conceptually similar to bronies (e.g., interest in walking, talking animal characters) with similar stereotypes (e.g., shy, introverted). Reysen and colleagues (2015) asked furries to rate their personality as a furry (e.g., their fursona) and their everyday self (e.g., when they're going to grocery store or post office). Across three studies, furries consistently showed significantly higher ratings of all five dimensions of personality (including extraversion) when talking about their "furry self" rather than their non-furry self. In essence, their personality "changed" to match the stereotype of a furry—something that sport fans also did in the same study (e.g., becoming more extraverted and less agreeable in line with stereotypes of sport fans). The effect was even stronger for furries who strongly identified with being a furry.

In sum, the present chapter found evidence that bronies, on average, do seem to differ from non-bronies with respect to their personality. We also reviewed evidence that differences *among* bronies are related to differences in the way they consume the show, interact with other bronies, and in their motivations for engaging with the show in the first place. But it's worth keeping in mind that these differences are fairly small in the scheme of things: There are plenty of extraverted bronies out there and there are plenty of reasons why bronies create fan-made content besides simply being open to experience. It's important to maintain a healthy sense of perspective when discussing the "personality of a brony" so as to avoid painting all bronies with the same broad brush and to avoid the fallacy of treating personality as immutable fate. And, if you subscribe to a social psychological perspective, your personality is not "locked in"—it can absolutely change, both from situation to situation and throughout the course of your life.

Chapter 17

"Eww, bronies!" Stigma Toward the Brony Fandom

> *"But now, everypony is laughing at me. I'm nothing but a laughing stock! ... Leave me alone! I want to be alone! I want to wallow in, whatever it is that ponies are supposed to wallow in! Do ponies wallow in pity? Oh, listen to me! I don't even know what I'm supposed to wallow in! [sobbing] I'm so pathetic!"*
>
> —*Rarity* (*Season 1, Episode 14,* Suited for Success)

In Chapter 1 we discussed the history of the brony fandom. Most presently relevant, we introduced the idea that *MLP* fans have had to fight against the show's decades-long legacy of being a tool for selling toys to little girls. We also introduced the idea that bronies are seen by the public as an anomaly needing to be explained, since the largely-male, mostly-adult fandom falls well outside the show's target demographic.[1] Taken together, we have a group of people seen by society as having an unusual interest in something that's at best trivial and at worst wholly inappropriate. It doesn't take a social psychologist to see how this perception may lead to negative attitudes, beliefs, and behaviors toward bronies—something referred to as stigma.

As defined by social psychologists, stigmatized people are people vulnerable to discrimination or prejudice by virtue of belonging to a group deemed to be deviant (Crocker & Major, 1989). Stigmatized groups are usually thought of as members of racial or religious minorities. But any group can theoretically be seen as deviant by society at large, up to and including members of unusual fan groups.

At first glance, it's easy to dismiss or trivialize stigma. So what if others don't approve of the group you belong to?[2] As it turns out, however, stigma can have a tremendous impact on a person's life, including poorer physical and mental health, lower academic achievement, and barriers to economic advancement[3] (Major & O'Brien, 2005). Speaking to the first two points, our own research has shown that bronies who see themselves as stigmatized experience greater social anxiety and lower self-esteem.

So what's a member of a stigmatized group to do? Psychological research on a variety of stigmatized groups suggests that there *are* coping strategies available, including simply hiding your group membership when possible, leaving the group altogether, blaming your failures on discrimination rather than on oneself, and banding together with others in the stigmatized group for support (LeBel, 2008; Major & O'Brien, 2005). As we will see in the present chapter, bronies rely on many of these strategies.

But let's not put the cart before the horse. We'll begin this chapter by discussing research on stigma in the context of fan cultures—including two studies that happened to reference bronies. Next, we'll discuss the issues of bullying and the strategy of being selective in who bronies discuss their brony identity with. We'll also review research on the relationship between stigma and stronger group identification, showing how bronies may differ in their use of strategies to cope with stigma. We then ask whether bronies see themselves as more or less discriminated against after joining the fandom. Finally, we'll finish up by examining whether actually seeing the show for yourself changes your beliefs about bronies.

Fandom Stigma

Sports are ubiquitous across cultures. Almost everyone has, at one point in their life, attended a sporting event, seen or heard a sporting event on the radio or television, or seen newspaper columns, movies, and websites prominently discussing sport (Wann, Melnick, Russell, & Pease, 2001).[4] You'd be hard-pressed walk several blocks through the center of a city *without* seeing a symbol of a sport team on people's clothing, in store windows, or on billboards. This ubiquity even extends to psychology, where a search for research on fans yields mostly articles about sport fans.

So what about non-sport fans? Does this dominance of sport fans in culture affect how *non-sport* fans are viewed and treated?

Reysen and Shaw (2016) argue that people see sport fans as the "prototype" or "default" when it comes to fans. In a nutshell, this means that sport fans are the standard against which other fan groups are compared (Turner et al., 1987). This tendency to think in terms of prototypes is a basic principle of how our minds work. For example, when people think of the category "American," they think of a White person rather than a different ethnic minority (Devos & Banaji, 2005). And when asked to think about the category "sex," people think about heterosexual, vaginal intercourse (Reysen, Shaw, & Brooks,

2015). White people and straight, vaginal sex are the prototypes of these categories, the first thing that comes to most peoples' minds when it comes to these concepts. And, as such, they're the standard against which other entries in the categories are compared.

In and of themselves, prototypes aren't a problem—they're just something our brains do. After all, when we think "chair," the prototype of a four-legged chair probably comes to mind because most chairs we encounter *do* have four legs. Likewise, insofar as Americans are, statistically speaking, more likely to be White than not, it makes sense that the prototype of an American in their mind is White. The problem arises, however, when individuals who *don't* fit the prototype are considered. Studies show, for example, that a non-prototypical member of a group is more likely to face discrimination (Devos & Mohamed, 2014) and is more likely to be required to explain *why* they are different from the prototype (see Hegarty & Bruckmüller, 2013). Likewise, the mere existence of prototypes is often used to legitimize preferential treatment or status differences between majority and minority groups (e.g., Sibley, 2010; Wenzel, Mummendey, & Waldzus, 2007).

So what does this mean for fans? Well, if sport fans are the prototypical fan for most people, this means that non-sport fans are likely to experience many of the same problems that other minority groups experience. This includes experiencing greater discrimination for being different and being forced to explain why their interests differ from those of the more mainstream sport fans. In short, the prototypicality of sport fans leads to stigma toward anyone whose fan interest is not sport. And the more that interest differs from sport, the stronger the stigma is likely to be.

To see whether this theory holds water, Reysen and Shaw (2016) asked a group of college students to describe a typical fan to see whether it's true that most people consider sport fans to be the prototype. About half of the participants did exactly that, describing sport fans[5] more than any other type of fan (e.g., media, music, hobbies). Next, the participants were asked to rate 40 popular fan groups (of which bronies were one) on how typical they were as fans (1 = *definitely not a stereotypical fan*, 7 = *definitely a stereotypical fan*) and on how normal it is to be a fan of that interest (1 = *not normal*, 7 = *very normal*). Finally, they were asked how they felt toward fans of that interest (1 = *cold*, 10 = *warm*).

So how did bronies stack up against the other fan groups? Not well: They were seen as being among the *least* prototypical fan groups and being fairly *abnormal* when it comes to fan groups. In and of itself, being a bit strange wouldn't be that big of a deal, except they were also disliked more than almost any other fan group.[6] This wasn't a coincidence. Analyses revealed a pattern: The less prototypical a fan group was, the more negatively people felt toward it precisely *because* they were seen as abnormal. In short, fans of non-prototypical (i.e., non-sport) interests face greater prejudice as they get further and further away from sport as an interest.

Okay, so people might have a somewhat negative attitude toward non-sport fans—but that's just opinion. The bigger question is whether this *actually* leads to differences in the way members of these groups are treated. A follow-up study tested exactly this with respect to anime fans. Reysen, Plante, Roberts, Gerbasi, Mohebpour, and Gamboa (2016) found that non-anime fans who held prejudicial attitudes toward anime fans were opposed to the idea of dating an anime fan. A later study by Reysen and Plante (2017) found essentially the same for bronies, who were rated among the least mature and, as such, were among the least desirable to date.[7]

Up to this point, the evidence suggests that bronies are a fairly stigmatized group due to their having a non-prototypical, non-mainstream interest. But so far, we've only seen how this affects attitudes and behavioral *intentions* toward them in theory (e.g., willingness to date a hypothetical brony). That's a far cry from showing that bronies are *actually* treated differently in the real world. For evidence of this, we turn to our own studies of the brony fandom the next section.

Bullying and Hiding One's Brony Identity

We first tested whether bronies experience more bullying throughout their lives than non-bronies did. Specifically, we asked a sample of both bronies ($N = 9{,}386$) and non-bronies ($N = 930$) whether they had ever been the victim of bullying in their time in school. As shown in Table 17.1, bronies were considerably more likely to have been bullied than non-bronies. It should be noted, however, that this was an imperfect measure of past bullying, since it's entirely possible that bronies were bullied *prior* to becoming a brony. If this were the case, their being bullied would have nothing to do with their being a brony. Nevertheless, it at least suggests, in line with what has been found in prior research, that bronies as a group may be stigmatized, in whole or in part for their interest in *MLP*.

If it's true that bronies are stigmatized because of their being a brony, it makes sense that some would want to hide the fact that they're a brony from

Table 17.1. Experienced Bullying by Brony and Non-Brony Samples

Response	Non-Brony	Brony
Never Been Bullied	464 (49.9%)	3169 (33.8%)
Been Victim of Bullying	466 (50.1%)	6217 (66.2%)

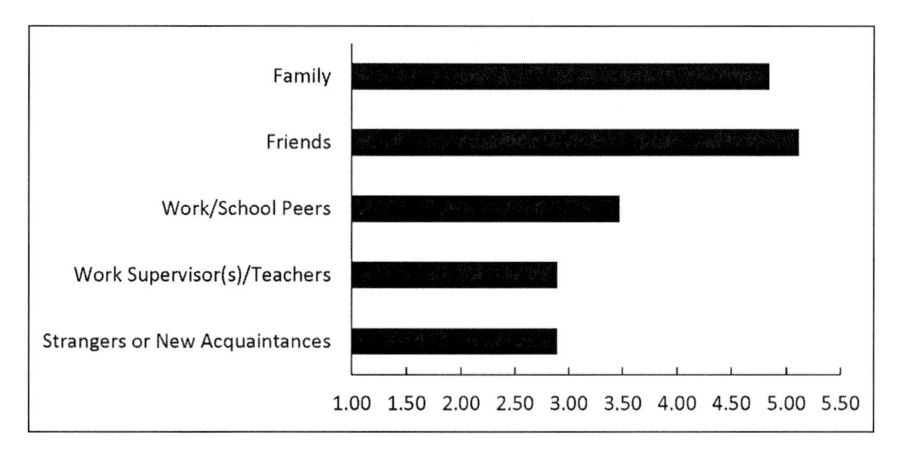

Figure 17.1. **Average extent to which bronies disclose their identity to non-brony others.**

others—especially those who are most likely to discriminate against them or who are in a position to inflict consequences on them for being a brony. To assess the possibility, we asked bronies to rate the extent that they disclosed their brony identity to non-brony (1) family members, (2) friends, (3) work/school peers, (4) work supervisor(s)/teachers, and (5) strangers or new acquaintances (1 = *strongly disagree*, 7 = *strongly agree*).

As shown in Figure 17.1, bronies are selective in who they disclose their brony identity to. Even among their friends and family, the people one would expect them to share the closest bonds with and feel the safest around, bronies only score a bit above the midpoint of the scale. This suggests that there are at least some friends or family members bronies feel the need to keep their brony identity hidden from. The need to conceal one's brony identity becomes more apparent when it comes to their peers or those in positions of power over them.[8] The story is the same for strangers and new acquaintances, perhaps due to the desire to make a good first impression and concerns about how misconceptions about bronies might affect others' perception of them if they discovered that they were a brony.

One might imagine that being able to conceal your stigmatized identity is a valuable tactic. After all, people who belong to stigmatized groups where they can't change their group membership and for whom their membership is clearly visible (e.g., race/ethnicity) can't use this tactic to avoid stigma. This *should* give bronies a strategy for avoiding stigma: Just hide or deny it. And it's true that being able to do this likely helps bronies avoid some unpleasant situations. But it does come at a cost, namely stress. Put simply, you have to be vigilant if you want to conceal some part of your identity from others. You need to watch what they wear, pay attention to everything you say, and constantly be looking over your shoulder to make sure no one sees you checking a brony-related e-mail or hanging out with bronies outside of work or school. And while it's easy to downplay the effects of stress, studies have repeatedly shown that stress is taxing to both our physical and mental health. So it's no surprise that people who are forced to conceal their stigmatized identities generally tend to report poorer physical and mental health (Chaudoir & Fisher, 2010). For example, research on furries finds that concealing one's furry identity is related to worse self-esteem (Plante, Roberts, Reysen, & Gerbasi, 2014a) and lower life satisfaction (Mock et al., 2013). In short, while bronies *can* conceal their brony identity from others, those who don't have to are likely better off both physically and psychologically in the long run.

So just who *is* open about being a brony? As noted in Chapter 13, the "more brony" someone is (fanship) and the more strongly they feel like a part of the brony community (fandom), the more open they are about being a brony to others.[9] These findings are consistent with Plante et al.'s (2014a) work on furries and disclosing their furry identity. Likewise, as noted in Chapter 16, bronies with more extraverted and open personalities are also more open about their brony identity. Taken together, these results suggest highly identified bronies and those looking to expand their friendship network to include other bronies among the most open about their brony identity.

But concealing one's brony identity isn't the only strategy for avoiding the stigma of being a brony. In the next section we look at another strategy: denying that you're the target of stigmatization in the first place.

Coping with Stigma: Denial of Personal Discrimination

In a 1978 study of working men and women in a Boston suburb, Faye Crosby found that, despite objective evidence that women were facing sexual discrimination, they rated their job about as positively as men did. In effect, women were denying the discrimination they were experiencing (Crosby, 1984). This finding is far from being a fluke or coincidence: Hodson and Esses (2002) have similarly found that African Americans, Haitians in Canada, and single mothers similarly deny being personally discriminated against despite the objective existence of discrimination against their group. While researchers do not yet agree on an explanation for these findings, what *is* certain is that members of stigmatized groups routinely think that discrimination occurs less for *them* than it does for *their group*.

Leshner and colleagues (2018) tested whether this same denial of personal discrimination occurs in fan groups. They did so by surveying furries, bronies, anime fans, and undergraduate college students who were fans of a variety of interests (i.e., sport, media, music, hobby fans). Each participant indicated whether they thought their fan group was discriminated against and whether they had *personally* been discriminated against for being a member of that group. Of all the groups studied, bronies scored the second-highest on group discrimination (behind only furries, who scored the highest). More importantly, in all of the groups, fans rated their *own* personal discrimination significantly lower than their group's discrimination. In other words, members of fan groups (even higher-status fan groups like sport fans) seem to see themselves as having dodged the discrimination that their group was facing. This means that the average brony, while acknowledging that bronies as a group experience discrimination, may be in denial about, or selectively remembering, instances of discrimination that they have personally experienced. Alternatively, they may be recalling instances of extreme discrimination against other members of their group and thinking "well, I guess I don't have it so bad!" Since research consistently shows that seeing oneself as the victim of prejudice is bad for one's psychological well-being (Schmitt, Branscombe, Postmes, & Garcia, 2014), this sort of downplaying or outright denial of discrimination may well protect bronies from some of discrimination's negative effects.

Coping with Stigma: Rejection Identification

Yet another strategy for coping with stigma toward one's group is to simply embrace it. This paradoxical strategy is known as rejection identification model (Branscombe, Schmitt, & Harvey, 1999). In effect, this means that the more society rejects or disapproves of your group, the more strongly you feel a sense of connection with your group—banding together with your allies, so to speak (Wohl, Branscombe, & Reysen, 2010). This phenomenon in particular has been seen in some more recent research finding groups that showed both higher levels of cohesion and perceived stigma were also more likely to participate in online research about their communities (Edwards, Edwards, Knottek, Olsen, & Griffin, 2018).[10]

Research on rejection identification as a strategy has largely looked at it within the context of race/ethnicity, gender, and sexual identities. In theory, however, there's no reason why the same phenomenon can't occur in other groups. For example, Jetten, Branscombe, Schmitt, and Spears (2001) found that when people with body piercings were discriminated against, they identified more strongly with others who have piercings. Another study showed

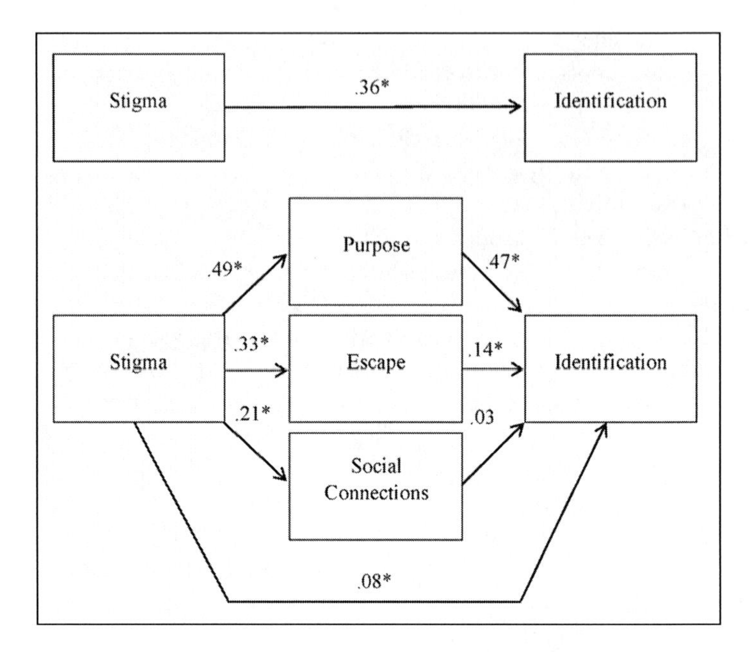

Figure 17.2. **The role of fandom function in the relationship between stigma and fandom identification in bronies. (*****This pathway is statistically significant.***)**

that atheists in the U.S. who feel more discriminated against also tend to identify more strongly with other atheists (Doane & Elliott, 2015).[11]

In the present research we examined whether bronies who were motivated to engage in the fandom for different reasons would differ in this rejection identification strategy (see Chapter 9). As shown in Figure 17.2, believing that others will treat you worse if they know you're a brony is related to greater identification with bronies (top pathway). This relationship is particularly strong for bronies for whom the fandom provides them with a sense of purpose and, to a lesser extent for bronies who use the fandom as a means of escapism. For those using the fandom as a way to meet others, this is not the case.[12]

Coping with Stigma: Change in Discrimination ("Things are getting better!")

Since there's a link between perceived stigma toward bronies and identifying as a brony, we wondered if some bronies perceived a change in the extent to which they were discriminated against *after* joining the fandom. To examine this possibility, we asked bronies to rate how frequently they expe-

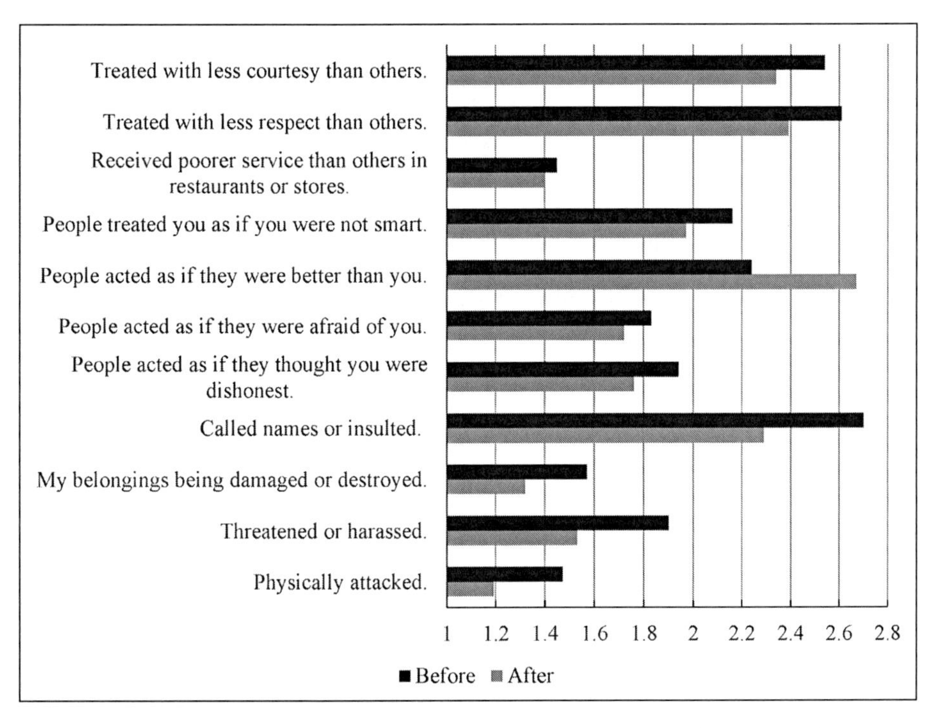

***Figure 17.3.* Comparing perceived discrimination before and after becoming a brony (measure adapted from Taylor, Kamarck, & Shiffman, 2004).**

rienced discrimination before and after they became a brony. As shown in Figure 17.3, with only one exception (people acting like they're better than you), participants felt like they had experienced *less* discrimination after becoming a brony compared to before.

It shouldn't be understated how surprising this finding is. After all, if bronies are stigmatized, it would seem to follow that joining the brony fandom should only make you a more visible target for discrimination and make it *harder* to hide being a member of this stigmatized group. Nevertheless, the opposite seems to be the case. Whether this is due to strength in numbers, bronies feeling less need to be in social settings where they're likely to experience stigma, or bronies denying personal discrimination remains to be seen.[13]

Reducing Stigma Toward Bronies: Non-Bronies' Exposure to *MLP*

Up to this point, we've focused on the effects of stigma and some of the strategies bronies have employed to combat discrimination toward them. In

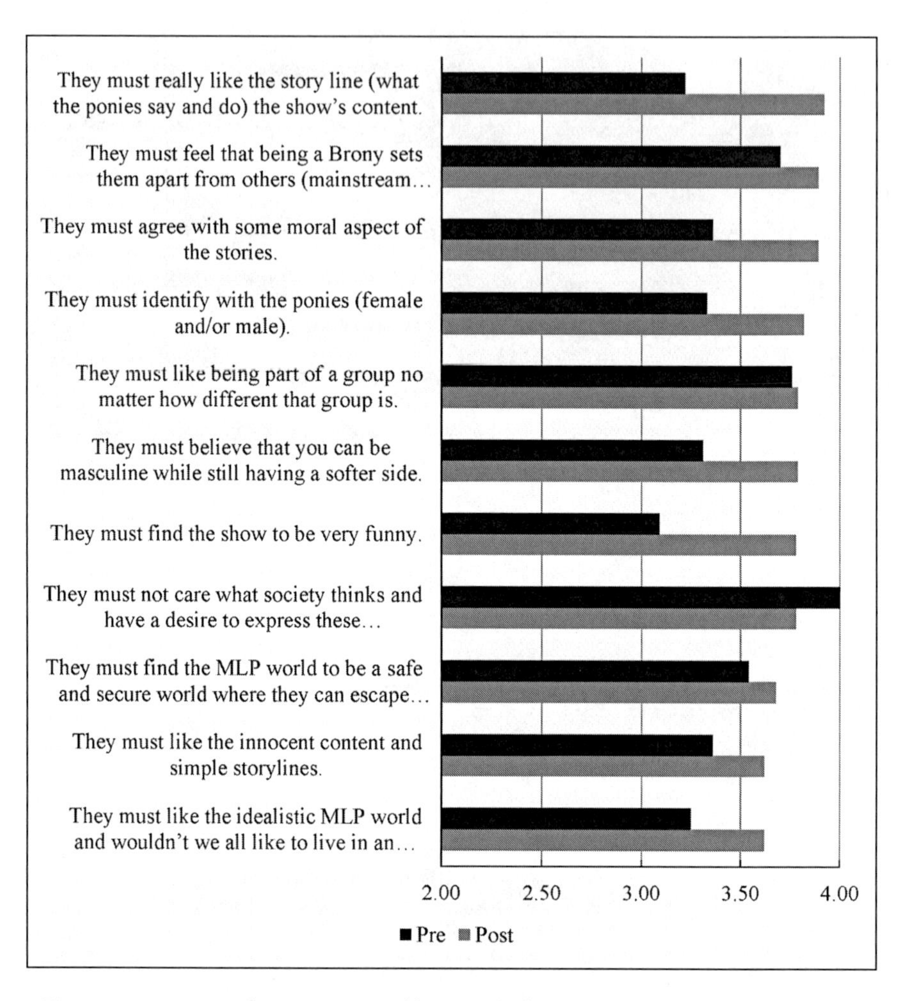

***Figure 17.4.* Perceived motivations of bronies before and after watching an episode of *MLP*.**

this last section, we'd like to shift our focus a bit and instead ask whether anything can be done to *reduce* stigma toward bronies. Can a little understanding go a long way, as conventional wisdom might suggest?

Numerous studies agree with this conventional wisdom. If people spend time with members of others groups, they tend to feel less prejudice toward those groups (Pettigrew & Tropp, 2006).[14] Interestingly, it turns out people don't even need to have in-person contact with members of these others groups. Having a friend who themselves are a friend of an outgroup member or "meeting" members of these groups through mass media can also reduce prejudice (Pettigrew, Tropp, Wagner, & Christ, 2011).[15] For example, fans of

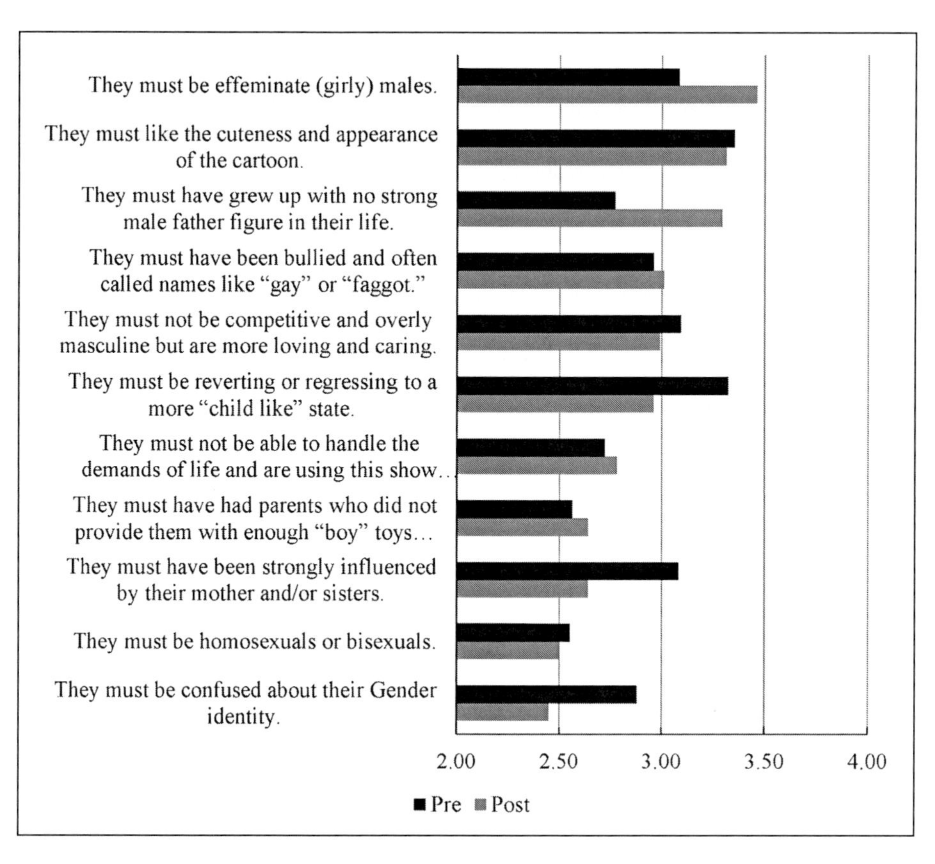

***Figure 17.5.* Perceived motivations of bronies before and after watching an episode of *MLP*—continued.**

the television show *Monk* who felt connected to the show's titular character—a detective with obsessive-compulsive disorder—endorsed fewer stereotypes and less prejudice toward those with the disorder (Hoffner & Cohen, 2012). As such, it's conceivable that the average non-brony could change their attitudes and opinions toward bronies simply by watching an episode of the show and getting some experience with it first-hand.

To test this possibility, we invited college students to first complete a measure which asked them to rate 22 different explanations for why they thought bronies were interested in *MLP*. Next, the participants watched half an episode of *MLP*.[16] The participants were then asked to complete the ratings again. The results have been split into two figures (Figure 17.4 and Figure 17.5).

It's worth noting that most of the biggest increases in beliefs about why bronies like the show are positive. For example, after viewing the show, viewers were much more likely to believe that bronies must watch the show because they found it funny. In contrast, viewers became less likely to endorse negative beliefs after viewing the show, such as the belief that bronies are confused about their gender identity. In sum, the results support the notion that even a small amount of exposure—in this case, about ten minutes of watching an episode—can help break down some of the prejudice directed toward bronies.

Conclusion

In the present chapter we reviewed evidence that bronies are stigmatized by non-bronies—including being seen as abnormal, immature, and poor dating partners. In line with prior research, bronies were found to use a variety of strategies to cope with this stigma, including hiding their brony identity, denying discrimination, and identifying more strongly as a brony. We also showed preliminary evidence that one way to potentially reduce this stigma is to encourage people to see the show for themselves. Given that the brony fandom itself owes its existence, at least in part, to curious people watching *MLP* and discovering it was better than they expected, these results might not be as surprising to bronies as they are to non-brony readers.

Chapter 18

Bronies: A Surprisingly Happy, Well-Adjusted Group of Fans

"There's one thing that makes me happy/And makes my whole life worthwhile/And that's when I talk to my friends and get them to smile."
—*Pinkie Pie* (*Season 2, Episode 18,* A Friend in Deed)

How are you?

There's a lot of ways to answer that question. For most of us, we might respond with our current mood, "I'm doing great!" or "It's not going so well." But that's not the only way to gauge our well-being. Alternatively, we could report on our physical health, firing off a list of aches and pains, griping about a cold that's coming on, or talking about how we've healed up nicely from a recent injury. Another way to respond might be to discuss not just yourself, but your relationships: "The kids are doing fine in school" or "Things haven't been great with my boyfriend." Still *another* way might be to talk about material or practical happenings in your life, such as the state of your stocks, an upcoming promotion at work, or whether your car battery needs replacing.

These examples illustrate just how broad and multifaceted the concept of well-being is. Indeed, psychologists find themselves running into the same problem many of us face when trying to answer questions about well-being: What, exactly, *is* well-being, and how do we measure it? (Linton, Dieppe, & Medina-Lara, 2016). For example, some psychologists (e.g., Dodge, Daly, Huyton, & Sanders, 2012) suggest that well-being refers to being in a state of having the resources (psychological, social, physical) we need to meet challenges. Others look at *subjective* well-being, whether you're happy, satisfied with your life, and have a positive sense of self-esteem (Veenhoven, 1991). Ryff (1989) suggests looking beyond subjective happiness, positing that well-being includes six components: (1) having a positive attitude about yourself, (2) interacting positively with others, (3) being autonomous and independent, (4) feeling competent in the things you do, (5) having a sense of meaning and direction in your life, and (6) feeling a sense of growth. These different ways of thinking about well-being, while related, are also quite distinct from one another (Keyes, Shmotkin, & Ryff, 2002; Lambert, Passmore, & Holder, 2015). In short, despite all being valid ways of assessing how one is doing in their lives, they can't all be lumped into the same category, nor can we use any one measure to infer the others.[1]

It's with this nuanced understanding that we're setting out to explore the well-being of bronies in the present chapter. We'll begin by reviewing what researchers have found about the well-being of other fan groups, including Wann's (2006) model of identification and well-being and the well-being of fans both at (and after) fan conventions. Next, we examine the *absence* of well-being in the brony fandom through the prevalence of different psychological conditions in the brony fandom. We then review some of the variables that may link being a brony with well-being (e.g., having a positive outlook, forming positive relationships). Finally, we'll finish off by asking whether bronies' well-being changed as a result of their joining the brony fandom.

Fandoms, Friendships and Well-Being: Wann's Model of Identification and Well-Being

Research has shown that being a sport fan is pretty good for one's overall well-being: It's linked to greater self-esteem and lower loneliness (Wann, Walker, Cygan, Kawase, & Ryan, 2005), lower depression and more positive feelings (Branscombe & Wann, 1991), and greater feelings of vigor, less tension, and less fatigue (Wann, Inman, Ensor, Gates, & Caldwell, 1999).[2] Indeed, Daniel Wann (2006) proposed a model linking fanship itself to psychological health. A key portion of his model argued that one of the reasons for this link was the formation of enduring friendships, which he proposed would improve some facets of one's well-being (e.g., life satisfaction) but not others (e.g., physical well-being[3]).

Wann and his colleagues found evidence for his model in studies of sport fans. For example, he found that fans who more strongly identified with a particular team felt a greater sense of trust in others (Wann & Polk, 2007), greater well-being (Wann & Weaver, 2009), and less loneliness (Wann, Rogers, Dooley, & Foley, 2011). He also found that sport fans at a game with other fans (vs. at watching at home) felt less lonely and more happy with their social lives in general (Wann, Martin, Grieve, & Gardner, 2008). That said, while Wann found a link between sport fandom and happiness, numerous attempts failed to find evidence that face-to-face friendships were the cause of this link (Wann, Waddill, Brasher, & Ladd, 2015; Wann, Waddill, Polk, & Weaver, 2011).

In later studies, Reysen and colleagues (2017b) tested Wann's model, not with sport fans, but with anime fans. The results found the same link between identifying as a fan and well-being, but this time found evidence that it was driven by face-to-face interactions with other fans (i.e., friends). In other words, Wann's (2006) hypothesis that being a fan improves well-being due to the friends you make in fandoms has been shown to work in non-sport fans. What's more, the same study also showed that these face-to-face interactions matter *more* than online interactions with other fans. As such, it seems fair to ask whether the most beneficial way for fans to interact with fellow fans is face-to-face at fan conventions.

Fan Conventions, Well-Being Highs and Post-Con Depression

As mentioned in the previous section, Wann and his colleagues (2008) found that sport fans report better well-being when they're at a game with other fans rather than sitting by themselves at home. With this in mind, Ray, Plante, Reysen, Roberts, and Gerbasi (2018) conducted a similar study with anime fans, who were either surveyed at an anime convention or online. The results showed that fans at the convention reported lower feelings of loneliness and higher well-being than anime fans sampled online.[4] More importantly, this difference was driven by the fact that being at the convention led to more face-to-face interactions which, in turn, reduces feelings of loneliness and, ultimately, improves feelings of well-being. In short, as any fan can attest to, being surrounded by like-minded others makes us feel good.

But sooner or later the sun sets, the cast takes a bow, the movie comes to an end, and the convention has its final day. After the blissful high that comes from being at a convention, what happens to fans when they return to the real world. Do they experience what some fans have called "post-con depression"?

Plante and colleagues (2016) looked for evidence of post-con depression in a sample of convention-going furries. The participants completed a variety of measures of well-being at a furry convention and then several days later. The results were clear: Furries showed more symptoms of depressed mood and less happiness after the convention. In an examination of participants' open-ended comments, Roberts and colleagues (2017) similarly found that people at a convention feel positive emotions and a sense of escapism. After returning home, however they express, among other things, negative emotions such as stress, loneliness, isolation, and a lack of energy. In short, while there is an upside to convention attendance, it's not all sunshine and rainbows. Many convention attendees experience a mental "crash" upon returning home that one could call a post-con depression. And while this phenomenon hasn't been studied specifically within the brony community, there is little reason to believe that furries and bronies differ dramatically in their susceptibility to this phenomenon. Ultimately, further research is needed in this area, both to test whether these effects do carry over in other fan groups and, more importantly, to examine how long symptoms of post-con depression may last.

For now, let's change gears a bit and focus on the flip-side of well-being—psychological conditions and dysfunction.

Prevalence of Psychological Conditions in Brony Fandom

In Chapter 17 we discussed the causes and consequences of stigma directed toward a group. As part of that discussion, we mentioned that the more a fan group differs from the prototype of a fan group, the more the group is seen as abnormal and negative. Related to this, we also explained that members of non-prototypical groups are often forced to explain or defend their group membership (Hegarty & Bruckmüller, 2013). In other words, if someone differs from what's "normal," people need to come up with an explanation for that deviance.

With this in mind, it makes sense why some people might look for a pathological explanation for bronies as a phenomenon. After all, other types of unusual behavior (e.g., talking to people who aren't present) can be explained by psychological conditions (e.g., schizophrenia). The logic looks something like this: Most adult males do *not* watch *MLP*. Yet, here's a group of adult males who really like and regularly watch the show. Something must *clearly* be wrong with them to explain why they engage in such strange behavior.

So what does the research say? Is there any evidence that bronies are more likely to have a psychological condition than anyone else?

To address this question, Reysen, Plante, Chadborn, et al. (2018) asked members of three different fan groups (furries, anime fans, and bronies) to report on whether they had ever been diagnosed with a mood disorder (e.g., depression), anxiety disorder (e.g., generalized anxiety disorder), attention-deficit/hyperactivity disorder (ADHD), or autism spectrum disorder (ASD). To avoid the problem of self-diagnosis, fans were specifically asked whether they had been *formally diagnosed* by a licensed practitioner and, if so, what they had been diagnosed with.

The results found that, compared to the other fandoms, bronies showed lower rates of mood disorders and anxiety disorders than anime fans and lower rates of ADHD than furries. They did, however, show significantly higher rates of ASD than anime fans and furries.

It's worth noting that these results were only comparing bronies to other fan groups—they say nothing about whether bronies are more likely to have been diagnosed than the average American.[5] To address this, bronies' prevalence rates for these conditions were also compared to the lifetime prevalence rates of these conditions in the U.S. population. Bronies were found to have lower prevalence rates of mood disorders, anxiety disorders, and ADHD than are found in the U.S. population. They were also found to have significantly higher prevalence rates of ASD than is typically found in the U.S. population.[6]

Given that most bronies *don't* have a psychological condition, there doesn't seem to be any reason to believe that being a brony is "caused" by a psychological condition. But before concluding, we need to acknowledge some rather large limitations of this study. First, the data relied on self-report: Participants may have omitted diagnoses, forgotten to list a diagnosis, or may have a disorder but not yet been diagnosed by a licensed professional. Second, the rates of mood disorders, anxiety disorders, and ADHD were all compared with U.S. *lifetime* prevalence rate, meaning they represent the number of people in the U.S. who have been diagnosed with the condition at *some point* in their life. Technically speaking, about half of the U.S. population could be diagnosable with a mental disorder at *some* point in their life (Kessler & Wang, 2008). Since bronies, as a group, are relatively young (their early to mid 20s), it's entirely possible that many of them could be diagnosable later on in their life.

In short, these results should be taken as a snapshot of what is going on in the fandom now, not what will occur over fans' lifetimes. Current rates of these conditions are quite low (even for ASD; despite being higher than the U.S. population, rates are still well below 10 percent), likely because some people in these fandoms haven't developed a disorder yet. Nevertheless, there doesn't seem to be any reason to suspect that psychological conditions "cause" people to become bronies, or even to suspect that they're more prevalent in the brony fandom than in any other fandom. Or, to put it another way, you're more likely to encounter people who have or have had a psychological conditions if you walk down the street than you are if you walk into a brony convention.

Identifying as a Brony and Well-Being

As mentioned previously, numerous psychology studies of sport fans have found that those who identify more strongly with their favorite team also tend to show the highest well-being (e.g., Wann, 2006). We wanted to test whether this was the case in the brony fandom, specifically with regard to measures of bronies' positive feelings and attitudes (e.g., "On most days I feel happy and content"). In addition, we wanted to look at three possible reasons for *why* this link might exist: (1) The brony fandom gives bronies a chance to seek advice and help from others, (2) The brony fandom gives bronies a place where they can be themselves without having to hide their brony identity, and (3) *MLP* gives bronies an outlet to turn to for advice or simply as a way to cheer themselves up when they're in a bad mood.

As shown at the top of Figure 18.1, the more strongly bronies identified with the fandom, the more they experienced positive feelings and attitudes. Importantly, this effect was driven, at least in part, by the fact that those who more strongly identify as bronies *also* share and seek advice from other bronies and also disclosure their brony identity. Interestingly, while highly identified bronies also use *MLP* as a way to deal with their problems, the

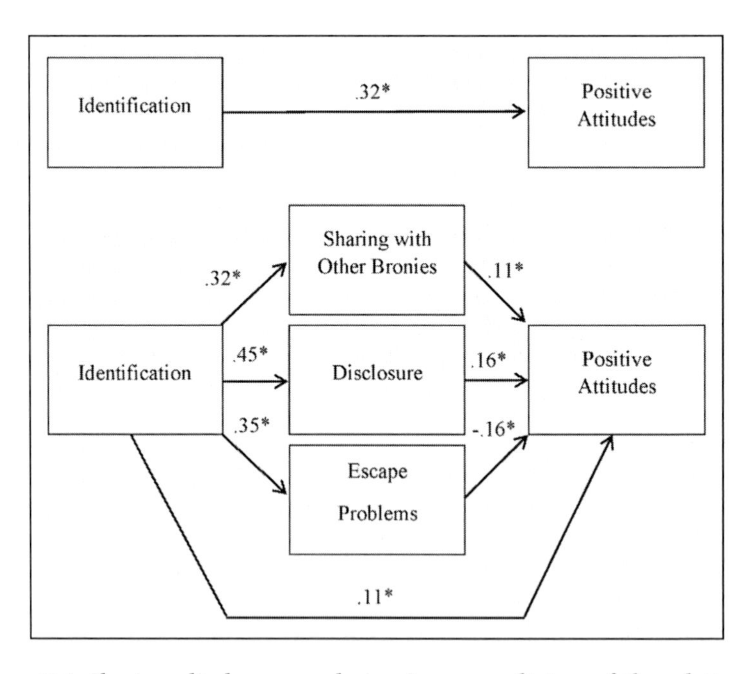

***Figure 18.1.* Sharing, disclosure, and escapism as mediators of the relationship between perceived identification and positive attitudes. (**These results are statistically significant.*)**

extent to which they did this was actually associated with *lower* positive feelings and attitudes.

These results largely match those found in both non-fandom research and in research on fan groups (e.g., Wann, 2006). Being part of the brony fandom offers its members a source of social support and a place to be themselves without having to stress out about hiding it from others. However, those who rely the show as a crutch when times are difficult or as an escape from problems may be using a poor or ineffective coping strategy.

Perceived Change in Well-Being

While the previous results seem to suggest that more strongly identifying as a brony may be good for your well-being, they don't directly address the question of whether becoming a brony has a positive effect on someone's life. To assess this, we asked bronies to complete numerous measures of well-being with respect to how they were before and after becoming a brony. If it's true that belonging to a fan group is related to better mental well-being, we'd expect to see drops in their measures of negative well-being (e.g., anxiety) and increases in their measures of positive well-being (e.g., happiness) *after* becoming a brony.

As shown in Figure 18.2, bronies reported less dysfunction (physical, emotional, and school/work) after becoming a brony as compared to before, with the largest change observed for emotional functioning. Bronies also reported more happiness after becoming a brony. In terms of maladaptation, bronies reported less social anxiety, depression, and generalized anxiety after becoming a brony. These findings are in line with findings from earlier in this chapter showing that bronies were less prone than non-bronies to psychological conditions such as mood or anxiety disorders. Finally, bronies reported significantly higher general well-being after becoming a brony than before they became a brony.

Together, these results suggest that bronies see themselves as better off after joining the fandom compared to before, regardless of how you measure well-being. As a note of caution, one should keep in mind that these results were provided by bronies *after* they had already joined the fandom. As such, bronies may have felt pressure to respond in ways that show improvement regardless of whether they had, in reality, improved. In addition, participants may simply be unable to remember how they were *actually* doing prior to joining the fandom. That said, very little change was observed for physical and school/work dysfunction, which seems to work against these possibilities (e.g., pressure to see oneself improving in general.) Despite these limitations, the results generally fit with the overall body of research showing that being

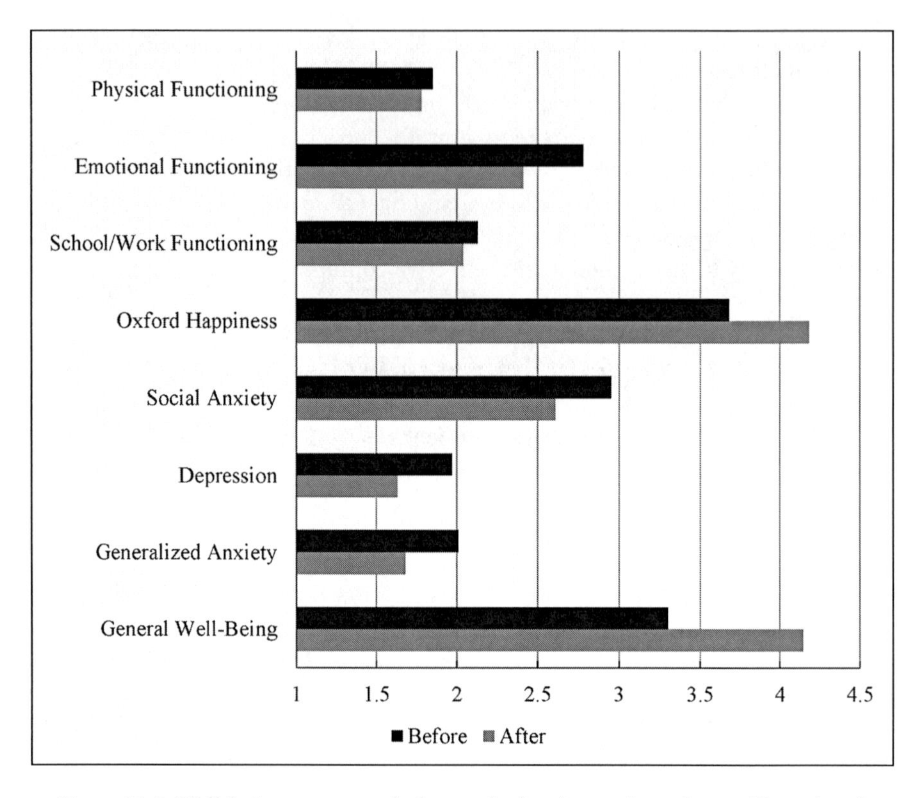

***Figure 18.2.* Well-being measures before and after becoming a brony. Note that for physical, emotional, and school/work functioning, higher scores indicate *worse* functioning (Physical, Emotional, School/Work Functioning, Varni, Seid, & Kurtin, 1999; Oxford Happiness, Hills & Argyle, 2002; Social Anxiety, Rodebaugh, Woods, & Heimberg, 2007; Depression, Kroenke, Spitzer, & Williams, 2001; Generalized Anxiety, Kroenke, Spitzer, Williams, Monahan, & Löwe, 2007; General Well-Being, Keyes et al., 2008; Lamers, Westerhof, Bohlmeijer, ten Klooster, & Keyes, 2011).**

part of a fandom, regardless of what that fandom is, tends to be good for one's psychological well-being.

Conclusion

In the present chapter we discussed research on bronies' well-being. After briefly reviewing the existing research in psychology on fandoms and well-being, we reviewed the results of a study looking at the prevalence of psychological conditions in the brony fandom. Bronies were found to report lower prevalence of mood, anxiety, and ADHD than U.S. population, although they did show a higher likelihood of being on the autism spectrum. Sharing advice and seeking help from other bronies (i.e., social support) and being free to disclose one's brony identity to others seems to underlie the benefits of being a brony on well-being, while using *MLP* as a means of escaping problems seems to be maladaptive. Finally, evidence suggests that becoming a brony has the overall effect of improving the well-being of bronies across a wide range of measures. There seems to be some truth in the idea that "friendship is magic," regardless of whether those friends are those with whom you go to sporting events, dress up in fuzzy costumes, or watch your favorite show about magical horse princesses.

Chapter 19

Making the World Better, One Kind Act at a Time

"Dear Princess Celestia, sometimes you can feel like what you have to offer is too little to make a difference, but today, I learned that everypony's contribution is important, no matter how small."
—*Fluttershy* (*Season 2, Episode 22,* Hurricane Fluttershy)

Say what you will about the *My Little Pony* series (e.g., it exists to sell children's toys, it's saccharine-sweet, sappy, and sentimental), the show *does* espouse a message most people can get behind: The world is a much better place when people show kindness and friendship to one another. But do these prosocial platitudes fall on deaf ears when it comes to fans of the show? Do fans the show *actually* practice what the show preaches? Do bronies follow the fandom's mantra of "love and tolerate"?[1]

In this chapter we explore the prosocial behavior of bronies, starting with a brief review of what prosocial behavior is (e.g., charity, volunteering, collective action) and what psychological research can tell us about it. Next, we briefly summarize what decades of research on media effects tells us about how people are affected by the media they consume.

We then discuss what research on helping behavior in fan groups specifically has to say, followed by a dive into research on helping behavior in bronies specifically, including how bronies themselves view the show's morals and values and whether the show itself is related to their helping behavior. We finish up with a look at the potential role that being part of a stigmatized group may play in bronies' willingness to engage in helping behavior.

From Charity to Protest: Why People Help

Helping someone can be as simple as lending them a quarter or as involved as rescuing someone from a burning building. Given the wide range of different ways to help, it should come as no surprise that there are also a wide range of factors influencing when, where, and how people choose to help. These factors include both individual-level factors (e.g., your mood) and societal factors (e.g., cultural beliefs about the importance of helping).

Illustrating the importance of considering both types of factors, a study was done testing whether there was truth to the idea that New York City is one of the most unhelpful cities in the world (Levine, Norenzayan, & Philbrick, 2001). To test whether this was the case, researchers dropped a pen while walking down the streets of various cities. In New York City in particular, only 15.4 percent of people told the experimenter that he had dropped his pen. In and of itself, this would seem to suggest that New Yorkers are not particularly helpful. But when the experimenter wore a shirt with the symbol of the democratic party, this number jumped to 57.7 percent (see Reysen & Levine, 2014). These results show that it's important to consider various factors such as culture (the city of New York) and group membership to get a full picture of when and why people help one another. In this section we'll look at some of the factors that lead people to give to charity, volunteer, and participate in social movements.

As a general rule, research has shown that the most charitable people are older, educated, religious, financially secure, married, have children, and show a great deal of empathy toward others (Bekkers & Wiepking, 2011a). Other factors that increase helping behavior include (1) being aware that someone is in need, (2) being asked to help, (3) standing to benefit personally from helping, (4) having an altruistic personality, (5) having your reputation boosted for helping, (6) getting to feel better about yourself afterward, (7) having prosocial/social justice values, and (8) feeling like you can make a difference (Beekers & Wiepking, 2011b). Perhaps most presently relevant, the groups we belong play an important role in our willingness to give to charity: Sport fans give more to a charity associated with their own team than they do when it's a charity associated with a rival team (Platow et al., 1999).

But giving to charity is just one type of helping behavior, one that's fairly quick and easy to do. In contrast, volunteering requires considerably more effort and is more time consuming than simply cutting a check or handing someone some change. Research suggests that these differences matter, as the things which motivate a person to give to charity may not motivate them to volunteer (Lee & Chang, 2007). For example, one study found that people who feel a sense of belonging to a community are more likely to spend more time volunteering (Choi & DiNitto, 2012).[2]

A third way people can help is through collective action: "Actions undertaken by individuals or groups for a collective purpose" (Brunsting & Postmes, 2002, p. 527). Activists usually seek to improve the world through their collective efforts, which can include everything from signing a petition to being arrested at a sit-in. Researchers have found several key variables that predict who will engage in these sorts of collective actions: the extent to which one perceives an injustice, feels like they can create change, has a strong stance on an issue, and feels a sense of anger or outrage (van Zomeren, 2013; van Zomeren, Postmes, & Spears, 2008; van Zomeren, Postmes, Spears, & Bettache, 2011). For just one example of these predictors affecting collective action, angrier consumers' were more likely to endorse protesting Wal-Mart (Cronin, Reysen, & Branscombe, 2012).

Taken together, these findings should make it clear that there's no *one* factor which causes people to engage in prosocial behavior. Like with most behaviors, a combination of factors interact to cause a person to help, whether that help involves donating money to a charity, volunteering at a soup kitchen, or going out to protest an injustice in the world. With this in mind, let's turn out attention to some of the characteristics of the brony fandom which may make them more likely than other groups to engage in these sorts of helping behaviors. To start, we'll look at whether it's even possible for a television show to affect our behavior.

Media Effects

Although we discussed media effects briefly in Chapter 17, we should elaborate on them further here. Much of the research on this subject has traditionally focused on the *negative* effects of media.[3] Taken together, more than a thousand studies since at least the 1960s have collectively shown that, yes, peoples' thoughts, feelings, and behaviors can be affected by the media they consume (e.g., Anderson et al., 2010).[4]

While researchers and news outlets alike have tended to focus on the *negative* effects of media consumption, however, there is also considerable evidence that prosocial media can have *beneficial* effects on consumers as well (Gentile et al., 2009). For example, playing a video game where the goal is to *help* other characters rather than kill them can reduce players' antisocial thoughts, increase their empathy for others, and reduce the enjoyment they might otherwise feel at the suffering of others[5] (Greitemeyer & Osswald, 2009; Greitemeyer, Osswald, & Brauer, 2010). In addition to changing thoughts and feelings, prosocial games can also affect real-world behavior, such as the amount of time they spend helping a researcher with a study or their willingness to step in to break up a fight (Greitemeyer & Mügge, 2014; Prot et al., 2014).

But the effects of prosocial media have also been studied outside the realm of video games. In one study, for example, participants read a story that modeled helping behavior (Johnson, 2012). The researcher then "accidentally" dropped some pens on the floor. Participants who became more immersed into the story were more likely to help the experimenter pick up the pens. Likewise, Greitemeyer (2009) found that listening to songs with prosocial lyrics makes people more likely to engage in prosocial behaviors, in part because the songs increased peoples' sense of empathy toward the suffering of others.

Children's media is perhaps the first thing many people think of when they imagine a show or game filled with prosocial content (Smith et al., 2006).[6] Nevertheless, the link between prosocial media and helping behavior isn't limited to children: It's been found across all age groups, including being particularly strong for young adults (18–25 years of age).

In short, there is abundant psychological evidence suggesting that the more prosocial media someone consumes, the more empathy they tend to experience and, by extension, the more likely they are to engage in prosocial behavior themselves. Given the centrality of *MLP*—a show with considerable prosocial messaging—to the brony fandom, it would seem to follow that bronies should experience greater empathy and more prosocial behavior by virtue of watching the show.

But before we test whether this is actually the case, let's look at one more reason why bronies may be particularly likely to engage in helping behavior.

Fandom and Helping

Traditionally, fan activism has been thought of as fans joining together to keep a beloved show from being cancelled. In recent years, however, fans' social causes have broadened to include important real-world issues, up to and including stopping genocide (Jenkins, 2012). Numerous celebrities have used social media to encourage their fans to engage in activism and charities (e.g., Lady Gaga; Bennett, 2012, 2014).[7] Andersen-Peters (2016) analyzed Markiplier's (a YouTube celebrity) social media stream and found that he inspired his fans to donate to charity: 97 percent of his fans said they learned about a particular charity through Markiplier, while 40 percent had actually donated during one of his Markiplier's livestreams. And Markiplier is certainly not the only celebrity to directly encourage charitable behavior. Bussie (2018) surveyed Beyoncé fans and finds that most had seen her post on social media about various social causes and about 20 percent intended to donate to a charity she endorsed.

But fans don't *need* a celebrity to rally them to action. As it turns out, fans themselves often encourage other fans to join in a cause (Chauvel, 2014). For example, Harry Potter fans have taken it upon themselves to harness the messages from the books and films to motivate real-world civic engagement through the Harry Potter Alliance (Hinck, 2012). And Twilight fans, despite their questionable taste in literature, created The Fandom Gives Back, which raised money for the Alex's Lemonade Stand Foundation—an organization which combats cancer in children (O'Brien, 2015).[8]

In short, charitable behavior in fans stems both from the fan interest itself (e.g., messages in the media, messages from the content creators) and from the fan community itself. All of these sources contribute to norms within fandoms stating that fans are *expected* to endorse and engage in prosocial actions.

And now, patient reader, let's turn our attention at last to the brony fandom to see whether these same forces are at play among bronies.

Moral Message

While *MLP* is generally considered by the public to be one long, treacly message of love and kindness, we wondered whether bronies themselves saw the show as containing prosocial messages. We tested this in our first study of the brony fandom. Bronies were asked to what extent they felt the show supports various virtues (e.g., friendliness) on a 5-point response scale, from 1 = *not supportive* to 5 = *very much supportive*. The results in Figure 19.1 are clear: Bronies feel that the show supports all of the prosocial values we asked about, as indicated by the fact that the average response for each item was *well above* the midpoint of the scale. Only one such virtue—faithfulness—stood out from the others as being somewhat less-endorsed, though it was nevertheless above the midpoint.

In short, bronies are indeed picking up on the fact that *MLP* contains the sorts of prosocial values that it's known for having. But can this tell us anything about the values and morals of bronies themselves, who spend so much time watching the show itself?

Moral Foundations and Perception

We next wondered whether bronies' morality would be related to their perception of the show as having prosocial virtues. Researchers believe that there are at least five moral dimensions that humans may value: (1) harm/care, (2) fairness/reciprocity, (3) ingroup/loyalty, (4) authority/respect, and (5) purity/sanctity (Haidt & Graham, 2007; Haidt & Joseph, 2004). We tested whether

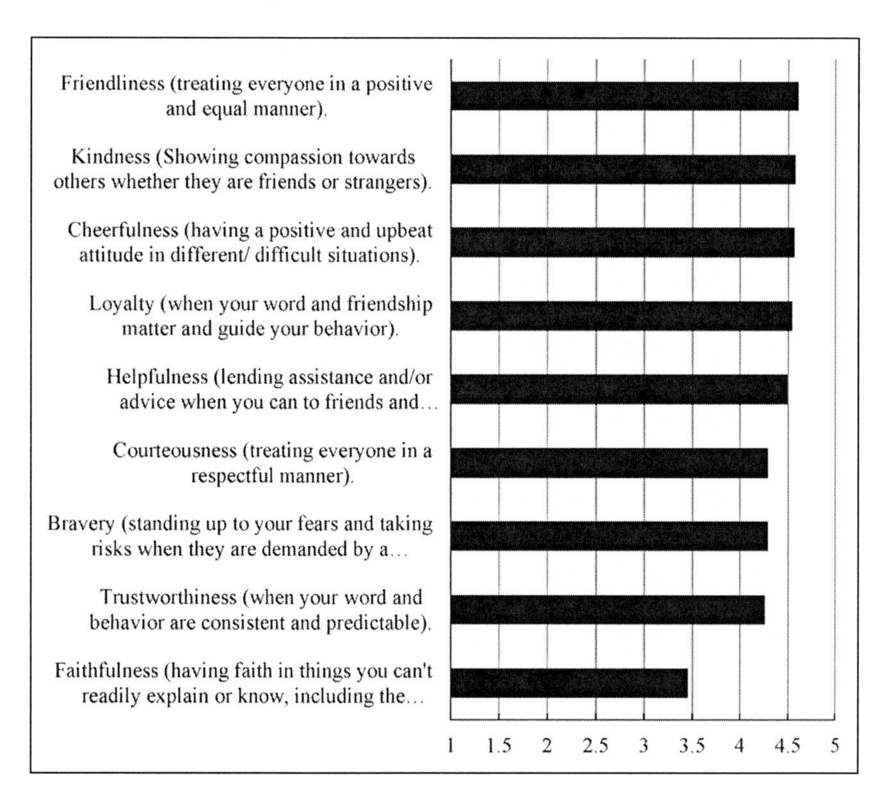

***Figure 19.1.* Bronies' perception that *MLP* endorses different values.**

the extent to which bronies themselves felt these different dimensions were related to their perceiving the virtues of helpfulness, friendliness, and kindness in the show itself (Kirchner, Griffin, & Edwards, 2017).

Figure 19.2 reveals that the moral dimensions of harm/care and fairness/reciprocity are the only moral foundations associated with seeing the show as containing prosocial virtues. Of note, the harm/care moral dimension was by far the most strongly associated with perceiving prosocial virtues in the show. In other words, to the extent that bronies value caring and protecting others, they tend to see the show as prosocial promoting prosocial values.

Reason for Liking the Show

So bronies certainly consider *MLP* to be a show espousing the virtues of prosocial behavior. But do they like the show *because* it contains these prosocial virtues?[9] To test this possibility, we examined whether bronies who felt the show promoted prosocial virtues also liked the show more. We also

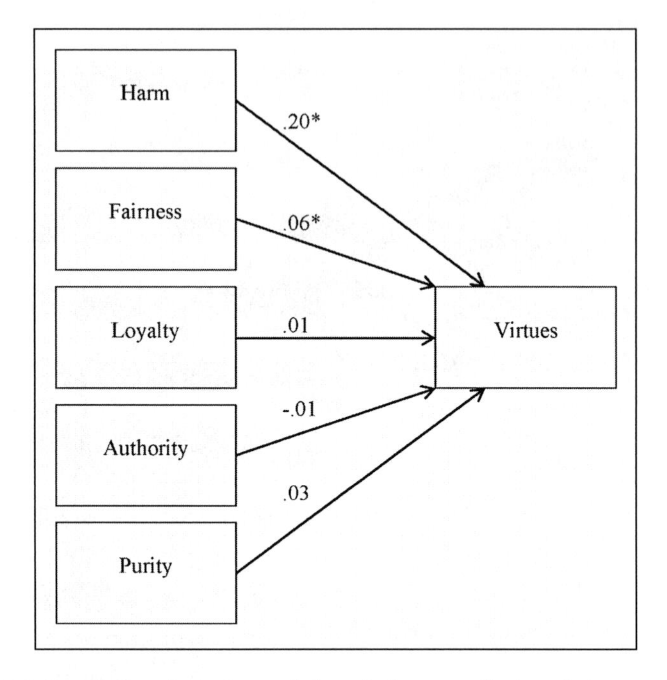

***Figure 19.2.* Bronies' endorsed moral foundations predicting their perception of virtues in *MLP*. (**This pathway is statistically significant.*)**

looked at whether this was driven, at least in part, by the fact that the show's moral message might have given bronies a sense of purpose or meaning.

As shown in Figure 19.3, there is a fairly robust link between seeing the show as having prosocial virtues and liking the show more. This association is driven in part by the fact that, at least for some bronies, *MLP* gives them a sense of guidance and purpose in their life—something to aspire to which, in turn, drives them to like the show all the more.

Fandom Comparison

To this point we've seen that bronies clearly appreciate the show for having prosocial virtues. But this is a far cry from saying that bronies themselves *engage* in prosocial behavior. We tested this directly in a study of bronies and fans of the popular Internet video producer Rooster Teeth (Plante, Chadborn, Groves, & Reysen, 2018).[10] Both groups rated how frequently they watched the show associated with their fan interest (i.e., *MLP* or Rooster Teeth) and completed measures of empathy and past charitable giving (e.g., "I have donated money to a charity"). The results showed that while bronies did not

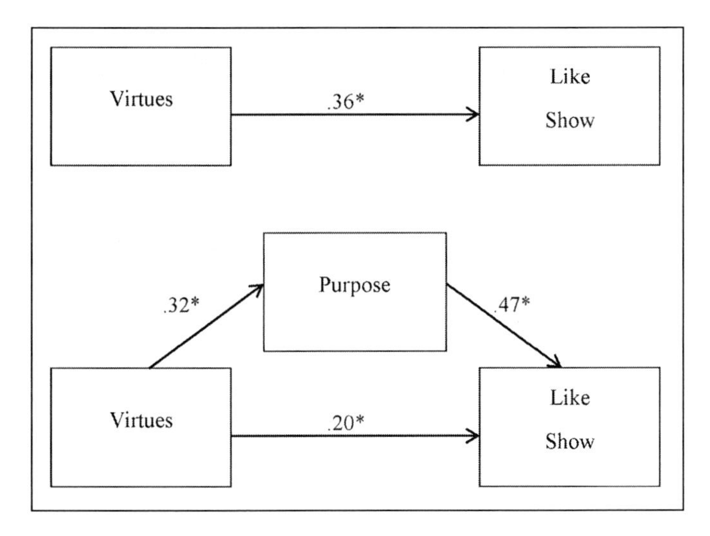

***Figure 19.3.* Purpose as a mediator between perception of the shows prosocial virtues and liking for *MLP*. (**This pathway is statistically significant.*)**

engage in *more* charitable giving than Rooster Teeth fans, bronies who watched more *MLP* engaged in more helping behavior. The same could not be said for Rooster Teeth fans. Follow-up analyses showed that, at least for bronies, more watching *MLP* was associated with stronger feelings of empathy which, in turn, was associated with more helping behavior. These findings are perfectly in line with other research on the effects of prosocial stories (Johnson, 2012) and music with prosocial lyrics (Greitemeyer, 2009).

Change in Helping

Since *MLP* has been shown to contain prosocial messages, and since past research shows that prosocial media leads to more prosocial behavior, the next logical step was to see whether bronies engaged in more prosocial behavior after joining the fandom. Bronies were asked how frequency they engaged in various prosocial behaviors in their community (e.g., "I have done something to help raise money for a charitable cause") and online (e.g., "When you play computer or console games, how often do you help or guide other players").

As shown in Figure 19.4, bronies stated that they helped others more—both in erson and online—*after* joining the brony fandom. Of course, this should be taken with a grain of salt: Without actually measuring the number of helping behaviors people engaged in before and after becoming a brony,

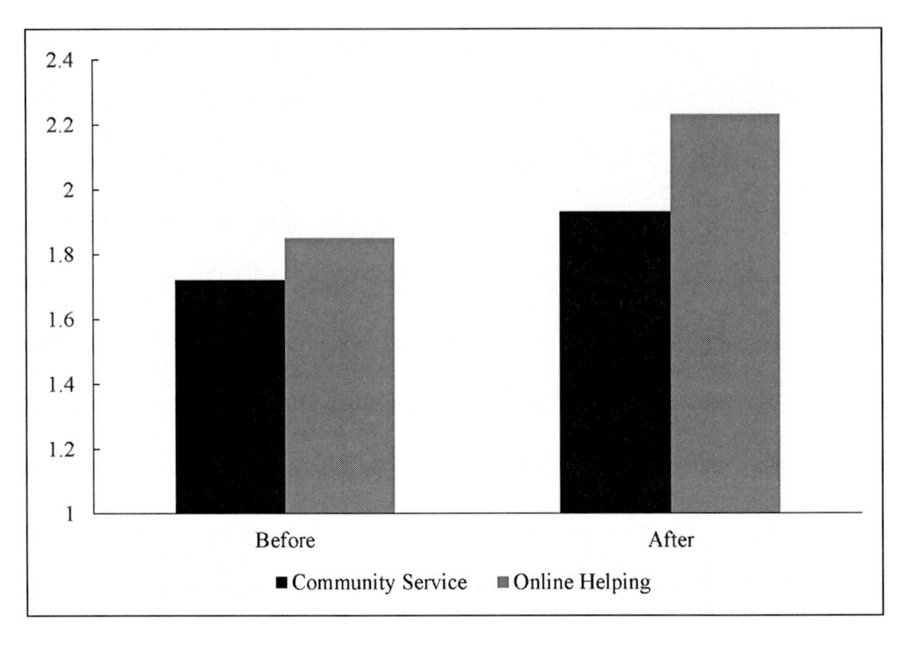

Figure 19.4. **Community service and online helping behaviors before and after becoming a brony.**

we're forced to rely on bronies' own reports of how much helping they've done and how much they've changed. Nevertheless, the findings, at very least, show that bronies *feel* like they've become more helpful after joining the fandom, and they're certainly in line with what we'd *expect* to find based on the reviewed research.

Giving and Receiving Help Within the Brony Fandom

All of the evidence seems to suggest that bronies engage in charity and helping behavior targeted toward those outside the fandom (e.g., donating to charities, helping strangers online). But what about helping others *within* the fandom? Certainly there are notable cases of bronies helping other bronies in need. If you recall from Chapter 1, we discussed two notable examples of bronies providing tremendous moral and financial support to two young boys who were bullied for loving the show and their families. Were these simply isolated cases, or is there evidence that, as a general rule, bronies help other bronies in need?

We assessed both the extent to which bronies reported *giving* help to

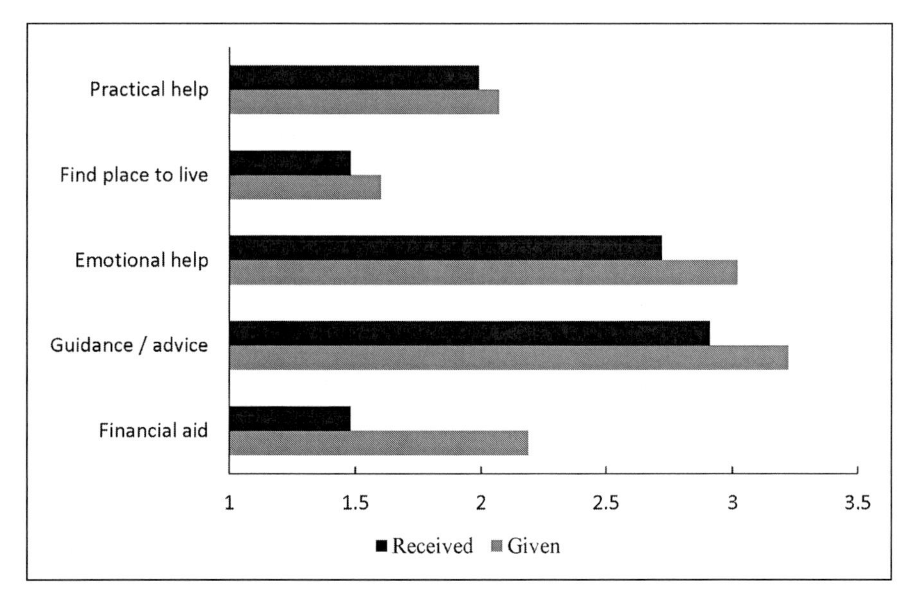

Figure 19.5. **Help given to and received from the brony fandom as rated by bronies.**

others in the fandom (e.g., "I have given help to bronies finding a place to life when they asked for it") and *receiving* help from others in the fandom (e.g., "I have received help finding a place to live from bronies when I asked for it") on a 5-point scale (1 = *never*, 5 = *frequently*). As shown in Figure 19.5, the most frequently given and received forms of help included emotional help and guidance/advice, which the average brony reported giving/receiving at least sometimes. When it comes to other kinds of help, such as financial aid, bronies are less likely to have received such help, though they do seem to report having given such help. This may reflect a sort of self-serving bias, where people want to see themselves in a positive light (i.e., having given more than they've received). Alternatively, bronies who were the recipients of money may not have participated in this study for one reason or another.[11]

Prosocial Fandom Norms

Let's take a final look at a possible contributor to bronies' prosocial behavior: fandom norms. This idea builds off the social identity perspective we introduced in Chapter 13. In a nutshell, the theory argues that threatened members of a group should more strongly adhere to the norms, values, and stereotypes of their group. To test this in bronies, Chadborn, Plante, and Reysen (2016) measured whether bronies felt a sense of stigma for being a brony, the extent to which they identified as a brony, their beliefs about norms in the brony fandom (e.g., "How many people within your fandom donate to charity because of direct appeals from other fans") and their own charitable behaviors (e.g., "performed volunteer work for a charity," "donated blood").

The results of the study revealed that bronies who saw their fandom as being particularly stigmatized identified more strongly with the brony fandom. They also saw the norms associated with the brony fandom (e.g., being charitable) as being stronger. This, in turn, was associated with individual bronies engaging in more charitable behavior. Interestingly, these results show that while stigma can often have harmful effects on bronies (see Chapter 17), it can also rally them to engage in acts of kindness and charity—in line with what the brony fandom demonstrated in the aforementioned anecdote about stepping in to provide support for the two young bullied members of their fandom. In short, bronies may be using the backlash against their fandom to embolden them to do better.[12]

Conclusion

Like other shows aimed at children (Smith et al., 2006), *MLP* contains numerous prosocial themes and morals. And, in line with research showing that prosocial media leads to more empathy and prosocial behavior, watching MLP and engaging with the brony community is associated with bronies' helping others. Not only do bronies recognize *MLP*'s prosocial messages (and liked the show for this reason), the extent to which they watch the show was associated with more empathy for others and ultimately more helping behavior. When it comes to helping within the fandom itself, bronies tend to do so primarily through providing advice and emotional support.

Importantly, the content of the show is not the only factor that contributes to bronies' helping: The fandom itself has numerous prosocial norms, including, among other things, love and tolerance and the norm to help one another out. Bronies are well aware of these norms, which in turn seem to influence the amount of prosocial behavior bronies engage in. While this link between fandom and kindness may not be entirely unique to brony fandom, it's nevertheless an important benefit to being a member of the brony community.[13]

Chapter 20

All Good Things: The Future of Friendship and the Fandom

"I have something extremely important to tell you about the future...."
—*Twilight Sparkle (Season 2, Episode 20,* It's About Time)

As we near the end of our look at the brony fandom, it only seems fitting that we finish up by talking about, well, the end. Or, more specifically, the end of *MLP:FIM* and the shape of things to come.

Midway through writing this book we were hit with two different announcements in rapid succession: the announcement of the last BronyCon and the announcement that season 9 would be the show's last. At first we were—as all good scientists should be—a bit skeptical of the rumor mill. After all, since at least 2012 there've been those decrying the end of days for the show and the fandom: from the fallout over "Derpy Hooves," to Twilight Sparkle getting her wings.[1] Who could have predicted that the show would eventually go to complete a nine-season run, a full-length motion picture, and a spin-off series with its own tie-in movies?[2]

This time, however, it seems like more than just idle rumors—the show really *is* going to come to an end—at least the current generation of it. So what does that mean for bronies and the fandom they've spent the better part of a decade creating?

One thing worth keeping in mind is that fan cultures have always been about more than the show itself. While there are always "neigh-sayers"[3] who'll argue that the fandom is nothing more than people who like a show, our own work—as well as the work of many other researchers—has made it clear that fandoms transcend their medium. This is true whether we're talking about television shows, literature, sporting events, or online communities (Ross, 2011; Stein, 2015; Williams, 2011). We don't deny that the conclusion of the show will mark the end of an era for the brony community. But it's hard to imagine that after nearly a decade the show itself will completely vanish—it will always be available somewhere online and on the hard-drives of diligent bronies who've stored every episode. More importantly, however, the communities which have spent years developing will continue on in at least some capacity—at least if other fandoms are any indication (Williams, 2015).[4]

This doesn't mean things won't be change, however. Some members of the fandom will leave, to be sure. The norms and routines fans have become accustomed to will certainly shift, as will the focus of the fandom. With the end of official *MLP:FIM* content, the focus of the fandom may shift to emphasize fan-made work more than the original show over time. But it's hard to know for sure. The future is sometimes scary for all its uncertainty. In this last research-focused chapter, we hope to address some of what we've learned about bronies' perception of the changing fandom, including looking back at some of those early discussions about the show's future, to see how the where the fandom sees itself now and where it sees itself going in the future.

With this in mind, our goals in this chapter are to first discuss what bronies expect regarding their future involvement in the fandom and what might affect it. Next, we'll delve into some of the reasons why bronies think people leave the fandom—in no small part so we can better understand who might stick around and why. Finally, we'll end this chapter by looking at what we might be able to glean about the future of the brony fandom based on past findings, including nostalgia, the direction of the fandom, finding a new home among related fan communities, how the fandom will maintain itself in the future, and what fans in the future should expect after the final curtain.

Expectations of Future Involvement

As we have previously discussed, when Dr. Edwards and Dr. Redden first started this research, they began by trying to organize bronies into different categories based on how open they were about being a brony and how strongly they identified with the fandom. As time went on, we began to notice a change in the frequency of these different "types" of brony in the fandom: an increase in "Social" bronies (highly identified, highly disclosing) and "Secret" bronies (highly identified, non-disclosing), to be specific. We also saw a drop off in Independent/Hipster fans (low identified, high disclosure) fans, which we suspected was a sign of losing people who were only on the brony bandwagon while it was popular.[5] Figure 20.1 demonstrates this effect as the

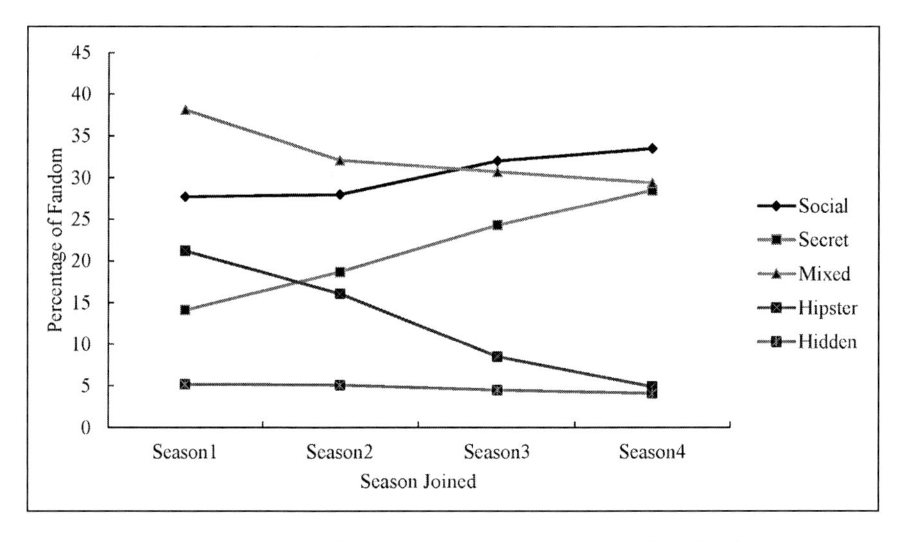

Figure 20.1. **Percentage of the fandom by typology joining within the first four seasons.**

Bronies joining early on compared to later in the early seasons saw a drastic shift between the "Hipster" and the "Mixed fans across the first few seasons."[6]

Through these changes, along with the controversies and drama that follows any fandom, the brony fandom has endured. If anything, it's a story of relative stability despite the storm. As a result, we're left with a large amount of information on current fans of the show. Unfortunately, due to the relative stability of the fandom and a lack of any mass exodus, it's actually been remarkably tough to study fans who leave. As such, we've been forced to rely on existing bronies to discuss their own experience with people leaving the fandom based on others they've seen leave the fandom or their own first-hand experience with considering leaving the fandom at some point.

From such studies we've found that fans have, for quite some time, predicted that they will have a fairly consistent trajectory in the fandom—namely, that they will continue to increase their involvement and interest in it over time (see Figure 20.2.)

If that's the case, who, if anyone, is likely to leave, and who can we expect to stick around for the long haul?

Predicting Future Involvement

Figure 20.2 seems to suggest that fans are pretty stable in their belief that they'll be around in the fandom forever—never planning to get off the ride, so to speak. But these average scores don't tell us the whole story: There

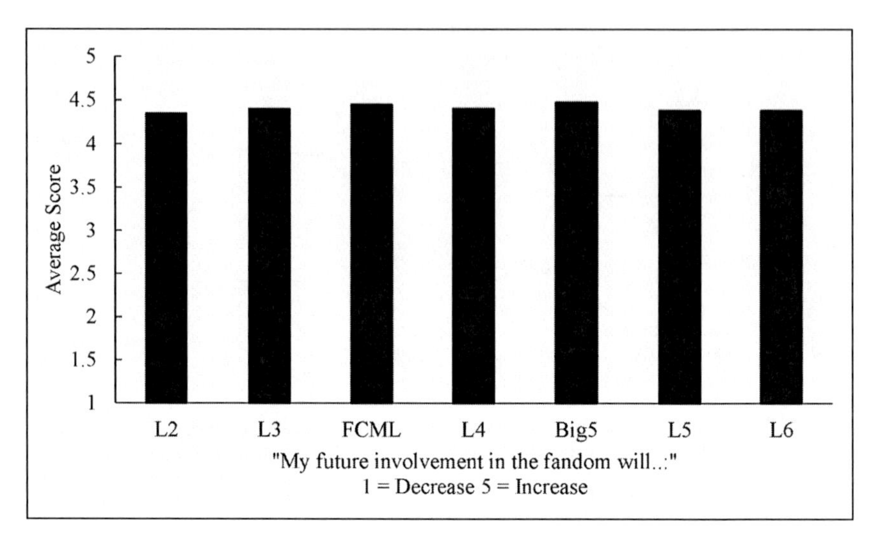

Figure 20.2. **Bronies predicting future involvement with the fandom.**

was variation within each wave. Specifically, some fans saw the writing on the wall and expected their own involvement in the fandom to decrease in the near future.

So how did these people differ from those who expected to stick around? Well, the people most likely to stick around were the ones who were driven to the fandom primarily for entertainment purposes, rather than for belongingness purposes. This makes a certain amount of sense: Those here because the show and its fan content are enjoyable are likely to stick around on the assumption that the content will continue to be enjoyable. In contrast, if you're in the fandom simply as a place to belong, you can get these same benefits from other communities as well.

And, perhaps to the surprise of no one, those who were the *most* interested in the show and its fandom were the ones most likely to expect to *continue* to be involved with the fandom in the future. Of course, intentions don't *guarantee* that these folks will actually stick around. But if research on other types of groups is any indicator, people's *intentions* to stick with a group typically translate into actually sticking with the group (Ouellette & Wood, 1998; Terry, Hogg, & White, 1999).

Why Do People Leave the Fandom?

Throughout this book we've discussed some of the various reasons bronies join the fandom. And you don't just have to take *our* word for it—studies of *other* fan groups have similarly shown that there are all sorts of reasons why people join their various fan communities (Ridings & Gefen, 2004).

What's far less understood is why people *leave* groups—fan groups or otherwise. Psychologists do know a bit about why people leave non-fandom groups: Something causes them to identify less with the group itself (Van Vugt & Hart, 2004), they start to lose interest in the subject (Wilhelm, Dewhurst-Savellis, & Parker, 2000), or simply having no commitments or ties to the group itself, which makes it easy enough to leave at the drop of a hat (Tajfel, 1974).[7] But rarely has anyone studied why fans leave their fan groups. And it's not hard to see why: It's pretty tough trying to get data on former fans.[8] So instead of focusing on *former* bronies, we focused our attention instead on bronies' own knowledge of why fans may leave the community.

Table 20.1 lists the questions we asked about why bronies might leave. For each of these possible reasons, we asked fans how much each of these issues have influenced *their own* interest in the fandom and whether they think these same factors influence other fans to leave. We've broken the results down in Figures 3 through 8 to make the results a little easier to digest. What they show, in a nutshell, is that the biggest issues for current bronies are also thought to be the same reasons that likely drive other bronies to leave.

So which of these factors was seen as the biggest problem for bronies, the one driving them to think about leaving the fandom? As it turns out, it's drama. As we can see in Figures 20.3 and 20.4, specific concerns about the show itself did edge out drama as a contributing factor. But, as seen in Figure 20.9, taken as a whole, drama was a bigger factor. It's also worth noting that these two may well be tied to one another: Bronies arguing about the show online (e.g., the show's future, issues with specific writers or plot points, complaints about character development) may well create drama. This is hardly unique to the brony fandom—comparable research on the furry fandom has similarly found that drama is the second-most common reason why furries leave their fandom.

Bronies may not like drama, and they may *say* that it's enough to drive them out of the fandom. But is there any evidence that drama is *actually* related to fan involvement? In short, yes. Of all the above-listed factors, drama was the *only* one that was significantly related to fans having less interest in the show and in the fandom itself. Drama was even related to fans watching fewer hours of the show. For all of the other issues, while fans may not have *liked* these problems, they didn't seem to affect how fans actually engaged with *MLP*-related content.

There are at least two ways to explain this relationship between drama and engagement. On the one hand, fans who see more drama in the fandom may find themselves associating that negativity with the show and generally be put off by it as a result (e.g., not being able to enjoy the show knowing

Table 20.1. Bronies' Perception of Why Bronies Leave the Fandom

Question	Factor	
1	Show/Season Issues	Anger and frustration at the show's direction.
2		Handling of specific events by the production team.
3		Feeling that the quality of the show has declined.
4		Boredom or indifference towards latest season.
5		Frustration with season length or breaks b/w seasons.
6	Drama	Too much drama between fan subgroups.
7		Obsessed fans arguing or putting others down.
8		Fandom elitist, shunning female fans.
9		Fan community doesn't engage in "love and tolerance."
10		"Love and tolerance" used to excuse negative behavior.
11		Fandom not becoming more positive/becoming cynical.
12	Loss of Interest	Loss of interest and inspiration from the show.
13		Interest blocks aspects of personal life.
14		Show/fandom no longer serves a useful purpose.
15		Too few new Bronies are joining the group.
16	Embarrassment	Embarrassment of vocal minority in fandom.
17		Discomfort at size/growth of the fandom.
18		There is too much media attention.
19	Seasonal Fans	Original Bronies have left/distanced themselves.
20		Many fans are seasonal.
21		Left because they can no longer contribute.
22	Other Reasons	Creative fans are seeking commercial outlets.
23		Fandom has lost its "shock value."
24		Caught up in the "fandom is dying" panic.
25		Community too big, no criteria for membership.
26		Desire to leave while the fandom is "on top."
27		Too much going on, oversaturation of events/meetups.

fans are arguing about it). Likewise, drama may make it hard to participate in the community, which might only serve as a reminder of the drama that's happening. On the other hand, it might be the case that those who watch more of the show and who more strongly identify with the fandom are simply *buffered* from the effects of drama and infighting in the fandom. While we don't yet know for sure which, if any, of these explanations for the link between drama and fandom involvement is true, future studies will hopefully shed some light on this subject.

Since drama seems to be related to less interest in the show and the fandom itself, is it also the case that drama causes bronies to see the fandom as shrinking and destroying itself? Not so much. Analyses suggest that a different factor seems to contribute to bronies' belief that the fandom is shrinking:

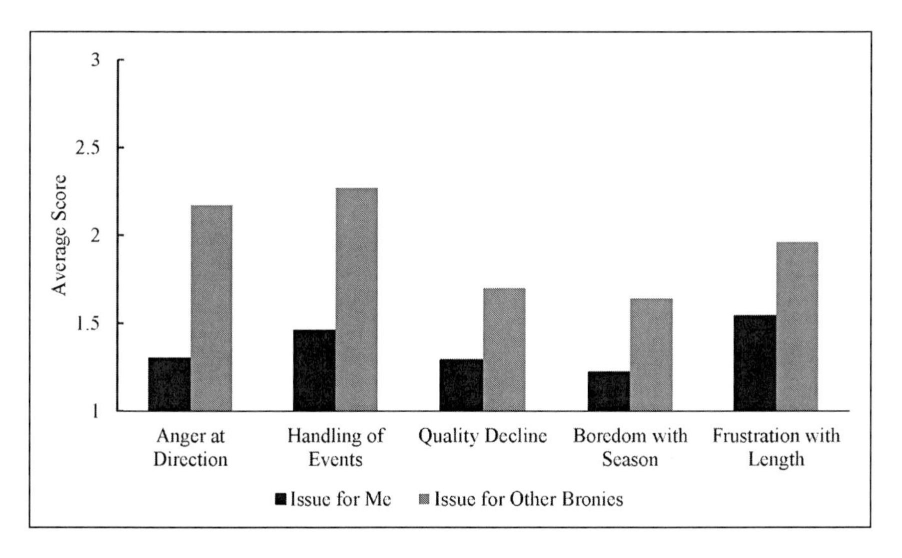

Figure 20.3. **Reasons why bronies leave: show/season issues. 1 = not an issue, 3 = strong issue.**

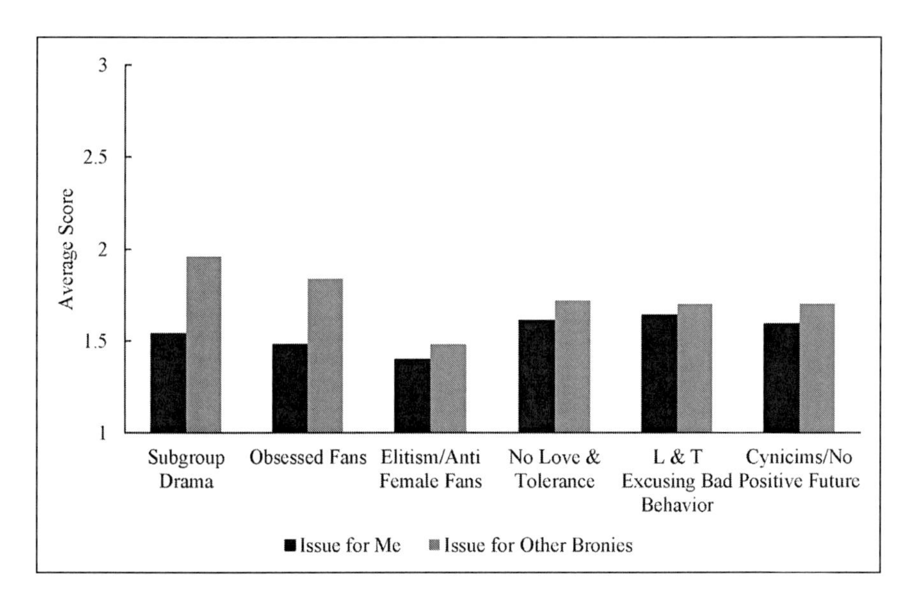

Figure 20.4. **Reasons why bronies leave: drama, 1 = not an issue, 3 = strong issue.**

Issues with the show itself (e.g., problems with how the show's creators handled issues like the character "Derpy Hooves," perceived drops in the quality of the show's writing and development, hiatuses between seasons that were too long). Community embarrassment also played a role in bronies' belief

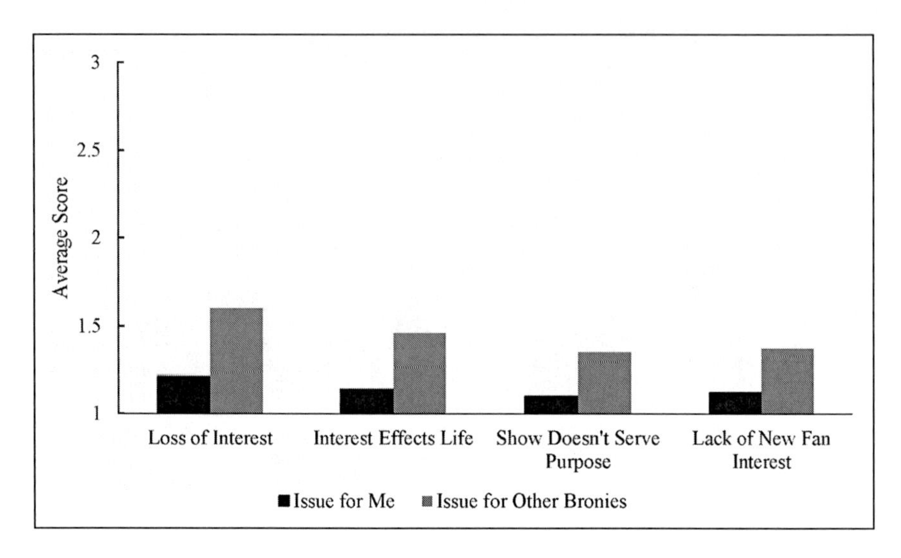

***Figure 20.5.* Reasons why bronies leave: loss of interest, 1 = not an issue, 3 = strong issue.**

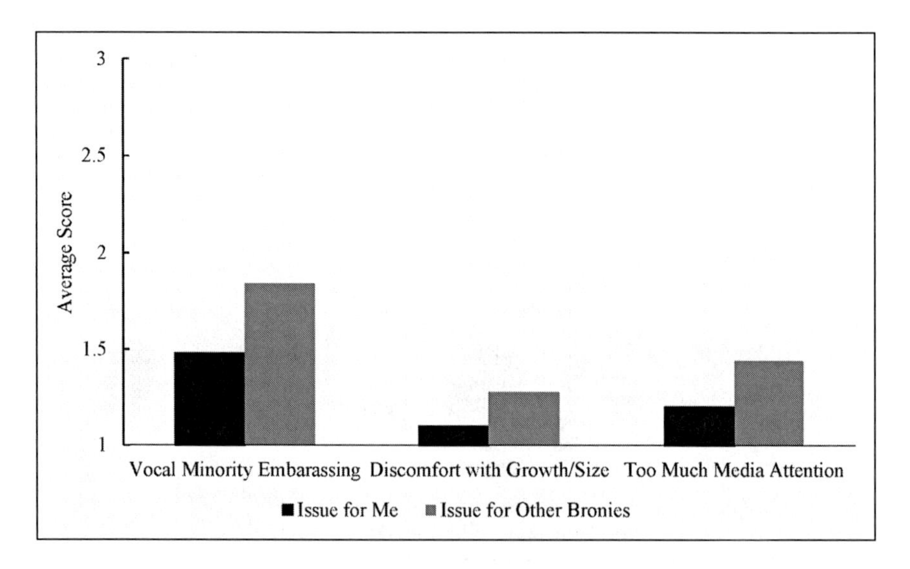

***Figure 20.6.* Reasons why bronies leave: embarrassment, loss of interest, 1 = not an issue, 3 = strong issue.**

that the fandom was shrinking (e.g., a vocal minority is causing conflict or making the fandom look bad).

In a nutshell, these findings suggest that drama (real or perceived) has the potential to sour bronies' *own* enjoyment of the show and their desire to

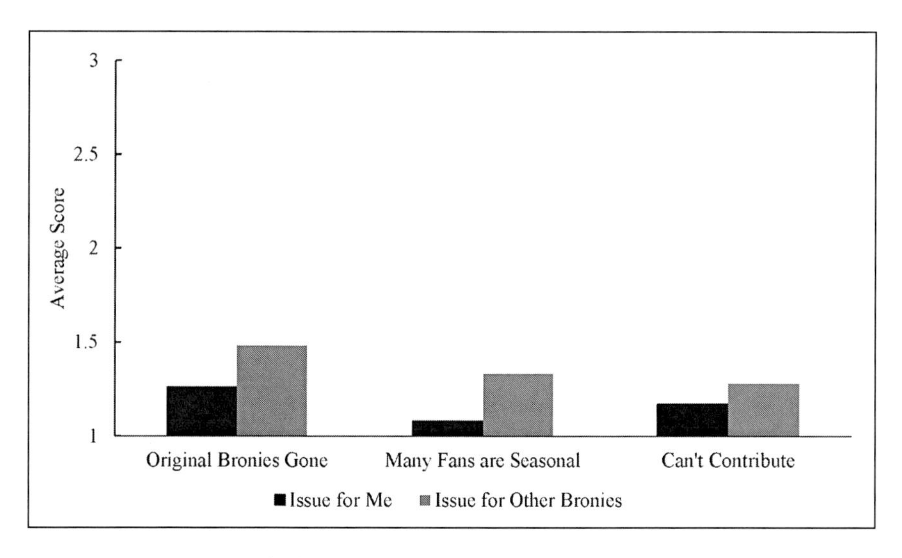

Figure 20.7. **Reasons why bronies leave: seasonal fans, 1 = not an issue, 3 = strong issue.**

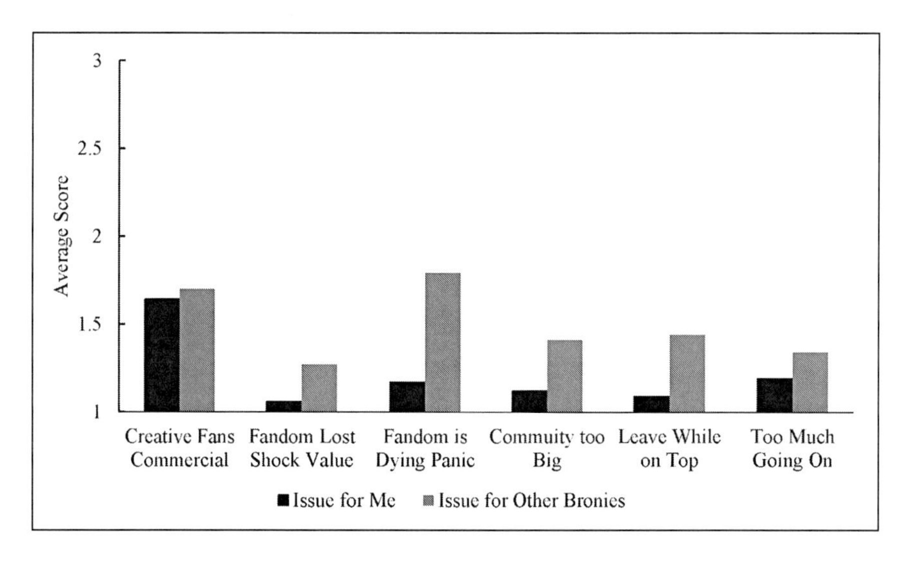

Figure 20.8. **Reasons why bronies leave: other reasons, 1 = not an issue, 3 = strong issue.**

be part of the fandom. But perceptions about the show itself seem to tie to bronies' view that the fandom itself shrinking.[9]

While these results offer a pretty good first look at why bronies may leave the fandom or whether the fandom itself is dying, it's been a hard subject

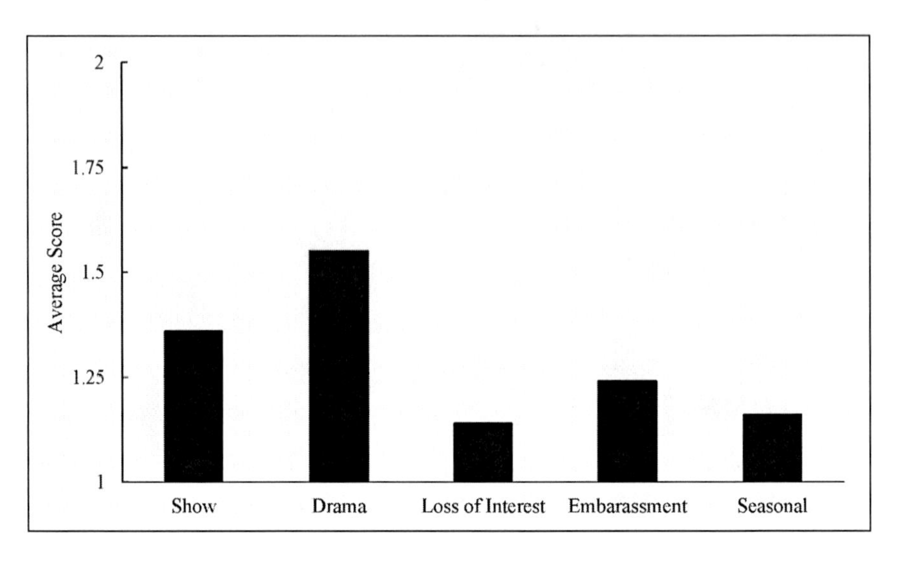

***Figure 20.9.* Bronies' own perceived problems with the fandom: all factors, 1 = not an issue, 3 = strong issue.**

to study. The topic is not a particularly fun one for bronies to discuss. After all, it's hard to be critical and accept the flaws and ugly parts of something someone loves. Nor is particularly fun to realize that the ride will eventually come to an end. In fact, in a recent survey, we found that the threat of the fandom ending significantly reduced bronies' willingness to even label themselves as a brony.

And yet, as we've seen in other fandoms, the end of the show does not have to mean the end of the fandom itself.

What the Future Holds

The end is not always the end. True, threats of the fandom ending certainly create drama and panic surrounding the uncertainty of the fandom's future. But history is also full of anecdotes and sayings about the bittersweet nature of loss. "'Tis better to have loved and lost than never to have loved at all," said Alfred Lord Tennyson. Or, in a more contemporary example, Mae Borowski, the main character of the *phenomenal* video game *Night in the Woods*, states, "When my friends leave, when I have to let go, when this entire town is wiped off the map, I want it to hurt. Bad.... Because that means it meant something."

There's something to be said for how bronies see their fandom—past, present, and future. We can learn something from their feelings on these subjects and give some potential advice (and yes, even some hope!) to those who want the community to continue long after the show's finale. Not all of this advice is positive, but even the negative points offer warning signs or cautionary tales and can give us some insight into what the future of the fandom may hold.

Nostalgia's One Hell of a Drug

Nostalgia has a *huge* influence on our behavior, as recent studies have begun to show. For example, feelings of nostalgia can boost crowdfunding campaigns for cancelled shows (Booth, 2015) and increase the value of an artifact among fan collectors (Geraghty, 2014). Anyone who's dug up an old movie or game from their past *knows* how "nostalgia goggles" can help us look past something's faults and see it for the gem that it is.[10] Our vision of childhood movies and the way things used to be is so well-known and so impactful that advertisers have used it for decades to influence our buying decisions (Havlena & Holak, 1991; Reisenwitz, Iyer, & Cutler, 2004).

Our own data shows that bronies themselves are not without a sense of nostalgia: Those who've spent more time in the fandom experience more nostalgia for the way things used to be in the fandom. But nostalgia is a double-edged sword. On the one hand, these feelings of nostalgia in older fans may create resistance to new and exciting directions for the content.[11] On the other hand, nostalgia can be a powerful muse, sparking the creativity and productivity of fan creators (Sedikides & Wildschut, 2016; van Tilburg, Sedikides, & Wildschut, 2015).[12] A 2016 study found that nostalgia also increases optimism and self-esteem (Cheung, Sedikides, & Wildschut, 2016).

What this means for bronies is that nostalgia, while able to cloud their judgment in some areas (i.e., spending way too much on a Twilight Sparkle plushie), can also create feelings of hopefulness, optimism, and even connection and community with other fans who share that same passion.

And hey, if *Futurama* fans have taught us anything, it's that a show can be brought back long after its original end if enough nostalgic fans create a demand for it!

Sharing Spaces

We mentioned that one of the potential downsides to nostalgia is a reluctance or closed-mindedness to change. We may well be seeing this in the mixed reception of bronies to the idea of embedding themselves within other fan communities in the future.

Every year thousands of fan conventions take place around the world, incorporating fans from a wide variety of communities who come together for the sake of sharing their interests.[13] Many modern conventions are a shared space for many different fan communities to coordinate, interact, and even recruit new members. This doesn't mean that there *aren't* fandom-specific conventions like BronyCon for bronies, Anthrocon for furries, and Otakon for anime fans. But these conventions typically require a "critical mass" of fans to be able to sustain the convention. And as the largest of the brony-specific conventions enters its last year, and in the face of falling convention attendance numbers, the brony community is faced with the question of whether they should consider opening traditionally "brony only" conventions to other, related groups (e.g., furries, *Stephen Universe*, other cartoon series).

When we asked bronies how they felt about sharing convention space with other fan groups, they were fairly mixed on the subject, as seen in Figures 20.10 and 20.11. In general, bronies seem to somewhat oppose the idea of welcoming non-bronies into brony conventions, or even the very idea that brony conventions may need to include other fan communities to survive. That said, in a bit of a contradiction, they also seem to disagree that brony conventions should be entirely filled with *MLP* and *Equestria Girls* content.

How these attitudes might influence the fandom and its conventions in the future is still anyone's guess. Bronies may not be strongly against other fan content at their conventions, although they're still bothered by the fact that it's there. Whether this is because it's a threat to bronies' sense of identity or simply due to it being a reminder that the brony fandom may not be growing the way it once was remains to be seen. While bronies may be a little conflicted on the subject, these views may change once the show has come to an end. Other fandoms (e.g., the *Star Trek* fandom) may serve as a useful model for bronies seeking to continue having brony meet-ups and conventions long after the show itself has concluded. Or perhaps bronies will buck the trend and shore up the continued support needed to keep brony-only conventions afloat well into the future.

Protecting the Fandom

We'll finish up with two topics that paint an optimistic future for the brony fandom. In this first topic, we turn to previous research showing that people who strongly identify with a group are highly motivated to act in ways that protect the group. Bronies are no different from other groups in this regard. This includes a greater willingness to attend a rally or protest if the fandom were threatened, to take action if threats were ever leveled at the fandom, to write letters of support to Hasbro, and to be willing to speak publicly in defense of the fandom.

Perhaps even more interesting, however, is the fact that this willingness to defend the fandom seems to be driven by bronies' hope for the future of

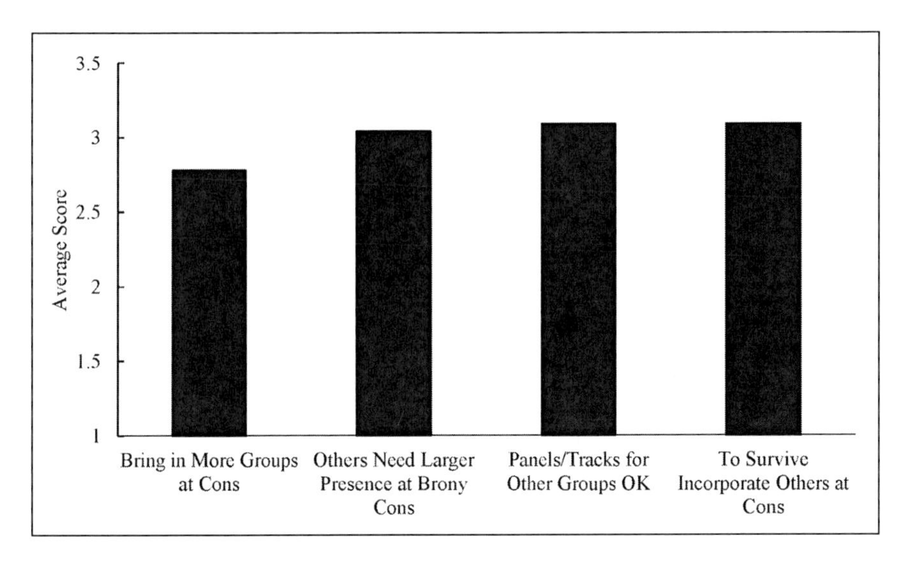

***Figure 20.10.* Bronies' attitudes toward shared space: including others, 1 = strongly disagree 7 = strongly agree.**

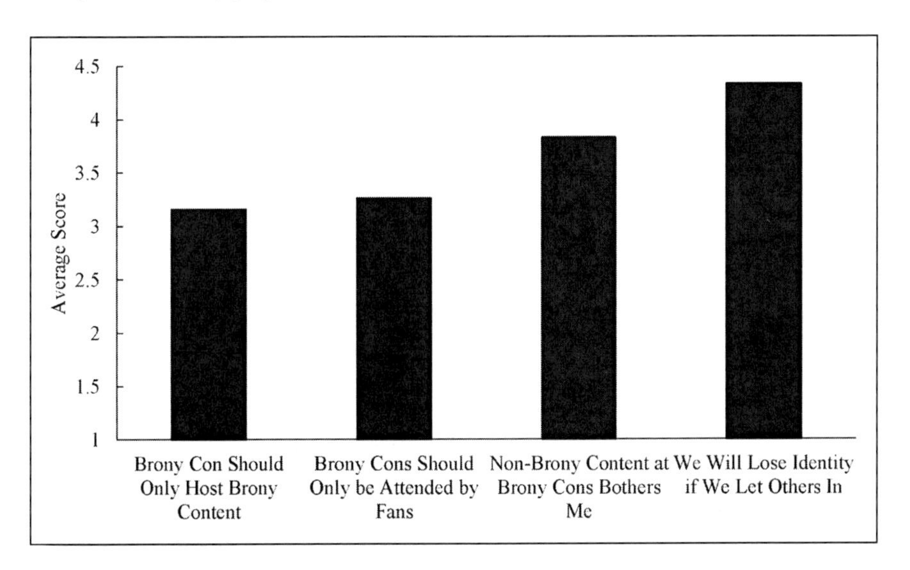

***Figure 20.11.* Bronies' attitudes toward shared space: bronies only, 1 = strongly disagree, 7 = strongly agree.**

the fandom. In other words, strongly-identified bronies are also the most hopeful about the fandom's future, and are thus the most likely to take action themselves to make it happen.

What this means is that the future of the brony fandom is likely to be carried by those who are both the most passionate about *MLP* and those who have the most optimism about the fandom as a whole. While identifying as a brony alone isn't likely to drive fans to action, believing that the fandom has a future may well drive letter-writing campaigns, efforts to create new fan conventions, and the desire to maintain the fan community long after the show has ended.

The Show and the Fandom

While identifying as a brony, in and of itself, may not drive bronies to act to protect their fandom, it *does* predict other facets of future involvement. Our own research has found that there are differences between being a member of the brony community (fandom) and simply being an avid watcher of the show (fanship). In short, the future of the fandom is more closely tied to fandom identity than with fanship. Whether looking at convention attendees or bronies gathered at a local meet-up, we've consistently found that identifying with the brony community is related to greater confidence in the survival of the fandom, more meetup and con attendance, and greater involvement in the fandom in general. Bronies, as a group, are motivated to stay active and involved in the fandom and to want to keep these things going, rather than simply tuning out and finding something else to watch once the show is no longer around.

Conclusion: All Good Things

Change is the only constant in life. It's as true for the rise and fall of empires as it is for fandoms. But even as fandoms reach their peak and inevitably decline, this doesn't mean they necessarily fade into nothingness. There are fandoms today which have existed for more than a century. Railroad enthusiasts are as old as rail itself. The first science fiction convention, World-Con, dates back to 1939. *Star Trek* has spanned 6 series, more than a dozen movies, and has had an active fandom the entire time. For bronies, the end is likely far from the end. If you take anything from this chapter, let it be that bronies have reason to be optimistic about their future. It can be hard for bronies to see it this way, especially as, for many, the brony fandom marks their first foray into fandoms themselves. But they can rest assured that the *MLP* fandom is far from the first to have had its source material end. Nor was it the first to have to deal with drama and trolls in their ranks: Diogenes plucked a chicken and called it a human to troll Socrates,[14] Anne Rice sent cease-and-desist orders to fanfiction writers in her fandom, and pretty much *everyone* seemed to have a problem with George Lucas after the *Star Wars* prequel trilogy. And when it comes to cringeworthy, embarrassing public fan behavior, it's hard to beat Sherlock Holmes fans.[15] Specifically, the ones who actually wore black and held mock funeral services in public after his death at the Reichenbach Falls.[16] Bronies have gone through, and will continue to go through, what nearly every fandom has at one time or another. And while it may seem like it's on the verge of ending, it's unlikely to be going anywhere anytime soon.

We hope you leave this chapter with hope regarding the future of the brony fandom. Bronies themselves—at least the highly identified ones—have this same sense of hope, emboldened by their nostalgia for the "golden age" of the fandom and their desire to maintain the community in the future. And who can blame them? If there's anything that makes the brony fandom distinct from other fandoms, it's the overall positivity of it all: from Pinkie Pie encouraging us all to smile to Twilight's lessons on Friendship; from Fluttershy's reminders that we should be kind to Rarity's assertion that we shouldn't be afraid to shine. Rainbow Dash taught us to be awesome along the way and Applejack ... well ... she taught us that apples are pretty good.[17]

This sort of positivity and optimism is what's going to keep the brony fandom going for years to come.

> *I may not know what comes next for you, but whatever it is, I promise I'll always be there for you.*
>
> —*Twilight Sparkle* (*Season 7, Episode 1,* Celestial Advice)

Chapter 21

Dear Princess Celestia: Parting Words from Bronies and the Research Team

"From this day forth, I would like you all to report to me your findings on the magic of friendship, when, and only when, you happen to discover them."
—Princess Celestia (Season 2, Episode 3, Lesson Zero)

In 2011 we began a simple project to understand a group of fans who seemed unusual in their love of a television show about colorful ponies. Little did we know that this investigation would lead us down a rabbit hole of friendship, knowledge, and far more work than any of us imagined! We've had a few missteps along the way, but we've also had some amazing triumphs. Unlike Twilight, who reported her findings to Celestia as she discovered them, science in the real world—and the reporting of it—takes a bit more time. So much so, in fact, that many of us have changed considerably since the start of the project.[1]

We've learned so much *about* this community and *from* this community. Much of this we'll never be able to fully spell out in research papers or talks. So instead we figured we'd finish this book with some of our last insights, conclusions, and personal thoughts about what we've learned from our work. We'll start with some words from fans to us, which we hope will help offer a better understanding of what bronies get from their involvement in the community. We'll then finish up with our own thoughts about what we've learned since from the brony community.

Dear Brony Study

Early on our focus was on why bronies joined the community and gradually evolved to look at the benefits that the community provided for them.

Being a part of a community, especially one with strong norms of giving, inclusiveness, and friendship, is a boon for people who may otherwise have trouble feeling accepted.

In our survey on "How the Fandom Changed My Life" we noted many of the positive changes bronies experienced as a result of "joining the herd." Since the beginning of the study, Dr. Redden has been managing our emails and contacts with fans, parents, concerned participants, and anyone coming across our website. In our newer surveys, Drs. Chadborn and Plante have similarly listened to questions and comments from the brony fandom. Through all these mediums, bronies have reached out to us and offered us their thoughts, positive suggestions, thanks, and encouragement. And, most relevant of all, they told us first-hand how the fandom changed their lives.

This is, of course, just a small sample of what we've received over the years from fans, but we hope that it gives you, the reader, some further insight into what being a brony has meant to members of the fandom.[2]

While at the time of writing, he still did not feel comfortable sharing his interest openly with others, a brony from the Midwest United States described the show as the "best form of anti-depressant" helping him cope with bullying and depression.

After a period of isolation and mistrust of others, finding the show through a friend, an brony from the Southwest United States described the show as "so innocent and sweet, and allowed me to feel happy and safe in a world where I hadn't been able to feel those things in a long time … but watching the show helped remind me of what pleasant interpersonal interactions could be like. My anger quieted, my happiness returned. It quite literally helped me get my life back after I had fallen into a very dark place."[3]

We heard this from an 20-year-old brony: "Personally, ever since I became a brony, I never been so happy to be part of an amazing fandom full of all kinds of creative, fun, awesome people.... But more so because.... I never had so many friends in my life." A female brony from Australia told us, "I'm happier, more social, more open, more confident, more ME.... I have no idea what I would have done without ponies."

A brony from Western Europe, discussing his life and difficulties in general after finding the show, said, "Ever since becoming a brony ive experienced the best I could imagine, but also the worst. Occasionally I ask myself if its worth it, I always come to the same conclusion. It sure is."

At BronyCon in 2012, a father, in tears, discussed with Dr. Edwards his son's reversal from isolation, depression, and suicidal ideation through his engagement with the fandom. Another 16-year-old fan wrote: "The day I was going to kill myself was the day I became a Brony … the show saved my life and I am grateful for it, I have yet to tell them how I became a Brony and more than likely I wont. but there is my story and how a bunch of multicolor ponies changed and saved my life." A 17-year-old from Western Europe reported after years of bullying: "...my life gets even better when I took of for Japan the last summer's holliday with people I didn't know, while in Japan I plainly assumed my Brony statement by wearing a T-shirt ... and cap ... with the inscription 'BRONY' ... and nobody was judging me, well some ask why I enjoy the show but they didn't judged me, I was REALLY HAPPY, that was the first time in my life that strangers accepted me as I am!!"

We bring up these stories not to portray the brony fandom as a cure-all for depression or mental illness, but to illustrate what we've learned from our work. For many outsiders it's hard to see the how beneficial it is to interact with like-minded individuals, even if the thing you have in common is your favorite show. And while they could likely get the same benefit out of belonging to any other group, the brony fandom may be particularly supportive to those feeling isolated or down, as has been shown for other stigmatized communities (Frable, Wortman, & Joseph, 1997; Reysen, Plante, & Chadborn, 2017).

Other fans have discuss experiences and benefits of the brony fandom that have *nothing* to do with mental health. One brony told us, "I became a brony after having researched why grown men would like the show *MLP*. I soon decided to watch an episode myself and to my surprise it wasn't so bad. I enjoyed the show in a recreational sense but even more impressed by what the fandom had to offer. ......The fandom has so many resources to help others develop skills—whether it be in animation, art, music, brony friends."

After seeing the show while his sister watched it, a fan from Appalachia reported, "This scared me to death. I didn't allow myself to watch it for a good 3 months." After some derogatory comments by a family member about boys who watch the show, he did some research. Now he views the program as a relief from stress and gave him a new perspective on the value of friendship. It also has helped him deal with bullying and has led to expanding his interests in creativity. Another brony from North America shared, "*MLP* introduced me to a great TV show that I look forward to watching ... and gave me opportunities to better myself as an individual and open up socially ... I have made four brony friends ... even befriended a few non-bronies." He got a promotion at work and went from "a shy, insecure boy who didn't know what he was going to do with his life, to a sociable, confident man who's set his sights on an engineering degree.... I'm confident that watching My Little Pony: Friendship Is Magic, was one of the best decisions I ever made." An 18-year-old from the Eastern United States commented, "*MLP* and the fandom has helped me think about things more. Not to take my first impression. I also feel generally happier."

And finally, an anonymous brony had this to say: "Before I became a brony, I tended to be more skeptical about new experiences, was a more picky eater, and was ok with many gender stereotypes that were and still are very common.... After becoming a brony, I realized that I was wrong about many things I thought were normal and right. I became more open to new experiences and foods. My tastes in music, movies, and reading material changed.... I sought more information about people/events before I formed opinions on them. That moment of opening up to a "show for six-year-old little girly girls' showed me that many times preconceptions about things like *MLP* and other things can lead you away from something you'll love. The lessons on friendship have also improved my interpersonal skills and I'm not quite as socially awkward as I used to be."

Dear Princess Celestia

To finish off, we here are our own last words about what we've taken away from our experience studying the brony fandom. In the tradition of Twilight and her friends, we would like to issue this final report of our findings on the science and psychology of the brony fandom.

Dear Princess Celestia and the Brony Fandom,

I cannot speak for everyone on the team, but my journey with Brony Study has been tied heavily to my journey in psychology. I started shortly after achieving my master's degree and being a part of this study and then moving on and working with some of the other members has helped me to grow as a researcher, writer, and psychologist.[4] Outside of the science aspects of my experience, my experience with fan research in general, publications, and interactions with the bronies, as both friends, acquaintances, and research participants has broadened my perspective and aided in how I interact and deal with others, especially those who don't like the same things as I do. Honestly, the biggest thing that I have learned from engaging in fan research with bronies, or reading through the research on cosplayers, anime fans, Furries, Trekkies, sport fans and many others is that the core aspects of what makes a person a fan runs fairly consistent throughout all groups. Some of the motivations may differ (entertainment vs. belonging vs. several others), but in the end any group you look at is as diverse as any other, with the only difference being what their collective interest is. There are variations amongst fans regarding their level of enjoyment, engagement, and interest. There are differences in demographics, backgrounds, and future trajectories and that many of them also find themselves fans of video games, sports, literature, and several other communities. What this has taught me is that what people enjoy is just a part of who they are. We can have debates over why music today is or isn't as good as music twenty years ago, what television show is the best, or whether the latest *Star Wars* movie lived up to the previous ones. The big takeaway though is that the fans of all these things are drawn by the same underlying psychological benefits and, outside of toxic communities or those perpetuating harm to others, the effects are generally positive. Over the last decade of research and reflection, heavily motivated by my interaction with fans who love the show and those who would demean and degrade those who like something they don't, I would say the biggest thing I learned was to enjoy things for what they are and to not hate someone for liking something I don't.[5]

In the end, through my work with Brony Study I have grown, learned, and taught and will continue to do so. I hope for continued interaction with the fans, other communities, and the psychological community which has been sometimes skeptical, often shocked and confused, but mostly accepting after explanation when confronted with our brony research. In the future I would like to see a continued examination of meaning and purpose in fandom research, its expansion to larger studies and group comparisons, and the growing examination of fan communities outside of sport. While the future can be uncertain, I am hopeful that both our study and the fandom will march on. Just as we have learned about friendship, fan science and psychology can also be magic.[6]

Sincerely,
Daniel Chadborn, Ph.D.

~ ~ ~

Dear Princesses Celestia and Luna and to their followers and fans

Over the course of my life, I have learned to "Never say never" as we can never know what the future holds. When my 16 year old son shared with me that he was a Brony I followed my scientific curiosity and initiated an online research project studying the Brony fandom. If someone had told me that I would become one of the world's foremost experts on a fandom, be featured in two documentaries, present research at over 40 regional and national Psychology conferences as well as eight fan conventions (BronyCon 2012–2018). I would have shook my head and said "no way"!

I would like to thank my son, my fellow researchers and the thousands of Brony fans who completed my online surveys and attended my BronyCon panels. Without your support this book would not exist!

I often share with my students the advice to "be certain, but humble." We should be certain about who we are and what we believe and cherish, but humble because others how differing beliefs and experiences. I find that this advice helps lessen criticism of people who hold different viewpoints, different likes and dislikes. While I have an extensive background in psychology (having taught for 34 years at the college and university level), I approached this exploration of the fandom with an open mind, with the plan of letting the fans educate me. I was surprised when one of the first bronies I interviewed told me about the WWBD statement ("What Would a Brony Do?"). I immediately recognized that this represented a guidance function, where fans find answers to questions about friendship and social interactions. I believe there is an important lesson embedded in this finding, as I have found indications of similar functions (guidance) within other fandoms (Disney Princesses, *Star Trek*, anime, Marvel superheroes, etc.). I believe that fans of different fandoms may have more in common (functionally) than they have differences.

The brony fans and the BronyCon gatherings have provided me with both a source of inspiration and a hope for the future. I have had numerous parents and individual brony fans tell me how the fandom fueled positive changes in their lives, even to the point of "saving" their lives. In a world where adolescents and young adults face tremendous adjustments as they search for an identity and a sense of intimacy, in their family and school environment, being a brony appears to have helped many of them. Our research indicates that social groups like the brony fandom can provide a significantly stable and safe place for fans to grow, develop, and heal.

I like to think that the Brony Study has played a small, but significant role in the growth and development of the fandom. Our early research findings help to dispel various false/negative stereotypes about the fandom and highlighted the positive prosocial nature of the group.

It saddens me to think that the fandom may decline with the end of *MLP: FIM*. However, like Pinkie Pie, in the video *Will the Real Pink Pony Please Sit Down*, I believe that as long as brony artists, music producers and fan fiction writers continue their creative efforts and the fan continue to embrace the message of love and tolerance, the fandom will live on. I hope that this book will contribute to that survival.

Extending thanks and acknowledgments,
Pat Edwards, Ph.D., "Dr. Psych Ology," Brony Study Founder

~ ~ ~

Dear Princess Twilight Sparkle,[7]

Like many bronies, I never *expected* to become a brony. I started off as a curious social psychologist. The signs were all there, and in retrospect, it should have been pretty obvious that I'd wind up in the fandom sooner or later. I was a furry for years, and an ardent fan of cartoons. If it was animated and had walking talking animals in it, I liked it. So when a friend sat me down and made me watch an episode of *My Little Pony: Friendship Is Magic* years ago, I did it "for science." It was an intellectual exercise, a chance to better understand the mindset of a group that, I admit, I thought was pretty weird.[8]

I couldn't have known that one episode would lead to another, which would lead to another season, which would lead to my discovering the University of Waterloo Brony Club, which would lead to my traveling to BronyCon, which would ultimately lead to my jumping on-board to study the brony fandom in conjunction with my research on the furry fandom. Call it a pleasant surprise,[9] but I'm eternally grateful that I gave the show a chance, because it's been a humbling experience for me.

From the moment I had jumped on board with the research, I was already convinced of the benefits that a fandom could have. Years in the furry fandom had taught me just how important it was to have people in your corner, someone to be there for you when the chips were down and life was tough. But, somehow,

I still had it in my head that this was something you only saw in the furry fandom. That the friendships and connections I had seen first-hand there couldn't *possibly* exist anywhere else, let alone in a group as strange as the brony fandom.

If I've learned nothing else, it's the fact that I'm really, really good at being wrong! Despite the apparent differences between furries and bronies, they have *so* much in common. And, as our work continues, it becomes increasingly apparent to me that while there's something "magical" about the brony fandom, it's certainly not *unique* to bronies. The story of bronies isn't a story about how "weird" or "different" they are. It's a story about just how much they have *in common* with everyone else. It's a story about how a fandom centered around colorful ponies can feel so *human*. We all want to fit in, whether we're talking about little girls, grown men, and everyone in between and beyond existing dichotomies. We all want to have people who care for us and who we can rely on. We all want to feel like we matter and to share the things we love with others.

So I suppose that's my lesson: Bronies aren't so different from the furries that I had come to know and love and rely upon. They're not so different from church groups or work friends or the pals you have a drink with while watching the game. Bronies, despite their surface-level weirdness, are surprisingly well-adjusted, healthy, and, above all else, *normal*.

Now, if you'll excuse me, I'm off to re-read some *Fallout Equestria*—I just can't get enough magical, colorful friendship horses surviving in the hellscape of post-apocalypse Equestria. You know, a perfectly normal hobby.

Your Faithful Student,
Courtney "Nuka" Plante, Ph.D.

~ ~ ~

Dear Princess Celestia,

First, let me thank you for your time, effort and guidance of the herd of ponies through *My Little Pony: Friendship Is Magic*. The timeliness, variety of lessons, and presentation in a way that was interesting and engaging can not be overstated. Personally, it provided a unique way of teaching those lessons that I wish I had had when I was a therapist.

I would particularly like to thank you for encouraging the bronies to write and share their stories, suggestions and criticisms with the Brony Study research group. I enjoyed reading these and communicating with the fandom. Communicating with those who showed interest at conventions and BronyCon was also enlightening and enjoyable.

In closing, it is my hope that you continue with your very important work and guidance of your ponies.

Gratefully yours,
Marsha Howze Redden, Ph.D., "Dr. Sci Entific"

~ ~ ~

Dear Princess Celestia,

During this project I've grown fond of the brony fandom. As stated many times throughout this book, fandoms, regardless of what they happen to be centered around, are psychologically similar to one another. The research shows that bronies, in general, are similar to other fan groups—they certainly have more in common with them than they have differences. Nevertheless, there are several unique aspects about the brony fandom that make me glad the brony fandom exists, including its prosocial norms and the way it weaves lessons about being a good person into both the show and the fandom itself. In short, the world could use more fandoms like the brony fandom in it.

Sincerely,
Stephen Reysen, Ph.D.

Chapter Notes

Preface

1. Otherwise, you'd be holding "Part One" of a very, *very* long series of books!

2. We love 'em! They make us laugh until our voices are *hoarse*.

Chapter 1

1. For those keeping track at home, Dr. Chadborn and Dr. Plante are our self-identified bronies.

2. In some contexts, the term "pegasister" (a portmanteau of the terms "pegasus" and "sister") is sometimes used to refer to women who would otherwise meet the definition of the term "brony." Our decision to treat the term "brony" as a catch-all has been done for brevity's sake—it's far easier to write "brony" than it is to write "bronies and pegasisters," especially since most people in the fandom use the term "brony" regardless of their gender.

3. We can't help but feel that writing statements like these are tempting Discord and any other lords of chaos to intervene!

4. That, or they picture an oscillating mechanical device with spinning blades that circulates air. It makes for interesting conversations when you tell people that you "study fans." Funnily enough, people are often confused that anyone devotes their career to studying fans *regardless* of which type of fan we're talking about.

5. For our European readers, the term sports fan may conjure up images of football hooligans boisterously drinking, fighting, and rioting while donning the jerseys and scarves of their favorite club or team.

6. In early studies asking "what it means to be a brony" we found that the items split between self-labelers (those that watch and like the show and label themselves bronies) and the gatekeepers (those that put more restrictions on what it takes to be a brony). See Chapter 15 for more.

7. Dr. Edwards once met a fan who had seen every episode twice, but was totally not a brony.

8. Except the occasional ribbing he takes from those who *despise* licorice.

9. As Connelly put it so eloquently in her book, this was *MLP*'s "original sin"—something that critics of the series would use to trivialize or dismiss it out-of-hand.

10. It certainly didn't help Hasbro's case that *My Little Pony 'n' Friends* featured numerous skits with characters from other Hasbro-owned lines of toys. This further cemented the public's belief that *MLP* was about selling toys, not about telling a story.

11. It should be pointed out that the show also left a more positive legacy for future fans of the series—it marked the introduction of the characters Applejack and Spike, who would find themselves a fan following among bronies in Generation 4 of the show!

12. In fact, viewers of G1 were intended to identify with the human character, not with the ponies.

13. It's important to note that few of these collectors would use the term "brony"

to describe themselves, for reasons we'll describe in the next section.

14. Including, but not limited to, Pinkie Pie, Rainbow Dash, Rarity, Fluttershy, Sweetie Belle, Cheerilee, and Scootaloo.

15. Many fans of the show saw the creation of a "core seven" as a sign of the inevitable decline of the show. This is ironic considering the love that bronies have for the "mane six" in G4.

16. Perhaps even less subtly, an advertisement appeared on the Hub singing a song called *Equestria Girls*, which included a reference to "Our bronies."

Chapter 2

1. It might surprise you to discover that none of us *planned* to become brony researchers when we grew up!

2. Yeah, it's hard to believe that Season 1, Episode 1 aired October 10, 2010!

3. The *Star Trek* fandom is arguably one of the longest and best-studied media fan groups, and has been around for *decades*!

4. Dr. Edwards had a bit of shock and confusion when first turning to the original show online. He had to be gently corrected by his son that *My Little Pony* had gone through some drastic changes since the 80s.

5. Funnily enough, our work would later show that this same disbelief was all-too-common for bronies discussing their interests with their families, schools, communities, and friends.

6. Also colloquially known as "haters."

7. Except for sport fans. Surprisingly, up until the last decade or so, the psychological research on fans has focused almost *exclusively* on sport fans.

8. While it goes without saying that our studies could not exist without the support of the brony community, special recognition needs to be given to the hardworking people running EquestriaDaily.com, who've helped us from the beginning and without whom this research might never have gotten off the ground!

9. For context, a typical psychology study might pull in 250 participants over the course of a semester, even when we offer participants class credit or gift cards!

10. And who can blame bronies, given all the negative press they were used to getting!

11. You can find more information at www.mane6.com, where the developers continue to work tirelessly on the game, now entitled *Them's Fightin' Herds*.

12. One of the attendees who questioned and filmed Dr. Edwards was Brent Hodgee. This interaction was a basis for the Hodgee Production film: A Brony Tale. Eventually Drs. Edwards and Redden were featured in both of the Brony fandom documentaries.

13. Specifically, he was studying fans of Dungeons & Dragons, a franchise which, in a weird coincidence, is also now a Hasbro-owned property.

14. As of fall 2018. By the time this book is published, these numbers will have increased.

15. Okay, maybe a *little* bit for bragging purposes! The Mythbusters got to start each episode of *their* show by showing off their credentials, so why can't we?

16. Fun Fact: Dr. Chadborn's time as a member of the fan community was done under the moniker "Professor Uponium" to match the original characters (OCs) of the other team members, including Dr. Edwards' "Dr. Psych Ology." He even has a long abandoned pony "ask blog."

17. More information in the IARP can be found at furscience.com.

18. Fun Fact: His favorite pony is Twilight Sparkle, something he shares in common with Drs. Chadborn and Edwards. For those keeping score at home, Dr. Griffin's favorite pony is Rainbow Dash and Will Edwards's favorite is Pinkie Pie.

19. We wanted to go with a stand alone complex but could not think of a good Ghost in the Shell reference to accompany it.

20. These are represented by the social (high disclosure/high meaning), secret (low disclosure/high meaning), hipster (high disclosure/low meaning), hidden (low on both), and mixed (moderate scores across questions). See Chapter 4.

21. To date, this has been our most controversial topic of study. We are very aware this is not a topic many members of the community want to discuss. That said, it is worth bringing up, mainly because it helps to dispel misconceptions about the brony fandom and allows us to compare bronies to other fandoms in this regard. See Chapter 11.

Chapter 3

1. Hey, if nothing else, you can say this chapter taught you a neat $20 word that you can throw around to make yourself sound really smart!

2. If this were true, Dr. Plante would be a certifiable genius!

3. "I would rather have questions that can't be answered than answers that can't be questioned."—Richard Feynman

4. It helps to think about a scientific theory as a model explaining how the world works. This is very different from the layperson's understanding of the word "theory," which often simply means "a guess or hunch about something." Scientific theories are often grounded in years of systematic observation and testing!

5. This, by the way, is why scientists are often hesitant to say they've *proven* something. Nothing is ever definitively *proven* in science—we can only find increasingly strong evidence that something is *not yet disproven.*

6. Scientists often display three characteristics: curiosity, skepticism, and humbleness (humble because over time ideas and theories are challenged, changed, or replaced).

7. Sorry to our American readers, but scientists measure these things in metric, the language of science!

8. And, in fact, this approach *has* been tried before in the field of psychology! A movement, known as *behaviorism*, essentially set out to *only* measure things which could be easily quantified, like the number of times a pigeon pecked a screen or the number of times a rat pressed a lever.

9. Just imagine trying to weigh a feather on a scale designed for trucks—or to measure a truck on a scale used to measure feathers!

10. Which is precisely what the authors of this book, who are all scientists themselves, spent years doing as part of their formal education!

11. Contrast this against short-term, in-lab studies where researchers create artificial settings to measure participant behavior (e.g., having participants watch an episode of *MLP* in a sterile lab room before handing them some money to see whether they keep it or put it in a conveniently-placed donation box). It lacks a certain "real-world" element when you *know* researchers are watching your every move, doesn't it?

12. In much the same way, it's *technically* possible to flip a coin 200 times and get heads every time. While it's certainly *possible*, it's not very *probable*.

13. Nearly all research conducted on human participants (and certainly all of the research in this book) is conducted under the supervision and approval of an ethics review board which considers whether the study itself is ethical. An important qualification for ethical research is that people are both aware that they are being studied and have agreed to do so. As such, it's important that we make crystal clear that our participants *agreed* to be studied of their own free will!

14. At this point, it's perfectly normal for readers who are science-inclined to find themselves having somewhat of a "crisis of faith" when it comes to science. We remind you to breathe. Relax. Graduate students, and even professors go through this same realization throughout their careers! It should tell you something that we remain scientists *despite* this realization!

15. And, in the spirit of encouraging future scientific inquiry, if you find yourself disagreeing with the results of one of our studies, you should conduct your own study and gather your own data! Science advances when scientists conduct studies to disprove one another! Nothing gets done, however, if critics merely lob stones at scientists but provide no alternative explanations, theories, or data to support their own position!

Chapter 4

1. Pun intended?

2. Understanding *why* this misinformation spreads is another question entirely, and there have been entire books written on the topic. The short version is that there is no one reason: Some people are trolls who revel in it, some have an axe to grind, some may have had a bad experience with a single member of the community, and others may know nothing and try to "fill in the gaps" with what they've heard from others.

3. We also saw this in practice with our study exposing undergraduate students to

an episode of *My Little Pony: Friendship Is Magic*, whose initial reactions to the show and its fans changed after that exposure.

4. Including a little taste at some early approaches and understanding of the difference between bronies in terms of their motivations and understanding of themselves as a brony.

5. We apologize to any fans who refer to themselves as Trekkers and prefer it. To the best of our knowledge, "Trekkie" is Roddenberry's preferred term, and it's a bit of a debate in the community. The *real* debate, as we see it, is who the best Captain is (it's Picard).

6. Our data, while including thousands of participants, can only tell us about the bronies who took our surveys. While we can probably assume that some of these characteristics also apply to bronies who didn't take our survey, this *is* still an assumption. Likewise, we are only speaking in terms of *averages*. Average tendencies are not statements about what *ought* to be, nor do they reflect every outlier and exception. Remember, if you're a brony and these findings don't perfectly describe you, you aren't any more or less of a brony!

7. We should also note that we're not the only researchers to track these demographics in the fandom: Coder Brony and the Herd Census (herdcensus.com) have similarly collected a lot of data on the demographic composition of the fandom.

8. Presently, we are using the term sex to refer to a person's self-reported biological male/female/intersex identity. As psychologists, we use the term gender to refer to a person's identification with masculine/feminine traits. In our earlier studies, before standards had begun to shift in research, we did not assess non-binary, genderfluid, or other gender identities. In more recent surveys, we have since addressed these limitations, informed by LGBTQ+ groups.

9. A term which we're thankful for, since it's *so* much easier than writing "fans of *My Little Pony: Friendship Is Magic*" every time!

10. We should also mention the term "pegasister," a term which not only shows the fandom's endless creativity when it comes to show-related puns, but also reflects the preferred designation of some female fans of the show.

11. We have in the past conservatively said about 75 percent male, though in reexamining the data it would be safer to say about 85 percent male as an accurate estimate.

12. Something which is, unfortunately, a still all-too-common oversimplification in psychological research.

13. A huge shout out to the edgy participant who, in nearly every study, identified as a 69-year-old attack helicopter who has been in the fandom for 420 years. We get it, you like memes. Unfortunately, since your responses indicate that you weren't taking the study seriously, they were omitted from our analyses. (We wish we were kidding here: Nearly. Every. Single. Study.)

14. A big part of being a good scientist is owning up to your mistakes!

15. You can say they "Keep Calm and Flutter On"! Or, as some on 4chan's/mlp/ board would put it, "the ride never ends." And who can blame them for sticking around: In Dr. Plante's opinion, the show's eighth season was among its best!

16. It's interesting to speculate about whether this may also explain the seemingly tumultuous start of the brony fandom, which may have had a fair number of members who were unfamiliar with the rules, norms, and other facets governing most fan cultures.

17. Whether this refers to board gamers, video games, or other kinds of games remains to be seen.

18. It seems that friendship is not only magic, it's a gateway to other cartoons!

19. We strongly recommend taking a look at the Gallup Poll write-up on sex and gender changes in the U.S from 2012 to 2017. Since our data comes from these same points in time, it is interesting to ponder whether bronies are simply just "ahead of the curve" with regard to inclusion of LGBTQ+ people.

20. Typology is just a fancy word categories or groups within a larger group. Like personality traits, but for types of bronies in this case.

21. Ironic, skeptical, and excited respectively.

22. Think of this as being invested in the fandom (meaning/direction) and whether or not you are "in the stable" or not in terms of being open about your identity as a brony.

23. If you are a brony and so inclined to place yourself in this brony Typology, however, do not be distressed or overly critical if you do not find an exact fit. Many individuals tend to find themselves somewhere between categories and don't fit neatly into one "type."

24. It's what Dr. Edwards calls the guidance function and is tied to convention attendance (Chapter 8), moral aspects tied to fandom and the show (Chapter 19), and the motivating factor of seeking purpose (Chapter 9).

Chapter 5

1. For example, the stereotype of the overweight brony, unemployed and living in the basement of their parents' house—a stereotype that's often applied to many other online communities.

2. Despite the fact that the show is officially available worldwide including, but not limited to, Singapore, Malaysia, the United Arab Emirates, South Korea, Japan, and throughout Europe.

3. Mainly, social bronies are more likely to be in larger and more urban areas, with secret bronies in smaller and more rural areas. Essentially, if you live in a denser area you are more likely to know another brony which might increase disclosure.

4. Two points worth mentioning: This census data also considers college dorms "living with parents," and it lumps 18- to 25-year-olds with 26- to 34-year-olds. We imagine the rate of people living with their parents would be even higher if *only* the 18- to 25-year-olds were considered—the approximate age range of the average brony.

5. Applejack might be considered falling into this category, as she and her siblings help her grandmother, Granny Smith, run the family farm.

6. In Twilight's case, "spreading her wings" can be taken quite literally—much to the chagrin of those fans who lamented her transformation into an alicorn (a unicorn with wings).

7. This represents the lowest and highest percentages across *all* studies.

8. A small number of these full time students are 18-year-old high school students.

9. Around 25 percent of participants did not choose any option; this could mean several things, including having already indicated that they were a student (full or part time) or being unable to work due to disability.

10. Put yourself in the shoes of a 12-year-old with a new hobby. Imagine how long you would stick with your hobby if you discovered that your parents disapproved of it or if your siblings and peers mocked you for it.

11. Dr. Plante notes how little closet space he would have left if he were forced to hide his pony plushie collection there every time his parents came over to his apartment!

12. Roosterteeth is an Internet video production studio. (roosterteeth.com)

13. As we asked it here, "conservative" refers to adhering to existing norms and resistance to change, while liberal involves openness to change and accepting of those who challenge norms. We realize this is a grossly oversimplified take on politics (e.g., libertarians are fiscally conservative but socially liberal), and largely American in its concept of political orientation (something our European participants have let us know *quite* vocally!).

14. It's worth noting that the university students in this sample were drawn from a university in southern Louisiana, which may explain why they don't look "as liberal" as one might expect a sample of university students to look.

15. We suspect that bronies will tend to fall quite liberal on social issues, but more conservative on fiscal issues. The seemingly moderate political orientation of bronies observed in these findings may well reflect this "compromise."

16. Cadence, of course, is the princess of love, while Twilight is the princess of friendship. Both seem to get the short end of the stick, as there's hardly as much reverence for them as there is for Celestia and Luna (Celestia in particular!).

17. This rules out the possibility that bronies are simply people who were raised in non-religious households. These data suggest that, regardless of how religious their particular home was, bronies are simply less religious than their parents were.

18. The exception to this rule being gen-

der and sexual orientation, with bronies being much more likely to be LGBTQ compared to the general population and census data. This too, however, may be more a product of generational differences (e.g., millennials in general) than simply being a brony.

Chapter 6

1. SJW stands for Social Justice Warrior, a term which, itself, has nearly as many interpretations and definitions as does the word feminism.

2. It's worth noting that the same sexism that has long plagued women seeking break down traditional gender norms has also condemned bronies, who like a cartoon "for girls."

3. Including numerous e-mails from bronies emailing us to *warn us* about what feminism *really* is.

4. We have no social justice agenda to fulfill, honestly! Though, in retrospect, that's *exactly* what a nefarious SJW agent would say! (But seriously, we don't....)

5. For an example of what we mean by this: Men are taller than women on average, but the difference isn't *so* large that we can't imagine a short man or a tall woman, nor is it inconceivable to imagine a woman who is taller than a man. While differences exist, the two groups overlap *considerably*, and thus shouldn't be treated as two entirely distinct categories.

6. It's like a difference between an 8 out of 10 and a 9 out of 10 on a scale of how important these features are to you.

7. As with any ideology or social movement, people will argue about what the "true" definition of feminism is. A full and nuanced discussion about this is beyond the scope of this book, and likely not what the reader signed up for.

8. While it could be a livestock pun, the term refers to a type of statistical control where participants are matched, in this case a number of demographic features before being compared.

9. This is the kind of thing psychology profs do when you give them power!

10. In other words, you can lead a horse to water, but you can't make it drink.

11. Hostile sexism refers to believing overtly sexist statements like "Women are worse at math" or "Women should stick to being homemakers." Benevolent sexism refers statements that, on the surface, sound positive, but contain many of the same gender stereotypes, such as "A man needs a good woman to take care of him at home" or "Women need to be protected by men."

Chapter 7

1. Actually, we're often asked another question before either of these two: "Seriously, that's your *job*? Don't you have a Ph.D. or something?"

2. Psychology is chock-full of these sorts of crisis-inducing existential realizations!

3. This was precisely how both Dr. Plante and Dr. Chadborn were lured into their liking of the show: Each had a friend who spoke highly of the show and recommended they watch it, despite initial reservations about watching a "show for little girls." Psychologists aren't immune to stereotypes and misconceptions!

4. That's the /co/ board, for those who are familiar with 4chan. People who are only passingly familiar with 4chan may have heard of its reputation as a somewhat lawless place where people post completely random content anonymously. This is true of 4chan's most infamous board, /b/—the "Random" board. The /co/ board, like most of the other boards, is far more heavily moderated. These days, 4chan has an /mlp/ board, due to popular demand.

5. For example, a number of pony spammers, either fans or trolls, have ensured that ponies have popped up on a number of forums and websites at according to Will Edwards, in many of the sites he came across looking for Mortal Kombat videos.

6. If you've ever found yourself hating a commercial because you resent the fact that someone is trying to get you to do what they want, you've experienced this firsthand.

7. More often than not, this was indicated to be a female relative—a sister rather than a mother, by an almost 3-to-1 ratio. Given that the brony fandom is predominantly male, statistically speaking, more of these sisters and mothers were probably not bronies themselves.

8. Dr. Edwards has often explained this route of discovery as a "virus vector" route, where one person catches the "bug" and passes it on to their friendship network. Not all friends will become Bronies, however, those that don't are likely to become "brony tolerant."

9. This is, in fact, how Dr. Plante became a long-time fan of the animated television series *Pokémon*. While he was not a fan initially, his younger brother and sister were *huge* fans, watching the show every day. Eventually, it got to the point where Dr. Plante knew the lyrics to the theme song and knew many of the characters by name just by being in the next room while his younger siblings watched. He eventually buckled and watched an episode with them. He ended up becoming a fan himself, albeit reluctantly.

10. … and the flexibility of your morality, not to mention your penchant for obeying the law.

Chapter 8

1. You apparently have a lot of friends with a very diverse set of interests!

2. Something else which surprises may laypersons is the narrative complexity of a show intended for a young audience—including many genuinely shocking plot twists. Without spoiling anything in particular, brony readers will recognize the episodes *Crusaders of the Lost Mark* and *The Perfect Pear* as particularly noteworthy examples of the sorts of bombshells viewers can have dropped on them.

3. Our apologies to any readers who are jazz fans, but let's be real, this is what jazz music sounds like to people who aren't fans of jazz.

4. Dr. Plante recently experienced this while on a trip to New York City with a friend. They visited The Guggenheim, a modern art museum, where Dr. Plante spent several hours alternating between bored and confused while his friend seemed awed by every piece.

5. This may have driven much of the fan backlash against the *Star Wars* prequel trilogy, which ran counter to many popular fan-created stories about what had come before the *Star Wars* films.

6. Dr. Plante has a particular soft spot for the background pony Vinyl Scratch/DJ Pon-3 who, while silent in the show, is recognized by many bronies as "unofficially" being voiced by the talented voice actor Jesse Nowack.

7. Dr. Plante's own hardcover copy of *Fallout Equestria* is sitting on the bookshelf next to his desk as he writes this. Sitting atop the book is an adorably out-of-place Twilight Sparkle plushie.

8. While on the surface, this may seem somewhat silly, there is a considerable body of research showing that emotions involve a powerful social component: We laugh harder, feel a stronger urge to cry, and get more excited when in groups than we do when we're by ourselves.

9. This isn't an unreasonable amount for a fan to spend on their hobby, especially when you consider the costs associated with other fandoms (e.g., concert tickets, sport jerseys, or DVD box sets).

10. "Praise the sun," anyone?

Chapter 9

1. Cake is also a powerful motivating factor.

2. Unlike bronies, it's not very hard to find sports fans, regardless of where you are in the world.

3. As the brony scoffing Sonic the Hedgehog cosplayer found out when asked a similar question by Dr. Edwards at a local fan convention.

4. Much like how the typology discussed in Chapter 4 may differ in other communities as sports fans for instance don't have much of a reason to not disclose their identity and may not get the same meaning and guidance from their favorite teams.

5. Any brony who's been to a brony convention can attest to the fact that, if anything, fan activities can be *incredibly* detrimental to one's personal finances! It's *far* too easy to spend money on merchandise—so much so that we imagine few fans of the show could ever consider their interest to be "profitable."

6. Without getting into the nitty-gritty details, think of a factor analysis like a series of correlations between items on a scale. The analysis looks at whether scores on some items tend to vary alongside other items.

For example, you can imagine that if I asked participants about the extent to which they felt "happy," "smiley," and "good," they would probably answer in a similar fashion on all three items: If they scored high on one, they probably scored high on the others, and if they scored low on one, they probably scored low on the others. A factor analysis allows us to condense these three items into a single dimension—something that all three of these terms (happy, smiley, and good) have in common—in this case, positive feelings.

7. This last point isn't particularly surprising, given the fantasy theme of the show and its characters.

8. The authors are reminded of an old series of commercials for Apple Jacks cereal. A perplexed adult would ask kids why they enjoyed Apple Jacks cereal despite the fact that it didn't taste like apples. The kids would reply in a matter-of-fact fashion, "We eat what we like." This same answer could be applied to bronies, whose enjoyment of the show and surrounding fandom doesn't seem to be for any clear, measurable benefit; they simply like it.

9. In a nutshell, a regression analysis allows researchers to simultaneously look at the relationship between one or more "predictor" variables (in this case, the four fan dimensions) and some outcome of interest (e.g., giving help to others) while statistically controlling for the fact that the predictor variables may "overlap" with one another. The further a number is from 0, the stronger the relationship between those two variables. A positive number means a positive relationship (i.e., as one variable increases, so does the other) while a negative number means a negative relationship (i.e., as one variable increases, the other decreases).

10. If you're noticing that many of these "needs" overlap with some of the models we've discussed throughout this chapter (e.g., Wann's eight motivations of sport fans, Deci and Ryan's self-determination theory), you're correct. Science often involves making small changes or tweaks to existing theories rather than creating something entirely different. While it can sometimes be frustrating, making it seem like everyone's essentially saying the same thing over and over, it *does* have the benefit of allowing different researchers to conceptually replicate others' work to see whether the findings hold true in other samples and within other theories.

Chapter 10

1. When you put it this way, I think a lot of us can identify with Snuzzle, can't we?

2. Given that the author of this chapter (Dr. Plante) cites Twilight Sparkle as his favorite of the Mane 6 ponies, the *real* winner here is the fandom for choosing correctly!

3. It should be noted that there are a *lot* of characters in the *MLP* universe: 68 different background characters were stated as being at least one participant's favorite. And this was before several seasons and the movie!

4. For curious readers, this is the reason why Dr. Plante, Dr. Chadborn, AND Dr. Edwards all chose Twilight Sparkle as their favorite pony! We're a bit biased towards the academic types!

5. In the anime fandom, this is sometimes known as having a "waifu"—that is, a fictional character from a story whom one is romantically attracted to and with whom one strongly feels like they are in a relationship. Some brony forums occasionally refer to the idea of having a "pony waifu," though this is more often than not a tongue-in-cheek allusion to the anime fandom.

6. Lest you think this idea is absurd, think about how many athletes were inspired by the training montages from the *Rocky* films, including the iconic scene of the film's titular character running up the stairs in front of the Philadelphia Museum of Art. The scene resonated with viewers so much and is now so well-known that a statue of it was built beside the steps themselves!

Chapter 11

1. Sorry bronies! But you have to admit, if a bunch of people all tell you *not* to look at something, that sparks some curiosity about the subject, don't you think?

2. It is also important to note that when it did come up as a topic to be discussed, it was mainly out a need to reduce the stereotypes of bronies being much more into it then they are. So while most didn't want the discussion, those that did wanted it as a

means to reduce stigma (Edwards & Cimoszewicz, 2017).

3. As scientists, it seems pointless to *only* study things that no one really cares about. If we wanted to do that, we'd all become geologists! (Sorry, geologists and fans of Maud Pie.)

4. Yes, we do mean *all* fandoms. If you're skeptical about this point, let us assure you that there is *most definitely* adult-themed fanfiction written about your favorite sport, film, and music stars, as well as characters from *any* show or film—animated or live-action. Be under no illusions: *Nothing* is safe from this fact, as a quick Google search of your favorite childhood show will attest to.

5. We take this stance both because it's just good science to remain neutral and amoral on questions about "what is morally right," and, for more pragmatic reasons, because it's in our best interest to not take sides on what *ought* to be. To quote the Jedi Obi-Wan Kenobi, "I'm not brave enough for politics."

6. And yes, we realize that we are in violation of these rules by virtue of having explained them.

7. The full slogan in any "official" messages reads: "We are Anonymous. We are Legion. We do not forgive. We do not forget. Expect us" (Rosen, 2009).

8. At the time of writing this Bowzette, or a combination Princess Peach/Bowser was taking the Internet by storm.

9. Conveniently, Rule 35 takes care of exceptions to Rule 34: "If no porn is found at the moment, it will be made."

10. The code is more what you'd call "guidelines" than actual rules.

11. And, in accordance with Rule 35, pointing out that porn does not *currently* exist of something or that porn *should not* exist of something will only motivate someone to create it. This is an excellent demonstration of what psychologists call *psychological reactance* and was perfectly exemplified when the social media company Twitter asked its users *not* to anthropomorphize its iconic bird logo. The result, like clockwork, was a deluge of anthropomorphic art of the Twitter logo—often explicit, in line with Rule 34—under the hashtag #tweetfur.

12. It can be argued that some is done for pure shock value.

13. With anthropomorphic animals existing that far back, this may be definitive proof that furries are a centuries-old fandom!

14. Early statues of Pan copulating with goats, general sex acts on pottery, and the Pompeiian wind chime (tintinnabula) in the shape of a flying, two legged, well hung phallus make it clear that early cultures had at least a fair appreciation for erotic art.

15. No one begrudges Michelangelo's David for baring it all or the Venus de Milo for being topless. Well, except maybe Pope Pius IX (look it up!).

16. If you thought sexual depictions of underage characters was a recent invention, think again.

17. Renamed "Tit's a Wonderful Life" and "A Tale of Two Titties," respectively. Years later, we see that this genre is alive and well in films like "Playmate of the Apes" and "Game of Bones." There was also no name change for *The Honeymooners*, they just put Ron Jeremy in it.

18. No citation for this one, though it wasn't for a lack of searching, much to the dismay of our university's IT department.

19. While we often treat the term fanfiction a product of the modern era, it actually dates back to at least the 1930s among fans of fictional characters like Sherlock Holmes.

20. Safe search helps.

21. SAFE SEARCH HELPS. And if you need more convincing, if ever given the chance, ask Dr. Edwards about his online encounter with Papa Smurf....

22. A group of fans organized around going through Google safe searches for fan content and characters and flagging any lewd and not suitable for work content.

23. In an analogous fashion, Dr. Plante is an avid fan of the *Fallout Equestria* series because it imbues the familiar characters and settings of the show with a decidedly *unfamiliar*, but nevertheless fascinating context of gritty, dystopian, post-apocalyptic realism.

24. Not that there would be anything wrong with someone who *did* have such a fetish. This is not intended to kink-shame or tell people what they ought or ought not to be attracted to. We're merely stating that it would be *inaccurate* to characterize the brony fandom as a group of people with an *MLP* fetish.

25. Even so, Figure 11.5 would suggest that even among these folks, only a *fraction* would say that pornography was the *reason* for their interest in *MLP* and the brony fandom.

26. You can take a look at other communities centered around shows like *Steven Universe*, *Gravity Falls*, *Pokémon*, et cetera to see similar discussions raging around pornographic content within these fandoms as well. As we said, *nothing* is safe from Rule 34.

27. Ask people who read *Fifty Shades of Grey* if they consider it to be porn. You're likely to get a wide range of answers!

28. The words of Supreme Court Justice Potter Stewart come to mind, who stated about pornography, "I shall not today attempt further to define the kinds of material I understand to be embraced within that shorthand description; and perhaps I could never succeed in intelligibly doing so. But I know it when I see it."

29. Then again, the same could probably be said about *most* of our Internet search histories or other personal details that we would never share with our parents. As a general rule, most people probably don't want their parents/friends/coworkers/boss to know what stokes their fire.

30. Which, let's be real, if anyone tried, would likely fail. See our earlier note about Twitter and the ineffectiveness of trying to censor the anthropomorphic depiction of its mascot. Or, for a classic demonstration of the ineffectiveness of banning something online, look up "the Streisand Effect."

31. If you've ever seen some of the unsettling things that make their way into Rule 34 content, you know that it's enough to make fully-grown adults cringe, retch, or struggle to get the image out of their heads. Probably not a bad idea to keep those sorts of images from children.

32. If it's not apparent by now, every horse-themed pun in this book is absolutely intentional. And we are absolutely unapologetic for each and every one.

Chapter 12

1. This was certainly the expectation of at least one of the author's parents, who believed that this was what he was going to a brony convention to do. "Why can't you just watch the show at home—why do you need to travel across the country just to watch it with some other people?"

2. Often referred to as an "OC."

3. In fact, it's fairly common at most brony conventions to have cosplay contests to determine who has the best-constructed or most unique cosplay.

4. Given that the *MLP* franchise itself was designed for the purpose of selling merchandise as a "lifestyle brand," there is no shortage of things for collectors to collect!

5. To better understand this, imagine walking into a room full of people who were different from you—a white person walking into a room full of black people or a young person walking into a room full of old people. Before anyone says a word to you, some part of you immediately begins to wonder whether you've made a mistake and whether you're in the wrong place.

6. Though probably not all at the same time.

7. Tom may, for example, enjoy rock-climbing or bouldering. This aside is *far* funnier for bronies than it is for non-bronies, for reasons that would take too long to explain.

8. For reasons of trademark violation, the game's creators were eventually forced to change the characters to non-*MLP* characters, although Lauren Faust *did* step in to help design the new characters.

9. Examples of this abound, for example, in the fan-created animated series *Doors*.

10. A particularly poignant example can be seen in the *Friendship is Manly* YouTube series by KanashiiPanda, in which the shows characters are drawn in a hyper-masculine fashion that parodies anime style.

11. This also leads to interesting debates from within the brony and furry fandoms about the relationship between furries and bronies. Many bronies take umbrage with the idea of being labeled a furry, as do many furries with the idea of being "lumped in" with bronies. This likely owes to the fact that both fandoms experience considerable stigma, and neither wants to take on the additional baggage of being associated with the other's stigma.

Chapter 13

1. It's not uncommon for psychology students to feel like psychologists seemingly make mountains out of molehills. While this *is* sometimes the case, we *usually* have a pretty good reason for doing so!

2. This isn't to say that there are *no* differences between groups, of course! Groups may well differ with regard to *why* people engage in the group (e.g., Schroy et al., 2016) or the stereotypes or beliefs about the personality of group members (Jenkins, Reysen, & Katzarska-Miller, 2012; Reysen, Plante, Roberts, & Gerbasi, 2015). But while these motivational factors or stereotype content may differ from group to group, the same social identity process should still operate within all of them.

3. As a stark example of this, sport fans are more likely to help an injured person if they are wearing a shirt with the symbol of their favorite sport team compared to wearing a shirt of a rival team (Levine, Prosser, Evans, & Reicher, 2005).

4. Don't worry if you find this distinction between fanship and fandom difficult! As it turns out, the distinction is also often lost on fan researchers themselves, leading to incidents where researchers use the term "fanship" when what they're really measuring is fandom (Lock & Heere, 2017).

5. Although there *are* rivalries within the *MLP* fandom over which pony is the best pony.

6. Instead of asking questions about sport-specific content, the scale asks questions in a much more general way, such as "I am emotionally connected to my interest" and "I strongly identify with my interest." In this case, "my interest" could be filled in with pretty much *any* fan interest, from model train enthusiasts to music or television fans.

7. As noted previously in this book, the brony fandom is predominantly male. We wondered if perhaps women in the fandom may feel less belongingness within the fandom given this fact.

8. This analysis was inspired by the fact that, as noted in Chapter 12, the brony fandom includes a fair number of artists and writers.

Chapter 14

1. If that particularly rough day happens to be today, we sincerely hope that you feel better soon!

2. As an illustrative example, if you've ever travelled to a foreign country by yourself, you may have felt loneliness and vulnerability. As social creatures, we're usually motivated to avoid situations where we don't have allies at hand should we need them.

3. For examples of this, look no further than the pushback schools and organizations often experience when they implement uniforms. It can feel stifling to be reduced to a number or to be treated as just another face in the crowd, especially in American culture, where tremendous pressure is put on people to stand out and be an individual.

4. It should be noted that we're *not* talking about delusion in this case. We're *not* talking about bronies who actually think they are small, colorful horses from the land of Equestria. Instead, we're talking about feelings of similarity or connection to a fictional character with the explicit knowledge that one is, in fact, a human being.

5. These questions are similar to a measure used by Roberts, Plante, Gerbasi, and Reysen (2015) designed to measure the nature of furries' connection to their fursona species, and to distinguish furries—fans of media featuring anthropomorphized animal characters, from therians—people who identify *as* non-human animals in a spiritual or metaphysical manner (Plante, Reysen, Roberts, & Gerbasi, 2018). In short, research on furries and therians suggests that at least *some* people wish to become, or feel completely, that they are a non-human animal.

6. Lest you think this is a bit absurd, ask yourself why people are drawn to the science fiction or fantasy genres in the first place—or indeed, why people watch films or plays games about others who lead more interesting lives than they do! To at least some extent, it's probably motivated by some sort of wish-fulfillment or desire to experience, however temporary, something outside the realm of normal experience! These data merely suggest that for some people, they may wish that feeling could carry on after the show ends.

7. It should be noted that we're not going delve into the realm of navel-gazing or philosophy, nor do we claim to have any answers about the meaning of life or why any of us are here (indeed, people far smarter than us have devoted much longer books than this to that very subject!). Instead, we're talking about whether people *feel* like they have a sense of purpose or meaning—regardless of what that purpose or meaning might be.

8. Given that people spend, on average, almost as much time looking at screens as they do sleeping on any given day, few would argue that screen media represents a fairly important leisure activity for most of us.

9. Another way to think about it is to imagine wine tasting: One person may take the time to savor the aroma and appreciate the delicate and interplay of nuanced flavors while another simply up-ends the glass and asks for more. The authors won't point out which category each of them falls into.

Chapter 15

1. Psychology researchers are often criticized for studying what many people consider to be "common sense." Findings such as these certainly make it *seem* that way, don't they?

2. This is assuming, of course, that we're talking about a group you can *choose* to belong to. Some groups, like a person's nationality or race, are groups they have no control over.

3. Funnily enough, members of stigmatized fan groups aren't immune to this tendency to make downward social comparisons either. Anime fans, in turn, often thumb their noses at furries and bronies as a way of deflecting criticisms of their own fandom: "Sure, we may be weird, but at least we don't dress up in mascot costumes or watch shows for little kids!"

4. Dr. Plante purposely wears *MLP* t-shirts with the intent of having them recognized by other bronies. He also finds himself chatting more with students on campus who wear *MLP* t-shirts or who have other *MLP* apparel.

5. Whether or not the fans' suggestions would be an improvement over Lucas' own ideas is an *entirely* different matter, of course! The point is that long-time fans of the show felt that they should be given a say in the direction of a story that was not their own.

6. Think of it this way, as we discussed before many fans fall into the category of brony as long as they watch the show, like it, and label themselves a brony while others viewed it more like a traditional more restrictive fan community.

7. It should be noted that Dr. Plante only agreed to do so as an academic exercise, of course! As a social psychologist, he wanted to understand what all the fuss was about. It wasn't until he was finished watching the first season that he realized he was well past the point of merely watching the show "for research's sake."

8. This too is not unique to the brony fandom. For example, fans of the indie computer game *Undertale* have similarly earned a reputation for being persistent in trying to get reluctant friends to experience the game for themselves. Because it's good. You should really play it! (For real!)

Chapter 16

1. Or, to put it another way: Personality traits are fairly stable in people, and tend to cluster together in predictable ways. A person who is relatively open-minded in their younger years will also tend to be fairly open-minded in their later years. Likewise, open-minded people are also more likely to fantasize, to be adventurous, and to empathize with others. These consistencies add a sense of order and predictability to the study of personality.

2. And you thought *your* job was boring and repetitive!

3. For example, friendly, genial, cordial, warm, sociable, gregarious, and outgoing are *all* describing pretty much the same type of person. Because of this, one could keep the word "friendly" and throw away the others as repeats.

4. In other words, to feel like they were in a relationship with an athlete despite the athlete not knowing them personally. As a classic example of an extreme parasocial interaction, imagine a celebrity stalker, a fan of a celebrity who loves the celebrity and believes that they share the same feelings for the fan.

5. Or, to put it another way, personality is not *fate*: A person who scores high in extraversion or agreeableness is not *guaranteed* to act or feel a certain way. Personality traits are simply one small piece of the puzzle!

6. To paint an image of what this may look like: Imagine you're struggling to find a job, can't pay rent next month, and are having relationship problems. Dealing with those issues is tough and can be overwhelming. It's far easier to just turn on your favorite show and *forget* about your problems—at least for awhile.

7. Fluttershy, for example, is the literal embodiment of the element of kindness!

8. Putting our cards and biases on the table: Most of the authors of this book are social psychologists by training. As such, it's very possible that a personality psychologist would disagree with our assessment of this point or the conclusions we reach. Just something to keep in mind as a critical reader!

Chapter 17

1. To see real-world evidence of this, look no further than the title of a 2012 documentary entitled *Bronies: The Extremely Unexpected Adult Fans of My Little Pony*. While the documentary itself was positive in its portrayal of the brony fandom, it doesn't shy away from framing the group as unusual.

2. This belief is especially likely to be espoused in cultures that encourage individualism, telling people to just be themselves and to not care what others think. In practice, however, this sentiment is more accurately put "be yourself—as long as it's not too different, too weird, or makes others feel uncomfortable."

3. If you doubt this last point, ask yourself this: Could a politician or a CEO *really* be open about being a brony? Remember the public's reaction to Bill Clinton being "outed" as a brony in Chapter 1?

4. In fact, these days there are multiple networks dedicated to 24-hour sport coverage, including entire channels devoted to just one sport (e.g., The Golf Channel, the NHL Network).

5. To the interested sport fans reading this chapter, the most prototypical sport fan was the football and basketball fan.

6. One of the only fan groups *more* disliked than bronies was juggalos—fans of the musical group Insane Clown Posse.

7. Once again, bronies shared the bottom rung of this desirability ladder with juggalos. As a pro-tip for the curious: Fans of cooking as a hobby were rated among the most mature and dateable!

8. Anecdotally speaking, we've spoken to bronies serving in the armed forces or who were government employees that have stated explicitly that they would *never* let their co-workers or supervisors know that they were a brony for fear of ridicule, abuse, or losing their jobs.

9. Whether this is because they feel more confident in sharing this part of themselves with others or because it's simply *harder* to hide being a brony if you're a bigger fan has yet to be studied!

10. This may be due to the need to "set the record straight" and allow the researchers (as long as there are legit in their credentials) to help make the case for them as long as the data really is positive.

11. This approach, while paradoxical at first, makes a certain amount of sense. If you see you and your group as an embattled minority, taking on the world, and you don't feel like you can (or want to) abandon the group, the next best thing is to stick together and provide a united front against your attackers.

12. One possibility for this might be that bronies motivated to make friends may see this stigma as hurting their chances to make other, non-brony friends. As such, they may seek to avoid or deny the stigma altogether to maximize their chances of making *any* friends.

13. One of the authors has experienced something similar to this first-hand as a furry. If he were to wear his fur suit out in public by himself, he would be the lone target of ridicule or discrimination. But if he went out as part of a group of 50 fursuiters, it would be a very different story. For one thing, people would be less willing to confront or attack a group of 50 people than a lone person. But even if someone were so bold, the risk of being personally targeted would be dissipated, since there are 49 other targets around!

14. As a simple example, it's harder to

hold homophobic views if you end up befriending several gay people or have a family member who comes out gay. Sadly, this doesn't make it *impossible*.

15. It could be argued that shows like *Will and Grace*, *Ellen*, and *Glee*, which prominently feature gay people or characters, have gone a long way to improving societal attitudes toward the LGBTQ+ community.

16. Specifically, the excellent episode *Super Speedy Cider Squeezy 6000*.

Chapter 18

1. As a simple example, you could imagine being in good physical health and doing well at school while having problems with your partner and feeling a general sense of stress and frustrated. Being high in one of these does not necessarily mean being high in the others!

2. Within the fandom, we had examined these effects early on, pushed on by stories, anecdotes, and eventually data to add support to the idea that being a part of a larger community influenced mental well-being (Redden, Edwards, Griffin, & Chadborn, 2015).

3. Given the diet often associated with sport fans in America (e.g., nachos, beer, wings, pretzels), this shouldn't come as a surprise.

4. You could probably file this one under the "well, duh!" category. That said, with the proliferation of the Internet, researchers and laypersons alike have asked whether online relationships can be a substitute for, or entirely replace, face-to-face interaction. The results of this study would seem to suggest they can't.

5. It's possible, for example, that anime fans, furries, and bronies are *all* higher than the general population on these conditions.

6. Important: Although bronies showed higher ASD rates than the U.S. population, the same was true for anime fans and furries. As such, it doesn't seem to be something unique to bronies. In fact, given that one of the defining features of ASD is an intense interest or fixation on something, higher rates of ASD may well be present in *most* fan groups.

Chapter 19

1. Funnily enough, despite this being an oft-stated mantra of the brony fandom, these words are never uttered in *MLP:FiM* itself.

2. If you remember back to Chapter 13, bronies feel a greater psychological sense of community with the brony community than they do with their local community. This suggests, at very least, that bronies may feel compelled to volunteer or help those within their own community.

3. This is due, in no small part, to societal concern about the rapid proliferation of television in the 1970s and 1980s and, later, the growth of video games in the 1990s and 2000s, as well as the increasingly extreme violent and sexual content in these media.

4. It's important to note that media violence researchers are *not* claiming that violent media turns people into violent murderers. Instead, they're saying that violent media is a *risk factor*—just one of many (and not even the largest) that increases a person's *likelihood* of having aggressive thoughts, seeing aggression in the world around them, and behaving aggressively.

5. A term also known as schadenfreude.

6. For good reason: Disney films average about one prosocial act per minute (Padilla-Walker, Coyne, Fraser, & Stockdale, 2013).

7. For fans of Lady Gaga, she's seen as more than just a performer: She's seen as a role model who inspires and shapes their attitudes and political beliefs (Click, Lee, & Holladay, 2017).

8. Sorry, Twihards. Consider it a friendly jab from one stigmatized fandom to another!

9. Anecdotally speaking, this would seem to be the case: In several of the brony groups of which one of the authors is a member, fans protested the show stopping its tradition of ending each episode with a moral message in the form of a letter to Princess Celestia.

10. In the interest of full disclosure, at least one of the authors of this book was a *huge* fan of Rooster Teeth's breakthrough Machinima series *Red vs. Blue* in his high school years!

11. Given that most of our research is conducted through online surveys or convention-

based sampling, it's possible that a brony who could not afford to pay for Internet access or attend a brony convention would not end up represented in our sample.

12. Dr. Plante notes that the motto "do better" was adopted by the *Fallout Equestria: Project Horizons* character Blackjack, a long-suffering character who channels her suffering into a desire to help make the world a better place.

13. And certainly one that Fluttershy herself, the element of kindness, can get behind!

Chapter 20

1. As the fandom is fond of jokingly saying, "*Thanks* M.A. Larson!"

2. Two more seasons than *Star Trek: The Next Generation*, which ended with an episode title that was just too good to pass up as a title for this chapter: "All Good Things."

3. Puns to the bitter end! Stop your groaning!

4. The *Star Trek: The Original Series* fandom is alive and well *despite* being off the air for decades!

5. They may also have been people calling themselves bronies simply for the shock value that came from being a fan of something unusual. Once the show and the fandom became somewhat more mainstream—or at very least less surprising—the novelty likely wore off, causing these folks to leave.

6. A more hopeful hypothesis, taken with the stability of the fandom over time reported in Chapter 4 would be to say that they joined for the irony and stayed for the show/fandom, which may also be why we see a high reporting of being a "mixed" fan over time.

7. "Ties" to the group include how visibly-identifiable you are as a member of that group and whether you can change this. You can choose to be a member of some groups (e.g., a church group), but not others (e.g., your race/ethnicity).

8. For one thing, fans who've left the fandom typically don't go to fan conventions or frequent fan websites, where researchers typically recruit fan participants.

9. Along with embarrassment about the fandom itself. This makes sense: While *you* might be willing to stick with the group through an embarrassing media fiasco, you understand why others may be inclined to leave as a result.

10. Dr. Plante recently found himself defending the classic video game *Goldeneye* to his much-younger students. While they decried the game's graphics controls as laughably bad by today's standards, Dr. Plante crankily insists that "kids today wouldn't know a good game if it came up and bit 'em in the face!"

11. We saw this in the initial reluctance of many bronies to the *Equestria Girls* spin-off of the show. And, currently, can hear the cries of some bronies shouting "Give Generation 5 of the show a chance!"

12. Remember that Lauren Faust herself was driven to create *MLP:FiM* in no small part because of her own nostalgia for *MLP* from when she was a child!

13. Conventions like San Diego Comic Con or DragonCon regularly approach or exceed 100,000 attendees and are not limited to any one fandom, series, or genre.

14. What, people can be fans of their respective scholarly disciplines. And we take our theoretical perspectives seriously!

15. And not just those who stalk Benedict Cumberbatch these days, but those who pestered Sir Arthur Conan Doyle, the character's creator.

16. Just imagine how people would have reacted to this if it were posted on Tumblr or Reddit.

17. Sorry Applejack fans—we went this *whole* book without taking a dig at you!

Chapter 21

1. For example, Dr. Chadborn has since received his Ph.D., Will Edwards has gone on and completed his Bachelor's degree, and Dr. Edwards has begun publishing his own series of fantasy novels inspired by his experiences as a clinician and fan researcher.

2. We have, in some cases, paraphrased statements to reduce their length and avoid this chapter taking up half of the book's word count! We have also avoided changing the original punctuation or grammar to preserve the original statement as much as possible.

3. He does mention that he doesn't offer

full credit to the show—getting out of a toxic job helped a lot. But is community interaction certainly helped accelerate his healing process.

4. Like Twilight I have moved from student to mentor and teacher myself. I cannot be a Princess of Psychology, though I am happy with my Ph.D. as an acceptable substitute.

5. It's a live and let live mentality, a respect for others, and a push to be more accepting of our differences—something heavily promoted in the show itself.

6. In the medieval alchemical sense. So basically, just science.

7. I have chosen to address my letter directly to the Princess of Friendship, given the relevance of my topic to her area of expertise.

8. Yeah, I know, this is pretty ironic coming from a furry, isn't it?

9. Serendipity is magic!

References

Abbey, A., Abramis, D. J., & Caplan, R. D. (1985). Effects of different sources of social support and social conflict on emotional well-being. *Basic and Applied Social Psychology, 6,* 111–129. doi:10.1207/s15324834basp0602_2.

Abrams, D. (2009). Social identity on a national scale: Optimal distinctiveness and young people's self-expression through musical preference. *Group Processes and Intergroup Relations, 12,* 303–317. doi:10.1177/1368430209102841.

Agneessens, F., Waege, H., & Lievens, J. (2006). Diversity in social support by role relations: A typology. *Social Networks, 28,* 427–441. doi:10.1016/j.socnet.2005.10.001.

Aiken, K. D., Bee, C., & Walker, N. (2018). From passion to obsession: Development and validation of a scale to measure compulsive sport consumption. *Journal of Business Research, 87,* 69–79. doi:10.1016/j.jbusres.2018.02.019.

Andersen-Peters, J. (2016). *Charitable YouTube discourse: Markiplier and the elements of online communication* (Undergraduate paper). University of Central Florida, Orlando, FL. Retrieved from: http://writingandrhetoric.cah.ucf.edu/stylus/files/kws4/kws4_Andersen-Peters.pdf.

Anderson, C. A., Shibuya, A., Ihori, N., Swing, E. L., Bushman, B. J., Sakamoto, A., Rothstein, H. R., & Saleem, M. (2010). Violent video game effects on aggression, empathy, and prosocial behavior in Eastern and Western countries: A meta-analytic review. *Psychological Bulletin, 136,* 151–173. doi:10.1037/a0018251.

Andrijiw, A. M., & Hyatt, C. G. (2009). Using optimal distinctiveness theory to understand identification with a nonlocal professional hockey team. *Journal of Sport Management, 23,* 156–181. doi:10.1123/jsm.23.2.156.

Angel, R. (2012, October 1). Adult male My Little Pony fans? Bronies are true rebels. *The Guardian.* Retrieved from https://www.theguardian.com/commentisfree/2012/oct/01/my-little-pony-bronies-rebels.

Ashmore, R. D., Deaux, K., & McLaughlin-Volpe, T. (2004). An organizing framework for collective identity: Articulation and significance of multidimensionality. *Psychological Bulletin, 130,* 80–114. doi:10.1037/0033-2909.130.1.80.

Bacon-Smith, C. (1992). *Enterprising women: Television fandom and the creation of popular myth.* Philadelphia, PA: University of Pennsylvania Press.

Beaton, C. (2016, September 6). 6 millennial myths that need to finally die. *Forbes.* Retrieved from https://www.forbes.com/sites/carolinebeaton/2016/09/06/6-millennial-myths-that-need-to-finally-die/#9adba884fa0c.

Bekkers, R., & Wiepking, P. (2011a). Who gives? A literature review of predictors of charitable giving part one: Religion, education, age, and socialization. *Voluntary Sector Review, 2,* 337–365. doi:10.1332/204080511X6087712.

Bekkers, R., & Wiepking, P. (2011b). A literature review of empirical studies of philanthropy: Eight mechanisms that drive charitable giving. *Nonprofit and Voluntary Sector Quarterly, 40,* 924–973. doi:10.1177/0899764010380927.

Bennett, L. (2012). Fan activism for social mobilization: A critical review of the literature. *Transformative Works and Cultures, 10.* doi:10.3983/twc.2012.0346.

Bennett, L. (2014). "If we stick together we can do anything": Lady Gaga fandom, philanthropy and activism through social media. *Celebrity Studies, 5,* 138–152. doi: 10.1080/19392397.2013.813778.

Birtel, M. D., & Crisp, R. J. (2012). "Treating" prejudice: An exposure-therapy approach to reducing negative reactions toward stigmatized groups. *Psychological Science, 23*(11), 1379–1386. doi:10.1177/0956797612443838.

Bizman, A., & Yinon, Y. (2002). Engaging in distancing tactics among sport fans: Effects on self-esteem and emotional responses. *The Journal of Social Psychology, 142,* 381–392. doi:10.1080/00224540209603906.

Bodet, G., & Bernache-Assollant, I. (2011). Consumer loyalty in sport spectatorship services: The relationships with consumer satisfaction and team identification. *Psychology & Marketing, 28,* 781–802. doi:10.1002/mar.20412.

Booth, P. (2015). Crowdfunding: A Spimatic application of digital fandom. *New Media & Society, 17*(2), 149–166. doi:10.1177/1461444814558907.

Branscombe, N. R., & Wann, D. L. (1991). The positive social and self concept consequences of sports team identification. *Journal of Sport and Social Issues, 15,* 115–127. doi:10.1177/019372359101500202.

Branscombe, N. R., Schmitt, M. T., & Harvey, R. D. (1999). Perceiving pervasive discrimination among African Americans: Implications for group identification and well-being. *Journal of Personality and Social Psychology, 77,* 135–149. doi:10.1037/0022-3514.77.1.135.

Brewer, M. B. (1991). The social self: On being the same and different at the same time. *Personality and Social Psychology Bulletin, 17,* 475–482. doi:10.1177/0146167291175001.

Brewer, M. B. (1999). The psychology of prejudice: Ingroup love and outgroup hate?. *Journal of Social Issues, 55*(3), 429–444. doi:10.1111/0022-4537.00126.

Brockmyer, J., Fox, C., Curtiss, K., McBroom, E., Buckhart, K., & Pidruzny, J. (2009). The development of the Game Engagement Questionnaire: A measure of engagement in video game-playing. *Journal of Experimental Social Psychology, 45*(4), 624–634. doi:10.1016/j.jesp.2009.02.016.

Brunsting, S., & Postmes, T. (2002). Social movement participation in the digital age: Predicting offline and online collective action. *Small Group Research, 33,* 525–554. doi:10.1177/104649602237169.

Bureau of Labor Statistics. (2018, April 26). College enrollment and work activity of high school graduates. *Economic News Release.* Retrieved from https://www.bls.gov/news.release/hsgec.toc.htm.

Busselle, R., & Bilandzic, H. (2009). Measuring narrative engagement. *Media Psychology, 12,* 321–347. doi:10.1080/15213260903287259.

Bussie, B. (2018). *How celebrities like Beyonce use social media to influence effective charitable change* (Unpublished master's thesis). Southern Illinois University Carbondale, Carbondale, IL.

Cain, S. (2012). *Quiet: The power of introverts in a world that can't stop talking.* New York, NY: Crown Publishers.

Chadborn, D., Edwards, P., & Reysen, S. (2017). Displaying fan identity to make friends. *Intensities: The Journal of Cult Media, 9,* 87–97.

Chadborn, D. P., Plante, C. N., & Reysen, S. (2016). Perceived stigma, social identity, and group norms as predictors of prosocial giving in a fandom. *International Journal of Interactive Communication Systems and Technologies, 6,* 35–49. doi:10.4018/IJICST.2016010103.

Chadborn, E., Edwards, P., & Reysen, S. (2016). Reexamining differences between fandom and local sense of community. *Psychology of Popular Media Culture, 7,* 241–249. doi:10.1037/ppm0000125.

Chaudoir, S. R., & Fisher, J. D. (2010). The disclosure processes model: Understanding disclosure decision-making and post-disclosure outcomes among people living with a concealable stigmatized identity. *Psychological Bulletin, 136,* 236–256. doi:10.1037/a0018193.

Chauvel, A. (2014). Fandom and civic engagement: From fan fiction to fandom led social causes. In A. Chauvel, N. Lamerichs, & J. Seymour (Eds.), *Fan studies: Researching popular audiences* (pp. 99–109). Oxford, UK: Inter-Disciplinary Press.

Cheung, W. Y., Sedikides, C., & Wildschut, T. (2016). Induced nostalgia increases optimism (via social-connectedness and self-esteem) among individuals high, but not low, in trait nostalgia. *Personality and Individual Differences, 90,* 283–288. doi:10.1016/j.paid.2015.11.028.

Choi, N. G., & DiNitto, D. M. (2012). Predictors of time volunteering, religious giving, and secular giving: Implications for nonprofit organizations. *Journal of Sociology and Social Welfare, 39,* 93–120.

Cialdini, R. B., Borden, R. J., Thorne, A., Walker, M. R., Freeman, S., & Sloan, L. R. (1976). Basking in reflected glory: Three (football) field studies. *Journal of Personality and Social Psychology, 34*(3), 366–375. doi:10.1037/0022-3514.34.3.366.

Clarke, J. R. (1998). *Looking at lovemaking: Constructions of sexuality in Roman art, 100 BC–AD 250.* Berkeley, CA: University of California Press.

Click, M. A., Lee, H., & Holladay, H. W. (2017). "You're born to be brave": Lady Gaga's use of social media to inspire fans' political awareness. *International Journal of Cultural Studies, 20,* 603–619. doi:10.1177/1367877915595893.

Cohen, J. (2001). Defining identification: A theoretical look at the identification of audiences with media characters. *Mass Communication and Society, 4,* 245–264. doi:10.1207/S15327825MCS0403_01.

Connelly, S. (2017). *Ponyville confidential: The history and culture of My Little Pony, 1981 2016.* Jefferson, NC: McFarland.

Connor-Smith, J. K., & Flachsbart, C. (2007). Relations between personality and coping: A meta-analysis. *Journal of Personality and Social Psychology, 93,* 1080–1107. doi:10.1037/0022-3514.93.6.1080.

Cooper, B., Cox, D., Lienesch, R., & Jones, R. P. (2016, September 22). Exodus: Why Americans are leaving religion—and why they're unlikely to come back. *Public Religion Research Institution.* Retrieved from https://www.prri.org/research/prri-rns-poll-nones-atheist-leaving-religion/.

Coppa, F. (2008). Women, Star Trek, and the early development of fannish vidding. *Transformative Works and Cultures, 1.* doi:10.3983/twc.2008.044.

Costa, P. T., Jr., & McCrae, R. R. (1997). Longitudinal stability of adult personality. In R. Hogan, J. Johnson, & S. Briggs (Eds.), *Handbook of personality psychology* (pp. 269–292). San Diego, CA: Academic Press.

Crocker, J., & Major, B. (1989). Social stigma and self-esteem: The self-protective properties of stigma. *Psychological Review, 96,* 608–630. doi:10.1037/0033-295X.96.4.608.

Cronin, T., Reysen, S., & Branscombe, N. R. (2012). Wal-Mart's conscientious objectors: Perceived illegitimacy, moral anger, and retaliatory consumer behavior. *Basic and Applied Social Psychology, 34,* 322–335. doi:10.1080/01973533.2012.693347.

Crosby, F. (1984). The denial of personal discrimination. *American Behavioral Scientist, 27,* 371–386. doi:10.1177/000276484027003008.

Cuesta, U., Martinez, L., & Cuesta, V. (2017). Effectiveness of narrative persuasion on Facebook: Change of attitude and intention towards HPV. *European Journal of Social Sciences Education and Research, 11,* 100–109. doi:10.26417/ejser.v11i2.p100-109.

Deci, E. L., & Ryan, R. M. (2000). The "what" and "why" of goal pursuits: Human needs and the self-determination of behavior. *Psychological Inquiry, 11,* 227–268. doi:10.1207/S15327965PLI1104_01.

de Grey, R. G. K., Uchino, B. N., Trettevik, R., Cronan, S., & Hogan, J. N. (2018). Social support and sleep: A meta-analysis. *Health Psychology, 37,* 787–798. doi:10.1037/hea0000628.

Devos, T., & Banaji, M. R. (2005). American = White? *Journal of Personality and Social Psychology, 88,* 447–466. doi:10.1037/0022-3514.88.3.447.

Devos, T., & Mohamed, H. (2014). Shades of American identity: Implicit relations between ethnic and national identities. *Social and Personality Psychology Compass, 8,* 739–754. doi:10.1111/spc3.12149.

Dhaenens, F., Van Bauwel, S., & Biltereyst, D. (2008). Slashing the fiction of queer theory: Slash fiction, queer reading, and transgressing the boundaries of screen studies, representations, and audiences. *Journal of Communication Inquiry, 32*(4), 335–347. doi:10.1177/0196859908321508.

Dibble, J. L., Hartmann, T., & Rosaen, S. F. (2016). Parasocial interaction and parasocial relationship: Conceptual clarification and a critical assessment of measures. *Human Communication Research, 42,* 21–44. doi:10.1111/hcre.12063.

Doane, M. J., & Elliott, M. (2015). Perceptions of discrimination among atheists: Consequences for atheist identification, psychological and physical well-being. *Psychology of Religion and Spirituality, 7,* 130–141. doi:10.1037/rel0000015.

Dodge, R., Daly, A. P., Huyton, J., & Sanders, L. D. (2012). The challenge of defining wellbeing. *International Journal of Wellbeing, 2,* 222–235. doi:10.5502/ijw.v2i3.4.

Edwards, P. W., Scher, S., Griffin, J. (April, 2016). *Manifestation of net generation characteristics in the brony fandom.* Presented at the meeting of the Southeastern Psychological Association, New Orleans, LA.

Edwards, P.W. & Cimoszewicz, O. (March, 2017). *Factors impacting stereotypes towards an atypical Internet fandom.* Presented at the meeting of the Southeastern Psychological Association, Atlanta, GA.

Edwards, P.W., Chadborn, D., Griffin, J., & Redden, M.H. (March, 2014). *The fan functions survey: What motivates the brony fandom?* Poster session presented at the meeting of the Southeastern Psychological Association, Nashville, TN.

Edwards, P.W., Edwards, W., Knottek, J., Olson, S., Griffin, J. (March, 2018). *Group stigmatization and cohesion: Willingness to participate in online research.* Presented at the meeting of the Southeastern Psychological Association, Charleston, SC.

Edwards, P.W., Griffin, J., Chadborn, D., & Redden, M. (March, 2014). *Fan typology: "Who are the bronies? Are they all alike"?* Poster session presented at the meeting of the Southeastern Psychological Association, Nashville, TN.

Edwards, P.W., Griffin, J., Langley, J., Redden, M.H., & Chadborn, D. (March, 2015). *A validation of the brony fan typology.* Poster session presented at the meeting of the Southeastern Psychological Association, Hilton Head, SC.

Faust, L. (2010, December 24). My little non-homophobic, non-racist, non-smart shaming pony: A rebuttal. *Ms. Magazine Blog.* Retrieved from http://msmagazine.com/blog/2010/12/24/ my-little-non-homophobic-non-racist-non-smart-shaming-pony-a-rebuttal/.

Frable, D. E., Wortman, C., & Joseph, J. (1997). Predicting self-esteem, well-being, and distress in a cohort of gay men: The importance of cultural stigma, personal visibility, community networks, and positive identity. *Journal of Personality, 65,* 599–624. doi:10.1111/j.1467-6494.1997.tb00328.x.

Freud, S. (1955). *The standard edition of the complete psychological works of Sigmund Freud, Volume XVIII (1920–1922): Beyond the pleasure principle, group psychology and other works,* 1–283. London, England: The Hogarth Press and the Institute of Psychoanalysis.

Fry, R. (2016, May 24). For the first time in modern era, living with parents edges out other living arrangements for 18-to-34-year-olds: Share living with spouse or partner continues to fall. *Pew Research Center: Social & Demographic Trends.* Retrieved from http://www.pewsocialtrends.org/2016/05/24/for-first-time-in-modern-era-living-with-parents-edges-out-other-living-arrangements-for-18-to-34-year-olds/.

Funder, D. C. (2007). *The personality puzzle.* New York, NY: W. M. Norton and Company.

Funder, D. C., & Fast, L. A. (2010). Personality in social psychology. In S. T. Fiske, D. T. Gilbert, & G. Lindzey (Eds.), *Handbook of social psychology* (5th ed., pp. 668–697). Hoboken, NJ: John Wiley & Sons.

Funk, D. C., Ridinger, L. L., & Moorman, A. M. (2004). Exploring origins of involvement: Understanding the relationship between consumer motives and involvement with professional sport teams. *Leisure Sciences, 26,* 35–61. doi:10.1080/01490400490272440.

FY & Lolrus. (2017). Rules of the Internet. *Know Your Meme.* Retrieved January 2, 2019, from https://knowyourmeme.com/memes/rules-of-the-internet.

Gates, G. J. (2017, January 11). In U.S., more adults identifying as LGBT. In *Gallup Social & Policy Issues.* Retrieved from https://news.gallup.com/poll/201731/lgbt-identification-rises.aspx.

Gau, L.-S. (2013). Development of a model connecting self-directive value and satisfaction of sociability needs in sport spectators. *Social Behavior and Personality, 41,* 795–804. doi:10.2224/sbp.2013.41.5.795.

Gentile, D. A., Anderson, C. A., Yukawa, S., Ihori, N., Saleem, M., Ming, L. K., ... Sakamoto, A. (2009). The effects of prosocial video games on prosocial behaviors: International evidence from correlational, longitudinal, and experimental studies. *Personality and Social Psychology Bulletin, 35,* 752–763. doi:10.1177/0146167209333045.

Geraghty, L. (2014). *Cult collectors.* London, England: Routledge.

GLADD. (2017). Accelerating acceptance 2017: A Harris Poll survey of Americans' acceptance of LGBTQ people. Retrieved from https://www.glaad.org/files/aa/2017_GLAAD_ Accelerating_Acceptance.pdf.

Godlewski, L. R., & Perse, E. M. (2010). Audience activity and reality television: Identification, online activity, and satisfaction. *Communication Quarterly, 58,* 148–169. doi:10.1080/01463371003773358.

Goldman, M. M., Chadwick, S., Funk, D. C., & Wocke, A. (2016). I am distinctive when I belong: Meeting the need for optimal distinctiveness through team identification. *International Journal of Sport Management Marketing, 16,* 198–220. doi:10.1504 IJSMM.2016.077930.

Gosling, S. D., Rentfrow, P. J., & Swann, W. B., Jr. (2003). A very brief measure of the big-five personality domains. *Journal of Research in Personality, 37,* 504–528. doi:10.1016/S0092-6566(03)00046-1.

Green, M. C., & Brock, T. C. (2000). The role of transportation in the persuasiveness of public narratives. *Journal of Personality and Social Psychology, 79,* 701–721.

Greitemeyer, T. (2009). Effects of songs with prosocial lyrics on prosocial behavior: Further evidence and a mediating mechanism. *Personality and Social Psychology Bulletin, 35,* 1500–1511. doi:10.1177/0146167209341648.

Greitemeyer, T., & Mügge, D. O. (2014). Video games do affect social outcomes: A meta-analytic review of the effects of violent and prosocial video game play. *Personality and Social Psychology Bulletin, 40,* 578–589. doi:10.1177/0146167213520459.

Greitemeyer, T., & Osswald, S. (2009). Prosocial video games reduce aggressive cognitions. *Journal of Experimental Social Psychology, 45,* 896–900. doi:10.1016/j.jesp.2009.04.005.

Greitemeyer, T., Osswald, S., & Brauer, M. (2010). Playing prosocial video games increases empathy and decreases schadenfreude. *Emotion, 10,* 796–802. doi:10.1037/a0020194.

Gwinner, K., & Swanson, S. R. (2003). A model of fan identification: Antecedents and sponsorship outcomes. *Journal of Services Marketing, 17,* 275–294. doi:10.1108/08876040310474828.

Haidt, J., & Graham, J. (2007). When morality opposes justice: Conservatives have moral intuitions that liberals may not recognize. *Social Justice Research, 20,* 98–116. doi:10.1007/s11211-007-0034-z.

Haidt, J., & Joseph, C. (2004). Intuitive ethics: How innately prepared intuitions generate culturally variable virtues. *Daedalus, 133,* 55–66. doi:10.1162/0011526042365555.

Harandi, T. F., Taghinasab, M. M., & Nayeri, T. D. (2017). The correlation of social support with mental health: A meta-analysis. *Electronic Physician, 9,* 5212–5222. doi:10.19082/5212.

Harlow, H. F. (1958). The nature of love. *American Psychologist, 13,* 673–685. doi:10.1037/h0047884.

Haslam, S. A., Jetten, J., Postmes, T., & Haslam, C. (2009). Social identity, health and well-being: An emerging agenda for applied psychology. *Applied psychology: An International Review, 58,* 1–23. doi:10.1111/j.1464-0597.2008.00379.x.

Havlena, W. J., & Holak, S. L. (1991). "The good old days": Observations on nostalgia and its role in consumer behavior. *Advances in Consumer Research, 18,* 323–329.

Hegarty, P., & Bruckmüller, S. (2013). Asymmetric explanations of group differences: Experimental evidence of Foucault's disciplinary power. *Social and Personality Psychology Compass, 7,* 176–186. doi:10.1111/spc3.12017.

Heider, F. (1958). *The psychology of interper-*

sonal relations. Hoboken, NJ: John Wiley & Sons Inc.

Heijnders, M., & Van Der Meij, S. (2006). The fight against stigma: an overview of stigma-reduction strategies and interventions. *Psychology, Health & Medicine, 11,* 353–363. doi:10.1080/13548500600595327.

Heine, S. J., Proulx, T., & Vohs, K. D. (2006). The Meaning Maintenance Model: On the coherence of social motivations. *Personality and Social Psychology Review, 10,* 88–110. doi:10.1207/s15327957pspr1002_1.

Hills, P., & Argyle, M. (2002). The Oxford happiness questionnaire: A compact scale for the measurement of psychological well-being. *Personality and Individual Differences, 33,* 1073–1082. doi:10.1016/S0191-8869(01)00213-6.

Hinck, A. (2012). Theorizing a public engagement keystone: Seeing fandom's integral connection to civic engagement through the case of the Harry Potter Alliance. *Transformative Works and Cultures, 10.* doi:10.3983/twc.2012.0311.

Hodson, G., & Esses, V. M. (2002). Distancing oneself from negative attributes and the personal/group discrimination discrepancy. *Journal of Experimental Social Psychology, 38,* 500–507. doi:10.1016/S0022-1031(02)00012-4.

Hoffner, C., & Buchanan, M. (2005). Young adults' wishful identification with television characters: The role of perceived similarity and character attributes. *Media Psychology, 7,* 325–351. doi:10.1207/S1532785XMEP0704_2.

Hoffner, C. A., & Cohen, E. L. (2012). Responses to obsessive compulsive disorder on Monk among series fans: Parasocial relations, presumed media influence, and behavioral outcomes. *Journal of Broadcasting and Electronic Media, 56,* 650–668. doi:10.1080/08838151.2012.732136.

Hogg, M. A., & Turner, J. C. (1985). Interpersonal attraction, social identification and psychological group formation. *European Journal of Social Psychology, 15,* 51–66. doi:10.1002/ejsp.2420150105.

Hogg, M. A., & Williams, K. D. (2000). From I to we: Social identity and the collective self. *Group Dynamics: Theory, Research, and Practice, 4,* 81–97. doi:10.10371/1089-2699.4.1.81.

Hughto, J. M. W., Reisner, S. L., & Pachankis, J. E. (2015). Transgender stigma and health: A critical review of stigma determinants, mechanisms, and interventions. *Social Science & Medicine, 147,* 222–231. doi:10.1016/j.socscimed.2015.11.010.

Igartua, J. J., & Barrios, I. (2012). Changing real-world beliefs with controversial movies: Processes and mechanisms of narrative persuasion. *Journal of Communication, 62,* 514–531. doi:10.1111/j.1460-2466.2012.01640.x.

Jenkins, H. (1992). *Textual poachers: Television fans & participatory culture.* London, England: Routledge.

Jenkins, H. (2012). "Cultural acupuncture": Fan activism and the Harry Potter Alliance. *Transformative Works and Cultures, 10.* doi:10.3983/twc.2012.0305.

Jenkins, S. T., Reysen, S., & Katzarska-Miller, I. (2012). Ingroup identification and personality. *Journal of Interpersonal Relations, Intergroup Relations and Identity, 5,* 9–16.

Jetten, J., Branscombe, N. R., Schmitt, M. T., & Spears, R. (2001). Rebels with a cause: Group identification as a response to perceived discrimination from the mainstream. *Personality and Social Psychology Bulletin, 27,* 1204–1213. doi:10.1177/0146167201279012.

Jin, S.-A. A., & Park, N. (2009). Parasocial interaction with my avatar: Effects of interdependent self-construal and the mediating role of self-presence in an avatar-based console game, Wii. *CyberPsychology & Behavior, 12*(6), 723–727. doi:10.1089/cpb.2008.0289.

Jindra, M. (1994). Star Trek fandom as a religious phenomenon. *Sociology of Religion, 55*(1), 27–51. doi:10.2307/3712174.

John, O. P. (1990). The "big five" factor taxonomy: Dimensions of personality in the natural language and in questionnaires. In L. A. Pervin (Ed.), *Handbook of personality: Theory and research* (pp. 66–100). New York, NY: Guilford Press.

John, O. P., & Srivastava, S. (2008). The big five trait taxonomy: History, measurement, and theoretical perspectives. In L. A. Pervin & O. P. John (Eds.), *Handbook of personality: Theory and research* (pp. 102–138). New York, NY: Guilford Press.

Johnson, D. R. (2012). Transportation into a story increases empathy, prosocial behavior, and perceptual bias toward fearful expressions. *Personality and Individual Differences, 52,* 150–155. doi:10.1016/j.paid.2011.10.005.

Jones, E. E., & Harris, V. A. (1967). The attribution of attitudes. *Journal of Experimental Social Psychology, 3,* 1–24. doi:10.1016/0022-1031(67)90034-0.

Kahle, L. R., Kambara, K. M., & Rose, G. M. (1996). A functional model of fan attendance motivations for college football. *Sport Marketing Quarterly, 5*(4), 51–60.

Kahn, R. L., & Antonucci, T. C. (1980). Conveys over the life course: Attachment, roles, and social support. In P. B. Baltes & O. Brim (Eds.), *Life-span development and behavior* (Vol. 3, pp. 253–286). Boston, MA: Lexington Press.

Kaptein, M., Markopoulos, P., De Ruyter, B., & Aarts, E. (2015). Personalizing persuasive technologies: Explicit and implicit personalization using persuasion profiles. *International Journal of Human-Computer Studies, 77,* 38–51. doi:10.1016/j.ijhcs.2015.01.004.

Kessler, R. C., & Wang, P. S. (2008). The descriptive epidemiology of commonly occurring mental disorders in the United States. *Annual Review of Public Health, 29,* 115–129. doi:10.1146/annurev.publhealth.29.020907.090847.

Keyes, C. L. M., Shmotkin, D., & Ryff, C. D. (2002). Optimizing well-being: The empirical encounter of two traditions. *Journal of Personality and Social Psychology, 82,* 1007–1022. doi:10.1037//0022-3514.82.6.1007.

Keyes, C. L. M., Wissing, M., Potgieter, J. P., Temane, M., Kruger, A., & van Rooy, S. (2008). Evaluation of the mental health continuum-short form (MHC-SF) in Setswana-speaking South Africans. *Clinical Psychology and Psychotherapy, 15,* 181–192. doi:10.1002/cpp.572.

Kim, Y., Kim, S., & Kim, Y.-M. (2017). Big-five personality and motivations associated with sport team social networking site usage: A cluster analysis approach. *Journal of Global Sport Management, 2,* 250–274. doi:10.1080/24704067.2017.1389249.

King, R. A., Racherla, P., & Bush, V. D. (2014). What we know and don't know about online word-of-mouth: A review and synthesis of the literature. *Journal of Interactive Marketing, 28,* 167–183. doi:10.1016/j.intmar.2014.02.001.

Kirchner, K., Griffin, J., & Edwards, P.W. (March, 2017). *Are the atypical brony fans "just a bunch of liberals"?* Presented at the annual meeting of the Southeastern Psychological Association, Atlanta, GA.

Kistler, M., Rodgers, K. B., Power, T., Austin, E. W., & Hill, L. G. (2010). Adolescents and music media: Toward an involvement-mediational model of consumption and self-concept. *Journal of Research on Adolescence, 20,* 616–630. doi:10.1111/j.1532-7795.2010.00651.x.

Kroenke, K., Spitzer, R. L., & Williams, J. B. W. (2001). The PHQ-9: Validity of a brief depression severity measure. *Journal of General Internal Medicine, 16,* 606–613. doi:10.1046/j.1525-1497.2001.016009606.x.

Kroenke, K., Spitzer, R. L., Williams, J. B. W., Monahan, P. O., & Löwe, B. (2007). Anxiety disorders in primary care: Prevalence, impairment, comorbidity, and detection. *Annals of Internal Medicine, 146,* 317–325. doi:10.7326/0003-4819-146-5-200703060-00004.

Lambert, L., Passmore, H.-A., & Holder, M. D. (2015). Foundational frameworks of positive psychology: Mapping well-being orientations. *Canadian Psychology, 56,* 311–321. doi:10.1037/cap0000033.

Lamers, S. M. A., Westerhof, G. J., Bohlmeijer, E. T., ten Klooster, P. M., & Keyes, C. L. M. (2011). Evaluating the psychometric properties of the mental health continuum-short form (MHC-SF). *Journal of Clinical Psychology, 67,* 99–110. doi:10.1002/jclp.20741.

Lawn, R. B., Slemp, G. R., & Vella-Brodrick, D. A. (2018). Quiet flourishing: The authenticity and well-being of trait introverts living in the west depends on extraversion-deficit beliefs. *Journal of Happiness Studies.* doi:10.1007/s10902-018-0037-5.

LeBel, T. P. (2008). Perceptions of and responses to stigma. *Sociology Compass, 2,* 409–432. doi:10.1111/j.1751-9020.2007.00081.x.

Lee, Y.-K., & Chang, C.-T. (2007). Who gives what to charity? Characteristics affecting donation behavior. *Social Behavior and Personality, 35,* 1173–1180. doi:10.2224/sbp.2007.35.9.1173.

Leonardelli, G. L., Pickett, C., & Brewer, M. B. (2010). Optimal distinctiveness theory: A framework for social identity, social cognition, and intergroup relations. *Advances in Experimental Social Psychology, 43,* 63–113. doi:10.1016/S0065-2601(10)43002-6.

Leshner, C., Reysen, S., Plante, C. N., Chadborn, D., Roberts, S. E., & Gerbasi, K. C. (2018). "My group is discriminated against but I'm not": Denial of personal discrimination in furry, brony, anime, and general interest fan groups. *The Phoenix Papers, 4*(1), 130–142. doi:10.17605/OSF.IO/27PZG.

Levenson, A. R. (2010). Millennials and the world of work: An economist's perspective. *Journal of Business and Psychology, 25,* 257–264. doi:10.1007/s10869-010-9170-9.

Levine, M., Prosser, A., Evans, D., & Reicher, S. (2005). Identity and emergency intervention: How social group membership and inclusiveness of group boundaries shape helping behavior. *Personality and Social Psychology Bulletin, 31,* 443–453. doi:10.1177/0146167204271651.

Levine, R. V., Norenzayan, A., & Philbrick, K. (2001). Cross-cultural differences in helping strangers. *Journal of Cross-Cultural Psychology, 32,* 543–560. doi:10.1177/0022022101032005002.

Lilienfeld, S. O. (2011). Public skepticism of psychology: Why many people perceive the study of human behavior as unscientific. *American Psychologist, 67*(2), 111–129. doi:10.1037/a0023963.

Linton, M.-J., Dieppe, P., & Medina-Lara, A. (2016). Review of 99 self-report measures for assessing well-being in adults: Exploring dimensions of well-being and developments over time. *British Medical Journal Open, 6,* e010641. doi:10.1136/bmjopen-2015-010641.

Lo, S.-K., Wang, C.-C., & Fang, W. (2005). Physical interpersonal relationships and social anxiety among online game players. *CyberPsychology and Behavior, 8,* 15–20. doi:10.1089/cpb.2005.8.15.

Major, B., & O'Brien, L. T. (2005). The social psychology of stigma. *Annual Review of Psychology, 56,* 393–421. doi:10.1146/annurev.psych.56.091103.070137.

Marison, C., Vieno, A., Moss, A. C., Caselli, G., Nikčević, A. V., & Spada, M. M. (2016). Personality, motives and metacognitions as predictors of problematic Facebook use in university students. *Personality and Individual Differences, 101,* 70–77. doi:10.1016/j.paid.2016.05.053.

Markman, K. D., & Hirt, E. R. (2002). Social prediction and the "allegiance bias." *Social Cognition, 20,* 58–86. doi:10.1521/soco.20.1.58.20943.

Martin, K. W. (2015, October 30). Masculinity, marines, and My Little Pony: Did the repeal of don't ask, don't tell open up space for military bronies in our armed forces? *Pacific Standard.* Retrieved from https://psmag.com/social-justice/masculinity-marines-and-my-little-pony.

Maslej, M. M., Oatley, K., & Mar, R. A. (2017). Creating fictional characters: The role of experience, personality, and social processes. *Psychology of Aesthetics, Creativity, and the Arts, 11,* 487–499. doi:10.1037/aca0000094.

Maslow, A. H. (1943). A theory of human motivation. *Psychological Review, 50,* 370–396. doi:10.1037/h0054346.

McAdams, D. P. (1997). A conceptual history of personality psychology. In R. Hogan, J. Johnson, & S. Briggs (Eds.), *Handbook of personality psychology* (pp. 3–39). San Diego, CA: Academic Press. doi:10.1016/B978-012134645-4/50002-0.

McCain, J., Gentile, B., & Campbell, W. K. (2015). A psychological exploration of engagement with geek culture. *PLoS One, 10,* e0142200. doi:10.1371/journal.pone.0142200.

McCutcheon, L. E., Lange, R., & Houran, J. (2002). Conceptualization and measurement of celebrity worship. *British Journal of Psychology, 93,* 67–87. doi:10.1348/000712602162454.

McKnight, P. E., & Kashdan, T. B. (2009). Purpose in life as a system that creates and sustains health and well-being: An integrative, testable theory. *Review of General Psychology, 13,* 242–251. doi:10.1037/a0017152.

Meerwijk, E. L., & Sevelius, J. M. (2017). Transgender population size in the United States: a meta-regression of population-based probability samples. *American Journal of Public Health, 107*(2), 1–8.

Meyer, I. H. (2003). Prejudice, social stress, and mental health in lesbian, gay, and bisexual populations: Conceptual issues and research evidence. *Psychological Bulletin, 129,* 679–697. doi:10.1037/2329-0382.1.S.3.

Milhaven, J. (1977). Thomas Aquinas on sexual pleasure. *The Journal of Religious Ethics,* 5, 157–181. Retrieved from http://www.jstor.org/stable/40017725.

Milne, G. R., & McDonald, M. A. (1999). *Sport marketing: Managing the exchange process.* Sudbury, MA: Jones and Bartlett Publishers.

Mock, S. E., Plante, C. N., Reysen, S., & Gerbasi, K. C. (2013). Deeper leisure involvement as a coping resource in a stigmatized leisure context. *Leisure/Loisir, 37,* 111–126. doi:10.1080/14927713.2013.801152.

My Little Pony: Friendship Is Magic. Wiki. (2018, November 14). *Character appearances.* Retrieved from http://mlp.wikia.com/wiki/Character_appearances.

Nettle, D. (2006). Psychological profiles of professional actors. *Personality and Individual Differences, 40,* 375–383. doi:10.1016/j.paid.2005.07.008.

O'Brien, A. A. (2015). *Negotiating the interconnections of sociality, identity, fan activism and connectivity within the Twilight community* (Doctoral dissertation). Available from ProQuest Dissertations and Theses database. (No. 3722429).

O'Connor, E. L., Longman, H., White, K. M., & Obst, P. L. (2015). Sense of community, social identity and social support among players of massively multiplayer online games (MMOGs): A qualitative analysis. *Journal of Community and Applied Social Psychology, 25,* 459–473. doi:10.1002/casp.2224.

Obst, P., Zinkiewicz, L., & Smith, S. G. (2002a). Sense of community in science fiction fandom, Pt. 1: Understanding sense of community in an international community of interest. *Journal of Community Psychology, 30,* 87–103. doi:10.1002/jcop.1052.

Obst, P., Zinkiewicz, L., & Smith, S. G. (2002b). Sense of community in science fiction fandom, Pt. 2: Comparing neighborhood and interest group sense of community. *Journal of Community Psychology, 30,* 105–117. doi:10.1002/jcop.1053.

Oliver, M. B., & Bartsch, A. (2010). Appreciation as audience response: Exploring entertainment gratifications beyond hedonism. *Human Communication Research, 36,* 53–81. doi:10.1111/j.1468-2958.2009.01368.x.

Oliver, M. B., & Bartsch, A. (2011). Appreciation of entertainment: The importance of meaningfulness via virtue and wisdom. *Journal of Media Psychology, 23,* 29–33. doi:10.1027/1864-1105/a000029.

Oskamp, S., & Jones, J. M. (2000). Promising practice in reducing prejudice: A report from the President's initiative on race. In S. Oskamp (Ed.), *"The Claremont symposium on applied social psychology": Reducing prejudice and discrimination* (pp. 319–334). Mahwah, NJ, US: Lawrence Erlbaum Associates Publishers.

Ouellette, J. A., & Wood, W. (1998). Habit and intention in everyday life: The multiple processes by which past behavior predicts future behavior. *Psychological Bulletin, 124,* 54–74. doi:10.1037/0033-2909.124.1.54.

Ozer, D. J., & Benet-Martínez, V. (2006). Personality and the prediction of consequential outcomes. *Annual Review of Psychology, 57,* 401–421. doi:10.1146/annurev.psych.57.102904.190127.

Paasonen, S. (2017). The affective and affectless bodies of monster toon porn. In P. G. Nixon & I. K. Düsterhöft (Eds.), *Sex in the Digital Age* (pp. 10–24). London: Routledge.

Padilla-Walker, L. M., Coyne, S. M., Fraser, A. M., & Stockdale, L. A. (2013). Is Disney the nicest place on earth? A content analysis of prosocial behavior in animated Disney films. *Journal of Communication, 63,* 393–412. doi:10.1111/jcom.12022.

Pearson, R. (2010). Fandom in the digital era. *Popular Communication, 8,* 84–95. doi:10.1080/15405700903502346.

Pettigrew, T. F., & Tropp, L. R. (2006). A meta-analytic test of intergroup contact theory. *Journal of Personality and Social Psychology, 90,* 751–783. doi:10.1037/0022-3514.90.5.751.

Pettigrew, T. F., Tropp, L. R., Wagner, U., & Christ, O. (2011). Recent advances in intergroup contact theory. *International Journal of Intercultural Relations, 35,* 271–280. doi:10.1016/j.ijintrel.2011.03.001.

Pimental, R. W., & Reynolds, K. E. (2004). A model for consumer devotion: Affective-commitment with proactive sustaining behaviors. *Academy of Marketing Science Review, 5,* 1–45.

Plante, C. N., Chadborn, D., & Reysen, S. (2018). "When entertaining isn't enough": Fan motivation and word of mouth spreading of fan interests. *Journal of Digital and Social Media Marketing, 6,* 168–180.

Plante, C. N., Chadborn, D., Groves, C., & Reysen, S. (2018). Letters from Equestria: Prosocial media, helping, and empathy in fans of *My Little Pony. Communication and Culture Online* 9(9), 206–220.

Plante, C. N., Gentile, D. A., Groves, C. L., Modlin, A., & Blanco-Herrera, J. (2018). Video games as coping mechanisms in the etiology of video game addiction. *Psychology of Popular Media Culture.* Advance online publication. doi:10.1037/ppm0000186.

Plante, C. N., Reysen, S., & Chadborn, D. (2018). *Fan dimensions.* Manuscript in preparation.

Plante, C. N., Reysen, S., Roberts, S., & Gerbasi, K. (2017). "Welcome to the jungle": Content creators and fan entitlement in the furry fandom. *Journal of Fandom Studies, 5,* 63–80. doi:10.1386/jfs.5.1.63_1.

Plante, C. N., Reysen, S., Roberts, S. E., & Gerbasi, K. C. (2016). *FurScience! A summary of five years of research from the International Anthropomorphic Research Project.* Waterloo, Ontario: FurScience Publications.

Plante, C. N., Reysen, S., Roberts, S. E., & Gerbasi, K. (2018). "Animals like us": Identifying with nonhuman animals and support for nonhuman animal rights. *Anthrozoös, 31,* 165–177. doi:10.1080/08927936.2018.1434045.

Plante, C. N., Roberts, S., Reysen, S., & Gerbasi, K. (2014a). Interaction of socio-structural characteristics predicts identity concealment and self-esteem in stigmatized minority group members. *Current Psychology, 33,* 3–19. doi:10.1007/s12144-013-9189-y.

Platow, M. J., Durante, M., Williams, N., Garrett, M., Walshe, J., Cincotta, S., Lianos, G., & Barutchu, A. (1999). The contribution of sport fan social identity to the production of prosocial behavior. *Group Dynamics: Theory, Research, and Practice, 3,* 161–169. doi:10.1037/1089-2699.3.2.161.

Pressman, S. D., Matthews, K. A., Cohen, S., Martire, L. M., Scheier, M., Baum, A., & Schulz, R. (2009). Association of enjoyable leisure activities with psychological and physical well-being. *Psychosomatic Medicine, 71,* 725–732. doi:10.1097/PSY.0b013e3181ad7978.

Prot, S., Gentile, D. A., Anderson, C. A., Suzuki, K., Swing, E., Lim, K. M., … Lam, B. C. P. (2014). Long-term relations among prosocial-media use, empathy, and prosocial behavior. *Developmental Psychology, 54,* 331–347. doi:10.1037/dev0000412.

Radetzki, P. (2018). Harlow's famous monkey study: The historical and contemporary significance of the nature of love. *Canadian Journal of Family and Youth/Le Journal Canadien de Famille et de la Jeunesse, 10,* 205–234. doi:10.29173/cjfy29349.

rainbowdashrules. (2018). Worst my little pony: Friendship is magic episodes. In *The Top Tens.* Retrieved October 27, 2018, from https://www.thetoptens.com/worst-my-little-pony-friendship-is-magic-episodes/.

Ray, A., Plante, C. N., Reysen, S., Roberts, S. E., & Gerbasi, K. C. (2018). "You had to be there": Convention attendance and well-being in anime fans. *The Phoenix Papers, 3*(2), 20–30.

Redden, M., Edwards, P.W., Griffin, J., & Chadborn, D. (March, 2015). *Can fandoms promote mental health?* Poster presented at the meeting of the Southeastern Psychological Association, Hilton Head, SC.

Redden, M., Edwards, P.W. (March, 2017). *The brony fandom: "They ain't been churched."* Presented at the meeting of the Southeastern Psychological Association, Atlanta, GA.

Reisenwitz, T. H., Iyer, R., & Cutler, B. (2004). Nostalgia advertising and the influence of nostalgia proneness. *Marketing Management Journal, 14,* 55–66.

Reyes, M. E. S., Davis, R. D., Panlilio, S. L. D., Hidalgo, P. R. A. S., Ocampo, M. C. D., Opulencia, M. R. D., & Que, J. R. P. (2017). Filipino cosplayers: Exploring the personality traits linked with fantasy proneness and dissociative experiences. *North American Journal of Psychology, 19,* 525–540.

Reysen, S., & Branscombe, N. R. (2010). Fanship and fandom: Comparisons between sport fans and non-sport fans. *Journal of Sport Behavior, 33,* 176–193.

Reysen, S., & Levine, R. V. (2014). People, culture, and place: How place predicts helping toward strangers. In P. J. Rentfrow (Ed.), *Geographical psychology: Exploring the interaction of environment and behavior* (pp. 241–260). Washington, D.C.: APA.

Reysen, S., & Plante, C. N. (2017). Fans, perceived maturity, and willingness to form a romantic relationship: Application of a short maturity measure. *Communication and Culture Online, 8,* 154–173.

Reysen, S., & Shaw, J. (2016). Sport fan as the default fan: Why non-sport fans are stigmatized. *The Phoenix Papers, 2*(2), 234–252.

Reysen, S., Katzarska-Miller, I., Nesbit, S. M., & Pierce, L. (2013). Further validation of a single-item measure of social identification. *European Journal of Social Psychology, 43,* 463–470. doi:10.1002/ejsp.1973.

Reysen, S., Katzarska-Miller, I., Plante, C. N., Roberts, S. E., & Gerbasi, K. C. (2017). Examination of anime content and associations between anime consumption, genre preferences, and ambivalent sexism. *The Phoenix Papers, 3*(1), 285–303.

Reysen, S., Plante, C., & Chadborn, D. (2017). Better together: Social connections mediate the relationship between fandom and well-being. *AASCIT Journal of Health, 4,* 68–73.

Reysen, S., Plante, C. N., Roberts, S. E., & Gerbasi, K. C. (in press). Sex differences in parasocial connection to favorite anime characters: A multifactor approach. *The Phoenix Papers.*

Reysen, S., Plante, C. N., Roberts, S. E., & Gerbasi, K. C. (2015). A social identity perspective of personality differences between fan and non-fan identities. *World Journal of Social Science Research, 2,* 91–103. doi:10.22158/wjssr.v2n1p91.

Reysen, S., Plante, C. N., Roberts, S. E., Gerbasi, K. C., & Shaw, J. (2016). An examination of anime fan stereotypes. *The Phoenix Papers, 2*(2), 90–117.

Reysen, S., Plante, C. N., Roberts, S. E., & Gerbasi, K. C. (2016). Optimal distinctiveness and identification with the furry fandom. *Current Psychology, 35,* 638–642. doi:10.1007/s12144-015-9331-0.

Reysen, S., Plante, C. N., Roberts, S. E., Gerbasi, K. C., Mohebpour, I., & Gamboa, A. (2016). Pale and geeky: Prevailing stereotypes of anime fans. *The Phoenix Papers, 2*(1), 78–103.

Reysen, S., Plante, C. N., Roberts, S. E., Gerbasi, K. C., Schroy, C., Gamboa, A., Gamboa, J., & McCarter, T. (2017). Routes to fandom discovery and expression of fan identity in furry, anime, and fantasy sport fans. *The Phoenix Papers, 3*(1), 373–384.

Reysen, S., Plante, C. N., Roberts, S. E., & Gerbasi, K. C. (2017a). "It just clicked": Discovering furry identity and motivations to participate in the fandom. In T. Howl (Ed.), *Furries among us 2: More essays on furries by furries* (pp. 111–128). Lansing, MI: Thurston Howl Publications.

Reysen, S., Plante, C. N., Roberts, S. E., & Gerbasi, K. C. (2017b). Anime fans to the rescue: Evidence of Daniel Wann's team identification-social psychological health model. *The Phoenix Papers, 3*(1), 237–247.

Reysen, S., Plante, C. N., Roberts, S. E., & Gerbasi, K. C. (2017c). Optimal distinctiveness needs as predictors of identification in the anime fandom. *The Phoenix Papers, 3*(1), 25–32.

Reysen, S., Plante, C. N., Roberts, S. E., & Gerbasi, K. C. (2018a). A brief report on differences in big five personality dimensions between anime fan cosplayers and non-cosplayers. *The Phoenix Papers, 3*(2), 46–53.

Reysen, S., Plante, C. N., Roberts, S. E., & Gerbasi, K. C. (2018b). "Who I want to be": Self-perception and cosplayers' identification with their favorite characters. *The Phoenix Papers, 3*(2), 1–7.

Reysen, S., Plante, C. N., Roberts, S. E., & Gerbasi, K. C. (2019). *Psychology and fursonas in the furry fandom.* Manuscript submitted for publication.

Reysen, S., Shaw, J., & Brooks, T. R. (2015). Heterosexual missionary as the sexual default and stigmatization of perceived infrequent sexual activities. *Advances in Social Sciences Research Journal, 2,* 93–104. doi:10.14738/assrj.25.1181.

Reysen, S. Plante, C. N., Chadborn, D., Roberts, S. E., Gerbasi, K. C., Miller, J., Gamboa, A., & Ray, A. (2018). A brief report on the prevalence of self-reported mood disorders, anxiety disorders, attention-deficit/hyperactivity disorder, and autism spectrum disorder in anime, brony, and furry fandoms. *The Phoenix Papers, 3*(2), 64–75.

Ridings, C. M., & Gefen, D. (2004). Virtual community attraction: Why people hang out online. *Journal of Computer-Mediated Communication, 10* (1). doi:10.1111/j.1083-6101.2004.tb00229.x.

Riketta, M. (2008). "Who identifies with which group?" The motive-feature match principle and its limitations. *European Journal of Social Psychology, 38,* 715–735. doi:10.1002/ejsp.534.

Roberts, S. E., Chong, M.-M., Shea, S., Doyle, K., Plante, C. N., Reysen, S., & Gerbasi, K. C. (2017). The highs, the lows, and post-con depression: A qualitative examination of furries' return home following an anthropomorphic convention. In T. Howl (Ed.), *Furries among us 2: More essays on furries by furries* (pp. 129–141). Lansing, MI: Thurston Howl Publications.

Roberts, S. E., Plante, C. N., Gerbasi, K. C., & Reysen, S. (2015). Clinical interaction with anthropomorphic phenomenon: Notes for health professionals about interacting with clients who possess this unusual identity. *Health & Social Work, 40*(2), e42–e50. doi:10.1093/hsw/hlv020.

Rodebaugh, T. L., Woods, C. M., & Heimberg, R. G. (2007). The reverse of social anxiety is not always the opposite: The reverse-scored items of the social interaction anxiety scale do not belong. *Behavior Therapy, 38,* 192–206. doi:10.1016/j.beth.2006.08.001.

Rosen, B. E. (2009, November 9). We are anonymous, we are legion. *Yale Law Review.* Retrieved from https://yalelawtech.org/2009/11/09/we-are-anonymous-we-are-legion/.

Ross, S. M. (2011). *Beyond the box: Television and the Internet.* Malden, MA: John Wiley & Sons.

Ryan, R. M., Rigby, C. S., & Przybylski, A. (2006). The motivational pull of video games: A self-determination theory approach. *Motivation & Emotion, 30*(4), 347–363. doi:10.1007/s11031-006-9051-8.

Ryff, C. D. (1989). Happiness is everything, or is it? Explorations on the meaning of psychological well-being. *Journal of Personality and Social Psychology, 57,* 1069–1081. doi:10.1037/0022-3514.57.6.1069.

Ryff, C. D. (1995). Psychological well-being in adult life. *Current Directions in Psychological Science, 4,* 99–104. doi:10.1111/1467-8721.ep10772395.

Salmon, C., & Symons, D. (2004). Slash fiction and human mating psychology. *Journal of Sex Research, 41,* 94–100. doi:10.1080/00224490409552217.

Scheier, M. F., Wrosch, C., Baum, A., Cohen, S., Martire, L. M., Matthews, K. A., Schulz, R., & Zdaniuk, B. (2006). The life engagement test: Assessing purpose in life. *Journal of Behavioral Medicine, 29,* 291–298. doi:10.1007/s10865-005-9044-1.

Schmitt, M. T., Branscombe, N. R., Postmes, T., & Garcia, A. (2014). The consequences of perceived discrimination for psychological well-being: A meta-analytic review. *Psychological Bulletin, 140,* 921–948. doi:10.1037/a0035754.

Schroy, C., Plante, C. N., Reysen, S., Roberts, S. E., & Gerbasi, K. C. (2016). Different motivations as predictors of psychological connection to fan interest and fan groups in anime, furry, and fantasy sport fandoms. *The Phoenix Papers, 2*(2), 148–167.

Sedikides, C., & Wildschut, T. (2016). Past forward: Nostalgia as a motivational force. *Trends in Cognitive Sciences, 20,* 319–321. doi:10.1016/j.tics.2016.01.008.

Shaw, J., Plante, C. N., Reysen, S., Roberts, S. E., & Gerbasi, K. C. (2016). Predictors of fan entitlement in three fandoms. *The Phoenix Papers, 2*(2), 203–219.

Shen, B. (2009). *Explicating para-social interaction: How para-social interaction interact with identification, similarity, affinity/liking, and imitation* (Master's thesis). Retrieved from ProQuest Dissertations and Theses. (No. 304839844).

Shokeir, A. A., & Hussein, M. I. (2004). Sexual life in Pharaonic Egypt: towards a urological view. *International Journal of Impotence Research, 16,* 385–388. doi:10.1038/sj.ijir.3901195.

Sibley, C. G. (2010). The dark duo of post-colonial ideology: A model of symbolic exclusion and historical negation. *International Journal of Conflict and Violence, 4,* 106–123. doi:10.4119/UNIBI/ijcv.55.

Skalski, P., Tamborini, R., Shelton, A.,

Buncher, M., & Lindmark, P. (2011). Mapping the road to fun: Natural video game controllers, presence, and game enjoyment. *New Media & Society, 13*(2), 224–242. doi:10.1177/1461444810370949.

Smith, L. (2009). Sex and obscenity in medieval art. *BMJ Sexual & Reproductive Health, 35,* 65–66. doi:10.1783/147118909787072342.

Smith, S. W., Smith, S. L., Pieper, K. M., Yoo, J. H., Ferris, A. L., Downs, E., & Bowden, B. (2006). Altruism on American television: examining the amount of, and context surrounding, acts of helping and sharing. *Journal of Communication, 56,* 707–727. doi:10.1111/j.1460-2466.2006.00316.x.

Soutter, A. R. B., & Hitchens, M. (2016). The relationship between character identification and flow state within video games. *Computers in Human Behavior, 55,* 1030–1038. doi:10.1016/j.chb.2015.11.012.

Stangor, C. (2010). *Introduction to psychology.* Boston, MA: FlatWorld.

Steger, M. F., Kashdan, T. B., Sullivan, B. A., & Lorentz, D. (2008). Understanding the search for meaning in life: Personality, cognitive style, and the dynamic between seeking and experiencing meaning. *Journal of Personality, 76,* 199–228. doi:10.1111/j.1467-6494.2007.00484.x.

Stein, L. E. (2015). *Millennial fandom: Television audiences in the transmedia age.* Iowa City, IA: University of Iowa Press.

Storrs, C. (2016, January 6). Bisexuality on the rise, says new U.S. survey. In *CNN Health.* Retrieved from https://www.cnn.com/2016/01/07/health/bisexuality-on-the-rise/index.html.

Sun, T. (2010). Antecedents and consequences of parasocial interaction with sport athletes and identification with sport teams. *Journal of Sport Behavior, 33,* 194–217.

Tajfel, H. (1972). Social categorization. In S. Moscovici (Ed.), *Introduction à la psychologie sociale* (pp. 30–37). Paris, France: Larousse.

Tajfel, H. (1974). Social identity and intergroup behavior. *Social Science Information (International Social Science Council), 13,* 65–93. doi:10.1177/053901847401300204.

Tajfel, H., & Turner, J. C. (1979). An integrative theory of intergroup conflict. In W. Austin & S. Worchel (Eds.), *The social psychology of intergroup relations* (pp. 33–47). Monterey, CA: Brooks/Cole.

Tajfel, H., Billig, M. G., Bundy, R. P., & Flament, C. (1971). Social categorization and intergroup behavior. *European Journal of Social Psychology, 1,* 149–178. doi:10.1002/ejsp.2420010202.

Taschler, M., & West, K. (2017). Contact with counter-stereotypical women predicts less sexism, less rape myth acceptance, less intention to rape (in men) and less projected enjoyment of rape (in women). *Sex Roles, 76,* 473–484. doi:10.1007/s11199-016-0679-x.

Taylor, T. R., Kamarck, T. W., & Shiffman, S. (2004). Validation of the Detroit area study discrimination scale in a community sample of older African American adults: The Pittsburgh healthy heart project. *International Journal of Behavioral Medicine, 11,* 88–94. doi:10.1207/s15327558ijbm1102_4.

Terry, D. J., Hogg, M. A., & White, K. M. (1999). The theory of planned behavior: self-identity, social identity and group norms. *British Journal of Social Psychology, 38,* 225–244. doi:10.1348/014466699164149.

Toder-Alon, A., Icekson, T., & Shuv-Ami, A. (2018). Team identification and sports fandom as predictors of fan aggression: The moderating role of ageing. *Sport Management Review.* Advance online publication. doi:10.1016/j.smr.2018.02. 002.

Tosenberger, C. (2008). Homosexuality at the online Hogwarts: Harry Potter slash fanfiction. *Children's Literature, 36,* 185–207. doi:10.1353/chl.0.0017.

Trail, G. T., & James, J. D. (2001). The motivation scale for sport consumption: Assessment of the scale's psychometric properties. *Journal of Sport Behavior, 24,* 108–127.

Tsay-Vogel, M., & Sanders, M. S. (2017). Fandom and the search for meaning: Examining communal involvement with popular media beyond pleasure. *Psychology of Popular Media Culture, 6,* 32–47. doi:10.1037/ppm0000085.

Turner, J. C., & Reynolds, K. J. (2012). Self-categorization theory. In P. A. M. Van Lange, A. W. Kruglanski, & E. T. Higgins (Eds.), *Handbook of theories of social psy-*

chology (Vol. 2, pp. 399–417). Thousand Oaks, CA: Sage.

Turner, J. C., Hogg, M. A., Oakes, P. J., Reicher, S. D., & Wetherell, M. (1987). *Rediscovering the social group: A self-categorization theory.* Oxford, England: Blackwell.

U.S. Chamber of Commerce Foundation. (2012, November 12). The millennial generation research review. *Foundation Reports.* Retrieved from https://www.uschamberfoundation.org/reports/millennial-generation-research-review.

van Tilburg, W. A., Sedikides, C., & Wildschut, T. (2015). The mnemonic muse: Nostalgia fosters creativity through openness to experience. *Journal of Experimental Social Psychology, 59,* 1–7. doi:10.1016/j.jesp.2015.02.002.

Van Vugt, M., & Hart, C. M. (2004). Social identity as social glue: The origins of group loyalty. *Journal of Personality and Social Psychology, 86,* 585–598. doi:10.1037/0022-3514.86.4.585.

van Zomeren, M. (2013). Four core social-psychological motivations to undertake collective action. *Social and Personality Psychology Compass, 7,* 378–388. doi:10.1111/spc3.12031.

van Zomeren, M., Postmes, T., & Spears, R. (2008). Toward an integrative social identity model of collective action: A quantitative research synthesis of three socio-psychological perspectives. *Psychological Bulletin, 134,* 504–535. doi:10.1037/0033-2909.134.4.504.

van Zomeren, M., Postmes, T., Spears, R., & Bettache, K. (2011). Can moral convictions motivate the advantaged to challenge social inequality? Extending the social identity model of collective action. *Group Processes and Intergroup Relations, 14,* 735–753. doi:10.1177/1368430210395637.

Varni, J. W., Seid, M., & Kurtin, P. S. (1999). Pediatric health-related quality of life measurement technology: A guide for health care decision makers. *Journal of Clinical Outcomes Management, 6,* 33–40.

Veenhoven, R. (1991). Questions on happiness: Classical topics, modern answers, blind spots. In F. Strack, M. Argyle, & N. Schwarz (Eds.), *Subjective well-being: An interdisciplinary perspective* (pp. 7–26). New York, NY: Pergamon Press.

Wann, D. L. (1995). Preliminary validation of the sport fan motivation scale. *Journal of Sport and Social Issues, 94,* 377–396. doi:10.1177/019372395019004004.

Wann, D. L. (2006). Understanding the positive social psychological benefits of sport team identification: The team identification-social psychological health model. *Group Dynamics: Theory, Research, and Practice, 10,* 272–296. doi:10.1037/1089-2699.10.4.272.

Wann, D. L., & Branscombe, N. R. (1993). Sports fans: Measuring degree of identification with their team. *International Journal of Sport Psychology, 24,* 1–17.

Wann, D. L., & Dolan, T. J. (1994). Spectators' evaluations of rival and fellow fans. *The Psychological Record, 44,* 351–358. doi:10.1007/BF03395919.

Wann, D. L., & Polk, J. (2007). The positive relationship between sport team identification and belief in the trustworthiness of others. *North American Journal of Psychology, 9,* 251–256.

Wann, D. L., & Weaver, S. (2009). Understanding the relationship between sport team identification and dimensions of social well-being. *North American Journal of Psychology, 11,* 219–230.

Wann, D. L., Carlson, J. D., & Schrader, M. P. (1999). The impact of team identification on the hostile and instrumental verbal aggression of sport spectators. *Journal of Social Behavior and Personality, 14,* 279–286.

Wann, D. L., Inman, S., Ensor, C. L., Gates, R. D., & Caldwell, D. S. (1999). Assessing the psychological well-being of sport fans using the profile of mood states: The importance of team identification. *International Sports Journal, 3,* 81–90.

Wann, D. L., Martin, J., Grieve, F. G., & Gardner, L. (2008). Social connections at sporting events: Attendance and its positive relationship with state social psychological well-being. *North American Journal of Psychology, 10,* 229–238.

Wann, D. L., Melnick, M. J., Russell, G. W., & Pease, D. G. (2001). *Sport fans: The psychology and social impact of spectators.* New York, NY: Routledge.

Wann, D. L., Rogers, K., Dooley, K., & Foley, M. (2011). Applying the team identification-social psychological health model to older sport fans. *International Journal of Aging and Human Development, 72,* 303–315. doi:10.2190/AG.72.4.b.

Wann, D. L., Royalty, J. L., & Rochelle, A. R. (2002). Using motivation and team identification to predict sport fans' emotional responses to team performance. *Journal of Sport Behavior, 25,* 207–216.

Wann, D. L., Schrader, M. P., & Wilson, A. M. (1999). Sport fan motivation: Questionnaire validation, comparisons by sport, and relationship to athletic motivation. *Journal of Sport Behavior, 22,* 114–139.

Wann, D. L., Waddill, P. J., Brasher, M., & Ladd, S. (2015). Examining sport team identification, social connections, and social well-being among high school students. *Journal of Amateur Sport, 1,* 27–50. doi:10.17161/jas.v0i0.4931.

Wann, D. L., Waddill, P. J., Polk, J., & Weaver, S. (2011). The team identification-social psychological health model: Sport fans gaining connections to others via sport team identification. *Group Dynamics: Theory, Research, and Practice, 15,* 75–89. doi:10.1037/a0020780.

Wann, D. L., Walker, R. G., Cygan, J., Kawase, I., & Ryan, J. (2005). Further replication of the relationship between team identification and social psychological well-being: Examining non-classroom settings. *North American Journal of Psychology, 7,* 361–366.

Watercutter, A. (2011, June 9). My Little Pony corrals unlikely fanboys known as "Bronies." *Wired.* Retrieved from https://www.wired.com/2011/06/bronies-my-little-ponys/.

Wenzel, M., Mummendey, A., & Waldzus, S. (2007). Superordinate identities and intergroup conflict: The ingroup projection model. *European Review of Social Psychology, 18,* 331–372. doi:10.1080/10463280701728302.

Wilhelm, K., Dewhurst-Savellis, J., & Parker, G. (2000). Teacher stress? An analysis of why teachers leave and why they stay. *Teachers and Teaching, 6,* 291–304. doi:10.1080/713698734.

Williams, P., & Lyons, J. (Eds.). (2010). *The rise of the American comics artist: Creators and contexts.* Jackson, MS: University Press of Mississippi.

Williams, R. (2011). "This is the night TV died": Television post-object fandom and the demise of *The West Wing. Popular Communication, 9,* 266–279. doi:10.1080/15405702.2011.605311.

Williams, R. (2015). *Post-object fandom: Television, identity and self-narrative.* New York, NY: Bloomsbury Academic Publishing.

Wohl, M. J. A., Branscombe, N. R., & Reysen, S. (2010). Perceiving your group's future to be in jeopardy: Extinction threat induces collective angst and the desire to strengthen the ingroup. *Personality and Social Psychology Bulletin, 36,* 898–910. doi:10.1177/0146167210372505.

Yip, J., Ehrhardt, K., Black, H., & Walker, D. O. (2018). Attachment theory at work: A review and directions for future research. *Journal of Organizational Behavior, 39,* 185–198. doi:10.1002/job.2204.

Yoshida, M., Gordon, B., Heere, B., & James, J. D. (2015). Fan community identification: An empirical examination of its outcomes in Japanese professional sport. *Sport Marketing Quarterly, 24,* 105–119.

Yoshida, M., Heere, B., & Gordon, B. (2015). Predicting behavioral loyalty through community: Why other fans are more important than our intentions, our satisfaction, and the team itself. *Journal of Sport Management, 29,* 318–333. doi:10.1123/jsm.2013-0306.

Zajonc, R. B. (1968). Attitudinal effects of mere exposure. *Journal of Personality and Social Psychology, 9,* 1–27. doi:10.1037/h0025848.

Index